The State of Speech

The State of Speech

RHETORIC AND POLITICAL
THOUGHT IN ANCIENT ROME

Joy Connolly

PRINCETON UNIVERSITY PRESS

PRINCETON AND OXFORD

Published by Princeton University Press, 41 William Street, Princeton, New Jersey 08540
In the United Kingdom: Princeton University Press, 3 Market Place, Woodstock,
Oxfordshire OX20 1SY

Library of Congress Cataloging-in-Publication Data
Connolly, Joy, 1970–
The state of speech : rhetoric and political thought in Ancient Rome / Joy Connolly.
p. cm.
Includes bibliographical references and index.
ISBN-13: 978-0-691-12364-6 (hardcover : alk. paper)
1. Cicero, Marcus Tullius—Criticism and interpretation. 2. Cicero, Marcus Tullius—
Political and social views. 3. Rome—Politics and government—265–30 B.C. 4. Latin
language—Rhetoric. 5. Rhetoric, Ancient. 6. Political science—Philosophy. I. Title.
PA6320.C66 2007
808.00937—dc22
2007007150

British Library Cataloging-in-Publication Data is available

This book has been composed in Sabon

Printed on acid-free paper.

pup.princeton.edu

Printed in the United States of America

1 3 5 7 9 10 8 6 4 2

For Michael, my particular friend

Art, great art, transformed courage, right decisions, magnificent oratory into something different and superlative . . . Neither action nor style could have accomplished the result alone. Everything felt the touch of his art—his appearance and gestures, the siren suit, the indomitable V sign for victory, the cigar for imperturbability. He used all the artifices to get his way, from wooing and cajolery through powerful advocacy to bluff bullying; yet he never overruled the Chiefs of Staff. What we are discussing here is not merely the direction of great affairs, but the creation and development of personality.

—Dean Acheson, *Present at the Creation*, 595–96

CONTENTS

ACKNOWLEDGMENTS

I BEGAN TO GRAPPLE IN EARNEST with the main themes of this book not long after September 11, 2001. Never had the distance between the daily practices of citizenship and the exercise of political power seemed to me so great, and for a long time, the things I wanted to say about public speech and civic identity in republican thought rang hollow to my own ears. The thanks I express here are all the more whole-hearted because each person reminds me of the value of clear thinking and commitment to humanist inquiry in anxious times.

Thanks go first to the Classics faculty at Stanford, who offered me a postdoctoral fellowship in Latin literature at an early stage in my turn toward the history of political thought, and who in subsequent years tolerantly encouraged my explorations into areas well beyond their original job description. I am especially grateful to my Stanford colleague by courtesy in the Department of Political Science, the late Susan Moller Okin, who gave me many helpful offprints and books and urged me to track down connections between ancient and modern treatments of rhetoric and citizenship. Thanks to the time and lovely space provided by a Laurance S. Rockefeller Fellowship at the Princeton University Center for Human Values in 2003–4, I was able to rewrite the draft from start to finish, benefiting throughout from contact with the Fellows and Princeton faculty in Classics and Politics. The company of my colleagues at my new home at New York University, not to mention the view of the Empire State Building from my study window, eased the final revisions. Over the years I have leaned heavily on the knowledge and encouragement of members of the Department of Classics at the University of Washington in Seattle, and I thank them warmly for welcoming me into my first faculty position and maintaining strong collegial links over the years. And I would not be writing these acknowledgments at all were it not for Bridget Murnaghan, Joseph Farrell, and Ralph Rosen, of the University of Pennsylvania, who guided my first forays into rhetoric and gender studies with keen criticism and goodwill.

My students in my courses on rhetoric and the history of political thought were excellent critics of some of the arguments made here, and I am grateful to them, especially the graduate students in my seminar on republicanism at Stanford in 2002, Marcus Folch, Lidewijde de Jong, Corby Kelly, Jack Mitchell, and Danielle Steen. For their perceptive comments on various chapters in progress, I thank audiences in Austin,

Chicago, Davis, Los Angeles, New York, Philadelphia, Seattle, and Stanford. Sasha Watson of the French Department at NYU provided prompt help at a critical point. Ann Bergren wisely convinced me to change my original title. Special thanks to those who read parts of the manuscript at different stages or offered other, less easily described forms of inspiration: Alessandro Barchiesi, Ruby Blondell, Barbara Fuchs, Maud Gleason, Alain Gowing, Michael Halleran, Stephen Hinds, Andromache Karanika, William Levitan, Michèle Lowrie, Stephen Macedo, Richard Martin, Daniel McLean, Andrea Nightingale, Josiah Ober, Patricia Parker, Michael Peachin, Jim Tatum, and Froma Zeitlin.

Bob Kaster read the next-to-last draft of the manuscript, supplied many pages of judicious comments, and saved me from many mistakes. Andrew Riggsby and one anonymous reader for Princeton University Press provided immensely useful comments and helped clear the way for the final revisions. The responsibility for any remaining errors is mine. I am very lucky to have worked with Chuck Myers at Princeton University Press, who maintained his support despite delays and unexpected changes of direction.

Debbie Tegarden shepherded the manuscript through production with expert grace. Marjorie Pannell's love of Latin and of clear prose made for learned, sensitive copy editing. Thanks finally to my affectionate, generous family. I owe a great deal to the encouragement of my mother in particular, whose early guidance in literature and art spurred my interest in classical culture.

In Cicero's greatest dialogue, *de Oratore*, a young man named Cotta asks his host, Licinius Crassus, what he needs to make the most of his talents. Crassus smiles and replies, "What else do you think, but zeal, and a truly passionate devotion? Without them, no one would ever achieve anything great in life." I love that answer, and the smile that goes with it, and I am happy to dedicate this book to someone who shares my appreciation. I thank Michael Strevens for his commitment to the world of ideas, his patience, and his many gifts of mind-opening books.

ABBREVIATIONS USED

The following abbreviations are used for journals and reference collections in the bibliography:

AJP	*American Journal of Philology*
ANRW	*Aufstieg und Niedergang der römischen Welt*
CA	*Classical Antiquity*
CIL	*Corpus Inscriptionum Latinarum*
CP	*Classical Philology*
CQ	*Classical Quarterly*
G&R	*Greece and Rome*
HCSP	*Harvard Studies in Classical Philology*
ICS	*Illinois Classical Studies*
JHS	*Journal of Hellenic Studies*
JRS	*Journal of Roman Studies*
ORF	*Oratorum Romanorum Fragmenta,* ed. H. Malcovati (Turin, 1953)
SVF	*Stoicorum Veterum Fragmenta,* ed. H. von Arnim (Leipzig, 1903–24)
TAPA	*Transactions of the American Philological Association*
YCS	*Yale Classical Studies*

The State of Speech

RHETORIC AND POLITICAL THOUGHT

JUST AS ROME'S LEGIONS left their mark on the map of Europe, Roman ideas about citizenship and constitutions helped frame Western political thought. The concept of individual liberty guaranteed by law, the beliefs that the end of political rule is the common good and that the community stands and falls on the civic virtue of its citizens, a strong notion of collective identity expressed in terms of cultural solidarity and common love for the fatherland—these compose the core of republican political ideas that, through the texts of Sallust, Cicero, Vergil, and Livy, were revived starting in the twelfth century by European thinkers seeking to develop alternatives to feudal government, and that remain matters of concern to political theorists today.[1] In this book I pursue a new approach to republican political thought in Rome, one that explores notions of civic virtue and collective identity in texts that seek to guide and govern public speech—in writings belonging to the discipline known since Plato's time as rhetoric. I treat rhetoric, especially the work of Cicero, as an extended engagement with the ideals and demands of republican citizenship. Above all, I concentrate on rhetoric's representation of the ideal orator, which I read as an exploration of the ethos of the ideal citizen. Just like the persuasive speech he utters, this citizen is a complex, paradoxical construction, at once imperious and responsive, masterly and fragile, artifical and authentic, who seeks civil concord through the exercise of seductive authority.

Active, reactive, and rich with resources for self-reflection, rhetoric in Rome always meant much more than learning to deliver a speech, which is why it has lived for so many centuries not in dusty library corners or the memories of curious antiquarians but at the center of European culture, in monasteries, rural schools, and royal courts. One of the three members of the trivium of the liberal arts, along with grammar and dialectic, rhetoric constituted the core of study for educated Romans by (at the latest) the first century BCE. With the emergence of a cosmopolitan Greek- and Latin-speaking elite in urban centers across the empire, rhetoric formed the pedagogical and political bedrock of a common imperial culture stretching from Spain to Syria and from southern Britain to north

---

[1] "We obey nothing and no one but our own laws," Sallust, *Hist.* 1.55; "all of us are slaves to the law so that we may be free," Cicero, *Cluent.* 146: discussion in Viroli, *Republicanism*, 47–52, 69–76, 79–90.

Africa, creating a literal language of *imperium* that was preserved by Rome's European and Byzantine descendants and their global colonies. Transmitted in the form of technical handbooks of logic and composition, the study of classical rhetoric spurred early modern practices of politics and political communication, and survives today in literary criticism, writing manuals, and even self-help books on fashion and public speaking.[2]

Rhetoric arises from the practice of oratory, acts of formal speaking before citizens gathered together—political orations, sermons, law court arguments—and also bears the influence of artistic performances and casual exchanges of conversation. All these practices, in different ways, influence the formation of civic identity and relate directly to the exercise of popular sovereignty and the achievement of social justice. Not only will we better understand classical Rome and the political work done by the spoken word in senate and Forum, we will also enrich our own political culture, I propose, if we examine Roman rhetoric's contribution to ideals of civic identity—if we explore the meaning, in rhetorical discourse, of dialogue, civility, and compromise, of the expression and the critique of traditional authority, the limits of reason, and love of country.

However remotely we sense the connection, each of us is a member of a political community. At the same time, we are all individual subjects, isolated bundles of sensation, imagination, memory, and desire. What shapes us as subjects from without, and enables us to reach out to other citizens from within, is language, the spoken word. "There is no way we could be inducted into personhood except by being initiated into a language," Charles Taylor asserts, citing George Herbert Mead's contention that we emerge as selves out of our common embedding in "webs of interlocution."[3] Concerned as they are with interlocution, rhetorical texts shed light on the process by which language connects human beings within the community and effects change in the world. Eloquence is power: the power to convey ideas and information, to persuade, and to bring pleasure: *docere movere delectare*.[4] "It is easily understood how much we owe to language," Thomas Hobbes wrote in *Man and Citizen*, echoing Isocrates and Cicero,

by which we, having been drawn together and agreeing to covenants, live securely, happily, and elegantly: we can so live, I insist, if we so will. But

---

[2] On the place of rhetoric in the early modern period, see Skinner, *Foundations of Modern Political Thought*, 23–48; a finer-grained picture emerges in Cox, "Ciceronian rhetoric in Italy, 1250–1360," esp. 284–88, and Ward, "Rhetorical theory and the rise and decline of *dictamen*," 192–93, 211–15. On the return of rhetoric in other fields, Bender and Wellbery, "Rhetoricality," provide a good guide and bibliography.

[3] Taylor, *Sources of the Self*, 36.

[4] "Eloquence is power": John Quincy Adams, *Lectures on Rhetoric and Oratory*, 1.26. To Gorgias, rhetoric is *dunamis* (*Encom.* 4); to Cicero, *vis* (*Brut.* 64).

language also hath its disadvantages; namely because man, alone among the animals, on account of the universal signification of names, can create general rules for himself in the art of living just as in the other arts; and so he alone can devise errors and pass them on for the use of others. . . . Therefore by speech man is not made better, but only given greater possibilities. (1.3)

No practice is more central to politics than communication, and to the Roman writers that I discuss in this book, as to Hobbes, no act of communication exists in isolation from moral judgment. If philosophy may be "divided into three branches, natural philosophy, dialectic, and ethics," Cicero declares in his dialogue *de Oratore* (*On the Orator*), "let us relinquish the first two," but, he continues, rhetoric must lay claim to ethics, "which has always been the property of the orator; . . . this area, concerning human life and customs, he must master" (1.68). It is crucial to understand from the start that Cicero is not principally concerned in his rhetorical writings with the ethical formation of the private individual but with a civic ideal whose dynamic constitution reflects the constitution of the republic, what I call the state of speech. This is a key difference between my work and that of previous studies of self-fashioning in classical rhetoric that have concentrated on the formation of the internal self, its construction through self-contemplation, and its grasp of its relation to the external world.

The resources rhetoric offers the republic are rich. Classical rhetoric nowhere offers a robust theory of knowledge that can compete with the epistemologies of Plato and other philosophers, but it seeks, in the competition it cultivates with philosophy, to understand and refine the processes by which citizens make decisions and consensus is forged—in short, the ways in which public knowledge, if not philosophical knowledge, is determined. Roman rhetorical writings are also, of course, the textual articulations of a particular political form: they constitute a theoretical and practical discourse of power in the republic (*res publica*).[5] The demanding blend of bodily and mental skills involved in rhetorical training, which combined and mingled rival discourses of traditional senatorial authority, logical reasoning, literary knowledge, deportment, theatrical strategies of popular appeal, and sheer pleasure in the grain of the voice, prescribed normative practices of identity formation designed to reflect the values of the Roman governing class and reinforce its traditional dominance.

It is not surprising that Roman rhetoric has played a historically significant role in welding what would come to be the Western ideal of

---

[5] I have avoided translating *res publica* with the English "state," given its modern bureaucratic implications. For the broader term *civitas*, I have generally preferred "polity" or "political community" and, when it is used to describe a Greek city (*polis*), "city-state."

civic identity, the *vir civilis*, to properties like glory-seeking and autonomy that are associated with masculinity—with important consequences for the cultures of modern democratic republics and the experiences of non-*viri* in them. Not every *homo* is a *vir*: all women stand outside the circle, in the company of the poor, immigrants, and other classes legally or culturally determined to lack the authority necessary to act in the political arena.[6] What is surprising, and what I seek to show, is how in its exposure of persuasive language's power to sway, mislead, theatricalize, distract, and delight, rhetorical discourse reveals unexpected (if often explicitly disavowed) points of resemblance between the reason and honorable authority of free citizen men and the confusion and abjection that is supposed to be everyone else's lot.

Rhetoric's peculiar power to absorb the other renders it a useful lens through which to observe and understand the workings of republican politics. Though it certainly seeks to discipline language and behavior according to standards imagined to embody elite norms, its appropriation of purportedly alien elements means that its prescriptions construct political power in terms of communication—as fundamentally *dialogic* in nature—thus illuminating how authority, resistance, and consent achieve expression and interact with one another in the world. Rhetoric sets limits on the arbitrary exercise of authority (itself an object of republican law, which protects citizens from arbitrary interference) by figuring it as a practice constrained in part by "natural law," in part by the consensual standard of public approval. Rhetorical discourse, I argue, directly reflects and mediates the historical negotiation of power in the Roman republic among members of the elite senatorial order and between that order and the citizenry, a relation expressed in the well-known formula *Senatus Populusque Romanus*.

Further, though it is constructed as an elite domain, rhetoric operates as a discourse of citizenship in a broader sense, the collection of rights and obligations that endows individuals with a formal legal identity as free, male, and Roman.[7] The gap that exists between the citizen-subject that rhetoric theorizes and any identifiable person in the real world is carefully fostered by writers who seek to preserve rhetorical training in the elite domain, and in this effort they largely succeed. It is a peculiarity of Roman education that many teachers were slaves or freedmen, but the

---

[6] Walters, "Invading the Roman body," points out that "not all males are men" in the sense that *viri* connotes: not only manly in behavior (and indeed some *viri* are not) but free and economically independent (32).

[7] On citizenship theory: Walzer, "Citizenship," broadly surveys the evolution of the notion; Turner, "Citizenship studies," discusses sociological theories of citizenship. Saxonhouse, *Fear of Diversity*, argues that the desire to exclude is the driving force behind political theory as such, a view that supports my treatment of rhetoric (a discourse intent on excluding improper modes of speech) as a mode of political thought.

enslaved and otherwise disadvantaged people were excluded from the student ranks. One of my aims, however, is to explore the ways in which the rhetoricians' ideas fail to make a perfect match with their elite agenda, thus creating an opening that more than a few readers, centuries later, would try to exploit.[8]

After a century or so during which rhetoric took a back seat to other areas of Western culture, classicists and scholars of early modernity have taken up its study with renewed energy.[9] Influenced by the New Historicism, cultural materialism, performance theory, and psychoanalysis, they have explored the ways in which oratory enables the "performance" of identity, the psychological antinomies embedded in the harsh self-disciplines of self-fashioning, and the relations between persuasion and ancient theories of optics, the origins of language, and epistemology. Studies of Latin drama, elegy, and epic have shown how rhetorical strategies originally designed for public persuasion seeped into literary texts, and vice versa.[10] Rhetoric's role in transmitting and inculcating masculinist and imperialist values, from the infant's first controlled vocalizations to the adolescent's advanced exercises in declamation, makes it a major resource for scholars seeking insight into the history of notions of class, gender, and national identity.[11] Cicero, always intensively studied for the light his work sheds on the chaotic political developments of the 60s through the 40s BCE and on Hellenistic philosophy, has recently found more readers for his rhetorical and political theory. He is being reread by scholars interested in the transmission of traditional ideology; his "invention" of Roman high culture in his dialogues, especially *Brutus,* a history of rhetoric, has played an important role in studies of intellectual life in Rome; and his abiding interest in self-promotion through self-presentation, once the object of withering accusations of self-importance, has enriched studies of Roman self-fashioning.[12]

---

[8] One provocative piece of this history is explored by Gustafson, *Eloquence Is Power,* which traces the way American colonies framed their own models of eloquence in order "to speak back to the imperial center" in narratives that brought (for instance) Native Americans into the domain of "republican" rhetoric (117).

[9] And other disciplines: Bender and Wellbery, "Rhetoricality," and Vickers, *In Defence of Rhetoric,* survey the rise and fall of the discipline in philosophical and literary studies.

[10] On the interaction between rhetoric and various literary genres, see the essays in part 3 of Dominik, *Roman Eloquence;* also Keith, "Slender verse," an insightful discussion of the overlap of aesthetic terms in elegy and rhetorical theory.

[11] On Roman rhetoric: Gleason, *Making Men;* Bloomer, *Latinity and Literary Society at Rome;* Gunderson, *Staging Masculinity* and *Declamation, Paternity, and Roman Identity;* Narducci, *Cicerone e l'Eloquenza Romana;* Richlin; "Gender and rhetoric"; Too, *The Rhetoric of Identity in Isocrates;* Vasaly, *Representations.*

[12] For example, on aristocratic values (including competition): Corbeill, *Controlling Laughter,* Hall, "Social evasion and aristocratic manners," Fantham, *The Roman World of Cicero's De Oratore;* on the construction of Roman cultural history: Habinek, "Ideology

While the story I want to tell about the political polyvalence of rhetoric draws gratefully on these developments, it is directly inspired by two different intellectual encounters with Roman antiquity, one in early modernity and the other currently under way. When the humanists of the fourteenth and fifteenth centuries gradually uncovered and circulated the full range of Cicero's and Quintilian's writings on rhetoric, their elation stemmed not only from the philological and exemplary value of the works but also from their obvious importance to developments in political thought that contemporary social and political changes rendered urgent and necessary—the emerging understanding of human social life "as a universality of participation rather than a universal for contemplation."[13] Classically educated men in early modernity viewed ancient rhetoric as a way to reframe questions of citizenship and the aims of the political community in terms of dialogue and persuasion rather than scripture or edict, and as a source of practical techniques for life in a world where the paradigm and the vocabulary of governance were undergoing radical epistemic change. From the medieval practice of teaching secretarial skills (concentrating on the production of official documents), new genres emerged, the most important being panegyric histories of city-states and political advice manuals, that were heavily indebted to Cicero and Quintilian. Scholars seeking to examine virtue outside the field of Catholic theology treated the rhetorical writings of Aristotle and Cicero as practical manuals for the application of their moral philosophy. In the 1260s, Brunetto Latini mixed Greek and Latin historical, philosophical, and rhetorical traditions in his claim that of the three types of government, the popular is the best, and "the chief science in relation to the government of cities is that of rhetoric, that is, of the science of speech."[14] Two centuries later, working within the classical tradition of panegyric rhetoric, the Florentine Leonardo Bruni found linguistic and ideological resources with which to bolster civic identity and to call citizens to take part fully in the life of the city: this is the driving force behind his *Laudatio Florentinae Urbis*, modeled on Aelius Aristides' Panathenaic oration in the early years of the fifteenth century, and his 1428 speech in praise of Nanni Strozzi.

The old argument over the aims and sources of work like Latini's and Bruni's—whether it should be given the political label of "civic humanism" or the ideologically nonaligned tag "rhetorical humanism"—does not

---

for an empire in the prefaces of Cicero's dialogues"; on Ciceronian self-fashioning, Riggsby, "Pliny on Cicero and oratory: Self-fashioning in the public eye"; now Dugan, *Making a New Man*, esp. 31–39, 104–68, 267–87.

[13] Pocock, *The Machiavellian Moment*, 75.

[14] Latini, *Li Livres dou Tresor*, cited in Skinner, *Foundations of Modern Political Thought*, I. 40.

diminish the fact that the two men and their contemporaries cast their revival of the classical rhetorical tradition as the reincarnation of a certain kind of political knowledge. These intellectual developments, against the turbulent background of papal, noble, and kingly conflicts, provided the foundation for modern political thought.[15] The self-contained, civil Roman of eloquence and reason praised by Castiglione, Puttenham, Elyot, Peacham, and Vives is the direct ancestor of the rational moral agent of Locke and Hobbes, Rousseau and Kant, and distant but related kin to the moral agent of Jürgen Habermas, Seyla Benhabib, and K. Anthony Appiah.

The second encounter with Rome that shapes this study began in the middle of the twentieth century, with the paradigm shift in American history and political thought that has been described as having a Kuhnian scale and dynamics.[16] At that time, "republicanism"—variously referred to as a vocabulary, a concept, a style of thought, a conception, a set of attitudes, a disposition—vaulted into dominance as a way of explaining the war of independence and subsequent developments in the making of the U.S. Constitution, and American political culture more generally.[17] Early in the twentieth century, American intellectual historians and political theorists had been split mainly according to their stand on the interpretation of American political culture advanced by Charles Beard just before and after World War I. Beard portrayed America as a nation-state constituted through an ongoing conflict of class interests, founded by men intent on warding off economic revolution and protecting their own extensive interests.[18] In subsequent decades, liberal historians seeking to do better justice to American cultural identity—its individualism, ambition, legalism, moderation, and high valuing of property and capital—enshrined John Locke as the source of American revolutionary identity and the constitutional thinking of the founders. Republicanism seemed

---

[15] An example worth examining is Marsiglio of Padua, whose allegiance to the Holy Roman Emperor led him (somewhat paradoxically) to produce one of the earliest revivals of classical republicanist notions of government and accountability, by way of Franciscan criticism of papal intervention in the secular sphere.

[16] Rodgers, "Republicanism: The career of a concept," 11.

[17] All terms regularly appearing in the three scholarly works that opened the floodgates of republicanism studies in the late 1960s and 1970s: Bailyn, *Ideological Origins of the American Revolution*; Wood, *The Creation of the American Republic*; Pocock, *The Machiavellian Moment*.

[18] Beard, *The Economic Interpretation of the Constitution of the United States* (1913), *Origins of Jeffersonian Democracy* (1916), and *The Economic Basis of Politics* (1922). Rodgers, "Republicanism," describes his work as the first modern paradigm of American history, followed by Louis Hartz's liberal response that American culture is notable for its consensus around key Lockean doctrines, ranging from the protection of property to preference for a relatively limited form of government, in *The Liberal Tradition in America* (1955).

to offer a third way between radical and liberal approaches; it explained much about the civic culture of the early United States, particularly its habit of citing ancient Rome as a model, and its persistent, paradoxical blend of tolerance and exclusionism, hopeful optimism and fundamentalist fear.[19] The paranoiac strains of Puritan oratory, the identification of white manly virtue with citizenship, institutionalizing prejudices against women and people of color, and the stubborn national penchant for "country" culture in an increasingly urbanized and cosmopolitan society—these are examples of phenomena that historians sought to explain by seeking the roots of the American experiment in the republican theorists of an earlier modernity, from Machiavelli to James Madison.

The intensity of this debate in American historical studies has faded, but not before exerting an enduring influence on political theory.[20] Two issues of importance in the move to recuperate the republican tradition are most relevant to this book: the intrinsic value of political deliberation and civic virtue. Political theorists exploring a middle way between liberalism and republicanism tend to be concerned with social fragmentation, widespread apathy among citizens, and the general impoverishment of political discourse, and they find an exemplary model of citizen activism in the classical republican tradition's definition of active citizenship as the best pursuit in life. One prominent advocate of democratic participation, Cass Sunstein, has blended the language of classical republicanism with deliberative democracy theory in his argument that the revolution in communication technologies makes possible new "town halls," flexible, virtual modes of political participation that bind citizens more tightly together in the shared enterprise of democratic government.[21]

---

[19] "Republicanism was the distinctive political consciousness of the entire Revolutionary generation": Kelley, "Ideology and political culture from Jefferson to Nixon," 536.

[20] Notwithstanding claims like those of Kymlicka, *Contemporary Political Philosophy*, who dismisses republicanism as an impossible ideal (294–98). Of the large scholarly literature critical of the modern "revival" of republicanism, milestones include the early response of Herzog, "Some questions for republicans," which argues that republicanism offers no advantages that it does not covertly draw from liberalism (490); and Nippel, "Ancient and modern republicanism," and McCormick, "Machiavelli against republicanism," both pointing out that it "guarantees the privileged position of elites more than it facilitates political participation by the general populace" (McCormick, 615). Ignatieff, "Republicanism, ethnicity, and nationalism," is skeptical about the republican love of country best expressed in Viroli, *For Love of Country*; Phillips, "Feminism and republicanism: Is this a plausible alliance?" sees republicanism as an "uneasy ally" for feminism because of its masculinist and military roots, its gendered definition of public space, and its downplaying of conflict of interests, but applauds it as a way to reconsider citizenship as a communal activity (esp. 293).

[21] Sunstein, *Republic.com*. A good example of this kind of thinking is Dagger's defense of compulsory voting, *Civic Virtues*, 145–50.

For deliberative democrats, civic knowledge and communication among citizens has emerged as an important area of study in its own right. Some scholars seeking a theoretical model for deliberation, such as Seyla Benhabib, have sought inspiration in Jürgen Habermas's theory of communicative action.[22] This posits communication as a practice that is doubly contingent, requiring that participants in dialogue reach intersubjective agreement regarding the validity of any utterance.[23] Drawing on speech act theory, Habermas distinguishes locution (the content of a speech act, which is subject to evaluations of truth value), illocution (the performative force of the locution), and perlocution (the effect of a locution on the hearer, such as fury or the desire to obey). He argues that speakers must meet corresponding standards of intelligibility, propositional content, and sincerity: effective deliberation is a matter of refining and maintaining these proper standards.

But what of the speaker whose communicative acts are compromised as a result of prejudice or incompatible standards of intelligibility? And what of the gap between perlocution and citizen action—a gap that rhetoric explicitly fills in its promise to move (*movere*) but that Habermas leaves to the operation of rational choice? We might, drawing on Aristotle's tripartite definition of the parts of rhetoric, define these as problems of *ethos* (character), *logos* (argument), and *pathos* (the intense feeling that moves audiences to action). In its attempt to protect modes of rational discourse from rhetorical "taint," Habermasian theory remains embedded in the tradition of Western philosophy that tries to "purify" communication of emotion and prejudice.[24] The greatest potential of the classical rhetorical tradition lies in the resources it offers citizens: strategies of 'framing' issues and arguments appropriate to various perspectives and experiences, moving citizens to action, and understanding how communicative standards reinforce social inequalities.[25]

[22] See Benhabib, *Situating the self* (89–120), and "Deliberative rationality and models of democratic legitimacy"; J. Cohen, "Discourse ethics and civil society"; Gutmann and Thompson, *Democracy and Disagreement,* with extensive references, 364 (note that Gutmann and Thompson do not adhere to Habermasian epistemological claims; see Hardin, "Deliberation: Method, not theory," 103, 107).

[23] Habermas, *Theory of Communicative Action*, vol. 1, 89–93, drawing on Goffman, *Presentation of Self in Everyday Life*, esp. 17–76.

[24] Further exploring this critique of Habermas is Young, *Inclusion and Democracy*, 65.

[25] Notable work to date includes Farrell, *Norms of Rhetorical Culture*, which pairs analysis of classical rhetorical theory with investigations of modern examples of rhetoric (Franklin Roosevelt, Mario Cuomo, others), and Allen, *Talking to Strangers*, 140–59. See also Hariman, *Political Style*: "The classical accounts of rhetoric, and particularly of stylistics and decorum, might be read as provisional solutions to perennial problems," 186 (see 177–95 more generally).

The second issue of relevance in contemporary republican theory is its promotion of the civic virtues of liberty, autonomy, tolerance, justice, and patriotism. If all but the last of these call to mind liberal values, republican theorists argue, they are not identical. Philip Pettit, a path-breaking voice in the field, has defined republican freedom not as the absence of interference (the classical liberal definition) but as nondomination. What is lacking in the liberal, rights-based definition of freedom, in his view, is that it overlooks conditions of oppression, like those experienced by the underpaid factory worker or a partner in a marriage with an unequal distribution of power (even if the employer or spouse happens to be benign).[26] Republicanism, by Pettit's lights, because it pays close attention to the interactions between human beings, places a high moral and legal standard on the bearer of power. In practice, this means reorganizing government around practices of accountability and inclusive contestation, with a heavy emphasis on popular deliberation.[27] Patriotism— the answer to the puzzle of what binds citizens together in the political collective, what gives them the sense of actually belonging to a polity— is a special case. No contemporary republican theorist would suggest that chauvinistic nationalist patriotism of the kind perpetuated largely by the forces of populism in modern nation states is desirable. One solution is to promote instead love of the political values on which the state is founded, especially political liberty, tolerance, personal commitment, and public accountability.[28]

My belief that these virtues may be understood as resting on communicative practices, and that speech must be a central concern of citizenship theory, informs my approach to Roman rhetoric. Following Isocrates, both Cicero and Quintilian define rhetoric as a normative system designed to produce the virtuous man through the practice of eloquence. The best sort of virtue, in their view, is that which is devoted, however indirectly, to regulating the *res publica,* especially in the microcosm of the law court, the guardian of justice and equality before the law. Virtue is fully

---

[26] Pettit, *Republicanism*, 52–66, 82–90.

[27] Springborg, "Republicanism, liberty, and the Cambridge historians," queries whether accounts like Pettit's have anything to do with the historical tradition of republicanism; Skinner, *Liberty Before Liberalism*, acknowledges the confusion the term can cause (22–23, 44–45); Viroli, *Republicanism*, offers a more sympathetic reading of Pettit and Skinner (45–55).

[28] Viroli, *For Love of Country*, emphasizes that he has no love for cultural homogeneity or nationalism. What concerns him is that the liberal polity cannot and does not generate a sufficient sense of affective connection: "no attachment, no love, no commitment" (13). His particular version of civic patriotism, however, is not the love of "historically and culturally neutral political principles" (a position advocated by Habermas) but allegiance to the "laws, constitutions, and ways of life of specific republics, each with its own history and culture" (*Republicanism*, 90; cf. 14, and Canovan's critical response, "Patriotism is not enough").

incarnated not in the individual's mastery of selfhood in isolation but in interactive communicative performances in the civic context.

Rhetoric emerges in Cicero as a practice of virtue located firmly in the *political* community—a significant issue that should encourage us to think carefully about to what degree the self in Cicero's work corresponds to modern liberal conceptions of what it means to be a self.[29] Moreover, ancient rhetoricians well understood the challenge implicit in Hobbes's observation (quoted above), that mastery of language is no automatic proof of virtue. Their insistence on the pursuit of oratorical perfection—an always unfinished and indeed unfinalizable task—simulates the always imperfect practices of citizenship and discloses the inconsistencies, gaps, and fissures in the political system the rhetorical treatise itself is designed to uphold.

In Quintilian's *Institutio Oratoria,* written late in the first century CE, this sense of imperfection is tied to the new political conditions created by autocracy. This is emphatically not to say that oratory fell silent under the Caesars; the younger Pliny, Plutarch, Apuleius, Philostratus, and others testify that Tacitus's report of oratory's demise is greatly exaggerated (*Dial.* 41).[30] Rather, by the end of the first century CE, the network of dispositions and expectations underpinning republican oratorical practice, which yoked public contests in the law court to electoral victory and status in the public eye, and in which the rhetoric of liberty and popular will played out the dramatic antagonism between senate and people that was the core trope of republican politics, had begun to assume a new shape. If it retained a certain consistency with tradition—and it is well-known that the principate's legitimacy lay substantially in its appropriation and reenactment of republican values and practices—these patterns were fundamentally different in that they identified the emperor as the figure of intercession between speaker and *populus,* and they derived the virtue

[29] On the relevant differences between ancient and modern views on citizenship, the modern *locus classicus* is Benjamin Constant, "The liberty of ancients compared with that of the moderns"; a harsher view is adopted by Fustel de Coulanges' 1854 *La cité antique.* Berlin, "Two concepts of liberty," (in *Four Essays on Liberty*), is the seminal twentieth-century analysis. All these works, which interrogate the way ancient and modern societies define freedom and autonomy, should inform our approach to the study of ancient subjectivity or selfhood, especially when we look to postmodern theories of the decentered or multiple self. Modern analyses should certainly not be barred automatically from application to premodern societies like Rome, but the fact that they are deeply rooted in the experience of the postindustrial (and post–world war) modern nation-state must be taken into careful account. An exception to the rule is the psychoanalytic approach (Gunderson's *Staging Masculinity,* for example), which adheres to a notion of the psychic self that is essentially ahistorical and which thus introduces a different if no less challenging set of methodological questions.

[30] On the survival of Roman oratory under the first century of autocratic rule, see Goldberg, "Appreciating Aper," Dominik, "Tacitus and Pliny on oratory," and Rutledge, "Oratory and politics in the empire."

and legitimacy of the *res publica* not in the performances of many citizens over time but in the body of the ruler, a new, singular body politic. Caesar is reported as having infuriated his contemporaries with his observation that "the republic was nothing, just a name with neither body nor form," but by the younger Seneca's lifetime the philosophical objections to engaging in political life were helping to make sense of the new political ethic: "What do you want, Cato? Liberty is off the table: it decayed a long time ago. The question is whether Caesar or Pompey will rule the republic" (*Ep.* 14.13).[31] This alteration in the horizon of perceptions and expectations in Roman elite culture of the first century CE means that postrepublican rhetoric, including Augustan declamation and Quintilian's *Institutio Oratoria*, are discussed only briefly in the last chapter of this book.

As Livy observed in a phrase often repeated by early modern political theorists, republican Rome was a self-governing community in which "the power of the laws (is) greater than that of men" (*imperia legum potentiora quam hominum*, 2.1.1). But politics exists in a space that is framed, not filled, by law. And for all the efforts to invent a civil science over the past four centuries, politics is not necessarily rational. On the contrary, to paraphrase Cicero, the nature of the republic defies reason (*vincit ipsa rerum publicarum natura saepe rationem*, *Rep.* 2.57). The space of politics is filled by dispute, contingency, inconsistency, unreason, and passion: here the arts of persuasion rule. Rhetoric is thus the key to untangling the legal and extralegal tensions shot through life in the community, where the networks of identity that make up the civic self intersect and blur together: the traits "proper" to masculinity and femininity, nature and culture, body and mind, obedience and autonomy, self-restraint and the rule of law, sincerity and hypocrisy, the competing interests of individual and community. Rhetoric might be said to make precise distinction between these terms impossible, resolving them as it does through invocations of the corporeal and the performative. Rhetorical texts represent the speaking body as the virtuous self, the highest fulfillment of human nature, an entity in which inheres the essence of "I" that we are now accustomed to imagine as our "private" internal self, as well as the expressive index of character that presents our selves to the world.

But this repository of virtue remains a living body, an entity always under construction over time, the aestheticized, fetishized object of the gazes of other embodied selves—a condition whose anxieties will claim my attention throughout the book. The rhetoricians' focus on identity formation through speech means that their imaginings of selfhood

---

[31] Caesar's comment in Suetonius, *Julius* 77: discussion in L. Morgan, "'*Levi quidem de re*,'" 25–30. On aristocratic ethics in the first century CE, especially in Lucan and Seneca, Roller, *Constructing Autocracy*, esp. 124–26.

always start from performative constraints, what we might call structures of discipline, coercion, unfreedom, the panopticon, the Law. But like all performances, spoken language and its effects are impossible fully to master, both in theory and in practice. The inevitable failure of self-mastery and the hopeless, compelling fantasy of mastery that always supplements it in rhetorical discourse forms the context in which each chapter scrutinizes the various ethical and epistemological conflicts that arise from the Roman coupling of virtue and performance.

Republican political ideology is both a product and a cause of the sense of failure immanent in Roman rhetorical discourse. For those familiar with Roman history, the most immediate failure that will come to mind in the context of the late republic is the meltdown of law and order witnessed by the first century BCE: the devastating Social War between Rome and its Italian allies from 91 to 89, the struggle between Marius and Sulla, then Cinna and Sulla, that peaked with massacres in Rome in 87 and 82, Lepidus's brief revolution in 78–77, the slave revolt of Spartacus in 73, the Catilinarian conspiracy during Cicero's consulship in 63, growing unrest and gang violence in Rome through the 50s, and two brutal rounds of civil war: in Tacitus's words, "the power of Pompey and Crassus swiftly yielded to Caesar, the armies of Lepidus and Antony to Augustus" (*et Pompei Crassique potentia cito in Caesarem, Lepidi atque Antonii arma in Augustum cessere, Ann. 1.1*).

In addition to the immense body of research into the upheaval of republican politics in the first century BCE, also significant for my study is the work of the Slovenian theorist Slavoj Žižek, who argues that the fear of failure, isolation, endings, and death at the level of the unconscious is the driving force behind political ideology in all its iterations. Ideology, in his view, functions as a discursive supplement to a unsettlingly perceptible constitutive lack in the human subject: the suturing of political signifiers within the ideological domain masks the terrible contingency and instability inherent in subjective experience.[32] Political thought, as a genre or discipline, is a series of representations that express desire for the always absent object: victory, unity, homogeneity, harmony, wholeness, immortality, even representation itself, in both the aesthetic and the political sense.

Along similar lines, the intellectual historian J.G.A. Pocock identifies the awareness of finitude, lack, and mortality as that which defines republicanism as a political theory and practice. This is what he calls "the Machiavellian moment," by way of contrast to medieval conceptions of

---

[32] Žižek, *Plague of Fantasies*: "We indulge in the notion of society as an organic Whole, kept together by forces of solidarity and cooperation" (6); see also *The Sublime Object of Ideology*, 5, 124–25.

an eternal, deity-derived and deity-sustained polity. "Only as a partnership in virtue among all its citizens could the republic persist; if virtue were less than universal, its failure at one point must in time corrode its existence at all others," he writes, concluding, "the aim of politics is to escape from time . . . the dimension of imperfection."[33] Pocock views the (re)invention of the humanist man of manners in early modern Italy, England, and North America (and their notional republics of letters) precisely as a response to republican fragility: the integrity of the civil man's personality becomes a normative control, a performed, visible source of stability, in a political order eternally poised on the brink of literal or ideological destruction. Beliefs about moral virtue and bodily beauty are consequently made to cohere; indeed, they become virtually indistinguishable; but as social practice becomes aestheticized, it takes on a paradoxical immunity from rational analysis and critique. And certain aspects of aestheticism, especially theatricality and ephemerality, emerge as flaws in the republican political unconscious. If the virtuous civic man created through rhetorical training is a potent construction, he is also a fragile one. What rhetorical discourse shows is that fragility, multiplicity, and artifice are the ideal citizen's greatest strength.

They are unlikely bedfellows, but Žižek and Pocock share what I see as a key insight into Roman rhetoric and the political ethos that is its concern: the looming awareness that the living web of communal virtue is always, somewhere, being torn apart by human vice and mortality; that the basis for legitimacy is slowly eroding; that the citizen and the state must die together. Rhetorical discourse enshrines the impossible: most obviously, in its quest for the best orator, who for Cicero (and even more so for Quintilian) remains eternally absent, inhabiting only the realms of the hopeful imagination or death, as in Cicero's *Brutus*, a history of Roman rhetoric written after the death of the great orator Hortensius, which deals only with dead men.[34] If the impossible quest for moral perfection that characterizes rhetoric and republican political thought alike is symptomatic of a weakness at the center of the republic, that quest also keeps rhetoric sufficiently flexible for the distinctive demands of republican politics. Eloquence, Cicero declares, is one of the greatest virtues (*eloquentia est una quaedam de summis virtutibus, de Orat.* 3.55, cf. 3.143). By identifying eloquence as the key connection between civic virtue and individual

[33] Pocock, "Civic humanism and its role in Anglo-American political thought," 87, 88. On the implications of this notion for aesthetics (see below), see Eagleton, *Ideology of the Aesthetic,* 37–38.

[34] It might be said that Quintilian's ideal is the dead Cicero, but the point remains essentially the same. Cicero makes a point of discussing only dead men in his own first-person "voice" in the dialogue (*Brut.* 249, 251): the admirable style of (the still living) Julius Caesar is discussed briefly by Brutus (his eventual assassin).

virtue, Cicero locks the future of the republic to the virtue of its speaking citizens: speech simultaneously stabilizes the republic and spurs the dynamic interactions of intra-elite competition and popular resistance.

This book does not provide a full-fledged account of Roman rhetoric as a product of late republican political policies. My interest in the normative and its discontents means that I will refer only briefly, and piecemeal, to Cicero's fifty-eight surviving speeches. Nor do I aim to explain the rhetoricians' personal motives in writing or to define "Roman values" wholesale. Recent years have witnessed a small flood of fine studies on Ciceronian and Roman self-fashioning, largely inspired by Pierre Bourdieu's work on bodily *habitus* in social practice, studies of the technologies of selfhood undertaken by Michel Foucault, Teresa de Lauretis, and other feminist theorists, and Stephen Greenblatt's essays on Renaissance writers such as Thomas More.[35] That rhetorical education "fashioned" the self is beyond question. My discussion of subjectivity in Roman rhetoric is trained on the conceptual questions emerging from the relationship between self-as-subject and self-as-citizen. Representations of cultural values and practices are an important ingredient in the book, but they are the means, not the end, of my analysis.[36]

Instead, by reading rhetoric in light of what Roman rhetoricians conceived as its natural arena, the *vita activa* of politics, we can glimpse the logics structuring Roman political thought, and to a certain degree its relevance for modernity. In the hope of advancing contemporary debates about civic identity and deliberative politics, I will occasionally handle rhetorical discourse in disarticulated form, as a living body of ideas, testing the Roman ethics of eloquence against some contemporary political theorists. This approach is perhaps closer to current habits of reading Latin poetry than prose. The dispute over the nature of the *Aeneid*, as Joseph Farrell has noted, finds its proximate origins in the wars of the twentieth century, meaning that recent philological readings of the epic prompt us to reexamine what we think about the social and political role of poetry while they teach us about Vergil's Latin.[37] The case is similar for psychoanalytic readings, the most successful of which are engaged in scrutinizing the self we bring to the text even as they examine representations of selves in ancient texts. We bring ourselves to studies of the past, and we

[35] Early and important work in this now well-studied area includes P. Brown, *Power and Persuasion*; Gleason's influential *Making Men*; and Richlin, "Gender and rhetoric."

[36] Alan Liu condemns the weaknesses of historicism in early modern cultural studies in "the power of formalism," arguing that scholars too easily find in the individual voices of the past a way to work out their own political fantasies: "In the mirror of desire named 'the Renaissance,' the interpreter can *fantasize* about subverting dominance while dreaming away the total commitments of contestation" (75, italics his).

[37] Farrell, *Latin Language and Latin Culture*, 3ff.

should never lose sight of our readings' motives. My main motive is to lift out of a historically grounded reading of Roman rhetorical texts questions that remain relevant today, questions about what it means to be a citizen. Each chapter identifies a familiar question in the rhetorical tradition—What is the best type of orator? Is rhetoric a product of nature or culture? What is the significance of style? Why is *decorum* so important?—and demonstrates how rhetoric's answers illuminate political problems. As Seyla Benhabib has observed, since tradition has largely lost the special legitimacy granted it by simply being part of the past, "the legitimacy of tradition rests now with resourceful and creative appropriations of it in view of the problem of meaning in the present."[38]

If a reception-focused approach risks our losing a grip on historical context, the risk seems worth taking, given its potential to prompt thought about issues of speech and civic identity that are as urgent today as they were in the first centuries BCE and CE. Today as in ancient Rome, talk is the interface between our public and private faces; the modification of bodily behaviors and attitudes remains a viable type of social resistance. Ancient rhetoric can help build a model of ethics that draws on postmodern and poststructuralist insights into performance and subjectivity but repudiates the obscurantist tendencies scattered through some performance studies and some recent directions in feminist theory. And it sharpens our understanding of the extent to which, historically, public speech has been conceived fundamentally as the proper tool of men and of elites. Work by Habermas and other critics of models of liberal citizenship that are based on the Enlightenment's construal of the nation-state reconsiders how theories of citizenship and selfhood may and must change in our rapidly shifting, globalized, commodified world. What if civic and personal identity worked itself loose from traditional national boundaries, from ethnic and religious ties, or even, through modern communication technologies, from the physical communities in which everyday life is lived? Surely this process is already happening, and equally surely we must look for new ways to invigorate civic bonds. Commitment to speech and shared debate—and to the right and ability for all to engage in debate—is one nexus of values that cuts across the personal and the civic, and it is central

---

[38] Benhabib, *Situating the Self*, 104. See also Rorty, "The historiography of philosophy: Four genres":

> [W]e are interested not only in what the Aristotle who walked the streets of Athens 'could be brought to accept as a correct description of what he had meant or done' [here he quotes Skinner's articulation of Cambridge-style intellectual history], but in what an ideally reasonable and educable Aristotle could be brought to accept as such a description. . . . It is perfectly reasonable to describe Locke as finding out what he really meant, what he was really getting at in the *Second Treatise*, only after conversations in heaven with, successively, Jefferson, Marx, and Rawls. (51, 54)

to many contemporary liberal projects, such as Habermas's effort to reinvent national patriotism as constitutional patriotism. In a limited sense, as I argue in my conclusion, Cicero is there before us.

I begin by looking back to the institutionalized origins of Roman rhetoric, from scraps of second-century speeches to the earliest extant treatises written in Latin, Cicero's *de Inventione* and the anonymous *Rhetorica ad Herennium*, both composed in the 80s BCE. Chapter 1 is most closely concerned with the rhetoricians' engagement with republican political practice, in particular their characteristic focus on dialogic argumentation. Exploring the connection between the study of rhetoric and periods of intense social and political stress, I address the consequences of the rhetoricians' treatment of speech as the civic act par excellence.

A central methodological concern in the study of rhetoric, and one that holds profound implications for my historical analysis, is whether we should approach it as a tool for those who seek power through emotional manipulation and misinformation—what we might call the Weberian charismatic model of rhetorical performance—or as a system of communicative practices intrinsically capable of escaping or transcending elite claims of exclusive ownership.[39] In addressing this issue, I hope to enrich the current debate among Roman historians over what label to apply to the *res publica* before the Caesars: oligarchy, democracy, or some variety of mixed regime. Two additional questions are relevant. The first belongs to contemporary cultural studies, especially the sociology of literature, and asks to what degree we may accurately say that ruling elites *master* language, from educational practices to literature, theater, and political communication in its conventional modes. Formalized language—song and drama no less than oratory—is deeply implicated in the maintenance of aristocratic hegemony, in Rome and perhaps in every human society.[40] Yet an excessively rigid view of language as the tool and property of the powerful curtails exploration of the mechanisms of

---

[39] In her defense of rhetoric as an instrument for an inclusive model of deliberative democracy, Young surveys the debate in political theory, from Thomas Spragens's critique of rhetorical passion in his *Reason and Democracy* to Jürgen Habermas's attempt to distinguish rhetoric from rational speech in *Theory of Communicative Action* to Plato's *Gorgias* (*Inclusion and Democracy*, 63–66). Farrell, *Norms of Rhetorical Culture*, admits that "nobody admits to liking rhetoric very much" but seeks to revise Habermasian discourse ethics by foregrounding issues of context and audience (230; see also 202–204, 232–275).

[40] On the "invention of Latin literature" as a buttress for aristocratic hegemony and the ground for cultural commodification in Rome's imperial expansion, see the provocative discussion in Habinek, *The Politics of Latin Literature*, 36 (and chap. 2 and 8 *passim*). Bloch, introduction, *Political Language and Oratory*, is a classic example of cross-cultural anthropological analysis of formalized language; Gellner, *Anthropology and Politics*, explores the implications of viewing stylized speech as the essence of the coercive power of the ruling classes (esp. 57).

change and encourages a deformed, overly static view of republican thought and practice. Here I am guided in part by work done in the context of Athenian democracy, especially Josiah Ober's exploration of oratory as the primary mechanism for airing tensions between mass and elite, as well as by scholarship on tragedy and comedy that has clarified the role of speech in constituting the polity and citizens' collective sense of belonging.[41] By these lights, speech is never simply an expression of dominance but an essentially dynamic interchange, a dialogue that may not name itself as such but that retains its characteristics nonetheless. The second question, related mainly to political theory, seeks to understand the privileged place of reason in political communication. Since Plato, theorists have appropriated rhetoric's structured modes of argumentation while seeking rational modes of political discourse that are cleansed of what they take to be the stains of oratorical performance, from passion to the "cosmetics" of style. Some recent work in political science has sought to recover the positive functions of these latter aspects of rhetoric, and I hope to contribute to this effort as well in my analysis of Cicero's *de Inventione* and the anonymous *Rhetorica ad Herennium*.

The next four chapters concentrate on Cicero's later rhetorical writing, especially his ambitious three books *de Oratore* (55 BCE) and the shorter *Brutus* and *Orator* (46 BCE), in dialogue with *de Republica* and *de Legibus*, composed in the middle to early 50s, and *de Officiis* (44).[42] Fresh from the completion of *de Oratore*, and embarking on *de Republica*, Cicero tells his brother Quintus that his new book is about "the best state of the republic and the best citizen," and the surviving fragments of the fifth and sixth books suggest that eloquence was a major theme (*Q. fr.* 3.5.1).[43] It is not simply the case that Cicero's treatment of the demands of republican citizenship shapes his prescriptions for a manly *ars rhetorica*, or vice versa, but that thinking about the republic sculpts the ideological imperatives of Cicero's rhetorical discourse, with rhetoric in turn leaving its own stamp on his theories of republican civic identity. His conceptions of citizenship and of public speech take shape together. In emphasizing the complexities of this relation, I hope to advance the insights of scholars such as Erik Gunderson and John Dugan, who focus on the nature of the masculine subject produced through oratorical training and represented in rhetorical texts,

---

[41] A good place to start is Ober, "Power and oratory in democratic Athens," which applies the broad perspective on oratory developed in *Mass and Elite in Democratic Athens* to Demosthenes 21 (*Against Meidias*). On the related performances of oratory, drama, and ritual, see Goldhill, "Programme notes." Morstein-Marx, *Mass Oratory and Political Power*, responds to Ober (14–15) and summarizes key theoretical issues (16–31).

[42] On the date of *de Oratore*, see *Att.* 4.13.5, which refers to the completion of a work in three books, and *Fam.* 1.9.23.

[43] Ferrary, "The statesman and the law," 49–50.

and especially Alberto Grilli, who has brilliantly limned the relationship between philosophy and rhetoric in the formation of Cicero's conception of the perfect "political man."[44] My concern is primarily with the ways in which speech about trained speech functions as a refractor of concerns about living in a polity—another human practice that, like persuasion, is subject to utopian fantasy and deep fear.

Romans are quick to remind themselves that Greeks, not Romans, invented rhetoric and imported it into the city and the culture of Rome.[45] Despite such protests, the combination of fear and fascination that colors Cicero's views of rhetoric has less to do with his suspicion of rhetoric as a Greek invention per se than with his insight into the conflicted nature of Roman civic identity, and the role of speech-making within it. In *de Oratore*, Cicero suggests that Greek philosophers and rhetoricians speak an unnatural, artificial language that bars them from the rolls of virtuous men and good citizens. He seeks to make the difference between virtuous Roman rhetoric and other types of speech an essential difference, one of nature rather than degree. As a result, his strategy exploits essentialist notions of national and gender identity in order to redescribe the artifices of trained eloquence as the quintessence of manly nature, which in Cicero's always universalizing hands becomes assimilated to Roman citizenship and, in turn, human nature. If Cicero aims to present his ideal orator and ideal citizen as undifferentiated, whole, pure, and uncomplicated embodiments of Roman virtue, however, these impressions are always undone from within. The good Roman, too, must speak the unnatural language of artifice and spectacle. What unfolds in chapters 2 through 5 is a portrait of the orator as a man who embodies the central tensions of republican citizenship: a construct of nature and culture, passion and restraint, emotion and reason, body and mind, autonomy and interdependence, consent and coercion.

Is eloquence an acquired art or a natural talent? Or, to put the question in a more practical vein, do eloquent men become so by means of innate character or external training, by nature or culture? Chapter 2 takes a new look at this old chestnut—Socrates' opening gambit in Plato's *Gorgias*—arguing that the importance of the nature versus culture debate in Cicero's rhetorical writings arises from his understanding of certain related tensions in republican civic identity. In a close reading of the interplay among Crassus, Antonius, and other interlocutors in Cicero's *de Oratore*, I show how Cicero constructs ideal *eloquentia* as a hybrid of *ars* and *natura*. In the dialogic conflicts of this work, Cicero's

---

[44] On the formation of identity in rhetorical discourse, see Gunderson, *Staging Masculinity*; Dugan, *Making a New Man*; and Grilli, "Cicerone tra retorica e filosofia."

[45] The Greeks, too, viewed rhetoric as a foreign import from Sicily, according to a now lost work of Aristotle, the *Synagoge Technon* (*Brut.* 46–48). See Cole, "Who was Corax?"

longest and most ambitious rhetorical treatise, a strategy I call the rhetoric of naturalization unfolds. Its conceptual progression is complicated and not without problematic inconsistencies, but in the end, the logic of the argument from nature wins over even Crassus, the speaker who, in the beginning, seemed to hold a different view. The chapter then turns to *de Republica* and other works to show that the hybridization of nature and culture in Cicero's account of the formation of the orator echoes his claim that nature forms the basis of the ideal polity, which has already, if tautologically, been cast in the mold of Rome. The drive to claim nature as both property and origin for the citizen orator grows out of a political fantasy of Roman purity and power.

The key to the citadel of the self, for Cicero and centuries of republican theorists after him, is oratory. But here an objection immediately interposes itself. Can a good orator be a good man? Cicero insists that he can, but a long tradition, beginning with Plato's *Gorgias* and *Republic,* stands against him. But where Aristotle, in his critical response to Plato's approach to politics, turned back to the household to cement "natural" channels of domination that retained sharp distinctions between male and female, Cicero chooses a more challenging course: the rewriting of masculine civic ideals in an ideal republican sensibility that embraces many of rhetoric's potentially unmanly, unfree aspects: its corporeality, its reliance on passion, and its fostering of multiple voices in the eloquent citizen. In chapter 3, points of contact with feminist theory are crucial to understand what I call Cicero's theory of the corporeal citizen, a usefully flexible if somewhat self-contradictory ideal. My point is to explain the implications of Ciceronian practices of self-fashioning for what they can tell us about the embodied, mortal nature of the republican community.

Chapter 4 turns to the virtue of *decorum*, which plays a central role in Ciceronian rhetorical and ethical discourse as the quintessential virtue-practice, since it involves not only action but reflection and demands constant attention to communal norms as well as individual sensibility and taste. Cicero's transformation (following the Greek Stoic Panaetius) of Greek philosophy's *sophrosune* (by most readings, a decidedly internal state), *decorum* is defined by an incompatible combination of the law of nature and social custom. It offers nonarbitrary aesthetic criteria on which to judge goodness as the visible enactment of the sociability that, in Cicero's Stoicizing view in *de Officiis*, makes communal life both possible and rewarding. This chapter rounds out and opens up the analysis of rhetorical discourse by reading Catullus against Cicero, in an effort to show how in both authors, the link between *decorum* and affection constitutes the emotional economy of the *res publica*. If the republican community is glued together in part by emotional sensibility, *decorum* in oratory and poetry help direct it, controlling the passions that in the wrong incarnation can destroy the state they make possible. Ciceronian rhetorical training offers a stylistics of living based in natural law; Catullan poetry probes and critiques the stylized life and the unfreedom prescribed by its laws.

Republican political thought and republican rhetoric perpetuate and are perpetuated by a complex, violent desire to define the natures and behaviors of the dominant against those of the disenfranchised: male *versus* female, Roman *versus* Greek or Asiatic, free *versus* slave, individual leader *versus* popular mass. Yet in practice, and even in theory, these categories defy their own distinctions. Chapter 5 turns to the role played by the disempowered and the weak in the formation of civic ethics, concentrating on the much-studied question of gender. In the ancient world, women did not possess full, autonomous political rights. Yet in more ways than ancient political theorists are prepared to admit, the ideal citizen resembles the ideal woman, and the bad citizen and the bad woman commit similar crimes. This explains the shattering effect of a "genuinely" perverted performance, the effeminate speech and behavior that Cicero abhors both in formal speech and in daily conversation. But the anxieties reflected in Cicero's gendered language, I argue, should be understood as a symptom of deeper concerns about the necessary deceits of civility and the affectations of oratorical style. The chapter concludes with a discussion of Cicero's ideal orator, the ornate grand speaker, and the troubling implications of his vision of a listening community bound together by the orator's passionate performance.

With Cicero's death comes the end of republican rhetoric, and the end of republican political theory. His successors are interested in different problems, especially the relation of elites to autocracy and the shifts in imperial governance that permanently altered the economic and political structure in Rome. Chapter 6 discusses early imperial rhetorical practice, beginning with declamation, originally a school exercise involving arguments for fictional cases and famous characters. In this changed world, imperial rhetoricians rework the core of Ciceronian rhetoric, exploring rhetoric's capacity to prompt experiments with language and values. I close with Quintilian's twelve-book handbook on Ciceronian rhetoric, the *Institutio Oratoria*, which reveals the proximity of ideals of republican citizenship and imperial courtly life—a proximity that unsettles Cicero's idealizing claims but helps explain the persistence of rhetoric into late antiquity and beyond.

Why write a book about Roman rhetoric? The view still to be found among literary scholars, intellectual historians, and some classicists, that Roman rhetoric is "de-intellectualized," "a rhetoric of trope, not persuasion," limited to the study of highly stylized and artificial forms, I hope my readers will join me in finding totally insupportable and in need of radical revision.[46] Nor do I think it possible to see rhetorical discourse as an endless elaboration of physical, social, or psychological repression. On the contrary, its disciplines must be viewed as moving along paths that defy and question dominant modes of being as well as uphold them, similar to the structures of confession and self-revelation that Michel Foucault studied in his late work on sexuality. Cicero is no democrat, but his belief in trained speech as a living and lived connector of citizen and community shares common ground with early modern theorists of natural sociability, such as Adam Smith, and contemporary theorists of deliberative democracy such as Amy Gutmann and Iris Marion Young. The Augustan declaimers are not performance artists in the modern sense, but their experiments with language and staged emotion test the limits of language in the transition from republic to empire and reveal ways in which rhetorical eloquence resists the rules with which practitioners seek to enforce language. Quintilian is no Cicero, but his reinvention of republican eloquence in an age of imperial autocracy helps explain the persistence of rhetoric in Roman society after its original conditions of production had disintegrated—as a pedagogy promising robust resources for that late antique self so occupied with the body, its health and appearance, even as it undoes the promises of republican rhetoric to preserve the state against the tyranny of autocracy.

My answer to the question, briefly elaborated in my conclusion, is that these writers, especially Cicero, helped shape our world—our educational system, our mixed admiration and suspicion of eloquence, our troubled relation to consensus and collective identity—and that the ways they wrestled with the inconsistences and incoherences of what it means to be a citizen can still enlighten us. Like the Renaissance readers who rediscovered these texts, we should approach the rhetorical tradition not only as readers and scholars but as writers and citizens, actors on a political stage both fractured and inspired by longing for full-fledged democracy. These pages express my commitment to bringing the study of antiquity to bear on contemporary debates about education and citizenship, and the questions asked in them should interest anyone committed to thinking through the vistas opened and the anxieties unleashed when we imagine the republic as a state of speech.

[46] Roland Barthes, "The old rhetoric," 24.

Chapter One

FOUNDING THE STATE OF SPEECH

> The successes of history belong to those who are capable of
> seizing rules, to replace those who had used them, to disguise
> themselves so as to pervert them, invert their meaning, and
> redirect them against those who had initially imposed them . . .
> so as to overcome the rulers through their own rules.
> —Michel Foucault, *Language, Counter-Memory, Practice*

WHAT GRANTS POLITICS LEGITIMACY? This is one of the great unresolved questions of political theory. To answer it, Hannah Arendt turned to classical antiquity, with special attention to Rome.[1] Defending a view of the republic to which I return several times in this book, she identified the source of Rome's endurance as the "trinity" of "religion, tradition, and authority."[2] This trinity had traction, she believed, because the ancient republic did not rest in any notion of God or eternal, absolute law but rather declared and constantly renewed itself in the recreation of the past, a past understood as the perpetual augmentation of a foundation that itself already fused innovation with tradition. For Arendt, this dynamism stood in sharp contrast with the sources of legitimacy cited by earlier theorists such as John Locke. Most readers of Locke focus on his argument that legitimacy rests in the consent of the people, but Arendt saw matters differently. She concentrated on what she saw as "the need for gods in the body politic" of Locke and other early liberal thinkers: their anticipation of the violent upheaval caused by revolution, she argued, drove them to appeal to a transcendent source of authority, whether God or the law of nature.[3] Against the absolutes of Genesis she set Vergil's *Aeneid* and Livy's *History*, where (as every reader knows) the foundation of Rome is represented not

---

[1] McClure, "The odor of judgment," discusses Cicero's influence on Arendt's conception of political judgment; Hammer, "Hannah Arendt and Roman political thought," surveys the presence of Vergil, the historians, and Cicero on Arendt's effort to mend the "Platonic separation of knowing and doing," 126.

[2] Arendt, *On Revolution*, 117, 201.

[3] Ibid., 184; see further 185–194. A key point in Arendt's argument is that seventeenth- and eighteenth-century theorists saw human reason (through which the social contract is formed) as God-given. For Locke on self-preservation as the will of God, see *Two Treatises of Government*, II.4; Hobbes on the human condition, *Leviathan* 70, 75–76,

as a pure, new beginning but as a refounding, first as Troy reborn and subsequently as a city reconstituted by Romulus, Brutus, the *decemviri* who composed the Twelve Tables, and the emperors, such as Augustus, who claimed responsibility for *res publica restituta*.[4]

Arendt interpreted this cycle as the core of republican politics, taking shape in practice through the long, senate-supervised, community-wide process of forming a common imagination that gives birth to laws, *leges*, which in turn become the object of communal contemplation and judgment. To flesh out this view of judgment, she appealed to Kant's third critique:

> But under the *sensus communis* we must include the idea of a sense *common to all*, i.e. of a faculty of judgment which, in its reflection, takes account (*a priori*) of the mode of representation of all other men in thought, in order, as it were, to compare its judgment with the collective reason of humanity, and thus to escape the illusion arising from the private conditions that could be so easily taken for objective, which would injuriously affect the judgment. This is done by comparing our judgment with the possible rather than the actual judgments of others, and by putting ourselves in the place of any other man, by abstracting from the limitations which contingently attach to our own judgment. . . . The following maxims of common human understanding . . . may serve to elucidate its fundamental propositions. They are: (1) to think for oneself; (2) to put ourselves in thought in the place of everyone else; (3) always to think consistently.[5]

Where Kant applied his conception of reflective judgment mainly to the realm of aesthetics, Arendt transfers it to the arena of politics. She approaches political judgment as an internal microcosm of the action that defines the public sphere: it begins with "a dialogue between me and myself" that "even if I am quite alone in making up my mind, [anticipates] communication with others with whom I know I must finally come to some agreement."[6] That dialogue within the self and with others is a fundamental element of political judgment explains the affinity Arendt

---

89–90, 111; and on the sovereign, 231. God plays a different central role in Sir Robert Filmer, whose *Patriarcha* traced the genealogy of government to the Hebrew scriptures: he sidestepped the question of reason with an account of politics as arriving with the making of Adam, the first father-ruler and the God-given model for human society for eternity.

[4] *On Revolution*, 210–211, worth reading in tandem with Miles, *Livy: Reconstructing Early Rome*, which explains the cyclical re-foundings in Livy's first pentad as a serial loss and reclamation of piety (75–109).

[5] Kant, *Critique of Judgment* 2.40. Kant's influence on Arendt is discussed in detail by Benhabib, *Situating the Self*, 132–33.

[6] Arendt comments further: "Freedom is a worldly reality, tangible in words which can be heard, in deeds which can be seen, and in events which are talked about, remembered, and turned into stories . . . whatever occurs in this space of appearances is political by definition, even when it is not a direct product of action" (*Between Past and Future*, 154–55).

glimpses between politics and the performing arts. In the theater of the political, language is the heart of political action. Just as dancers, actors, and musicians require an audience to display their virtuosity, so citizens need the presence of others, in a "space of appearances where they could act, with a kind of theater where freedom could appear."[7] Arendt's high privileging of the public sphere arose in part from her Aristotelian conviction that only "in public" are human beings able to cultivate internal dialogues that transcend the pettiness of isolation, leading to the "enlarged" ways of thinking that Kant describes in his *Critique*.[8] Political cultures organized in public, like the Roman *res publica* or the Greek polis, are guarantees "against the futility of individual life, the space protected against this futility and reserved for the relative permanance, if not immortality, of mortals."[9]

Arendt's notion of public space is controversial. Political precepts, she proposes, "arise directly out of the will to live together with others in the mode of acting and speaking."[10] But whom are we supposed to imagine acting and speaking? When Bonnie Honig compares Arendt's account of politics as performance to "the original performative, the divine utterance, 'Let there be . . .' ," she means to criticize Arendt's reinforcement of the traditional order, the implicit name of the Father, as the guiding source of politics—a reflection of the patriarchal exclusionism of her classical sources.[11] But Honig also rightly emphasizes that performance, by its nature, never perfectly or wholly reproduces human desire or will. The truth cuts another way. Alive, changeable, finite, the performance of authority is constituted in a fundamental instability.[12]

Though each act of performance seeks always to establish itself as beyond question, beyond the reach of alternatives, it rests on a consensual relation between performer and audience that is always subject to the interruptions of dissent, disengagement, or the excesses of the performance itself, which Roman writers tended to cast in terms of contestation and risk. The intense pressure to achieve fame through action competes with, and often defeats, the drive to self-memorialize (Sallust, *Cat.* 3.1–2). "I want all my triumphs, the ornaments of my office, the memorials of my glory, the symbols of praise to be built and founded *in your hearts*," Cicero declared, warding off the same anxiety as Horace

---

[7] Arendt, *Between Past and Future*, 154.

[8] Tambornino surveys the problem and seeks a middle ground in *The Corporeal Turn*, 19–23, 30–35.

[9] Arendt, *The Human Condition*, 56.

[10] Ibid., 245–56.

[11] Honig, "Declarations of independence," 206, 233.

[12] I develop this view of performance from Butler's account of the performative and its constitutive "unfixity" in *Bodies That Matter*, 187, 195.

("I have constructed a memorial more eternal than bronze").[13] The ephemeral nature of public culture engenders what scholar of rhetoric Robert Hariman calls "a strong sense of the transitory."[14]

Here is a partial explanation of the Roman effort to fix collective memory through sculpture, inscription, funeral oration, and eventually (especially in the hands of Cicero), the written text.[15] The Roman performance of traditional authority in oratory and a variety of written texts makes a powerful appeal to the past, notably through the use of models (*exempla*), in the effort to anchor itself in collective memory and renew that memory's force, but doing so is also a sidelong acknowledgment of the performance's subjection to the exigencies of the present, its incapacity to claim or embody, finally and fully, that to which it refers. Livy recognized this dynamic in the preface to his history, where his exhortations to imitate models of virtue are framed by expressions of concern about his text's failure to heal the morally decayed present. Half a century earlier, Sallust problematized the memorialization of the past with the "stunningly paradoxical" suggestion that Rome's decline gathered momentum because of the deeds of none other than the exemplary elder Cato.[16]

The historians' nostalgic gaze is funereal. And not only in the metatextual language of histories and in funeral orations, and not only in imperial texts, but whenever the Roman orator invokes and recreates ancestral *auctoritas*—in exhortations to war, reminders of ancestral greatness, or in the rhetorical figure of prosopopoeia, the assumption of a voice from the past (for example, Cicero's staging of Appius Claudius in *Caelio*)—his expression of desire for the absent object in which the audience is invited to share also replays the loss of that (idealized) past. In the public space of the law court or forum, this strategy prompts a collective recognition of absence or decline that may foster dismay or discontent, but this is not a necessarily revolutionary or subversive reaction. So long as the audience concludes that its duty is to join the orator with renewed energy in reconstituting the past, the performance that recreates loss will end by buttressing the traditional order even if it never stops functioning as a reminder of loss. In short, the temporal

---

[13] Cicero, *Cat.* 3.26: *in animis ego vestris omnis triumphos meos, omnia ornamenta honoris, monumenta gloriae, laudis insignia condi et conlocari volo*; Horace, *Carm.* 3.30.1: *exegi monumentum aere perennius.*

[14] Hariman, *Political Style*, 230 n. 32; also 110: "The republic that is constituted in discourse need stand no longer than the next speaker."

[15] Butler, *The Hand of Cicero*, stresses the connection between writing and fame in the late republic; Dugan expands this view into a reading of Cicero's effort to construct an inviolate "textual and discursive self within cultural writings" (13; also 47–58, 303–9).

[16] So Levene, "*Sallust's Catiline*," persuasively argues, showing that Sallust's subtle reminders of Cato's own moral campaign serve to undermine the notion of an archaic age of virtue (178).

dynamic at work in the republican performance of tradition at once ensures stability and change, whether for better or worse—both are built into the system "from the beginning." This is the dynamic of legitimacy articulated in the encounters between the members of the senatorial elite and the popular mass in the Forum and the law court, an outdoor venue open to the public. In all the ways that it enables communication in the civic sphere, oratory founds and refounds the republic as a state of speech.

Before considering Roman rhetoric as a mode of political thought, keeping in mind that rhetoric promises to train powerful speakers, we must examine the relationship between speech and power in republican political culture. This is related to the question of the nature of republican governance—a matter of debate in studies of Rome since at least the second century BCE, with Polybius's confession that Rome's mixture of kingship, aristocracy, and democracy presents a considerable challenge to regime analysts seeking to identify its true seat of power (6.4). In an important study of the sociology of literature, Thomas Habinek encouraged us to answer the question *cui bono?*, that is, to calculate the "interestedness of particular utterances," their role in sustaining elite structures of political and cultural authority.[17] In this chapter, I pose that question to expressions of traditional authority preserved in fragments of pre-Ciceronian oratory, but rather than parsing the interests of the Roman elite, I bring marxist and postcolonial analysis to bear on the elite-mass communicative encounter with the aim of illuminating the audience's investment in sustaining the performative legitimacy of republican government. After a brief historical survey, I lay out a theoretical model for interpreting expressions of authority in the republican context, focusing on the creation of the perception of equality and identification through moralizing speech. In the last part of the chapter, turning to the earliest rhetorical treatises written in Latin, Cicero's *de Inventione* and the anonymous *Rhetorica ad Herennium*, I propose that they respond to traditional practices of authority by drawing on Hellenistic rhetorical theory's rationalized, rationalizing system of civic communication. Their special focus on forensic oratory, long ascribed to the authors' pragmatic approach to rhetorical training, I read instead as casting rhetoric as the main player in a crucially important political fantasy of law and justice— a cyclical vision of society eternally split by antagonistic divisions and healed by the mediating power of eloquence. These treatises show that rhetoric is one of the means by which the republic takes its failures into account in advance.[18]

---

[17] Habinek, *The Politics of Latin Literature*, 9.

[18] Žižek speaks of the "fantasy" of society in these terms, *Sublime Object of Ideology*, 125–27.

The challenge of understanding the popular dynamics at work in expressions of traditional authority is brilliantly explored by the novelist V. S. Naipaul:

> The Europeans could do one thing and say something quite different; and they could act in this way because they had an idea of what they owed to their civilization. It was their great advantage over us. The Europeans wanted gold and slaves, like everybody else; but at the same time they wanted statues put up to themselves as people who had done good things for the slaves. Being an intelligent and energetic people, and at the peak of their powers, they could express both sides of their civilization; and they got both the slaves and the statues.[19]

A Bend in the River, set in a nameless West African country in the 1970s during the rule of an anonymous "Big Man" (in fact, Congo/Zaire under Mobutu Sese Seko), dissects the most enduringly destructive aspect of colonial imperialism: the white Europeans' combined control of the means of both material production—slave labor, rubber plantations, gold and diamond mines—and cultural production, by which they seek to define the whole "developing" world by "civilized" European standards. Naipaul's European colonizers are well aware that complex societies are not ruled by violent coercion alone. Their solution is to create finely tuned systems of what Ernst Gellner calls "coercion at a distance": the pervasive domination of life in all its aspects, legislative, ritual, economic, domestic, linguistic, and moral, in a fashion that identifies virtue and progress with the beliefs and practices of the ruling order. The class that controls the symbols of legitimacy, Gellner observes, in considerable measure controls "the crystallization of social cohesion and loyalty, and thus exercises great power."[20]

In Naipaul's novel, ownership of these symbols leads to the owner's self-deception, and ownership is never absolute. Under the colonial regime, symbols taken to signify "rightful" or "natural" dominance end up blinding colonizer as well as colonized. The white Europeans' serene conviction of their own moral authority (embodied, as they see it, in the material evidence of their technological and economic superiority, from bicycles to engines to capital) conceals even from themselves the murderous violence of their exploitative rule. "They got both the slaves and the statues," Naipaul's protagonist remarks, and we are meant to understand that "they" believed without a shadow of a doubt that they deserved them. Yet material things like mines and rubber trees can be destroyed by the people forced to work them, and in this sense, the fiction

---

[19] Naipaul, *A Bend in the River*, 12.
[20] Gellner, *Anthropology and Politics*, 162–63, 166 (source of quotation); on "coercion at a distance," 59.

of white Europeans' "ownership" of Africa rests on unstable ground.[21] The crucial insight of *A Bend in the River* is that just like material objects, symbols of legitimacy can be neither wholly owned nor contained by their original creators. Statues can be pulled down, or better, like mines, they can be copied or reused. Symbols, in short, are *communicated* in a process that implies the existence of a subterranean dialogue between ruler and ruled: it is only because they are part of a dialogue that they are available for appropriation and reinscription from "the bottom." This, for Naipaul, is the essence of the postcolonialist tragedy: the very symbols that the Europeans used to deceive its colonies, and which in turn deceived them, are the symbols taken up in the dialectic of postcolonialism for use by the colonized, who, tumbling into the cycle of symbolic self-deception, revive both tyranny and the shaky fictions of legitimacy and virtue that conceal it. Tracking the rise and fall of French, Greek, Indian, and finally Congolese characters, the novel shows how acts of power in the sphere of language always spiral outside the control and ken of their wielders.[22]

Through his preoccupation with the agonizing ironies that emerge from the colonized's appropriations of colonial values, where Western ideals such as self-determination and democracy flounder in postcolonial tyranny and poverty, and through his exposure of the loose epistemological moorings of hegemony, Naipaul upholds the essentially dialogic nature of ideology. Official language may be "owned" or controlled by the ruling order, but it is also what links ruler and ruled. It is both a key instrument in ensuring elite domination and popular obedience and a point of elite vulnerability and popular participation. "Our acts of power in communication are not wholly our own," John Pocock writes, since "language gives me power, but power which I cannot fully control or prevent others from sharing."[23] Expressions of power, symbolic or verbal, cannot deploy a perfect unilateralism; the spoken word does not exert force in a single

---

[21] The theme of African ownership is a central (and deeply problematic) theme in *A Bend in the River*, exemplified by circumstances of the foreign businessmen who are forced to sell their shops and restaurants to indigenous Zaireans in the course of the nationalization of the economy.

[22] The last chapter of the novel represents Sese Seko's recycling of the visual symbols of oppression as a reenactment of the European destruction of Congolese identity: "On the *newly painted white* wall was a *larger-than-life photograph* of the President, just the face—*that was a face full of life*. Below that face, Ferdinand [a young Congolese official] *seemed shrunken, and characterless in the regulation uniform* that made him look like all those officials who appeared in group photographs in the newspapers. *He was, after all, like other high officials*. . . . [Ferdinand addresses Salim, the protagonist:] 'They haven't done anything to you in jail. . . . but one day they will rough you up and *then they will discover that you are like everybody else*, and then very bad things will happen to you'" (my emphasis, 271–22).

[23] Pocock, "Verbalizing as a political act," 29, 31.

predictable and masterable direction. This is a key point in my approach to expressions of power and authority in republican oratory.

Politics in public

If recent work in Roman history has made one thing clear, it is that absolutist assessments of the republic are bound to miss the mark.[24] This is as true of Ronald Syme's contention, in 1939, that the regime was nothing more than a "screen and a sham" for the feudal rule of the senatorial oligarchy as it is of Fergus Millar's recent proposal that Rome should be considered a democracy.[25] Partly in response to Millar's provocation, Roman historians have brought more nuanced modes of analysis to bear on the internal relations of what Polybius and Cicero called the mixed regime of the *Senatus Populusque Romanus*, focusing in particular on how the Roman senatorial elite legitimized its authority through a variety of communicative practices, from inscriptions and ceremonies to public speeches.[26] They may be compared to scholars of democratic Athens who have turned away from what Brooke Manville calls the "old paradigm" of political history, which, concentrating on institutions and laws, viewed democracy as a static system of rights and duties. The new paradigm, by contrast, approaches Athenian democracy as a dynamic system of dispositions and practices, embedded in and advocating a particular system of social and moral values, constantly under examination and renegotiation by its citizens, especially regarding the balance of interest between the rich and the rest.[27]

[24] This brief account is included for convenience's sake; readers are encouraged to consult the references in n. 26.

[25] Syme, *The Roman Revolution*, 15. As Ober points out, Syme's view resembles Michels' "Iron Law of Oligarchy," which proposes a general tendency in democracies to prefer oligarchic rule (*The Athenian Revolution*, 18–19). The most recent and systematic expression of Millar's views is *The Crowd in Rome in the Late Republic* (esp. 11, 197–226), synthesizing earlier articles on the topic (listed in the bibliography).

[26] Morstein-Marx, *Mass Oratory and Political Power*, rightly views oratory as the instrument of establishing, perpetuating, and validating existing hierarchies rather than as a democratic forum for testing alternatives (285–86). Flaig synthesizes previous studies in *Die Ritualisierte Politik*, presenting the republic a system of consensus-building ritual practices, including funerals, games, and voting. Other major contributions include Hölkeskamp, *Senatus Populusque Romanus*; Jehne (ed.), *Demokratie in Rom? Die Rolle des Volkes in der Politik der römischen Republik*; Lintott, The *Constitution of the Roman Republic*, 191–219; Mouritsen, *Plebs and Politics in Late Republican Rome*; Nippel, *Public Order in Ancient Rome*; J. A. North, "Politics and aristocracy in ancient Rome"; Vanderbroeck, *Popular Leadership and Collective Behavior in the Late Roman Republic*; and Yakobson, "*Petitio et largitio*: Popular participation in the centuriate assembly."

[27] Manville, "Toward a new paradigm of Athenian citizenship," 22–27.

Athens compensated for inequalities of wealth and birth by establishing legal and political equality among free men. Regardless of status, all citizens voted, served on juries, and could (if they wished) speak in the assembly. In Rome, inequality was the bedrock of the political system: it was institutionalized in the census, on which the organization of senate and the popular assemblies was based, in the electoral process, and legal limitations on rights to public speech. Believed to have originated as an advisory council to the kings of Rome, the senate drew its numbers from the most prominent and wealthy citizens (Livy 1.43). Through Cicero's lifetime, the men modern historians often call the "senatorial order," whose ancestors had usually held office, hailed from a broader elite or dominant class made of up rich, land-owning families based in Rome and its local environs, some politically active, others not.[28] Men like Cato or Cicero, born to families without senatorial ancestry, could enter this group, but very rarely did a "new man" climb the ladder of yearlong magistracies (the *cursus honorum*) from the quaestorship to the high office of consul in a single generation.[29] The senatorial order established and reinforced its political authority by establishing patron-client relations, which created local and provincial networks of economic and social obligation; by retaining control of priestly colleges that oversaw the religious life of the city; by linking political magistracies to military leadership roles; and by competing for status.

Membership in a well-established family and accomplishment in the law court or on the battlefield dictated who ascended the *cursus honorum* and how quickly.[30] Magistrates were empowered to execute decrees so

[28] I will avoid the word "aristocracy" because (1) it ignores the fact that tribunes and "new men," important figures in public discourse, came from a broader group than the arguably "aristocratic" order of the ancient established families, and (2) it carries anachronistic overtones of hereditary court culture in medieval and early modern Europe (cf. the criticism of Millar, *The Crowd in Rome*, 4–6).

[29] On the importance of belonging to an ancient family for election to the highest office, see Badian, "The consuls: 179–49 BCE"; also Hopkins and Burton, *Death and Renewal*, 31ff.

[30] Holding minor offices responsible for roads, land surveying, the night watch, the mint, and miscellaneous services normally preceded election to the quaestorship; there were normally at least fifty of these functionaries active (Lintott, *Constitution*, 139; see 104–44 for general discussion). First was the quaestorship, a primarily financial post; next, the aedileship, which oversaw public games and city services, or (if the candidate was a plebeian) the tribunate. By the second century BCE, the tribunate regularly supplied men to the higher magistracies: many tribunes belonged to or were allied with the senatorial order and shared its economic and political interests. But because of its origins in the archaic struggle of the plebeian and patrician orders, the office was associated with defending popular interests: it offered opportunities for men seeking to build a popular base of support, or who wished to assume an intermediary role between senate and people. Next came the praetorship, whose holders presided over the courts and held high military command, and finally the consulship. Life membership in the "senatorial order" was

long as they did not conflict with existing law.[31] Their duties involved leading entourages around the city's public spaces, striking coins and building monuments that commemorated ancestors by name, and seizing opportunities to speak in the Forum on political issues or legal cases, from the Rostra, or from the steep steps of buildings like the Temple of Castor. In one particularly well-studied ritual, the funerals of leading men, actors donned the wax masks of the family's ancestors and paraded to the Forum, with attendants carrying the dead man's insignia of office, such as the bundled rods of *fasces* that symbolized elected magistrates' authority (Polybius 6.53).[32] The speech given in praise of the deceased wove his deeds into the fabric of collective history, instilling the memory of greatness in the whole audience and the desire for virtue in the younger generation (6.54). The pattern follows Max Weber's account of the institutionalization of charismatic authority, in which high family status combines with individual achievement to construct a social hierarchy that sustains what had originally been the charismatic leadership of one or a few individuals.[33]

Citizenship was held by right of birth by children born into Roman citizen families; slaves freed by Romans were enrolled as citizens at the time of manumission.[34] There were no property requirements for citizenship, but economic standing, recorded by the census, determined each citizen's place in the body politic. "Independence, power, and superiority to the less privileged were enjoyed most of all by the aristocracy, but the humblest citizen had some share in them."[35] Legally, the official role of the *populus Romanus* was limited to passing laws framed by members of the senatorial order and electing magistrates drawn almost exclusively from that same group. Voting in the *comitia centuriata* (which elected the higher magistracies and the censor) was organized by census class, heavily favoring the wealthy; in the *comitia tributa*, the

---

usually achieved by election to the quaestorship (a development formalized by Sulla), but just as the elected censors had the power to expel members, they could also enroll men of high status who had not held office. (Cicero served as aedile in 70. There is an element of special pleading in his first speech to the people from the Rostra, which he delivered while praetor, relatively late in his career: he describes the *contio* as the *locus ad agendum amplissimus, ad dicendum ornatissimus,* "the place offering the most scope for action and the most glory for speeches," and apologizes that he has not previously "dared" to speak there (*auderem, Man. Leg.* 1–2).)

[31] Lintott, *Constitution,* describes the concepts of *potestas* and *imperium,* 95–99.

[32] On funerals and material evidence, see Flower, *Ancestor Masks and Aristocratic Power in Roman Culture,* and Flaig, *Ritualisierte Politik,* 49–68.

[33] Weber, *Economy* and *Society,* 246–54.

[34] Further discussion of this complex issue in Sherwin-White, *The Roman Citizenship*; 322–34, and Gardner, *Being a Roman Citizen,* 7–51.

[35] Brunt, "*Libertas* in the republic," 297.

tribal assembly, the impact of the urban poor vote was limited by their enforced enrollment in just four of its thirty-five total tribes.[36] To the small merchant or poor laborer in the Roman *vicus* through most of republican history, Roman citizenship likely meant mainly the burden of long military service.[37] The extension of civic rights to residents of towns outside the city occurred slowly: even after the Social War of the early first century BCE, when free male residents of the Italian peninsula were granted full citizenship, exercising civic rights (notably voting) was limited by the necessity of being physical present in Rome. Free Roman women born into citizen families were also *cives*, and thus in an important respect were differentiated from slaves or foreigners, but they could not hold power (*potestas*) over other free citizens, since, as Jane Gardner points out, they lacked male citizens' definitive capacity to act or speak on behalf of others. While they could own property, marry, divorce, and (to a limited extent) utilize the courts, they could not adopt children, they did not wield an entirely free hand in legal or financial dealings, and—most important for my purposes—they could not participate in public life. "Women and slaves, not because they do not have the capacity to judge, but because it is received practice, do not perform civil functions" (*D.* 5.1.12.2).[38] Assuming responsibility for the welfare of others was the task of the jury and the popular assemblies, who passed judgment on people and proposals for the well-being of the republic; these institutions, the jury and the popular assembly, were barred to those whose legal and social status did not permit them that responsibility.

With the significant exception of senate meetings, Roman politics took place in the public eye. In formal voting assemblies (*comitia*), the people elected magistrates, passed laws, and occasionally sat in judgment over senators charged with bribery, abuse of power, or other misbehavior. Trials, *quaestiones*, drew juries only from the wealthiest census classes but were argued outdoors, in prominent public settings such as the steps of the Temple of Castor. Magistrates summoned "the People" to nonvoting meetings, *contiones*, where speakers might address policy (declarations of war, agrarian reform), rally support, abuse their rivals, swear oaths, or offer prayers.[39] Cicero's letters show that the *contio* made a useful rough

[36] Composition and responsibilities of the assemblies in Lintott, *Constitution*, 49–60, and L. R. Taylor, *Roman Voting Assemblies*, 11ff.

[37] See Nicolet, *The World of the Citizen*, 89–110, 149–206.

[38] Quotation of the *Digest* adapted from the useful discussion of Gardner, *Being a Roman Citizen*, 88; extended discussion of the basis of limiting women's roles and legal capacity, 94–107.

[39] Pina Polo, "Procedures and functions of civil and military *contiones* in Rome," 205–15.

gauge of public opinion. In 59, he happily informs Atticus that a crowd listening to Julius Caesar attack his consular colleague withheld their applause (*Att.* 2.21.5); two years later, enjoying a boost in public opinion after his return from exile, he notes that his rival Clodius provoked laughter when he melodramatically exhorted his contional audience to "defend their liberty" in the form of a shrine to Libertas that Clodius had built atop the ruins of Cicero's home (*Att.* 4.2.3).[40] Who regularly attended these events, and in what numbers, is today a matter of intense debate.[41] But even the majority of citizens whose role was limited to spectatorship and hearsay, whom Cicero dismissively describes as *imperiti*, "inexperienced men," would have known the centers of political action in the city: the Curia (senate house), the Forum, where most contional speeches were given and elections and trials were held, and other areas for voting, like the Campus Martius.[42] By the middle of the second century BCE, copies of some laws were being posted in public places on bronze plaques, with additional copies kept in public buildings.[43] The Curia stood adjacent to the Roman Forum, separated from it by the towering platform of the Rostra, where elected magistrates and anyone they chose to invite summoned and addressed *contiones*. In the Curia, members of the senate deliberated over *senatus consulta*, decrees that were not laws but rather the formal expression of the senate's views on an issue brought before it by a magistrate who had been elected by the *populus*, usually recommending that he follow a particular course of action.

Against the authority of the senate stood *libertas*, liberty. Since the early nineteenth century, civic liberty has been conventionally (if problematically) described in terms of negative and positive rights or freedoms: freedom from domination, in the sense both that citizens are by definition free, not slaves, and that they are legally protected from arbitrary coercion, especially coercion by a magistrate; and the freedom to realize

---

[40] Examples of popular reactions: reactions to public men at the theater (*Sest.* 115), a *contio* in 169 where antiheckling measures had to be carried out (Livy 43.16.8), whistling (whether in praise or criticism is unclear, *Att.* 1.16.11), hissing (*Att.* 2.19.2); additional references in Mouritsen, *Plebs and Politics*, 46–48.

[41] Summarized by Millar, *The Crowd in Rome*, 29–38.

[42] Cicero, *Flacc.* 2; *Amic.* 95; also "that repulsive, base filth of the people" (*apud perditissimam illam atque infimam faecem populi*, Q. Fr. 2.5.3), "the craftsmen and shopkeepers and all that filth of the city" (*opifices et tabernarios atque illam omnem faecem civitatum*, *Flacc.*18). On the merely "inexperienced" crowd: *Cat.* 4.17, *Mur.* 38, *Sest.* 139, 140, *Flacc.* 96–97, *Mil.* 90, *Phil.* 2.116. Discussion of Cicero's critical representation of the *contio* in Morstein-Marx, *Mass Oratory*, 62–63, 68–69, who points out the different tone Cicero adopts in speeches before the people (e.g. *Rab. Perd.* 18). On assemblies: Polybius 6.14.10; Lintott, *Constitution*, 3, 40–64.

[43] Harris, *Ancient Literacy*, 164–65, emphasizes word-of-mouth communication and points out (citing Cicero's complaint, *Leg.* 3.46) that with the exception of *plebiscita*, Roman laws were not systematically recorded.

one's potentialities through the pursuit of self-mastery.[44] P. A. Brunt's comment that "the liberty Cicero prized was that of a senator" captures not only Cicero's views on liberty but the slant of the development of the concept as a whole.[45] Republican liberty is best understood as a conceptual spectrum, with the poor citizen's freedom from mistreatment by a magistrate at one end and Cicero's notion (the freedom to participate in governing) at the other.

Libertas is a recurring theme in republican oratory. In Sallust, tribunes give fiery, well-received speeches about the damage done by the powerful and wealthy few to the liberty of the many.[46] Cicero, on the relatively rare occasions when he spoke in the Forum, used the rhetoric of popular *libertas* associated with the tribunate. This rhetoric is part of a popular culture that hated the degraded state of slavery and prized freedom, audible in the subaltern voices of Roman literature, like this group of poor men in Plautus's *Pseudolus*: "Hey, we may seem like poor and humble types to you," they say to a rich youth, "but we aren't tamely responsible (*obnoxii*) for what you love or hate ... we're free men (*liberos*), as is right and proper" (515, 517, 520). While ancient families like the Cornelii and Fabii were publicly revered in statues, triumphs, and crowded funeral processions, republican culture depended no less crucially on its memory of antagonism: the plebeian struggle from noble domination, memorialized in legends of cyclical fraternal strife. The legitimacy of republican political practices must be seen as deriving not only from the particular ways in which the distribution of power was institutionalized and naturalized, but also from the performative contexts for mass-elite interaction where elite interests were advanced in terms that summoned or at least were compatible with the rhetoric of popular liberty, a rhetoric that simultaneously revived and sought to bridge that antagonism.[47] This is oligarchy with a difference.[48]

[44] Brunt, "*Libertas* in the republic," 297, cites Cicero (among other sources) to demonstrate the casual lexical overlap between *ius* and *libertas*: "*O nomen dulce libertatis! O ius eximium nostrae civitatis*" (II *Ver.* 5.163); but see the persuasive critique by Roller, *Constructing Autocracy*, 231–33, which questions the relevance of the modern debate framed by Benjamin Constant and Isaiah Berlin. I take up the problem of liberty in greater detail at the beginning of chapter 4.

[45] Brunt, "Fall of the Roman Republic," 55; cf. 294–98; Wirszubski, *Libertas*, demonstrates the range in his treatment of the conflict between the *dignitas* held by a few and the *libertas* held by all citizens (74–79).

[46] Sallust, *Jug.* 31.4–5, 16–17; *Hist.* 3.48.1–4.

[47] Horsfall, *Culture of the Roman Plebs*, 37–42; Brunt, "*Libertas*," 330–50; Wirzubski, *Libertas*, 3–65; Mouritsen, *Plebs and Politics*, 8–13. Nippel, "Policing Rome," remarks on the "considerable loss of flexibility in the interaction between rulers and ruled" that Rome experienced under autocracy (20).

[48] Part of that difference derives from the massive investment of physical and economic capital in military conquest, which rendered necessary a political culture that granted great significance both to habits of popular obedience and to elite accountability. From

What bound the citizens of the city in a regime that, even as it called itself *Senatus Populusque Romanus*, was governed by a deeply entrenched, wealthy class, with power clustered in the hands of less than twenty families at any given time, were acts of public speech that actuated and advertised bonds of shared law and religion. From the middle of the third century BCE, as the Roman *imperium* stretched outward from peninsular Italy to clash with Carthage in Sicily, northern Africa, and Spain, the senatorial order had every reason to worry that the threads of traditional values as well as habits of communication that held together the fabric of domestic social cohesion were beginning to fray. From 241 BCE, the year that Rome won its first war with Carthage and completed the political organization of peninsular Italy south of Pisa, political reorganization took place in the city and its environs on a significant scale.[49] The unification of Italy, as far as it went, was initially effected by the establishment of circuit courts with prefects visiting the towns.[50] The Sabines inhabited the first municipal

---

the city-state's gaining control over the Italian peninsula in the fourth century BCE up to Augustus's consolidation of autocratic power, the Roman citizen army went to war nearly every year: from the beginning, proposals to draft citizens to fight were deliberated in public. Historians describe tense confrontations between elite and mass over military service, with a cluster of well-known examples occurring in the local Italian campaigns of the fifth century, and later, before and during the first and second Punic wars (Livy, 2.24.6); see the valuable discussion in Harris, *War and Imperialism in Republican Rome*, especially his discussion of aristocratic and popular attitudes toward war, 9–68: "ordinary citizens in the category of *assidui* came to exercise an important influence over external policy in the second century by means of their willingness or unwillingness to serve in person in particular wars" (42). Rich, "Fear, greed, and glory," helpfully surveys the debate between Harris's model of aggressive expansionism and the "defensive imperialism" view associated with Gruen, Sherwin-White, and Eckstein (among others): he recommends a modified version of Harris's position (65). This is not to say that the governing order necessarily favored war in the face of strong popular resistance. In 167 BCE, when the senate was divided over whether to initiate hostilities with Rhodes, the praetor M' Iuventius Thalna mounted the Rostra to appeal to the people for a declaration of war. According to Polybius, he met with enough success to drive the Rhodian ambassadors seeking peace with Rome to put on mourning clothes advertising their desperation (30.4.4). But Polybius also reports that a tribune (an elected office traditionally associated with the interests of the people) who supported peace with Rhodes silenced Thalna by dragging him bodily from the Rostra (30.4.6)—hinting that Thalna's appeal to the people is less evidence of popular bellicosity than a tactical move in the competition among politicians for popular attention. Though Polybius observes that the *populus Romanus* has the power "to deliberate about peace and war" (6.14.10–11), we know of no post-fourth-century case where a senatorial recommendation to go to war was voted down by the popular assembly—an important sign of the influence of the senate.

[49] This did not happen in the absence of resistance. In one notable case, the Etruscan city of Falerii revolted and was destroyed, half its land was confiscated, and the entire population was relocated four miles away (Poly. 2.19.7–13).

[50] Sherwin-White, *Roman Citizenship*, 52–53.

town to be granted the full political participation of the *suffragium*, or voting rights, a development that accompanied increases in the numbers of magistrates called *praefecti* in Sabine territory (to the north of Rome) and throughout Campania, to its southeast.[51] To handle these changes, the magistracy of *praetor peregrinus* was created, along with two new tribes, making a permanent total of thirty-five. By the beginning of the first century BCE, the *municipia* of Italy existed in a state of legal uniformity that had been established through the commission known as the *quattuorviri*, meaning that municipal magistrates assumed heavier responsibilities and were subject to greater oversight from Rome. Internal changes in republican institutions within the city seem to have been equally far-reaching. The *comitia centuriata*, the people's assembly organized by property ownership, which passed legislation, elected consuls, praetors, censors, military tribunes, and decemvirs, and which functioned as a court for cases of treason and capital offenses, underwent major reorganization at some time between 241 and 220 BCE.[52] By putting in place local prefects who oversaw the dissemination of Roman law, the Romans began to diffuse an administrative language that was crucial to security and the reinforcement of common identity among outlying territories.[53] At this time, the economic power of the *equites*, who belonged to the same census class as the senators but who did not hold formal office, began to grow, and signs of cooperation between the senatorial order and this newly powerful economic sector become visible.[54]

---

[51] "Prefects for Capua first began to be created with rules of law derived from the praetor, L. Furius, when in a time of civil discord they themselves had asked for both as a cure for their political disease" (Livy 9.20.5, describing an event dated to 318 BCE, cited in Sherwin-White, *Roman Citizenship*, 43). Sherwin-White (41, 51) emphasizes the confusion in the sources over the identity in the fourth and third centuries of towns like Capua as *socii* (allies) or *cives* (citizens). While the Romans were unwilling in this period to incorporate non-Latin communities completely in the Roman body politic (i.e., by giving them the vote), even the grant of a limited franchise did not signify great changes in the local structures of power.

[52] On elections: Livy 1.60, 3.33, 3.35, 5.52, 10.11, 10.22, 12.1, 7.22, 40. On legislation, Cicero, *Rep.* 2.31; on court cases, Cicero, *Rep.* 2.36, *Leg.* 3.34; Dio Cassius 37.27. See further L. R. Taylor, *Roman Voting Assemblies*.

[53] This is a key point in Habinek's *Politics of Latin Literature*, that Latin literature is "invented" in this period of stressful growth by the elite in their effort (successful, in his view) to consolidate elite hegemony (35). Ando, *Imperial Ideology and Provincial Loyalty in the Roman Empire*, applies the Habermasian model of communicative action to the "speech acts" of the empire, including inscriptions, notarized documents, local archives, and speeches (73–130).

[54] See, for instance, the Claudian plebiscite barring senators from owning large ships, which left trade open to the equestrian class (Livy 21. 63): Feig Vishnia, *State, Society, and Popular Leaders*, 48.

Formal modes of communication, between Roman and Italian, electoral candidate and voting citizen, and orator and juror, were the basis of the republican empire: this is the context for the rise of rhetoric as a discipline in the second century BCE. Rhetoric had been the province of Greek empires, from Athens to the Hellenistic world. The imperial tools the Greeks had abandoned the Romans now assumed (de Orat. 3.130, 137). Quintilian puts a date on the arrival in Rome of rhetoric proper: "The first Roman (as far as I know, anyway) to write something on this subject was Marcus Cato the censor; later Marcus Antonius began a similar project (for only one book of it survives, and it is unfinished)."[55] If Quintilian is right, the earliest Roman rhetorical handbook was written by the elder Cato at some time in the late third to the middle second century BCE: rhetoric is thus inaugurated as a discipline at the moment when foreign conquest and internal change place immense pressure on the traditional order. With the expansion of Roman power beyond the local comes the formal stylization of power through the spoken word, using techniques drawn, appropriately enough, from Hellenic culture.

In contrast to the democratic assemblies of Athens, where the principle of *isegoria* granted all citizens the right to speak, public speech in Rome was the domain of elected magistrates and those they invited to speak. As Robert Morstein-Marx concludes in his excellent study of late republican political culture, popular opinion did not exist, in an important sense, until a member of the elite summoned a public meeting and framed the issue in ways that reduced the audience's decision making "to a choice between champions" in whom they would invest trust. His close analysis of *contiones* shows that public oratory's main importance lay in its function as a communal discourse, in which traditional hierarchies were perpetuated and validated in a tone of "ideological monotony" that suppressed the presentation of alternatives in open debate.[56]

IDEOLOGY AND POWER

Because of the central place of ideology in the "new paradigm," exemplified by Morstein-Marx's trenchant formulation, it is essential to define the word properly. Economist marxism (the prevailing mode of marxist

---

[55] *Romanorum primus (quantum ego quidem sciam) condidit aliqua in hanc materiam M. Cato ille censorius, post M. Antonius inchoavit; nam hoc solum opus eius atque id ipsum imperfectum manet* (3.1.19–20).

[56] Morstein-Marx, *Mass Oratory*, 284 (and 279–87 generally). The word *contio* may refer to the public meeting as well as to the speech itself.

analysis through the early twentieth century) understands ideology as a superstructural system of ideas, produced and circulated by the ruling class, that conceals the relations of individuals and classes to the means of production. By this view, Roman oratory must be interpreted as a formal discourse of mystification, an instrument of mass false consciousness, designed to sustain and reinforce the status quo; the beliefs and dispositions of the citizen mass become the material through which the purposes of the senatorial elite are worked. Antonio Gramsci was among the most important early critics of the economist model, on the grounds that it allowed only cramped space for political and cultural change. His preoccupation with the model of change as the transformation of the collective will was fueled by his goal of conceiving a model of revolutionary leadership that would not simply replace the economic hegemony of the bourgeoisie with an exclusive intellectual and moral hegemony but would embody and express the will of the mass—itself produced not only through traditional bourgeois means of cultural production like the university but also through social practice and "common sense" belief on every level and in every aspect of life. This in turn engendered his critique of the conception of ideology as a superstructural system of beliefs, a critique pursued by (among others) Althusser.[57] Citing Marx's claim that "men become conscious of fundamental conflicts on the ideological terrain" of the superstructure, Gramsci proposed a totalizing notion of hegemony as a lived process, in which the intellectual, social, and cultural practices of the material world—one's identity, relationships, choices—are thoroughly saturated by and in the relations of domination and subordination, to the extent that for most people, hegemony constitutes their "common sense" of reality.[58]

In Gramsci's view, there is no "class" as such: the ruling class is the state. What makes a class hegemonic (as opposed to simply "ruling" or "dominant") is its successful articulation of a critical mass of ideological elements characteristic of a given social formation. This formation—and this is a crucial point for political analysis—is not limited to the practices and values of the rulers. On the contrary, it prevails when it manages to become "popular religion" or "the national-popular"—which Gramsci defines as the "link by means of which the unity of leaders and led is

---

[57] Althusser's essay "Ideology and Ideological state apparatuses" and other engagements with the postmarxist problem of ideology are collected and introduced in Žižek, *Mapping Ideology*.

[58] Marx, preface to *A Contribution to the Critique of Political Economy*, cited by Gramsci, *Prison Notebooks*, 158. Althusser, too, relies on this assertion in his psychoanalytic revision of the ideological basis for identity formation (known as "hailing" or "interpellation"). Guidance to Gramsci's argument in Williams, *Marxism and Literature*, 55–71, 109–12 (noting the problematic potential overlap of the terms "ideology" and "hegemony" in Gramsci, 112).

effected."[59] Hegemony and the ideology it articulates are thus composed of fragments that do not necessarily "belong" to or even directly advance the interests of the ruling class. To believe otherwise, he argues, is "to form the habit of considering politics, and hence history, as a continuous *marché de dupes*, a competition in conjuring and sleight of hand."[60] Gramsci's effort to identify the process by which social and political change occurs raises another salient point: if hegemony exists in the terrain of the popular, then it must be a dialectic of cross-cutting values and practices, logically including counter-hegemony—forms of alternative or oppositional cultural and political practice. Ideology, the meanings, values, and beliefs that make sense of the hegemonic order to its subjects, is subject to the same logic. Since the social field is always fluctuating, incomplete, and contested (the very qualities that allow ideology to be articulated through discourse in the first place), ideology always contains elements outside the hegemonic. It is impossible, then, for ideology to sing in only one tone.[61]

Consideration of the name "the Roman people" (*populus Romanus*), the sovereign citizen body of the *res publica*, clarifies Gramsci's point. Who are the Roman people? By an economist marxist reading, the ideological function of the *populus Romanus* or *Quirites* (as they are hailed in elite-produced speeches and histories) is to conceal the rule of the senatorial order via the mystifying force of the rhetoric of popular liberty. In a speech before the people that rehearses the traditional senatorial rejection of popular agrarian reform, Cicero dramatically claims that a recently proposed land law "shows the *populus Romanus* land, but rips away its liberty . . . and establishes kings in the city (*reges in civitate*, *Leg. Agr.* 2.15): his concern, he insists, is not land but the "traps set for your liberty under the guise of liberality" (*insidias libertati vestrae simulatione largitionis*, 2.16). Such "liberty" in the hands of a pro-senatorial speaker cannot be anything but a deceptive myth. So G.E.M. de Ste. Croix argues: that because the people are ignored and "the senatorial concept of *libertas* was tailored to fit the senatorial interest," there could be no meaningful change between republic and principate in the political field.[62]

But this interpretation only grazes the surface of the many meanings of a founding notion such as "the people." It is normal for orators to

---

[59] Gramsci, *Prison Notebooks*, cited and clarified by Mouffe, "Hegemony and ideology," 194.

[60] Gramsci, *Prison Notebooks*, 165.

[61] Morstein-Marx's use of the term *monotony* was important in my thinking through this question, but I should note that I am pressing a point that is essentially irrelevant to his (obviously fruitful) mode of analysis.

[62] de Ste. Croix, *Class Struggle in the Ancient Greek World*, 364, 70.

refer to "the people" as a unit with a single mind and purpose, as Cicero does in a speech addressed to a jury of senators: "I will embark on that course to which the *populus Romanus* has been calling me. For concerning citizenship and liberty, it considers itself the judge, and rightly so" (II *Verr.* 1.12–13). Other texts characterize the people as a mass whose size and diversity place it in dire need of magisterial or tribunal direction.[63] Writing to Atticus about a grain shortage, Cicero credits himself with the transformation of a hustling, agitated mass to an orderly assembly. At first, during two days of high food prices, "men (*homines*) rushed (*concurrissent*) first to the theater, then to the senate, and under the influence of Clodius, shouted that the shortage was my work" (*Att.* 4.1.6). Once Cicero suggests (via a *senatus consultum*) that the people pass a law empowering Pompey to deal with the crisis, they applaud in a show of controlled consensus, and he (re)summons them as an organized *contio*. His semantic choices refuse to recognize the men agitating against famine as a politically coherent collective, "as if the masses could dream of a full stomach but never of exercising power"—a representation that serves elite interests and self-justifications.[64] His implicit claim that popular action is possible only in the wake of elite-led consensus (whether the leader is the vicious Clodius or the virtuous Cicero) places mass politics beyond the borders of rational apperception, evaluation, and representation: hence, implicitly, outside the realm of self-knowledge, and ultimately beyond reason and politics itself.

At the same time, since the size and unpredictable flow of the multitude exceed any traditional measure of the body politic, tacit or open characterizations of the urban masses as violent grant recognition to the latent uncontrollability—and power—of the people.[65] Even in the fearful event of a hostile uproar, as Cicero's failed defense of Milo testifies, the speaker's only recourse was more talk: the grain-hungry mob he describes to Atticus, we note, succeeded in getting their problem solved.[66] The multiplicity naturally implied by the notion of "the people" acknowledges

[63] Cicero, *Rab. Perd.* 33–35, *Phil.* 6.17; Sallust, *Jug.* 31.1–5, *Hist.* 3.48.1–5. On Cicero in his guise as leader of the *populus*, Morstein-Marx, *Mass Oratory*, 207–40.

[64] Foucault, *Language, Counter-Memory, Practice*, 219.

[65] Hardt and Negri, *Multitude*, 196. Serres discusses the important role of multiplicity in the Romans' careful cultivation of Roman identity as "unknowable" in *Rome: The Book of Foundations*, esp. 98–114, 231–82. M. Beard reminds us of the (largely erased) polyphony of popular discourse, arguing that Plautus's *Amphitruo* "parodies and problematizes" the aristocratic hero of the triumph ("The triumph of the absurd: Roman street theatre," 39–43). More on the representation of crowds in republican politics in Connolly, "Crowd politics," 89–96.

[66] Accounts of the murder of Clodius are good illustrations of mob power (Asconius 32–52 C; Appian, *BC* 2.21). Millar, *Crowd in Rome*, 94–166, surveys the turbulent crowd politics of the late 60s and early 50s BCE.

awareness of a turbulence that resists analysis or total mastery even as the word suppresses that knowledge in the transformation of manyness into the singular *populus*. A speech Cicero delivered to a priestly college soon after his return from exile rewrites the diversity of the urban and rural masses as proof of its virtuous unity:

> The beauty (*pulchritudo*) of the *populus Romanus*, its real form (*illa forma*), was this . . . when all the leading men of the polity (*principes civitatis*) of all ranks and ages believed that they were voting on the safety not of one citizen but of the *civitas* itself, and when people (*homines*) came to the Field of Mars not when shops but whole municipalities were shut down. (*De Domo Sua*, 89–90).

In letters and orations in the senate—when he is not speaking in a public meeting or trying (as above) to construct the republic in terms of solidarity—Cicero stresses the essential difference of identity between ruling elite and the inexperienced mass. In practice, however, the line of demarcation between dominating and subordinate identities is neither clear nor immutable. Taken as a collection of individuals, "the people" incorporate ruling practices in their own lives, especially in the household, where the treatment of slaves and women enacts the polity in miniature, and in the public organizations (*collegia*) of guilds and clubs, whose inscriptions adopt the tone of official proclamations.

This is not to deny the power of the senatorial order as a ruling group but to emphasize that the situation cannot be understood as a matter of two identities and ideologies, one ruling, one ruled. If the separation of Romans into the two groups *Senatus* and *Populus* makes the division of political power *appear* rational and intelligible, the multiple nature of the mass and its microappropriations of elite habits of rule themselves compose the structure of hegemony. The distribution of power constitutes itself not through the binary division of "authority" and "obedience" or "submission" but as a process through which ruling class and mass partake of beliefs and practices that are, in the strictest sense, proper to both. The ideological articulation of hegemony is a political relation in a constant state of change, and as such cannot be conceived (in the phrase of Laclau and Mouffe) as "the irradiation of effects from a privileged point."[67] By my reading, Cicero's notion of *concordia ordinum* is an expression of an ideal that had been, in an important sense, in place throughout republican history— a broad social consensus that conceived the senate and the people as allies—a conception that, while it camouflaged harsh economic and

---

[67] Laclau and Mouffe, *Hegemony and Socialist Strategy*, 141. Their discussion of Gramsci is important for my earlier comments (esp. 65–71).

political inequalities, hailed the people as the moral and legal judges of their economic superiors, a role that, we shall see, senatorial speakers found it useful to underscore, and that seems to have resonated in popular culture.[68]

Let me note, by way of provisional summary of this section, three closely related points. My definition of ideology insists on ideology's constitutive "contamination" by the extrahegemonic; it grasps the fact that ruling practices (and their alternatives) make meaningful the lived experience of the whole society, and as such saturate the formation of identity at every level; and it denies the notion that members of the ruling order, as lone agents for their class, can articulate and mobilize an ideology that mirrors *only* or even *primarily* that order's desires and values with a view to sustaining its rule. On the contrary, ideology functions precisely because it inheres values and beliefs that stand in tension with the hegemonic. With this in mind, the analysis of popular elements in Roman politics—voting, participating in civic festivals, and especially (given our evidence) listening to speeches—assumes a new importance and must pursue a new direction.

This returns us to my starting point: the equation of eloquence and power. In the speeches they delivered in the senate and Forum, in their control of civic rituals such as games and triumphs, and in their patronage of the arts, especially the public productions of comedy and tragedy during civic festivals (*ludi*), the senatorial order spoke, and patronized the speech of others, with a view to maintaining the traditional dominance of the established families to which they already belonged or which they wished to join. The senatorial order did not, as a rule, implement its authority through the direct application of force, nor did it cultivate the intimate apparatuses of physical coercion or ideological enforcement characteristic of modern experience, such as the police or public education. To what degree is it accurate to say that the political and cultural horizons of the Roman citizenry were shaped by and for their political leaders?[69] I am suggesting that framing the question in these terms risks misrepresenting the complex operations of language in the public sphere. Elite efforts to shape public discourse through communicative acts should rather be seen as working in dialogue with the perceptions and beliefs of the citizen mass.

[68] Popular invective (*sine auctore notissimi versus*, Suet. *Aug.* 70.1) against late republican figures, where the singers claim moral superiority over the ruling class: Courtney, *Fragmentary Latin Poets*, frr. 1–7.

[69] "The cultural horizons of the aristocracy," as Horsfall notes (*The Culture of the Roman Plebs*, 65), is a chapter title in Beard and Crawford's history *Rome in the Late Republic*. (Ithaca, 1985).

Consequently, an interpretive approach based on the assumption that public speech functions primarily, let alone exclusively, as an instrument of traditional ruling authority tends to miss its effects as a popular discourse of identity formation; it generates conclusions that (in spite of themselves and their good intentions of liberal or radical political critique) reinforce the perspectives and desires of our elite sources. As scholars of language, we are apt to fantasize about the absolute power of language, constructing an *eidolon* of politics where language is the essential tool of class domination. Whether we then celebrate that language as a triumphal product of aristocratic virtue (as John Quincy Adams praised Roman oratory) or condemn it as a tool of political oppression, we remain embedded in the master narrative of elite language as elite property, reifying elite representations of power as a static exchange of aristocratic command and mass submission. We should consider terms like *authority* and *obedience* as presenting their own interpretive problems in the arena of public speech. The anthropologist José Gil paves the way with a bracing rejection of these binary terms. Seeking to explain the translation of speech into power, he sees the orator and audience as composing a "collective enunciative subject," through a "progressive conformity of 'responses' to 'demands'" so that the message "*is reflected back onto* the surface thus formed, such that the listeners' individual inscriptions on this body imply that they share the same aim."[70] In the course of the creation of the collective subject of enunciation, just as speakers gain status, influence, a particular policy, or a change in popular opinion, so audiences gain a payoff for their investment in the speech (their physical presence, their vocalizations (shouts, jeers), self-reflection, and conversation with fellow listeners). By recognizing the basic legitimacy of the spoken word as an expression of power as such (a recognition voiced even in hisses or shouts), they integrate themselves into the structure of the expression of power, becoming silent speakers of authority, consensual agents in the system.

The reaction to the expression of power thus manifests itself not as a simple response of obedience or resistance but in hybrid form. Wild approbation can diminish the leader when the assertion of the public's will leaves a more lasting impression than the initial exhortation. Grudging acceptance prepares the ground for future disobedience; angry rejection holds the seeds of consensus. In Livy, when Menenius Agrippa is sent as ambassador to soldiers who have withdrawn in protest of senatorial policy to the Sacred Mount, he tells a parable in which the republic is a body, with the senate as the belly and the people the limbs (Livy 2.32–33). Livy's details reveal that the soldiers' physical departure from

[70] Gil, *Metamorphoses of the Body*, 190–91 (his italics).

the city was not simply an act of resistance or rebellion. Though lacking
an officer to command them, and carrying only survival rations, they
built a camp where they lived in good military order (*communitis castris
quieti*, 2.32.4). Their hill physically mirrored the senatorial seat of
authority, the Capitol; their behavior proclaimed the temporary nature
of their disciplined withdrawal and their expectance of future authority.
In short, their movement of secession also performed an act of obedience
and an invitation of rejoining, which Menenius accepted. Eloquent
(*facundum*) and beloved of the people (*carum plebi*), Menenius embodied the *concordia* that, because it is rooted in the connection of speech
and the communal emotion speech arouses, serves both elite and mass
objectives. Even more dramatic is the strategy of Licinius Crassus, a
character in Cicero's *de Oratore*, who, early in his career, summoned a
contio, where he argued on behalf of repealing the law excluding senators from criminal juries. This speech, clearly focused on upholding the
political advantage of the senatorial order, turned on the rhetorical
redescription of the senate as willing slaves to the People's will: "Do not
let us be a slave (*servire*) to anyone, except to all of you collectively
(*vobis universis*), as we can and ought to be" (1.225). The teller of the
anecdote expresses shock at the rashness of Crassus's use of *servire*, but
his story anticipates Cicero's own habits in claiming common cause with
the popular audience *in contione*—not only his call for unity in the crisis of the Catilinarian conspiracy, but also his rhetoric of popular identification in the agrarian orations: "I am not the kind of consul who, like
many others (*ut plerique*), thinks it anathema to praise the Gracchi, by
whose counsel, wisdom, and laws I see many parts of the republic have
been strengthened" (*Leg. Agr.* 2.10).[71] In cases like this, interpretations
of the relations of language and power must move beyond the binary
oppositions of authority and obedience, rule and subjection, resistance
and passivity: power structures are reinforced in practice precisely by the
blurring of these terms.[72]

Of course, as we try to understand these structures, the state of our
evidence presents a major challenge. In the textual tradition, from official
documents to the literary canon, the ruler's voice is usually the only one we

[71] On Cicero as *popularis*, Morstein-Marx, *Mass Oratory*, 208–30.

[72] Mbembe, "Provisional notes on the postcolony," 3. His controversial piece on
Cameroonian politics inverts the Bakhtinian association between the masses and the
grotesque, arguing that the the postcolonial regime is one of control *and* conviviality, coercion *and* grotesque excess, which spins off whole vocabularies that run parallel to official
discourse, and in the process, break down standard Bakhtinian oppositions. I am also influenced by Foucault's critique of words like "control," "dominance," and "resistance" in his
work on the conventions of historical discourse, which systematically represents "control"
as an elite property and "resistance" as the violent, irrational reaction of the masses
(*Language, Counter-Memory, Practice*, 151; cf. 222).

hear.[73] The evidence for oratory from the Roman republic before the lifetime of Cicero, for instance, preserves for us the voice of the powerful senator Cornelius Scipio Nasica, summoned by a tribune before an angry multitude to explain the senate's handling of a grain shortage in the late second century BCE: "Silence, please, citizens! For I know better than you what is good for the republic" (*tacete, quaeso, quirites! plus ego enim quam vos quid rei publicae expediat intellego*, V. Max. 3.7.3). "When his voice was heard," Valerius Maximus continues, "all fell reverently silent, paying more heed to his authority (*auctoritas*) than to their own means of sustenance." We hear too Nasica's cousin Scipio Aemilianus, scornfully redescribing a crowd infuriated by the murder of the popular tribune Tiberius Gracchus as a motley collection of foreign ex-slaves: "Let them be silent, these people for whom Italy is a mere stepmother," he remarked, adding, "You can't make me afraid, you 'free' men I dragged here in chains" (V. Max. 6.2.3).[74] The powerful effects of the speech of an individual of immense charismatic authority transcend the particularities of an individual elite Roman's character or status. In the election of 214 BCE, in the middle of Hannibal's invasion of Italy, Fabius Maximus brought his *auctoritas* powerfully to bear in stopping the consular election when the electoral unit casting the first vote (the *centuria prerogativa*) chose generals he judged incompetent. A key tradition of Roman electoral practice was overturned: Fabius and his ally Claudius Marcellus were elected in their place (Livy 27.6.2–11).

Roman writings on rhetoric, especially the late works of Cicero and the imperial rhetorician Quintilian, concentrate on training voices of authority, such as those of Fabius and the Cornelii Scipiones, and legitimizing their claim to power. They express a substantial degree of regard for the audience's expectations, particularly as these relate to the audience's judgment of the speaker and its vulnerability to being emotionally moved by his speech: here the later Cicero and Quintilian both follow the tripartite scheme laid out by Aristotle in the *Rhetoric*, which places the presentation of the character (*ethos*) and the arousal of emotion in the audience (*pathos*) on a par with the development of arguments (*logos*).[75] In their

---

[73] Non-elite evidence: M. Beard, "Triumph of the absurd: Roman street theatre," and Horsfall, *Culture of the Roman Plebs*, which trenchantly attacks what he calls the "widely-credited model of Roman cultural life" of "an unquestionable and irreversible hierarchy" made up an "an aristocratic minority which exercises complete control" and the "bullied, exploited, poor" masses in 64–74 (quotation from 66).

[74] "'*Taceant*,' *inquit*, '*quibus Italia noverca est*' . . . '*non efficietis*' *ait* '*ut solutos verear quos alligatos adduxi.*'" For alternative accounts, see Vell. Pat. 2.4.4, Plutarch, *Mor.* 201e–f.

[75] Quintilian on Aristotle's division (3.1.14; cf. Cicero, *Inv.* 2.8). Aristotle criticizes the traditional method of organizing rhetoric under the parts of the speech (proem, narration, etc.), *Rhet.* 1354b16–1355a1, 1414b13–18, 1415b4–9; cited and discussed in Solmsen, "The Aristotelian tradition in ancient rhetoric," 38–39; useful discussion in Wisse, *Ethos and Pathos: From Aristotle to Cicero*, 77–93.

concern with the audience's ethical evaluation and emotional reactions, however, their overall aim is the negotiation of mass opinion and elite authority, how to gauge and react, shape and sway.[76] This is the logic behind Cicero's emphasis on the orator's capacity to whip up his listeners' emotions: it makes them susceptible to his direction.[77] Rhetorical texts reinforce the values and ensure the dominance of the senatorial order by giving prescriptive shape to traditional expressions of moral authority—expressions in which, as we shall see, the citizen mass holds a critical investment and whose role cannot be reduced to obedience or adulation.

EXPRESSIONS OF TRADITIONAL AUTHORITY

The most important contexts for a public meeting of mass and elite in republican Rome were three: the *contio*, the nonvoting public assemblies summoned in the Roman Forum and other public places, where magistrates and other members of the senatorial class competed for popular standing and public trust; the law court, where intra-elite disputes were resolved and elite individuals made known to the people; and a variety of other public gatherings, including the triumph.[78] Louis Althusser describes the formation of subjectivity as a process by which the subject is "recruited" or summoned or into being by ideology, through repetitive acts of hailing that transform the individual into a subject position predefined by existing discourses, such as law and education.[79] In these three contexts, the citizenry was summoned into being—it came to

[76] See further, chapter 3. On the history of this development, see Solmsen, "Aristotle and Cicero on the orator's playing upon the feelings," and Fantham, "Ciceronian *conciliare* and Aristotelian ethos," arguing that the *captatio benevolentiae* is a form of emotional appeal; also Fortenbaugh, "*Benevolentiam conciliare* and *animos permovere*," esp. 270–73, on the importance of Stoicism and forensic experience in Cicero's account of emotion.

[77] To his son's query about the number of elements in a speech, Cicero replies: "Four: two of them, narration and argument, serve to lay out the case; the other two, the opening and the peroration, serve to arouse the audience's minds" (*Part.* 1.4).

[78] Many of the latter fall under the official category of the *contio*, such as funeral orations; the speeches of victorious generals at the conclusion of their triumphs; the censors' report after the census; events connected with religious ritual, such as the nomination of replacement augurs; and various oath takings, including the swearing in (and out) of magistrates (Pina Polo, "Procedures and functions of civil and military *contiones*," and Morstein-Marx, *Mass Oratory*, who includes a thorough survey of the geography of the *contio* (10–11, 34–60). The senate house is obviously another important venue for deliberative speech but does not, of course, directly involve mass-elite relations.

[79] Althusser, "Ideology and Ideological State Apparatuses," 128–32.

understand itself as a citizen collective—through the communal experience of watching and reacting to elite men broadcasting their authority
and high status (*auctoritas, dignitas*), whose legitimacy the presence of
the mass in turn confirms. The physical quality of these crowd experiences is an important element in the story of how elite power maintained
popular legitimacy. In the triumph, for example, the material impact of
imperial conquest made itself sensually manifest through magnificent
parades of slaves, booty, and plundered art.[80] Rituals like the Saturnalia
similarly enacted an imperial conviviality that mixed together elite and
mass in an communal act of self-celebration. To the younger Seneca,
such occasions permitted "the many" to spread its disease of frenzied
license, threatening the putative integrity of elite self-government (*turba,
multi, Ep. Mor.* 7.1–2). His reaction suggests the degree—frightening,
from his perspective—to which the triumph succeeded both in celebrating the power and glory of the victorious general and in closing the distance between him and the corporeal excess of the crowded, festive
celebration, manifested in the triumphator's gaudily adorned, cosmetically enhanced face and body.[81]

The communicative encounter in the *contio* and law court did not
celebrate the convivial communal body in the same way the triumph
did. Instead, the orator reinforced his authority by offering the audience
the pleasures of moral agreement, pleasures that made possible the celebration of popular liberty. This involved, I propose, not a top-down
display of charismatic authority in the traditional Weberian mold but an
affirmation of the consensual fantasy of membership in an ideal civic
body.[82] At this stage we should recall that memories of the middle
republican orator shape the exemplar of the ideal orator in Cicero's
later work, and thus the model of the ideal prince and the *vir civilis* in
the European tradition. If I am right to explain moralism as an equalizing

[80] The conviviality on display at the triumph and other civic festivals sweeps up senatorial nobility and plebs into a shared celebration of the body politic in the most basic sense.
To step away from such celebrations is, in a sense, to deny life itself (no light observation
in the case of the plebs, for whom the distribution of food may have been an important, if
intermittent, source of nutrition).

[81] It is worth noting, however, that as claims of individual achievement, especially self-
sacrifice or military glory, are made to stand for "Roman virtue," in the context of the
community of the free male whole united by putatively shared values, two things happen:
the ruling class seeks to secure a grip on (publicizing) their actions, but the possibility
endures that a heroic individual outside that class may achieve great deeds according to
the dominant script—a fantasy kept alive by (for example) the legionaries mentioned in
Caesar's war commentaries (Petreius, *Gal.* 7.50) and perhaps the Roman gladiator (cf.
Barton, *Sorrows of the Ancient Romans*, 85–91).

[82] Weber's famous definition of charismatic authority: *Economy and Society*, 241–53; for
an influential account of Weberian charisma, see Giddens, *Capitalism and Modern Social
Theory*, 160–72.

element in republican discourse, it will alter our understanding of those models in the context of the evolution of political thought about citizenship and communication.

Cicero's history of Roman oratory, composed in 45 BCE, opens with a list of ten protoorators, from Brutus, the ancestor of Cicero's dedicatee and the founder of the republic, to M. Cornelius Cethegus, the first Roman for whom Cicero possesses textual evidence (*Brut. 57*).[83] Figured here as a belated art with origins in talent instead of craft, early Roman eloquence naturalizes the senate's traditional authority. Cicero's representation thus preserves the field of early Roman cultural achievement as Roman pure and simple, with no taint of foreign influence. His account makes no mention of rhetoric's periodic banishments from Rome: in 161, when the praetor M. Pomponius, with approval from the senate, expelled rhetoricians and philosophers, and in 92, when the censors' edict shut down the public teaching of rhetoric in Latin (Suet. *Rhet. 1*). Suppressed by Cicero here, the memory preserved in other texts of rhetoric's periodic expulsions reinforces its identity as a biddable art that exists at the sufferance of the ruling order, even as it reminds us of rhetoric's potentially subversive force. Instead, the early sections of *Brutus* showcase traditional senatorial privileges and authority in the face of popular unrest. Only one of Cicero's "canonical" ten is remembered for his speeches on behalf of the *populus* (G. Flaminius); three gained fame from their successful quelling of popular sedition.[84] The dictator Marcus Valerius "quiets" the plebeians after their secession to the Mons Sacer in 259 in protest of harsh debt laws and military service (*dicendo sedavisse discordias*, *Brut. 54*). L. Valerius Potitus "softened" the plebeians in the turbulent wake of the decemvirs' rule (*plebem mitigaverit*, 55). M. Popilius, informed of rioting while performing a ritual in his simultaneous roles as consul and *flamen*, "quieted" the crows still dressed in his priestly robes (assonance links the key words: *seditionemque cum auctoritate tum oratione sedavit*, 56).[85]

---

[83] The list of ten may reflect the influence of Caecilius of Calacte: I am persuaded by O'Sullivan's argument that Caecilius, whose work probably contributed to the creation of the "canonical" list of "ten Attic orators," is a contemporary influence on Cicero ("Caecilius, the 'canons' of writers, and the origins of Atticism").

[84] According to Livy, Brutus's first act in founding the republic was a public speech calling for revenge against the Tarquins (1.54). On the rest: Cicero's treatment of Manius Curius, a tribune of the early third century, emphasizes his role as an interlocutor between mass and elite: he helped negotiate a crisis during which a patrician consul had refused to accept a plebeian candidate for office, in defiance of the law (*contra leges*, *Brut. 55*). Of the remaining six described in *Brutus* 54–57, one is famous for his senatorial speeches (Appius Claudius), one for his work as an ambassador (G. Fabricius), and three are mentioned in passing (Tiberius Coruncanius, Q. Fabius Maximus, Q. Metellus).

[85] Nobility is much on Cicero's mind at this point in the text: he views preserved speeches as a textual resource for families eager to defend the memory of the great deeds of their house, but also to prove their nobility. Scraps of speeches are preserved, according to

The structure of the memories preserved in *Brutus* weaves the senatorial order's claim to be the religious, moral, and political arbiters of Rome into their claim to political leadership: as these speakers are shown as consuming all the available air of public discourse, politics itself becomes identified with their voices. The dialogue implies that their speeches create the frame within which "politics" properly occurs—within which popular opinion may be shaped and elite rivalries played out.

In content and style, extant fragments of middle republican oratory support the representation of political oratory in *Brutus* as an arena for the expression of traditional aristocratic authority. Of course, anecdotes of middle republican speech-making reveal not necessarily actual practice but what elite sources judged worth remembering. The form in which the tradition preserves these fragments, and the privileged place granted to moral themes, bespeak the elite investment in viewing senatorial public speech as a stylized projection of the republic as a "well-defined group which might be called a community of moral obligation."[86] How, precisely, do they grant legitimacy to the republican order and the dominant role of the senatorial elite?

One of the earliest partially surviving speeches in Latin was delivered by the elder Cato to the senate in 167 BCE. Rome had just defeated Macedon, in a war in which Rhodes had remained neutral, and the city sent an embassy to the senate to justify its neutrality and forestall Roman reprisal. When the senate reacted aggressively, Cato advised caution:

> I realize that in many men, at times that are favorable, successful, and prosperous, the spirit is exultant, and arrogance and self-assurance increase and grow great. For which reason this is now my greatest concern, that because this affair [the Macedonian war] has proceeded so successfully, something harmful may result in our deliberation, which would diminish these successes of ours—or that our happiness may become too self-indulgent. Adverse affairs tame and teach us what must be done, but favorable ones generally thrust men sideways from the straight way in deliberation and consideration.

> *scio solere plerisque hominibus rebus secundis atque prolixis atque prosperis animum excellere atque superbiam atque ferociam augescere atque crescere. Quo mihi nunc magnae curae est, quod res tam secunde*

Cicero, by families seeking to advertise their high social status, particularly at funerals (*quasi ornamenta ac monumenta*, 62). That religious documents are a part of elite efforts to institutionalize, through record keeping, their intertwined religious and political authority is suggested by Cicero's reliance on the records of a priestly college for his information about Tiberius Coruncanius (*valuisse*, *Brut.* 55).

[86] I borrow this formulation from Roller's discussion of traditional Roman ethics, *Constructing Autocracy*, 28.

processit, ne quid in consulendo advorsi eveniat, quod nostras secundas res confutet, neve haec laetitia nimis luxuriose eveniat. Advorsae res edomant et docent quid opus siet facto, secundae res laetitia transvorsum trudere solent a recte consulendo atque intellegendo (Gel. 6.3.14)

The rhyming and alliteration of phrases like *scio solere, prolixis atque prosperis*, and *edomant et docent* lend Cato's exordium the flavor of aphorism. Later rhetoricians would call these turns of phrase *sententiae*, but their effect goes further. The speech is evidence that Cato's message lies not only in his argument but also in the way it draws attention to the quality of the words as they roll off his tongue: the grain of their timbre, their intimate connection to Cato's physical being. Its sensual assonance and granulated crackles exert the power of the body beyond the limits of the body to demand assent. As it transforms the logical structures of rational argument into rhyme and ornament, the speech modifies "raw" authority and moral reasoning into a paradigmatic expression of what calls itself "political," "eloquence," "persuasion," and by that act of self-naming it seizes not only legitimacy but the very means by which legitimacy may be claimed or contested. Gramsci notes that histories of political thought generally leave out the notion of force or violence, as though political thought were the natural opposite or negation of violence, and not part of the ruling class's strategic justifications of hegemony.[87] Cato's speech has power not because it leaves out violence but because it gracefully modifies violence. A roundhouse punch that also offers the pleasure of rhyme and rhythm, his voice makes authority endurable, indeed attractive.[88] His style closes the distance between his *auctoritas* and his argument, and the result is intensified, transsomatized message—the essence of the "hyperclarity" of the traditional expression of authority.[89]

Cato's figures of speech incorporate and in turn reinforce the formulaic language of religious ritual.[90] The connection between eloquence and religious authority surfaces in Cicero's *Brutus*, too, which draws on sources preserved by a priestly college (*ex pontificum commentariis, Brut.* 55). In *de Agricultura*, Cato preserves prayers designed for recitation

---

[87] Gramsci, *Prison Notebooks*, 52.

[88] Lendon, *Empire of Honour*, brilliantly describes Roman honor as "a face-saving device, a way to describe the interaction of man and authority, to conceal greed and fear, to depict obedience in a world where slavery cast a stigma upon it . . . permitting the efficient exercise of brute power under an unobjectionable veil" (24; cf. 25–27, 39).

[89] Gil, *Metamorphoses of the Body*, 189.

[90] Leeman, *Orationis Ratio*, 45–46 compares this fragment to other Catonian fragments that share stylistic and structural elements, and analyzes it in light of Gellius's response to Cicero's secretary Tiro, whose criticism of the speech's lack of polish and erudition preserved certain key sections (Gel. 6.3.8–55). Useful discussion of names in prayer: Corbeill, *Controlling Laughter*, 68–74, and *Nature Embodied*, 15–20. Habinek, *The World*

before the harvest that include repetitions of *esto* and the phrases *bonas preces precor*, "I pray these prayers" and *porco piaculo*, "sacrificial pigs" (four times in a single sentence), and marked alliteration and homoteleuton, sometimes both in a single phrase, such as *porco piaculo immolando esto* (134.1–4, 139.1; cf. Gel. 4.6.3–10). A longer prayer to Mars, to be pronounced by a farmer purifying his land, displays the resonance of the ritual language:

> Father Mars, I pray and I seek that you be willingly favorable to me and my house and my household, for which reason therefore I have ordered a *suovitaurilia* (triple sacrifice of pig, ram, and bull) to be led around my field and land and farm, so that you keep off, defend, and remove disease, seen and unseen, barrenness and bleakness, disaster and unseasonable weather; and so that you allow my crops, grain, vines, and gardens to come out well, and so that you keep safe my shepherds and flocks, and give good health and vigor to me and my household and my family. . . .

> *Mars pater, te precor quaesoque uti sies volens propitius mihi domo familiaeque nostrae, quoius re ergo agrum terram fundumque meum suovitaurilia circumagi iussi, uti tu morbos visos invisosque, viduertatem vastitudinemque, calamitates intemperiesque, prohibessis defendas avveruncesque; utique tu fruges, frumenta, vineta virgultaque grandire beneque evenire siris, pastores pecuaque salva servassis duisque bonam salutem valetudinemque mihi domo familiaeque nostrae. . . . (141.2–3)*[91]

To the mature Cicero, these patterns are the essence of Latin archaism: unpolished and crude, harsh and old-fashioned.[92] They possess an almost hypnotic abundance of repetition, the sense of which is increased by asyndeton and alliteration. Spoken in the senate, they confirmed the solemn state of the assembly; spoken in public, they underlined the speaker's appeal to the Roman *mos maiorum*. His *Brutus* brings out

---

of Roman Song, aptly adduces Manilius's representation of song (early first century BCE) as drawing down authoritative knowledge from the cosmos (89–94), and cites Cicero's recognition (*Tusc.* 1.64) of the close interconnections between song and eloquence (94–102). Momigliano, "Perizonius, Niebuhr," argues that the earliest Roman historical memories were conveyed in *carmina*.

[91] Compare the augur's prayer, Varro, *L.* 7.8: *olla verba arbos quirquir est, quam me sentio dixisse, templum tescumque me esto in sinistrum* (repeated with substitution of *dextrum* for *sinistrum*).

[92] "Atticus" (Cicero's friend appears in character) remarks that the elder Cato was *impolitam et plane rudem* (*Brut.* 294); Cicero admits in his own voice that Laelius was *vetustior et horridior* than Scipio, because he took more pleasure in the archaic (*delectari mihi magis antiquitate videtur*, 83). His favorable comparison of Laelius to Stoic authorities in a nonrhetorical context may be the more pointed given the Stoics' well-known preference (in Cicero's view) for a plain and rough style of speech (*ND.* 3.5, 3.43).

these associations when it describes Aemilianus's close friend Laelius in 145 BCE delivering a similar speech, which used archaic diction in combination with arguments appealing to the old-fashioned simplicity of archaic religion successfully to oppose the innovative proposal of C. Crassus that priesthoods should be elected by the popular assembly (*Brut.* 83). In the next generation, the conservative historian Calpurnius Piso Frugi is said to have adopted a meager (*exiliter*) style, free from then-fashionable ornament, to describe the simple life of the *maiores*, at an important moment in the development of antiquarianism and the revival of archaic religious rites (*Brut.* 106).[93] While the diction and sentence structure of later fragments gain in complexity, Catonian habits of repetition and rhythm persist. The following passage is excerpted from a speech by Scipio Aemilianus, who was brought to trial before the people by a tribune eager to exact revenge for actions taken against himself during Scipio's censorship. Like Popilius (*Brut.* 56), Scipio appeared before the assembly cleanly shaven, clad in his white triumphal garb (Gel. 3.4.1–3).[94] His speech aggressively turns the tables on his accuser:

> All the evils, vices, and crimes that men commit exist in two things: malice and wastefulness. Against which do you defend yourself, malice or wastefulness, or both at the same time? If you prefer to defend against wastefulness, good: if you have squandered more money on one whore than what you reported at the census as the whole value of your Sabine estate, if this is so, who pledged the thousand sesterces? If you have dissipated more than a third of your paternal property and squandered it on vices, if this is so, who pledged the thousand sesterces? You do not want to defend against the charge of wastefulness. Come, then, defend yourself at least against the charge of malice. If you swore in pre-planned phrases consciously in your conscious mind, if this is so, who pledged the thousand sesterces?

> *omnia mala, probra, flagitia, quae homines faciant, in duabus rebus sunt, malitia atque nequitia. Utrum defendis, malitiam an nequitiam an utrumque simul? Si nequitiam defendere vis, licet; si tu in uno scorto maiorem pecuniam absumpsisti quam quanti omne instrumentum fundi Sabini in censum dedicavisti; si hoc ita est, qui spondet mille nummum? si tu plus tertia parte pecuniae paternae perdidisti atque absumpsisti in flagitiis; si hoc ita est, qui spondet mille nummum? Non vis nequitiam. Age malitiam saltem defende. Si tu verbis conceptis coniuravisti sciens scienti animo tuo; si hoc ita est, qui spondet mille nummum?* (Gel. 6.11.9)

[93] Rawson, "Scipio, Laelius, Furius," 83; and further on Piso, "The first Latin annalists," 257–67.

[94] The implication of Gellius's *cum esset reus*, "although he was a defendant," is that accused men allowed their beards to grow and wore dark clothing.

The impact of the repetition of *si hoc ita est, qui spondet mille nummum?*
and *nequitia, defendere,* and *absumpsisti* is enhanced by Scipio's use of
alliterative antithesis (*parte pecuniae paternae perdidisti* and *sciens
scienti*) and homoeoteleuton (*mala, probra, flagitia* and *malitiam,
nequitiam*).[95] The flavor of ritual and echo of prayer in this speech lend
its speaker a transhuman power.[96] Its ritualized style makes the language
of conventional morality and the political authority that expresses it
transcendent: the body of the speaker takes on charismatic significance
as the embodiment of moral rightness. The formalization of utterance
also gives a certain shape to the speaking body: by making it the
"proper" vehicle of the proclamation of moralistic pronouncements, it
both exploits and transcends the body's materiality. Speeches given by
men who were the embodiments of the political order—in the case of a
noble family, imagined to be literally descended from the roots of republican history—gave the republic discursive presence, the authority to
authorize (*auctoritas*); their speaking bodies provided the model for the
monuments and statues in which the *res publica* took artifactual shape.
Religious, legal, and political authority thus intersected and supported
one another, made visible and audible through common patterns of comportment and ritualized speech: the energy of verbal rhythm and repetition overdetermines hegemonic rule.

At the same time, as Manrice Bloch has argued, because it is associated
with rule or the idea of the ruler rather than with any particular member
of the ruling class, stylization also "removes the tie" between utterance
and particular event: it affirms the role of leader rather than that of the
leader himself.[97] If the stylization of power produces a nonspecific discourse whose universalist effect serves to naturalize the contingent social
order, it also restricts the ability of the speaker to improvise; it fixes him
in an enforceable position. And it disciplines public speech by demanding
a certain degree of public accountability and by funneling intra-elite
struggles into verbal contests over virtue. In 187 BCE, Tiberius Gracchus
attacked Scipio Africanus on the grounds that he had put the fortunes of
his brother (who had been accused of bribery) ahead of civic virtue, and
that where Scipio had once virtuously refused the people's offer of an
indefinite consulship and dictatorship, he had begun to behave like a

[95] Similar patterns of parallelism, repetition, and the use of multiple synonyms are visible in the *laudatio funebris* delivered by Scipio's grandson in praise of Scipio's closest
friend, Laelius, preserved in a scholia on Cicero's *pro Milone*.

[96] Now see Corbeill, *Nature Embodied*, 12–33: he may overstate the emphasis on the
authentic naturalness of recorded prayer, but his discussion of the overlap between religious and medical gesture is valuable (esp. 26–33).

[97] On this phenomenon in expressions of authority in Maori, African, and native
American culture: Bloch, *Political Language and Oratory*, "Introduction," 26.

tyrant (Livy 38.56). Aemilius Paullus, victor in Spain, Liguria, and
Macedonia, used the *contio* to advertise his virtuous piety, an act that
simultaneously increased Paullus's symbolic capital and reinforced the
moral standards of the *populus*, creating precedents according to which
future transgressors could be punished (V. Max. 5.10.2). By providing,
through public utterance, an image of virtuous rule as its own justification, the senatorial order not only shaped the world around itself but
shaped itself around that world.

Nor did invocations of religious ritual serve exclusively to underscore
elite power. According to A. D. Nock, a distinctive feature of Roman
religion was its emphasis on authoritative utterance, usually in the context of the popular assembly, which regularly voted on the proper form
and time of rituals: he contrasts the Eastern Orthodox formula, with its
passive construction, "N. *is baptized* in the name of the Father," with the
western Roman usage, "*I baptize you* in the name of the Father."[98]
Judgments of ritual efficacy and propriety rested with the people and
were granted permanence through inscription on stone or bronze tablets:
the discursive registers of Roman law and religion overlapped in the act
of public approval and public display. In the claim made by prayers and
other ritual utterances to give proper dispensation, certain Latin words
ubiquitous in prayers and acts of legislation—such as *esto*, "let it be"—
stood in contrast to Greek ritual expressions, which stressed continuity
with ancestral custom (along the lines of "this is how it has always
been").[99] The legal form of expressions of authority in Roman religion
reinforced the people's sovereign role as makers and remakers of the law.

Beyond prayer, other discursive ingredients evoked in the oratorical
performance cross lines of class. Cicero attests to the musical and rhythmic expectations of the popular audience (*Orat.* 168, 173; *de Orat.*
3.198). Popular proverbs, riddles, games, and worksongs used the diction, rhythms, and ornaments of prayer, such as the children's chants
rex erit qui recte faciet, qui non faciet non erit ("the good boy will be
king, the bad boy won't be"), *malum consilium consultori pessimum est*
("bad advice works out worst to the adviser," Gel. 4.55.5), and Varro's
repetitive jingle *novum vetus vinum bibo, novo veteri morbo medeor*
("New and old wine I drink up, by new and old wine I'm made well,"

---

[98] Nock, "A feature of Roman religion," 97. Dowden, "Rhetoric and religion: The instance
of prayer," agrees that the "I-ness" of the human speaker and the "you-ness" of the god is
emphasized in Roman, as opposed to Greek, prayer, and notes that Servius believed that
Roman orators as late as the Gracchi began all their speeches by invoking the gods (*ad Aen.*
11.301).

[99] Nock, "A feature of Roman religion," 88–91; see Rawson, "Scipio, Laelius, Furius,"
on the post-146 BCE fashion of research into and revival of archaic religious practices (that
is, after the end of the third Punic war), 80–82, 101.

L. 6.21).[100] Republican oratory is composed of a mingling of popular and elite sounds and rhythms. If educated ears heard the echo of a ritual whose exact words were known only to a few, others could interpret the simple repetitions of Cato's speeches as reflective of these popular modes of speech. An implicitly dialogic dynamic of authority emerges here, even a glimpse of the way these expressions of traditional authority could arouse, beyond consent, identification on equal terms.

THE RHETORIC OF EQUALITY

We tend to assimilate the rights and liberties of democratic citizenship with our shared belief in equality—moral equality, the belief that humans are equal, rights-bearing individuals by virtue of being human. This belief is a product of liberal political thought about rights as the intrinsic, inalienable property of human beings. However, this notion of liberty has no foundation in Roman thought or practice; as Wirzsubski puts it, the Romans "conceived *libertas* as an acquired civic right, and not as an innate right of man."[101] Although Roman citizens in the republican period enjoyed equality under the law and were protected from the arbitrary interference of others, including and especially magistrates, it is difficult to think of the republic as a regime of equality: candidacy for political office, jury duty, and participation in public speech were limited to men of substantial wealth; electoral voting itself was weighted according to wealth. How, then, may the prevailing influence of the senatorial order in setting the political agenda be reconciled with the value they seem to have laid on popular approval? And if the citizen mass played such an important role in approving, and occasionally opposing, the senatorial agenda, why were they satisfied with that limited, reactive role?

A popular anecdote sheds light on the question. In 187 or 185 BCE, anticipating the experience of his adopted son Aemilianus, Scipio Africanus was summoned to trial by a tribune before the assembly. Ignoring the charges against him (extortion and overstepping his authority), Africanus delivered a lengthy, lively speech that recounted his services to the state. Judgment was postponed—until the anniversary of Africanus's victory over Hannibal. Back on the Rostra, Africanus noted the coincidence and invited the crowd to accompany him to the Capitoline hill, where he would offer sacrifices to the gods, to whom he wished to pray that Rome would always have leaders like

---

[100] The children's song appears in Porphyrio, *ad* Hor. *Epist.* 1.1.59 (cited by Horsfall, *Culture of the Roman Plebs*, 46).

[101] Wirzsubski, *Libertas*, 3.

himself. The Forum emptied, leaving the tribunes alone with their assistants, and Scipio spent the day leading the people from temple to temple in festive celebration (Livy 38.51).[102] In the spectacle of the powerful man expressing unquestioned confidence in the virtue of his domination, by virtue of his domination, self-righteousness becomes the sign of legitimate authority. In the moment of his encounter with the public assembly, Scipio appeals to his own body as the symbol of truth, broadcasting a powerful sense of civic cohesion extending beyond any mere utterance.[103]

His speech recalls other senatorial invitations to a popular moralist consensus: Marcius Rutilius Censorinus rebuked the people in a *contio* for electing him to the censorship twice; Scipio Africanus chided them for wishing him dictator (V. Max. 4.1.3, Livy 38.56). Heroic values find a communal mode of expression in the *laudatio funebris*, or funeral oration, like the stoic performance given by Q. Fabius Maximus for his son, who died young (*Sen.* 12). Q. Caecilius Metellus, an early star in Cicero's *Brutus* (57), gave a *laudatio funebris* extolling his father's achievements and his list of maxims describing the goals of a good life (Pliny *Nat.* 7.139), whose flavor is captured by his speech warning that Roman virtue would be weakened by victory over Carthage (V. Max. 7.2.3).[104] When Sulpicius exhorted the reluctant *populus* to pursue the Macedonian war in 200, he uses the same rhetorical strategies as were used by Appius Claudius Caecus, the consul in 307 and 296 who would become a symbol of archaic style, when he harangued the senate to war against Pyrrhus.[105] We might conclude that such anecdotes are preserved because they showcase what Max Weber calls the "charismatic authority" of the

---

[102] "In the end, the tribune made his plea *apud populum sine populo*, before the People without any people; deserted, he stayed alone in the Forum . . . eventually, in order to escape his shame, he followed the parade to the Capitol, and from the accuser of Scipio became his admirer" (V. Max. 3.7.1g; cf. Gel. 4.18). Valerius Maximus (3.7.1a–1g) and Aulus Gellius (4.18) repeat garbled versions of several similar anecdotes about Scipio.

[103] Gil, *Metamorphoses of the Body*, 193–94.

[104] He was the target of the comedian Naevius's comment "by (sheer) luck the Metelli are consuls at Rome," *fato Metelli Romae fiunt consules*, to which Metellus was supposed to have replied *dabunt malum Metelli Naevio poetae*, "the Metelli will pay back the poet Naevius."

[105] Livy records Sulpicius' speech (31.7). Ennius paraphrases Appius Claudius: "Where have your minds turned, which used to stand up straight before, mindless now?" (*Quo vobis mentes, rectae quae stare solebant/antehac, dementes sese flexere?*, Cicero, *Sen.* 16). On the speech *De Pyrrho Rege*, see Plutarch, *Pyrrhus* 19.1: other sources in Malcovati, *ORF*, who surveys the debate over the authenticity of his work even in Cicero's time (*contra* Cicero's statement that he has read Appius's work, *Brut.* 61), pointing out that Cato is elsewhere agreed (by Cicero and others) to be the first to publish his speeches. On his special status as the earliest Roman orator: *apud Romanos Appius Caecus adversus Pyrrhum solutam orationem primus exercuit* (Isidore *Etym.* 1.38.2; cf. Seneca *Ep.* 114.13, Tacitus *Dial.* 21.7).

senatorial class.[106] Egon Flaig concludes that the republic revolved precisely around this dynamic: senatorial charismatic leadership and popular obedience (*Gehorsam*).[107] Triumphs, vote canvassing, and speeches—all the stagings and restagings of mass-elite encounters—reminded the masses of their duty to obey, a duty that the ritual nature of Roman politics transformed into political consensus.[108]

Achille Mbembe, in a compelling piece of postcolonial analysis of political practice in Cameroon, proposes a different approach. He explores how the government-sponsored ceremony and parade create a suspended moment in time during which everyone, including and perhaps especially the poor, the diseased, and the disenfranchised, is eager to sustain a bond, however brief, "of familiarity, of collusion even, with domination in its most heady form," so that the politics of coercion is sensed to lessen the burden of subjection.[109] Key to Mbembe's argument is the way moral authority kindles not simply terror or shame but an affirmation of the citizenry's strength in partnership with elite authority, an affirmation whose excessive, loud, vulgar expressions mirror the excessive nature of elite power and the transgressions that result from its exercise. The elite contest for prestige and authority contains "elements of crudeness and the bizarre that the official order tries to hide," Mbembe observes, but which the mass exposes in a "logic of conviviality" that appropriates the repertoire of elite power.[110] Africanus's prayer, which is also a boast, invites his audience to celebrate virtue in an extravagant mode, placing themselves in a position of moral superiority over the tribunes, the traditional (elite) voice of the people. The crowd climbs the Capitoline extolling the authority not only of Scipio but of themselves, in their capacity as moral judges who, in praising Scipio, appear to reclaim popular initiative from tribunician control.

The anecdote enriches our understanding of why *ethos*, the presentation of character and the invitation of moral judgment, must be the mainstay of republican oratory.[111] *Ethos* transposes elite rivalry into a

---

[106] Weber, "Charismatic authority," in *Economy and Society*, 241–54: see especially his comments on "hereditary charisma," where "recognition is no longer paid to the charismatic qualities of the individual, but to the legitimacy of the position he has acquired by hereditary succession . . . [by] traditionalization or legalization" (248).

[107] Flaig, *Ritualisierte Politik*, esp. 13–17, 83–88.

[108] Habinek, *Politics of Latin Literature* (esp. 36–39), similarly conceptualizes the command-obedience dynamic in his argument that Latin literature should be understood as the carefully constructed "invention" of the Roman aristocracy, who seek to maintain their hegemony over the masses through the coercion of culture.

[109] Mbembe, "Provisional notes," 20.

[110] Ibid., 8, 10.

[111] Of course, Aristotle had seen that *ethos* is always crucial: "Moral character, so to speak, constitutes the most effective source of persuasion" (*Rhet.* 1.2). The question is

moral key, rewriting political difference (expressed in policy disputes or legal cases) as moral difference.[112] This operation conceals signs of instability in the political order: by veiling the real fractures created by the internal struggle for power, the transposition recasts rivalry that threatens the stability of the polity as a cleansing moral force that promises, not incidentally, to heal the polity. Moralism also serves to pull the people more closely into its embrace: when citizens are persuaded that moral conflicts are at stake, they are more readily prepared to engage in political action.[113] As a language all politicians speak, moralism has the effect of ameliorating political difference itself: as much as audience members are distracted or entertained by the spectacle of moral competition, they are also comforted by the language of virtue and vice that unites elite with elite and elite with mass in a shared value system that putatively trumps the real intensity of intra-elite rivalry. Most important, moralist speech, by remaking the assembly in the forum or the crowd around the jury in the forum into a living microrepublic of virtue, constructs the ostensible equality of liberty in the republic, *by rendering citizens as equal in their capacity as moral judges*. This is the full significance of moralism in political discourse: it is proof and guarantor of republican liberty, because it creates the perception of equality.

The moralist Roman polices the sexual domain with special care.[114] Here Scipio Aemilianus speaks against Tiberius Gracchus's proposals for judicial reform:

> They are taught disreputable tricks (*praestigias inhonestas*), when accompanied by effeminates (*cinaedulis*), with a harp and a lute, they go to the actors' school (*eunt in ludum histrionum*), they learn to sing songs which our ancestors would prefer to be thought degrading—they go, I say, into the dancing school among the effeminates, freeborn girls and boys (*eunt, dico, in ludum saltatorum inter cinaedos virgines puerique ingenui*). When someone told me about this, I couldn't bring myself to believe it, that men of noble families were teaching their own children these things, but when I was brought to the dancing school, sure enough, I saw in that school five hundred boys and

---

why. Most studies explore Cicero's exploitation of *ethos* in the law court and are satisfied with the assumption that *ethos* "worked" in popular speeches because the Romans valued *auctoritas, gloria,* and *dignitas* (e.g., May, *Trials of Character,* 7–9)—to which we can ask "why?"

[112] Brilliantly evoked by Morstein-Marx, *Mass Oratory,* 258–76.

[113] So Flaig, *Ritualisierte Politik,* 184–201. My concern here is with pre-Ciceronian oratory: on moralism and the presentation of character in Cicero, see May, *Trials of Character,* and Dugan, *Making a New Man,* 55–62.

[114] On the regulation of sex and sexual language: Gellius 4.20, Plut. *Cato Maior* 29; Richlin, *The Garden of Priapus*; Corbeill, *Controlling Laughter,* 104–6, 128–73.

> girls, and among them one (this makes me pity the republic!) wearing a
> bulla, the son of a man seeking office, at least twelve years old, dancing with
> bells on, the sort of dance a shameless little slave could not have danced hon-
> orably (*impudicus servulus honeste saltare non posset*). (Macrobius 3.14.5)

Another Scipionic speech attacks Sulpicius Gallus as a *cinaedus* for wearing long tunics and heavy perfume, plucking his body hair, and sleeping
with men (Gel. 6.12.5–6).[115] Though it is not clear where these speeches
were delivered—senate, law court, or *contio*—both fragments establish
Aemilianus as the arbiter of morality as well as policy and law by cultivating an image of aggressive masculine virtue. With vivid imagery that
lingers on the representation of vice, Aemilianus's request that his audience
join in the banishment of the obscene and the vicious mounts a pleasura-
bly revolting portrayal of what it condemns. The indulgence of vice that
arises from vice's banning creates a moment of shared emotional intensity
where the elite demand for popular obedience voices itself as a call for
common self-restraint, a call that is itself expressed in terms of sexual vul-
garity, class hatred, and xenophobia. The language of paternal authority
passes judgment in the voice of aggrieved and aggressive masculinity ("I
couldn't bring myself to believe it"), acting as a connective bond between
the living bodies of speaker and audience, redressing the imbalance of
power between speaker and audience. The point is not only that
Aemilianus affirms and reinforces his own manly virtue, which is also the
essence of his moral authority; rather, the communicative context in which
he delivers his speech means that it affirms, reinforces, and magnifies the
manly virtue and moral authority of each listening citizen. The speech's
detailed concerns—education, sex, music, clothing, dancing—express the
putatively universal concerns of the domestic sphere, a brand of moralizing that invokes and celebrates paternal authority and extends its notional
overlordship to the republic as a whole. The moralizing senator's public
condemnation of the transgressive bodies of the dancers, actors, and free
youths who have been monstrously transformed into sexually objectified
slaves constructs a shared intimacy of moral agreement that grants the
people a sense of participation and empowerment; the dynamics of domestic authority are satisfyingly inscribed in the public domain via the shared
experience of paternal authority. Scipio's moralism amounts to an invitation to the less powerful to share in power by sharing in the language of
power—a language the audience already knows and celebrates.

As the artifactuality of moral agreement creates a fantasy of common
identity and civic liberty, the elite oratorical performance thus goes some

---

[115] He engaged in a contest with the tribune Claudius Asellus, whom he expelled from the
equestrian order. Leeman sees this as possible evidence of a culture war between the "conservative" Scipio and his enemies, the plebeian tribunes (*Orationis Ratio*, 52–53).

way to solving the complex negotiation of senatorial domination and popular assent. So strong is the power of the speaking body in this creation of consensus that speech loses its force when the body is absent. As Cicero says of the orator Galba, a contemporary of Cato, "when he wrote down his speeches, they lost their life (*motus*), and the speech went limp" (*flaccescebat oratio, Brut.* 93).

Moralist discourse, of course, is not the exclusive property of the senatorial order. It permeates Roman culture, inscribed on tombstones and graffiti, in comedy and tragedy. Horace suggestively comments that plays filled with familiar moralisms were popular even when they were less well written (*Ars* 319). Beginning with the earliest surviving Latin literature, largely translations or adaptations from Greek literature, Roman authors tended to increase the moralizing element from Greek originals. A character in Plautus's *Rudens* observes, "I've seen the comic actors, just like this, utter wise maxims, and get applause for them, when they point out these prudent habits to the people" (*spectavi ego pridem comicos ad istunc modum / sapienter dicta dicere atque eis plaudier / cum illos sapientis mores monstrabant populo*, 1249–50). Plautus increased the number and length of monologues in his comedies, especially those in the voices of slaves, which allowed extra scope for moralizing; Ennius's tragedies follow a similar pattern. Anthologies of "moral sayings," whether drawn from comedy or mime, such as the collection of the mime artist Publilius Syrus, or from the sayings of historical figures, were used as writing exercises in schools. Quintilian calls moral tags, or *sententiae, populares*, "popular" (5.13.42, 8.3.12).

Like satire and comedy, moralism invites laughter, a laughter that in the republican political context works the strange magic of communal identification in the act of recognizing the painful pang of disempowerment. In 167 BCE, at the end of the wars in the eastern Mediterranean, the soldiers of Aemilius Paulus, already annoyed by the general's refusal to indulge them with rewards of booty, were aroused by a military tribune named Galba to vote against granting him a triumph (Livy 45.35–36). The venerable ex-consul M. Servilius, seeking to secure the triumph for Paulus, summoned them to a *contio* in which he harangued the men in their dual identity as soldiers and citizens and reminded them of their own stake in the celebration of victory (45.38–39). He concluded by asserting his own moral claim to influence, with a gesture that brought the speech to an unexpectedly ecdysiastic climax:

> "Twenty-three times I have challenged and fought with the enemy; from all the men with whom I fought hand to hand, I brought back spoils; I have a body adorned with honorable scars, all of them facing front." Then, it is said, he stripped off his clothes, and specified in what war he had received which

wounds. While he was displaying these scars, because certain things were exposed which should have been kept covered, a swelling in his groin aroused a laugh from his audience (*adapertis forte, quae uelanda erant, tumor inguinum proximis risum mouit*). "This too, what you're laughing at," he said then, "I have because of sitting my horse day and night, and it does not shame or mortify me any more than these scars, since it was no obstacle to my good deeds for the republic at home and on the battlefield. I, an old soldier, have displayed this body of mine wounded by the sword to you young soldiers; let Galba strip and show you his gleaming smooth, unscarred body (*ego hoc ferro saepe uexatum corpus uetus miles adulescentibus militibus ostendi: Galba nitens et integrum denudet*). Tribunes, recall the tribes to the vote!"

As the sight of Servilius's swollen genitals arouses a ribald laugh that is (Livy implies) raucous and derisive, it also evokes a connection between elite and mass, centered precisely on the physical target of the moralist gaze that is supposed to supervise communal life. Servilius moves swiftly to turn the crowd's laughter into reverence by describing his condition as another honorable scar of battle, but the effort is scarcely necessary: the embodied discourse of moralism means that the ex-consul can persuade his audience not only through the theatrical display of authority symbolized by his history and bearing but also by inserting the grotesque into the very performance by which he accrues majesty.

Connected, in Livy's account, to the extravagant parades and feasts involved in celebrating a military triumph, the anecdote illuminates the important role played by the elite body (whether by accident or by design) in appropriating the vulgar, of working both "top" and "bottom"—a process that invites knowing laughter from the crowd precisely because it exposes the crudity of domination. This is the core of Mbembe's critique of Bakhtinian readings of carnival and the grotesque as authentically "popular," "low," and "vulgar"; on the contrary, he argues, obscenity constitutes a modality of power:

> The real inversion takes place when, in their desire for a certain majesty, the masses join in the madness and clothe themselves in cheap imitations of power so as to reproduce its epistemology; and when, too, power in its own violent quest for grandeur makes vulgarity and wrongdoing its main mode of existence.[116]

Obscenity is the other side of moralism's coin. We see a new side to the prevalence of body-focused abuse and invective in late republican oratory, especially Cicero's prosecutorial speeches: invective is not only a way to evoke the audience's sympathy by summoning it to frown or laugh at

[116] Mbembe, "Provisional notes on the postcolony," 29.

another but a rhetorical institutionalization of the crude physical vitality that fuels Roman imperial power. This is a complex operation. On the one hand, the politically dominant class can and does resort to violence to preserve their power (for example, during the Gracchan years); we might say, following Benjamin and others, that their power rests implicitly on their ability to employ the resources of the state to do violence.[117] On the other hand, as I have noted, violence was not a permanent state policy. On the contrary, the history of early and middle republican politics tracks the ways in which the people are protected from arbitrary violence at the hands of magistrates. If we take the governing order's occasional use of physical force in public space as the exception that proves the rule, then we can see how the moralism/obscenity dyad in public speech functions both as a reminder of the imminence of violence in the political order and as a mitigated, transferred artifact of that violence.[118]

The institution of republican government had produced a new kind of body politic: the ideal expressed by Menenius Agrippa in the fable he is supposed to have told the plebeians when they seceded from the patricians in the early years of republican history (Livy 2.32). This body is imagined as a free, masculine, aggressive entity made up of differentiated parts, a strict hierarchy of economic and social class. What kept the parts in line was proper behavior by all, but the lower parts, the popular masses, do not simply obey, like automata; they are each invested, according to the fable, in the survival and success of the whole body. Yet the sharp distinctions of class that characterized Roman politics openly disempowered the poorer classes and made the active role of the middling citizens something of an open question: this threatened to assimilate poorer citizens into the category of slaves, unraveling the master fiction of *libertas* that was supposed to be the possession of every citizen in the republic. When no one but the rich spoke, and the poorer citizens rarely if ever voted, what was left in the way of exerting popular power in the political sphere except rioting and other acts that elite-defined politics itself defines as beyond the law? The moralist discourse of the senatorial class helps conceal this inequality by placing the powerless on an ostensibly equal footing with the powerful. More than an

---

[117] Agamben, *Homo Sacer*, places Benjamin's essay "Zur Kritik der Gewalt," on the latent presence of violence in legal institutions in the context of work by Schmitt and Arendt (39–44).

[118] Analogies with the exercise of magisterial authority under normal circumstances in Nippel, "Policing Rome," who stresses the legal necessity for the magistrate's physical presence at the scene of a disturbance, and the lictors' task as "the symbolic representation of the magistrates' claim to obedience" (23). His essay (as well as his larger study, *Public Order in Ancient Rome*) is an invaluable study of the dominant order's strategies for preserving order (suppressing religious movements and night meetings, for instance), which, suggestively, they tend to justify publicly by appeals to morality (24–25).

opportunity to bind the community together in a common affirmation
of shared values, by constructing virtue—the virtue of the body politic,
which rests on that of the individual citizen body—as a principal object
of concern for the republican audience, moralist discourse creates a consensus of moral agreement that compensates for citizens' awareness of
disempowerment, their limited political influence, and the damage suffered through economic and social dependency.[119] Moral agreement
reinforces the fantasy of common identity and civic liberty, since everyone "freely" joins in condemnations of tyranny, effeminacy, and disso-
lution. Such is the nature of moral judgment: it is an autonomous act.
It offered a share in power to the citizens whose economic and social
status limited their participation in, and even their knowledge of, politics. It also helps explain why the Roman masses never agitated for their
own public voice. They already had one, in the familiar expressions of
paternalistic moralism that enabled the citizen mass to identify with the
senatorial order.[120] Moralism creates a world of meanings all its own, a
master fiction that conceals the reality of economic, social, and political
inequality, that offers the moralist equality as a compensatory replacement for political equality. Unlike modern, liberal, moral equality,
moralist equality is a static, conservative principle: it confirms existing
conventions of moral authority, that is, who can moralize, about whom,
and how.[121] Moralist equality, as it compensates for social, economic,
and political inequality, *displaces* the concepts of social, economic, and
political equality. Moral character trumps competence; moral excellence
exiles or debases rational argument.

Transforming political contest into the choice between virtue and vice
encourages citizens to limit the intellectual powers they bring to their
decision-making role to traditional beliefs and opinions about morals,
instead of weighing evidence, reasoning through arguments, and offering
judgment. The stylization of power through voice helps conceal the
horror of material conditions that undermined a central if self-idealizing
aspect of Roman self-perception: the limits of *libertas*. Suppressing the
antagonisms that traverse society, the acts of collective listening and
rendering moral judgment enable the audience to imagine itself as an

[119] Here I am directly inspired by Halperin, who traces the appeal of Aeschines' moralistic condemnation of Timarchus in the Athenian context in "The democratic body," 99.

[120] Richlin, *Garden of Priapus*, explores the importance of (the language of) sexual violence
in the Roman social order (esp. 65–69, 210–14).

[121] Moralism does not function as a rational basis for, or work actively toward, political or
social equality, as belief in moral equality clearly can: in the United States, since the early
nineteenth century, strong belief in the moral equality of all human beings, regardless of race
or gender, helped bring about the end of slavery and the first steps toward enfranchisement
for people of color and women.

organic whole, bound together by forces of solidarity and cooperation.[122] The fact that Roman education is training in contentiousness
bears witness to the repressed conflicts that underlie communal life.
Social values and national history come alive in the moralizing body that
embodies the collective power of the consenting mass.[123]

THE RATIONALIZED REPUBLIC

I have argued that the senatorial speaker legitimized his authority with
expressions of authority that drew on religious ritual and took the form
of invitations to judgment that constructed the republic as a community
of moralizing equals. In their style and organization, the oratorical performance projected the idealized values of the Roman ancestors, the
mos maiorum, and by extension, the equally idealized laws that the
ancestors first established, as the values and laws shared by all Romans.
If oratory may be called, in Austin's terms, performative discourse,
language designed to act on people and cause them in turn to act, the
performances of the orators previously discussed remind us of the
charismatic aspect of perlocution. These two fundamental modalities of
the rhetorical tradition—rhetoric as the training ground of persuasive
style, the honing of expressive actions that draw on established traditions of public authority, working in tandem with rhetoric as a discourse of law, the rational negotiation of difference—reinforce one
another. The tandem nature of their operation is designed to suit the
nature of political decision making and indeed the nature of the republic, at once a group united by practices of rational judgment and a tribal
collective founded on common prejudice.

Late republican intellectual history tracks the rise of moral philosophy,
law, historical analysis, and religion in writings like Varius Rufus's *de
Morte*, Brutus's *de Virtute*, Varro's research into Roman history and
language, Lucretius's *de Natura Deorum*, and Ciceronian dialogues.
Scholars of the period, notably Elizabeth Rawson and Claudia Moatti,
conclude that the overriding aim of the period was the quest, exemplified
by Caesar, for an absolute rational standard opposed to the arbitrary, to
prejudice, and human negligence. In his reforms of the calendar and his
call for a simplified, pure grammar that relied not on "vicious and corrupt habits of usage" (*consuetudinem vitiosam et corruptam*) but on systematic theory (*ratio*), Caesar sought to establish institutions and
practices, grounded in nature, that time and human vice could not

---

[122] On the constitutive role of antagonism in the state; see Žižek, *Plague of Fantasies*, 8, 10.
[123] On the relations of memory, power, and the collective, see Taussig, *Magic of the State*, 127.

destroy (*Brut.* 261).[124] In what follows, I propose that the earliest Latin
rhetorical treatises, the anonymous *Rhetorica ad Herennium* and Cicero's
de Inventione, belong to the rationalizing trend in late republican
thought, in their move beyond the vision of the moralist community as it
is represented in and by the earlier senatorial tradition of public speech.[125]
The two treatises are texts of amalgamation in two senses: they blend
competing (and contradictory) Greek traditions of rhetorical knowledge,
notably Aristotle, Isocrates, and Hermagoras, and they mix training in the
social codes of the Roman ruling elite with instruction in a rational system of language that grounds the orator's legitimacy not in his birth or
position but in his speech acts, his capacity to construct arguments.[126]
Their work frames the speeches in the court (especially), assembly, and
senate—as acts that bind the republic with the force of reason. The texts
implicitly seek to untangle the modality of rhetorical reason from
charisma, replacing the exemplary expression of elite authority that characterized current republican practice with a view of rhetoric as a primarily rational discourse subject to logical systematization and analysis.

De Inventione and *Rhetorica ad Herennium* were composed in the
years immediately following the Social War, when Rome's Italian allies'
demand for full citizenship rights led to a violent revolt, and in the midst
of the conflict between the factions of Sulla and Marius.[127] Against the
backdrop of this upheaval, the treatises seek to codify and standardize

---

[124] Rawson, *Intellectual Life in the Late Roman Republic*, esp. 317–25; Moatti, *La Raison de Rome*, 167–70.

[125] An analogy in religion: Murphy, "Privileged knowledge," rightly points out that the circulation of religious knowledge in the late republic was undergoing an uneasy transition from corporate embodiment in the senate to books "published by specialists who were not necessarily senators . . . none [of whom] wished to be seen as disregarding the protocols of instituted knowledge" (134).

[126] In his otherwise insightful study, Morstein-Marx slights the usefulness of the rhetorical works for understanding the political culture of republican Rome, calling them "jejune . . . textbook discussions and notes from the lecture halls" (61–62). He is right to spotlight the silence of Cicero and the author of the *Rhetorica ad Herennium* on what we now see as crucially important differences between deliberative contexts, speeches given in the senate and in the assembly (but see *de Orat.* 2.333–34). My argument that the rhetorical works benefit from close reading as political texts should be seen as supplementing his analysis of oratorical speeches, where speech acts create sociopolitical cohesion and interpellate the citizens as subjects (he rightly cites Althusser). For all that they enact a fantasy, however, the expectation and worldview in the Ciceronian language of *libertas*, in *de Inventione* and his later works, are no less real: they affect decisions and dispositions.

[127] The dates for both treatises are uncertain, but composition in the 80s seems likely: the *Rhetorica Ad Herennium* draws sample deliberation topics from the Social Wars ("shall-citizenship be granted to the allies?" 3.2). Cicero later dismisses *de Inventione* as drawn from unfinished student notebooks (*quae pueris aut adulescentibus nobis ex commentariolis nostris incohata, de Orat.* 1.5).

civic dialogue. Following Aristotle, they begin by identifying three sites for speech, the three *genera dicendi*, demonstrative, deliberative, and judicial. These sites define the orator as the dominant figure in civic space, in keeping with Aristotle's definition of rhetoric as the offspring (*paraphues*) of dialectic and ethical studies, with the latter "rightly called politics" (*Rhet.* 1.2.7), and Hermagoras's definition of rhetoric as "treating the proposed political questions (*politika zetemata*) as persuasively as possible" (Sext. Emp. *Math.* 2.62). The Auctor describes the orator's duty as speaking *ad usum civilem*, for "citizen usage" (1.2); Cicero characterizes rhetoric as a *civilis ratio*, a "citizen science" (*Inv.* 1.6).

George Kennedy, a master scholar of ancient rhetoric, dismisses *de Inventione* and *Rhetorica ad Herennium* as technical handbooks whose emphasis on systematization sets them apart from Isocrates' or Aristotle's investigations of the place of rhetoric in society.[128] This conclusion ignores the significance of Hellenistic theory as a written discourse that puts rhetoric forward as a model of rational and rationalized public discourse, helping legitimize it as a discourse of governance. The Latin treatises constrain the expression of authority by insisting that it agree with rules of logical argument and a learnable code of proper style. This is the significance of Hellenistic rhetorical theory for the republic: the modeling of civic performance, the externalization of the internal dialogues that constitute good political judgment. This amounts to a critical intervention in traditional oratorical practices.

The fact that the forensic genus holds pride of place in both treatises is often explained as a matter of practical convenience for the reader, who would, it is assumed, expect to prepare for a career in the law courts. Yet the Auctor declares that his discussion of judicial oratory is applicable to the deliberative and demonstrative genres (3.2.2, 3.6.10), a claim supported by Quintilian (3.6.1). More important, making forensic oratory the template for civic discourse in the broad sense crucially models all institutionalized modes of public speech after the Roman legal system. As deliberative and demonstrative speech are subsumed under the rubric of reason and justice that circumscribes judicial speaking, they are also assimilated to the broad project of governance. This anticipates Cicero's later treatment, in *Brutus*, of all activity in the forum and law court as synecdochically staging the republic's flourishing or decline. As

---

[128] Kennedy, *The Art of Rhetoric in the Roman World*, 116; *The Art of Persuasion in Greece*, 267. Hellenistic rhetoricians after Aristotle elaborated his three-way division of the elements of rhetoric (ethos, pathos, logos) into the quinquepartite division that shapes most surviving Roman rhetorical treatises: *inventio* (invention), *dispositio* (arrangement), *elocutio* (style), *memoria* (memorization), and *pronuntiatio* (delivery). *De Inventione* is limited to the first; *ad Herennium* covers invention in books 1–2 and 3.1–15; arrangement, 3.16–18; delivery, 3.19–27; memory, 3.28–40; and style, book 4.

Cicero reminds one jury, all eyes turn to the courts to see justice done
(II *Ver.* 1.12–15).[129] We should remember that the law court was one of
the first manifestations of republican government to appear throughout
Italy, creating a common forensic language for Rome's closest allies, and
that it offered a path to prominence for newly made citizens in the wake
of the Social War and foreign conquest.[130] The dominance of judicial
rhetoric in these texts reinforces the notion of the orator as the speaker
of the law. If, as they suggest, the law court is the stable source of authority for the community, then, by the same token, the community's legality
is upheld.[131]

By embracing the technical language of Hellenistic theory, Cicero and
the Auctor mount a critical intervention in Roman oratory as it was traditionally conceived and practiced. The Auctor does not object to moralizing in the course of making an argument: he is, after all, concerned with
the creation of consensus. But he sidesteps matters of character and
lifestyle, disavowing the role of moralistic instruction claimed by senatorial speakers (*non vivendi praeceptores videamur esse*, 4.25). When style
is subject to the same systematization and codification as logical argument, traditional practices are opened up for critical viewing. The Auctor
warns against the kind of prettified, rehearsed slickness that signals to
the audience the artificial nature of the speech (*artificii significandi*):
summarizing the argument is the moment for brevity and orderliness. By
contrast to Cicero's later work, which emphasizes the need to affect the
audience's emotions throughout the speech (e.g., *Part.* 15.52), the Auctor
limits the arousal of the audience (*instigatio auditorum*, 2.30.47) to
particular moments appropriate for embellishment. The ten "commonplaces" that provide the basis for embellishment frame the horizons of
acceptable civic discourse: the authority (*auctoritas*) of history, with a
focus on legal precedent, and the jury's awareness of itself as guardian of
the law and of the republic's future (2.30.48). Where traditional oratory
grounded authority in the charismatic transcendence of the elite body,
the Auctor frames a system by which the orator embodies the ideal politics of his period: not relying on ancestry or wealth, but recouping elite
charisma in a logical discourse of style.

This represents a divergence from Aristotle's system in favor of the
Hellenistic tradition. In response to the system of dividing the parts of
rhetoric according to the parts of speech (*moria logou*), a habit of

---

[129] Riggsby, *Crime and Community*, suggestively concludes that because all Roman
crimes were in a crucial sense understood as political crimes, "the courts existed not for
the sake of justice in the abstract . . . but for the good of the Roman people as a whole"
(157–58).

[130] Sinclair, "The *sententia* in the *Rhetorica ad Herennium*," suggests that the Auctor, like
Cicero, is a *novus homo* (565).

[131] Part of the argument in what follows appears in Connolly, "The new world order."

rhetoricians mentioned in Plato (*Phaedr.* 266d–67d), Aristotle had advocated a tripartite scheme of proofs (*pisteis*): argument (*logos*), presentation of character (*ethos*), and the arousal of emotions (*pathos*). Where Aristotle gave all three equal weight in the job of the orator, Cicero and the Auctor follow the Hellenistic tradition in confining the presentation of the orator's character (*ethos*) and the arousal of emotions (*pathos*) to the proem and epilogue.[132] The Auctor dismisses the *commiseratio*, the effort to drum up pity, with the dry observation that "nothing dries more quickly than a tear" (*nihil enim lacrima citius arescit*). While neither text denies the importance of audience entertainment (*Rhet. Her.* 1.6.10), their structure and organization reflect their emphasis on argument and proof (2.18.28). The Auctor (Cicero's discussion being limited to invention, the first part of rhetoric) presents style as a rationally organized system that must be employed only to aid the argument (*exaugendam et conlocupletandam*); he grounds similes in rational comparison (*ratio*) and defines proper exempla as those that reflect truth without exaggeration (2.46–50). He insists on accurate citation of precedents that must reflect judicial consensus: exceptional cases must not be cited as commonplace. Facts admitted by the other side should be taken as the starting point of common agreement between the opposing sides regarding the case; the orator must not amplify what he must prove (*item vitiosum est id augere quod convenit docere*, 2.30.47). If one man charges another with homicide he must not declare that there is no crime worse than homicide but rather prove that the homicide was committed in the way he alleges. The summary must survey everything clearly and honestly, in the proper order. And so on.

Above all, the treatises reduce the practices of persuasion to a learnable code. What fills the moralist gap, and provides a systematic standard by which civic speech may be produced and judged, is status theory, which lays out methods by which the speaker may analyze the "issue" at stake, in Latin *status* or *constitutio*, in Greek *stasis*, with the aim of discovering the appropriate arguments he should adopt in order to persuade his listeners (*Inv.* 1.10, *Rhet. Her.* 1.18).[133] This system, influentially elaborated by

[132] Solmsen, "Aristotelian tradition" (part 2), 178, points out the difference with Cicero's "maturer works," where "we find him assigning to the orator the threefold task *probare, delectare, permovere* (*de Orat.* 2.114, *Orat.* 69, *Brut.* 158, *Opt. Gen.* 3); and this new conviction, which must have grown out of his practical experience, is reflected in a readmission of *ethé* and *pathé* to a position on a par with the rhetorical argument. . . . [T]he revival of Aristotle's conception of the *loci argumentorum*, the return to the four virtues of diction [etc.] . . . lend substance to his claim that in *de Oratore* he renewed the *ratio Aristotelia* (along with the *ratio Isocratea*)." On Cicero's recovery of Aristotelian *pisteis*: May, *Trials of Character*, 3–12, Fantham, *Roman World* 161–85.

[133] In Cicero's later work and in Quintilian, the term *constitutio* changes to *status*. Quintilian remarks on the use of the Latin words *constitutio, quaestio, quod ex quaestione*

the second-century Greek rhetorician Hermagoras, may be presented in
the form of questions.[134] In the process of inventing and arranging the
speech, the orator asks, does the case turn on the truth or falsity of a statement (*constitutio coniecturalis, Inv.* 1.10, *Rhet. Her.* 1.18)? Or is it a question of how to interpret the law (*definitiva, Inv.* 1.11; *legitima, Rhet. Her.*
1.19)? Will the jury face a judgment of circumstance, such as Caepio's plea
in 105 BCE that his loss of an army was an accident (*generalis, Inv.* 12–15;
iuridicalis, Rhet. Her. 1.24)? Or (in the fourth Hermagorean status discussed by Cicero, but not the Auctor) is the legal process itself the issue,
such as the suitability of a jury to hear a case (*Inv.* 1.10, 1.16)?
Pedagogically speaking, status theory is designed to help the budding orator decide how best to organize his speech, what facts or claims to deploy,
and so forth. But the treatises also represent a normative vision of civic
knowledge and decision making, generously conceived, that is imagined to
apply not only in the law court but in other venues as well. By presenting
arguments in a systematic way to the jury, they may deliberate not only
on the case at hand but also on what is just and honorable, and on
the broader interpretation of the law: not only pragmatic concerns but the
state of moral issues are at stake (*Rhet. Her.* 2.10.14–15, 3.2.3). The
rhetorical treatise constructs public discourse as embodying order, a system
fleshed out by knowledge of history and custom but ultimately subject to
rational analysis that incorporates consideration of history, nature, custom, the good and the just (*Rhet. Her.* 2.10.15). This vision of the jury is
a microcosm of the just city: a community linked by consensus as to the
demands of justice.

Ad Herennium and *de Inventione* offer the orator tools to express the
will to consensus, through procedures for controlling and delimiting
language and belief, rooting the law in consensus, and consensus in the
law. They seek to protect the law through knowledge practices that
discard the element of chance, contingency, or charisma. Throughout
the treatises, the emphasis is on utility, and the goal, transparency of
language, both for the reader-orator and the rhetorician himself—a goal
reflected in the Auctor's acknowledgment that the orator will argue court
cases that are dishonorable (1.3.5) and his emphasis on the need for clarity

---

appareat ("that which may arise from the *quaestio*"), and *status* to refer to what had been
stasis in Greek (3.6.18).

[134] The Auctor's choice of *constitutio* to describe "types of question" is shared by Cicero
in the early *de Inventione*, but in later works Cicero prefers *status* (from the Greek *stasis*).
For a broad outline, see Clarke, *Rhetoric at Rome*, 26–27, 67–69. Bonner, *Roman
Declamation*, provides "case-study" examples from Roman rhetorical exercises (11–26).
Dieter, "Stasis," explores the potential for the *constitutio* to direct and regulate emotion;
Braet, "The Classical doctrine of status," pursues the productive, dialogic perspective *sta-
tus* theory offers.

and practicality (1.4.14; cf. 1.1.1).[135] Bad argumentation and generalities are out; logic and precise rules of proof and refutation are in (*Rhet. Her.* 1.18, 1.26, 2.33). We may compare Caesar's enthusiasm for rules of language in *de Analogia*.[136] The result is two treatises exhorting the reader's faith in the certainty of language, a certainty created by the orator who builds an audience's sense of conviction in the course of his oration, and that furnished by rhetorical discourse itself. While this discourse is constructed as thoroughly Roman—the *Rhetorica* utterly rejects Greek rhetorical authorities (1.1.2; cf. 4.1.1)—it identifies the things the orator "ought to have" not as *dignitas* and *auctoritas* but knowledge of the post-Aristotelian quinquepartite scheme of speech composition: *inventio, dispositio, elocutio, memoria,* and *pronuntiatio* (1.2.3). The point is that one cannot simply speak in any way: this system seeks to govern and limit how political discourse works. In those rules we glimpse the basis of a new way to conceive and represent the republic as the instrument of rational justice. And further: if we say that the Roman republic is an ensemble of institutional forms made possible because of the general governmentalization of its agents, the specific ways in which those agents become objects of knowledge and regulation and discipline take on new importance. The *res publica* does not grant power; it is the collection of people whose own discipline comes itself to stand for or characterize a structure called *res publica*, a structure that is then referred to and understood as standing apart or above, in a certain sense, from its individual human agents. The disciplining of the mind and voice in these treatises directs the polity to assume a rational form.

Not surprisingly, then, law enforcement through language is the central theme. Cicero classifies eloquence as "a kind of civic reason," "part of civil science" (*ratio civilis quaedam, civilis scientiae pars, Inv.* 1.6). The Auctor of the *Rhetorica ad Herennium* promises to cover only matters that are relevant to the *ratio* or system of public speaking (*pertinere,* 1.1.2), which deals with practices proper to citizenship and consensus (*ad usum civilem . . . cum adsensione auditorum,* 1.2.2).[137] Cicero theorizes the background to his approach in a preface that follows the fourth-century Athenian rhetorician Isocrates in locating the invention of

---

[135] Habinek, *Ancient Rhetoric and Oratory,* argues that the writing of a treatise was itself "a kind of rhetorical performance, a demonstration of mastery . . . equivalent to the 'masterpiece' of later schools of painting or the 'master-song' (*Meistergesang*) of the late medieval musical tradition" (45).

[136] Sinclair, "Political declensions," suggestively places Caesar's arguments for pure grammar in the imperialist context, showing that they may be seen as efforts to craft an accessible language for new citizens.

[137] Sinclair, "*Sententia,*" reasonably suggests that the Auctor is a "mature and well-educated Roman citizen" deeply familiar with "the standards and values of the Roman senatorial order," 563, 566.

politics in the discovery of eloquence.[138] Eloquence is the first step toward law, the necessary talent by which humans (benefiting from the leadership of the best men) may deliberate the best way to live in company with one another. The question of origins becomes a question of political subjection, a subjection enacted by a primitive yet recognizable oratory. The quotidian importance of eloquence as a performance that stabilizes and gives meaning to the republic surfaces in Cicero's claim that the paradisiacal state of human politics ended when the most powerful and learned men abandoned oratory for other pursuits (philosophy is implied): lesser men took their place, and the ship of state began to founder (*naufragia, Inv.* 1.4). The law court is introduced from the start not simply as the place where justice is done but as the place where the republic is renewed through the active participation of its best citizens. His argument implies that the most common practical application of rhetoric, forensic oratory, is the bedrock of the polity, the central practice of citizenship.

Both treatises foreground the capacity of language to resolve disputes that could otherwise divide and damage the political community. If rhetoric is not formal law in the sense of *lex* or *ius*, it is what makes the force of law felt in the world. Rhetorical techniques like status theory convert difference into consensus. By representing language at once as the capacity that makes humans human and as a practice to be systematized and regulated in a way that mirrors the laws that are the topic of oratorical debates themselves, rhetorical discourse naturalizes the regulatory forces governing the republic. In its role as handbook and manual, a pedagogical text, the rhetorical treatise creates subjects who not only conform to but enact and embody the law.

Cicero makes the aim to describe a rational language that will ameliorate civil discord explicit (*Inv.* 1.3), but nowhere is the emphasis on civic agreement stronger than in the presentation of status theory. Status theory transforms the struggles of the law court and the senate into debates focused on the problem of proof. Here, as Robert Kastely shows in a brilliant essay, rhetoric reveals itself as the channeling resolver of social antagonism; its genius arises from "its embrace of the source of political instability and its transformation of that source into a resource for a deeper, if continuously renegotiated, stability."[139] Status theory is dialogic,

---

[138] "In other capacities that we possess, we are not at all superior to other living things: but rather in speed, strength, and other resources we are indeed inferior to most; but because we possess the natural capacity to persuade one another and to clarify our desires to ourselves, not only have we escaped the life of wild beasts, but we have gathered together, founded cities, made laws, and invented arts" (Isocrates, *Antidosis* 253–54; cf. *Nic.* 48; Cicero, *Inv.* 1.1–1.5).

[139] Kastely, "The recalcitrance of aggression," 256–57.

transforming the roots of political instability into the foundation of order. As it trains the speaker to investigate the causes of civic dispute: as a matter of fact (what happened?), circumstance (under what conditions are criminal acts justified?), legal interpretation (what are the limits of written law?), and correct application of the law (what courts may sit in judgment, and which men may speak in public, and about what, and when?), it teaches the basics of civic education: how to evaluate evidence, the conflict of laws, and what influences fellow citizens (2.28). It allows the refinement of conflict, and ultimately its resolution: what separates people is identified and healed, reflecting a favorite founding story of Rome into action—the articulated, distinct dualized bodies of patricians and plebs. It gives linguistic form to the polity: a form of mutually agreed-upon strategies of communication. In an age as devoted to rational codification and categorization as it is bedevilled with civic discord, rhetoric does its best to make the resolution of civic disagreement rational and consistent over time, replacing the violence and contingency of republican politics with reason.

Antagonism—indeed, the necessity of antagonism, stated or implied—is a common theme in the representation of Roman political history. Marcus Antonius, a character in Cicero's *de Oratore*, observes: "I listed all the types of civil discord (*seditio*), their vices and dangers . . . and I concluded that all civil discords are pernicious, but nonetheless some are legitimate (*iustas*) and virtually essential" (*necessarias, de Orat.* 2.199). Examples like the story of Menenius Agrippa, a harmonious vision of civic division and its mediation, could be multiplied: Romulus's act of fratricide, the struggle to pass the Licinian laws establishing equality under the law for all citizens, the repeated memorializations of the goddess Concordia in stone and text. The notion of politics itself is founded on division; antagonism is as essential to the survival of the republic as the peace making that cures it. The articulation of language as a rationally organized system in *de Inventione* and *Rhetorica ad Herennium* suggest that public speech is the means of confronting and curing the republic's own impossibility: the antagonism baked into its earliest memories, the antagonism of competition among the ruling class and between rulers and ruled. In its positive, rationalizing presence, it responds to a certain blockage: it is both the cure for and symptom of the impossibility of society's achieving its notional telos as a homogeneous, harmonious collectivity. In response, these texts transform the codes of oratorical eloquence into a learnable system that embraces observation, common knowledge, gossip, hearsay, speculation, history, memory, and legend, rationalizing the ways in which knowledge is perpetuated and framed. Rhetoric's job is never done: it is a product of the ultimate unverifiability of political legitimacy. Cicero and the Auctor bring its action out of the sphere of the traditional claim on hegemony, the *auctoritas* of a Scipio, into the domain of reason. The authority gained by the reader of their texts is presented as effective precisely (perhaps only) because oratory is the instrument of law and deliberation. It is not a courtly practice or ritual separate from decision-making, like the aura created by a monarch on his throne; it absorbs deliberative practices into a larger system of traditional power.

"We know quite well that we do not have the right to say everything, that we cannot speak of just anything in any circumstances whatever, and that not everyone has the right to speak of anything whatever."[140] Michel Foucault proposes that the divisions of reason versus madness and truth versus falsity represent major steps in the early modern project of defining "knowledge." His point is not that the division between true and false is arbitrary or that truth and falsity themselves are historically contingent. Instead, we must explore the arbitrary and contingent nature of the *systems* by which beliefs, values, ideas, and information are transmitted and evaluated. These systems undergo constant modification: the dismissal of poetic knowledge by Thucydides and Plato shapes certain contours of historical and philosophical discourse; the side-by-side, competitive evolution of rhetoric and philosophy contributes to the particular standards by which truth value is judged. In their sketch of schemas of possible, observable, demonstrable, plausible knowledges, *Rhetorica ad Herennium* and *de Inventione* reveal the will to bridge the gap between "consensual knowledge"—the public agreement about what words mean and how their use relates to decisions in the world—and the rationalizing drive of philosophy. Both treatises impose on the reading subject a certain will to knowledge that is verifiable and practical. As Claudia Moatti concludes, the wisdom of the rhetorical schools is not equivalent to traditional knowledge, though it had enabled traditional hegemony: "we might say that eloquence is a wisdom of liberty, founded on persuasion, not authority. In this sense, it is opposed to the traditional mentality."[141] The significance, in these treatises, of reason (in the sense of public reasoning and their own systematic organization) suggests that their will to knowledge stands in a certain tension with traditional claims to knowledge expressed in senatorial oratory. They pursue the resolution that informed Isocratean rhetoric: to make the wisdom garnered by a moral philosophy available to the public through eloquence so that the individual members of the public would understand the essential connection between their

---

[140] Foucault, "The order of discourse," 109.
[141] Moatti, *La Raison de Rome*, 195.

individual identity and their membership in the republic.[142] When Roman ideals of autonomous manly achievement grind against the necessity of creating consensus, rhetoric eases the friction: it enables the manly citizen to win by obeying the law.

The goal of the rhetorical treatise is managing the communicative encounters between speaker and audience. Just so, Cicero and the Auctor are not engaged in an aggressive critique of tradition, but managing the encounter between Hellenistic theory and Roman practice. In the picture that emerges from their work, stylized speech is presented in terms of dialogue; dialogue implies a kind of equality; equality, a kind of liberty; liberty, security; security, communal concord; concord, shared identity. If Cicero and the Auctor represent educated rich speakers as republican citizens in the fullest possible sense—free from the domination of others in the fullest sense—they do not treat those who are only free to listen and vote as disenfranchised or as slaves but as free, though in a more limited sense. Their treatises may be seen as indirectly checking the potential tyranny of the governing class if they seek to infringe on the already limited freedom of the governed. This is Cicero's justification for the tribunate, when his brother Quintus attacks its powers: it acts to check the crimes of the senatorial order and help defend the rights of the people (*Leg.* 3.24–25). But this is only limited liberty.

Theirs, in Arendtian terms, is an augmenting intervention that makes reason and logic the guardian of republican law and order. While they draw heavily on the Hellenistic rhetorical tradition, they neither reject nor ignore the traditional Roman language of aristocratic *auctoritas* or *dignitas*. It is precisely their emphasis on negotiation and dialogue that allows them to claim a place in the elite literary tradition—by praising the qualities informing the *ethos* of the senatorial nobility, for instance—while envisioning a normative ideal of public speech that would balance aristocratic *ethos* with *logos*, reasoned argument. The two treatises thus mirror and negotiate the tensions of political legitimacy in the Roman republic. Their enshrining of traditional performances rewrites the performative in the realm of the rational, a treatment that both endows traditional authority with the prize of reason and subtly interrupts it. The Cicero who will go on to praise the *senatus auctoritas*, the authority of the senate (*Sest.* 95, 97), who develops a reputation for an ornate, passionate style, and who dismisses popular liberty as a matter of keeping up appearances (*Leg.* 3.24) emerges here as a young rhetorician concerned with the workings of the *ratio civilis*, the "civil science" of rhetoric, in the ebb

[142] Kastely, "Recalcitrance," 247.

and flow of public discourse (*Inv.* 1.6). This concern underlies
Cicero's subsequent vision of the orator as the model of republican civic
virtue: the active overseer of justice who balances honor and interest,
aristocratic dignity with popular approval, reason and emotional
engagement.

Chapter Two

NATURALIZED CITIZENS

WESTERN POLITICAL THEORY STILL BEARS the stamp of the early modern disagreement regarding the origins and basis of the state.[1] Are human beings compelled by nature to want to live with one another, as classical political theory claims, or does the state come into being as a contract between rational agents who see security and advantage in sheer numbers and the rule of law? Contractarianism tends to treat nature in negative terms—in Hobbes's famous phrase, as a state of war, which humans seek to escape in the formation of the civil state.[2] Classical theorists, by contrast, face a puzzle: nature (*natura*) is at once the source and sustenance of the political association and that which is replaced, either gradually or at the moment of the polity's inception, in the course of the development of the civilization (*cultus*) that political activity makes possible. If nature is the gateway to political life, the transition is never clean. Though the political association, its culture, and its arts define themselves as transcending or escaping nature, they persist in finding their roots and justification in it; the result, to borrow from Lacanian typography or the conventional image of the Roman *damnatio memoriae*, might be written, ~~natura~~, a term that persists through its own erasure.[3]

The problem is related to a broader issue of identity crystallized in this rebarbative remark: "You can be British without speaking English or being Christian or being white, but nevertheless Britain is basically English-speaking and Christian and white, and if one starts to think that it might become Urdu-speaking and Muslim and brown, one gets frightened and angry. . . . Such feelings are not only natural, surely—they are right. You ought to have a sense of your identity, and part of that sense

---

[1] The original Roman use of the word referred to the condition of the commonwealth, *status rei publicae* or *optimus civitatis status*: so Sallust Cat. 40.2; Cicero, *Off.* 2.3; Livy 30.2.8, Seneca, *Ben.* 2.20.4. On the evolution of the word in its modern usage via Jean Bodin's 1576 *République* and especially Hobbes's *de Cive* and *Leviathan*, see Skinner, "The state," 117–126.

[2] *Leviathan* 1.13: Compare the famous early formulation of contractarianism offered by Glaucon in *Republic* 2. Of course, I do not mean to imply that the contractarian understanding of nature is simple or unproblematic.

[3] I draw here on Grosz's psychoanalytic reading of metaphor in *Lacan*, 100, where the term falling below the bar becomes repressed, though not forgotten, and its replacement becomes its symptom.

derives from your nation and your race."[4] *Mutatis mutandis*, the Romans also ask the question of who belongs. Cicero, as a "new man," an outsider to the close-knit network of dominant Roman families, was forced to handle abuse from insiders like Catiline, who, according to Sallust, taunted the consul in the senate house as "a township citizen of the city of Rome" (*inquilinus civis urbis Romae, Cat.* 31.3).[5] A generation earlier, the eminent Marcus Scaurus was accused by a tribune, Varius Severus, of taking a bribe from Mithridates, the rebellious king of Pontus. Scaurus used the magisterial third person to attack his prosecutor, a fellow citizen, as a provincial outsider: "Varius Severus from the Spanish river Sucro claims that Aemilius Scaurus was corrupted by royal bribery and betrayed the empire of the Roman people; Aemilius Scaurus denies that he was an accessory to this crime. Which of the two do you believe?"[6] Catiline's and Scaurus's truculent mobilization of the language of identity politics exposes the potentially shaky ground on which assimilated peoples stand in the very court of law under which they were, as Roman citizens, supposed to be equal.

What does the word "natural" mean in the Roman context? The only possible answer lies in the particularities of the term's strategic deployment in a given text. "Nature" in the poetry and rhetorical writings discussed in this chapter defies fixed definition, emerging through a shifting array of signs, clustering around images of cosmic order and the notion, never clearly cut, of something ostensibly opposing "culture" or "art." In this lies its strategic value: its ambiguity exposes the useful flexibilities and internal contradictions in Cicero's Catonian conception of the virtuous man (*vir bonus*), who is also, as we shall see, the ideal orator, "the good man skilled in speaking," as Quintilian later put it (*vir bonus dicendi peritus*)—and the model for the republican citizen. This chapter explores the interpenetration of nature and its supplements (in Derrida's sense) in the discourse of citizenship, beginning with the *Aeneid*. An overview of the legal background sets the stage for my discussion of the programmatic

---

[4] *Spectator* editor Charles Moore in 1991, quoted in Appiah, *The Ethics of Identity*, 132. Modern notions of race, however, have no place in my discussion. On Rome as "a world in which expectations were not framed by the idea of race," see the useful comments of Dench, *Romulus' Asylum*, 258 (and more generally, 221–64).

[5] On the implications of Cicero's identity as a "new man" (*novus homo*), see Dugan, *Making a New Man*, esp, 40–43.

[6] *Varius Severus Sucronensis Aemilium Scaurum regia mercede corruptum imperium populi Romani prodisse ait, Aemilius Scaurus huic se adfinem esse culpae negat; utri creditis?* (V. Max. 3.7.8). Scaurus was not alone in attacking Varius: doubts about his civic status (*obscurum ius civitatis*) were expressed in his nicknames *Hispanus* and *Hybrida* (V. Max. 8.6.4). Sherwin-White: "the obstacles that hindered ambitious Italian provincials from achieving a *status dignitatis* . . . were political and social rather than any exact legal disqualification" (235).

prefaces of Cicero's political treatises and his major rhetorical work, completed in early 55 BCE, the dialogue *de Oratore*.

Nature and culture are central themes in most founding tales in Western history, and Vergil's *Aeneid* is no exception.

> "You have defeated me, and defeated, stretching out my hands,
> the Rutulians have seen me; yours is Lavinia to wife,
> stretch your hatred no further." He stood whetted for war,
> Aeneas, rolling his eyes, and restrained his right hand;
> now a little, now a little more, the argument had begun to sway
> him, standing doubtful there. . . .

> ". . . Vicisti, et victum tendere palmas
> Ausonii videre; tua est Lavinia coniunx:
> ulterius ne tende odiis." Stetit acer in armis
> Aeneas, volvens oculos, dextramque repressit;
> et iam iamque magis cunctantem flectere sermo
> coeperat. . . . (*Aen.* 12. 936–41)

In the poem's final scene, as the wounded Turnus begs Aeneas to spare him, the Trojan leader stands still, torn by conflicting impulses. But his glance falls on the baldric Turnus had taken as trophy from Pallas, a young warrior who had fought alongside the Trojans, and Aeneas's momentary restraint gives way to wrath (*furiis accensus et ira terribilis*, 12.946–7). He slays Turnus, the double of the heroes Achilles and Diomedes from whom Aeneas had barely escaped in Homer's *Iliad* and his own double in the present epic. His quest to found a city ends as it began in Troy, with violence.[7] Rome is founded in the act of blood-spilling, and not once, but in an agony of repetitive reenactment. In Roman legend and history, Aeneas initiates a string of Roman murders where like kills like, from Romulus and Remus down to the civil wars prophesied in *Aeneid* 6. For some, the scene represents the disintegration of Aeneas's carefully constructed persona as *pius pater*, a persona devoted to law and duty.[8] In a reversal of the epic's other famous political refugee, Dido, who appears in book 1 as the calm architect and judge of her newly founded city of Carthage before passion destroys her, Aeneas yields to frenzy at the moment he clears the way for the founding of Rome.

---

[7] Quint notes that Turnus's reaction to an omen at 12.867–68 precisely recalls Aeneas's own physical symptoms of terror earlier in the epic (2.773, 3.48, 4.280), *Epic and Empire*, 83.

[8] The seminal discussion is Parry, "The voices of Vergil's *Aeneid*": also Clausen, "An interpretation of the *Aeneid*," 85–86; Putnam, "Anger, blindness and insight"; Braund, "Vergil and the cosmos: Religious and philosophical ideas," 206–7; Fowler, "Epicurean anger," 30–35, and Gill, "Passion as madness in Roman poetry," 228–41.

But it would be a mistake to view Aeneas's exchange of indecision for action as a wholesale transformation of civilized restraint into wild impulse. In that brief moment of self-control, his rolling eyes disclose the desire to unleash violence, and in his fury he retains the capacity for coherent speech. His reply to Turnus invokes the cultural bond of male homosociality, indicating that in Pallas, it is not natural blood-kin Aeneas is avenging but a young man to whom he feels the obligations of a foster father, friend, political ally, and perhaps even lover.[9] If Aeneas's choice hints that a relation of essential necessity exists between the civilized act of founding a polity and the brutal extermination of obstacles that stand in its way, he himself is the point at which the civilizing drive ominously converges with nature, embodied in his fiery rage—ominously, because the promise of self-restraint hovers so near. Earlier in the poem, the Trojans were taunted for their cultural refinements, which strike the Rutulians as effeminate and soft. Now, Aeneas's just-repressed impulse toward human identification with Turnus and possibly clemency makes his execution of the Rutulian hero all the more terrible. Fiery wrath and social obligation melt into an unstoppable new element, the historical force and fantasy of the *imperium sine fine*, in which an eternal series of Aeneas's doubles will arise and conquer.

Leaving the poem as it does, in a heightened state of narrative and ethical enigma, Aeneas's decision recalls for the last time its central theme and drama, the hero's conflicting desires. From his desertion of Creusa in favor of his father and son to his abandonment of Dido in Carthage for the shores of Italy, Aeneas's options might seem at first to fall into easily recognizable oppositions that set women against men, affective connection against autonomy, leisure against action, privacy against public life, and freedom against self-denial. How are these categories aligned with the natural and the cultural? No longer is our answer as straightforward as "woman is to nature as man is to culture," the formula suggested by Sherry Ortner in her influential feminist article of 1974.[10] If the epic's narrative structure makes women symbolize passion and domestic obligation which the men, especially Aeneas, aim to transcend in their love of glory, war, and city-founding, the men continue to act passionately, and to care about domestic obligations. The *Aeneid* mingles and blurs these and all the aforementioned oppositions, foreclosing easy interpretations of their moral and political resonance.[11]

---

[9] Hints of a homoerotic bond between Aeneas and Pallas discussed in Putnam, "Possessiveness, sexuality, and heroism."

[10] "Is female to male as nature is to culture?" 67–87.

[11] Fowler: "Philosophy has to believe in solutions: literature often likes to stress that there are none" ("Epicurean anger," 34).

Twentieth-century readings of Aeneas have focused on his relationship to autocracy and Roman imperial identity, but the hero trapped in these oppositional shifts and clashes embodies the basic dilemma facing theorists of civic identity in the republican context. Aeneas anticipates the problem of a host of heroes praised in Cicero, Livy, Horace, and the neo-Roman tradition: Brutus, sending his beloved sons, his only blood descendants, to public execution when they plot against the newly founded *res publica*; Horatius, who murders his sister when she mourns for the lover he has just killed; Regulus, whose sense of honor conquers his affections for family and friends; and countless other examples in the republican imagination.[12] The "necessary" rape of the Sabine women, their conversion to membership in the Roman community, and Romulus's swift assimilation of their relatives symbolize the hybridity of the community from its birth in a different but related sense. These figures test the uncertain border defining the individual's allegiances to family, friends, and citizenry: the subordination of the self (and what kind of self is it?) to the "we" of the political community. They impute an unnaturalness, even a lack of humanity, to republican virtue, which stands in tension with the putative naturalness of the republic in classical political thought.

Nicole Loraux has explored the ways Athenian democracy mobilizes its local myth of autochthony on the dramatic stage for the purpose of giving roots in nature to that radical experiment in people power, the Athenian polis.[13] In Greek and Roman mythology, historiography, and epic, founding the city-state and giving it leaders are acts fluctuating between the competing pulls of nature and culture. Consider Chiron, the centaur-teacher, and the wolf-nurse of Romulus and Remus: humanized creatures who nurtured leaders, they fashioned them both out of nature and against it.[14] The acts of killing on which Athens and Rome were founded—Orestes, Aeneas, Romulus, and Brutus's sons—often resulted from struggles within the family, where the bloodshed, like a sacrifice, enabled the city to advance to its next stage: the founding of the Areopagus, the building of Rome's city walls, the reinforcement of republican over kingly government. As the deeply radical nature of their rebellion bore itself inescapably upon them, the founders of the early United States sought with increasing fervor to ground the new republic in natural law, despite the inconsistencies that arose in their thought and

---

[12] Jed, *Chaste Thinking*, lays out a strong case for the dehumanized quality of republican heroes, though with some overstatement (see below). On Brutus, see below; on Regulus: Cicero, *Off.* 3.102; Horace, *Carm.* 3.5.

[13] Loraux, *Children of Athena*, 3–21.

[14] Machiavelli discusses the centaur as a nature-culture hybrid in *Il principe* 18; see also the opening lines of Horace's *Ars Poetica*.

writing as a result. Why did Jefferson not write "These truths are self-evident" instead of the incongruous and implicitly self-contradictory "We hold these truths to be self-evident"? Hannah Arendt answers that the American founding walked a razor-thin edge between desire for divine sanction, implied by the invocation of divinely rational, externally irresistible, natural truths, and the populist cultural legitimacy of the main clause, "We hold."[15] No wonder that Washington's hagiographer, Parson Weems, made the young George's famous one-liner an expression of irresistible natural power: "I *cannot* tell a lie," and that Thomas Jefferson came to believe the future of the United States lay not in the urban metropolis but in the committed closeness of each literate citizen to his own plot of tamed and tended nature. In this context, Cicero's representation of the ideal orator, whose body is intensively trained out of its original, "natural" state so that it may act all the more "naturally," emerges as the textual repository of fantasies and fears about Roman cultural identity, subjectivity, masculinity, and power, which is to say, about republican citizenship.

THE NATURE OF REPUBLICS

The reality of Roman citizenship (*civitas, ius*) in Italy until the beginning of the first century BCE was a variegated patchwork in which cities and towns occupied different statuses depending on their historical relationship with Rome, and I can offer only a simplified overview of the topic here.[16] Under monarchical rule, full citizenship was restricted to citizens' children and emancipated slaves, sorted into categories under the Servian reforms. Of the Roman *municipia*, the self-governing villages and towns so named for the most important "single duty" (*munus-ceps*) they owed to Rome, namely, men to fight in the legions, some may have viewed the *foedus* (treaty) with Rome as an advantageous arrangement, others as a kind of bondage. *Civitas sine suffragio*, the "citizenship without the vote" granted to some of these communities, involved certain elements of integration, such as the local presence of prefects, common religious rituals, and the use of Latin, which likely contributed to a growing sense of incorporation with Rome, even a perception that this status was a stepping-stone to full citizenship.[17] Citizenship in the early and middle

---

[15] Arendt, *On Revolution* 192–96. Honig discusses the language of legitimacy in "Declarations of independence," 205–6.

[16] Dench, *Romulus' Asylum*, esp. 117–36, surveys the evolution of citizenship with careful attention to the way orators and historians bend earlier history to suit their own ends, viz. the case of the Spanish Balbus, whose rightful claim to citizenship Cicero defends, with "sweeping claims of unceasing ancestral generosity" (Dench, 118–19).

[17] Sherwin-White, *Roman Citizenship*, 52–53, citing Vell. Pat. 1.14.7 (on the Sabines as the first *municipes* to get the vote and enroll in a Roman tribe) and the first grants of full

republic was relatively openly bestowed, and it was not an immutable state: when Camillus went to Ardea, according to Livy, he greeted the Ardeates as "old friends, and now my new fellow citizens" (*veteres amici, novi etiam cives mei*, 2.2.10–11). Decisions on extending the citizenship lay with the popular assembly, though Livy hints at the senate's desire to preempt this power (38.36.8). Civic status was the crux of numerous legal cases in the second and first centuries (described as *amplissima* and *innumerabilia, de Orat.* 1.181). The consul G. Mancinus, for instance, after surrendering his army to Numantia, made a peace treaty with them that the senate subsequently refused to authorize. Mancinus was formally handed over to the Numantines by the senate, but when he returned to Rome that year, the dispute over his civic status was resolved only by the passing of a special law in the popular assembly that restored his rights (*de Orat.* 1.181–82). Another common case turned on the question of residence, such as freedmen who, having become Roman citizens after emancipation, returned to their native cities. If they intended to return to Rome, the jurist Pomponius says (citing the comments of Q. Scaevola, *D.*49.15.5.1–3), their civic rights should remain intact; if not, they would forfeit their Roman citizenship and take up citizenship in their native place.[18]

The picture through the third and second centuries BCE is one of local variegation in the service of imperial conquest: in Ennius's evocative description of the Roman legions fighting against Hannibal, "the Marsic men, Paelignian cohort, the Vestine virile force" (7.15).[19] Beginning in 90 BCE, the Social War between Rome and a selection of its Italian allies led the Romans to grant citizenship to the Italian allies of the peninsula.[20] In the next generation, Julius Caesar extended the civic status that had earlier applied to the Latins (*ius Latii*) to parts of Spain, Sicily, and southern

---

citizenship as a direct reward for military service, as in the case of the Sicilian and Spanish deserters from Hannibal (Livy 26.21.10–11). Livy is not always clear on the status distinctions (8.14, 10.1.3).

[18] See further Cicero on the case of Balbus, a prominent resident of Gades, whose citizenship was called into question in 56 (*Pro Balbo*, esp. 27–28, which refers to the case of the freedman by name).

[19] This is the conclusion of Dench, *Romulus' Asylum*, who cites the Ennius passage (124).

[20] Brunt, "Italian aims at the time of the Social War," argues persuasively that the Italians sought a "share in political power" (90), and dismisses the geographic obstacles to participation (104), but Mouritsen argues that Brunt's view (which reaches back to Mommsen) rests on the unproven assumption that Roman citizenship was desirable—a product of modern nation-state ideology—and that the reality was more likely Italian ignorance of or alienation from Roman political practice (*Italian Unification*, 6–9, 87–91). Dench is circumspect, but claims the evidence is stronger for *Latin* interest in citizenship (*Romulus' Asylum*, 130).

Gaul. He intended to establish a uniformity of procedure in granting citizenship and in supervising the "hotch-potch" of local governments ruling Italy and the provinces in the first two-thirds of the first century BCE.[21] The contemporary question of how to manage the far-flung province of Gaul, as we saw at the end of chapter 1, may have prompted reflection on the new meaning of citizenship at a time when it was becoming increasingly clear that previous standards of physical presence in Rome and active participation in elections and lawmaking could no longer apply. How would the new entrants into the Roman polity be integrated into the legislative and judicial system? What was a citizen if not a Roman, a Latin speaker, or a military ally of long standing? What role would the local governing elites, whose desire for a share in Roman political practice had brought war to Italy, play in the senatorial order? Most important for Cicero, did Romans of that order possess a natural aptitude for the performative practices of Roman politics, or were they arts to be acquired through training? A conceptual shift in thinking about citizenship occurred in the two centuries after Cicero's death as experts in jurisprudence began to articulate a notion of legal rights beyond the right to participate in politics, of which the most important were the negative freedom of immunity from arbitrary interference and guarantees regarding the ownership of property.[22] Rather than local attachments and actions, the "citizen" came to denote membership in a community of shared law, which had no necessary relation to contiguous territory or the Aristotelian political paradigm of citizens actively exchanging the roles of ruling and being ruled. Malcolm Schofield traces what may be the roots of the displacement of citizenship from the purely local in Cicero's argument that political legitimacy rests in the *fides* of magistrates to whom the *populus* "entrusts" itself.[23]

The variety of types of civic status imposed on conquered regions, and the enrollment of emancipated slaves in the citizen lists, distinguish the Roman republic from comparatively citizenship-protective polities like democratic Athens, which in the fifth century limited citizenship to those born of two Athenian parents. Instead, Roman political culture fostered civic ties (as varied in strength as the types of civic status allotted to

[21] Sherwin-White, *Roman Citizenship*, discusses Caesar's intention (170) and the confused condition of local governments in Italy (119–73) and the provinces (174–89).

[22] "The Augustan age ushered in the period in which the material importance of the *civitas* began to decline": Sherwin-White, *Roman Citizenship*, 236, on the challenge of integrating extra-Italian provincials into Roman government. A century after the death of Augustus, "the City itself is less the material Rome than an idea" and orators like Aelius Aristides can sponsor notions of Roman citizenship as "a form of unity which includes existing differences and distinctions without effacing them" (Aelius Aristides 26.63), 259.

[23] Schofield, "Cicero's definition of the *res publica*," 70–72.

Italian towns) through shared practices of voting, legislation, and law enforcement and through shared narratives of history and communal custom, although the challenge of sifting the evidence for this tendency is intensified by the habit of later writers of altering history to defend or counteract contemporary developments.[24]

Aetia, origin tales, renewed the values shared by the community, animating its telos, clarifying its difference from other types of associations, and warning of the dangers of adopting dissident values. "Imagining" the civic community through practice and narrative, however, raises a number of problems.[25] That which gives strength to cultural bonds, such as narrative, which operates through the mobilization of the imagination, also has the power to make them weak. Civic narrative is readily rewritten through censorship, whether enforced by the state or in less easily quantified ways; its resulting relativist, contingent feel lends a sense of precariousness to civic identity even as it enables a flexibility rendered necessary by social practice.[26] The civic ties of shared story-telling weaken noticeably when it is set up in opposition to, and then trumped by, blood. In *Blood and Belonging*, an impassioned analysis of modern nationalism and its effects, Michael Ignatieff examines the attraction (and the terrible consequences) of founding citizenship on the identity of one's parents, for instance, or extended kin group—on biological ties of any and all kinds. In the past century, in Germany, in the region once known as Yugoslavia, in parts of Iraq, Iran, Turkey, and Syria inhabited by Kurds, in Sudan, in the United States, and in other places, people sharing a tie of blood, often heavily reinforced by a common religion, have called for the consolidation of a state based on blood alone. The relatively simple test of kin relationship, a test whose results are, not inconsequentially, usually difficult to escape or deny, creates a strong ideological frame on which to hang membership in a state. But in the modern world, where history has bequeathed regions with diverse protocitizen inhabitants, blood citizenship is an impossible formula. When blood is treated as

---

[24] Useful essays in McKinnon and Hampsher-Monk (eds.), *The Demands of Citizenship*, esp. Philp, "Motivating liberal citizenship," which compares classical civic virtue models with modern, active, pluralist models, and Ivison, "Modus vivendi citizenship," which measures the degree of "consensus or community" a liberal democratic society needs to maintain political goods.

[25] Said examines the challenge of writing history in territories where competing versions overlap and intertwine in *Culture and Imperialism*.

[26] On the difficult balance of local and global narratives and identifications, see the argument of Appiah, *The Ethics of Identity*, that the sense of rootedness lent by investment in shared language and traditions is fully compatible with a cosmopolitan awareness of the value of diversity (esp. 237–46). The tension between the obligations of city-state and cosmopolis, too complicated to address here, is Nussbaum's subject in "Duties of justice, duties of material aid" (with particular attention to *de Officiis*).

"making" the citizen, especially in societies already destabilized by oppression and poverty, violence is rarely far away. At worst, the dominant civic power comes to see ethnic cleansing as its only solution—a final solution, in the Hitlerian sense of the word—for a state needing the stability of homogeneity that only blood is imagined to offer. This is nationalism, based on the tribal sense of *natio*, at its least humane. Its worst tragedy is that blood ties are themselves a fiction, though one constitutively invested in not disclosing itself as such. Looking at the map of Gaza or the West Bank, for instance, Palestinians and Israelis no longer agree on the story of the region, from names on maps to how and why the names got there. So diverse are the tales of the events that shape the area that the possibility of a common history seems foreclosed; civic narrative, the story that could serve as the legitimate basis and justification for common citizenship, cannot emerge; blood, and the religious affiliation that speaks itself as a matter of blood, is what matters. Appealing to nature and to putatively natural bonds, especially family, heals the sense of breach and alienation produced by extrabiological notions of citizenship.

We are all bodies, sacks of skin, blood, bone, and organs with a history made manifest in genes and physical experience, and we use our bodies as the base on which to forge links of identification and community with others. Family, the first and primary community for most, strikes us as special because the lived experience of family transforms the simple fact of blood ties into something greater: a shared frame of reference that offers refuge and defies rupture (*Fin.* 3.62, *Off.* 1.12).[27] Notwithstanding its fantastical aspect, being in its way as imaginary a collective as the nation-state, the family persists as the most important template for civic polity in ancient political theory. In the classical account of citizenship in Aristotle's *Politics*, the hierarchies of the *oikos* or household are treated as structures of nature. To Aristotle the family is more than a biological union of female and male that produces offspring: he makes it a fortress of divisions and inequalities putatively based in nature and its designs. Here he derives his influential definition of the citizen (*polites*), the patriarch of a household, who is free to leave his household behind to take up, with his equals, the political relationships of ruling and being ruled. The male head of the family and its only member to qualify "naturally" by virtue of his superior physical and mental attributes, the citizen is unique, the only inhabitant of the polis who is at once a product of nature and capable of transcending nature to live the truly good life.[28] Naturally dominant over the naturally dominated (women, slaves, and children), and

[27] On natural kin-groups in Cicero, see Wright, "Cicero on self-love and love of humanity," 180 n. 21, 23.

[28] In "Sex and essence in Aristotle's metaphysics and biology," Deslauriers points out that his account of citizenship in *Politics* 1 is not based in essentialist biology. W. Brown

relying on the labor of production and reproduction that women and slaves perform in the natural world, Aristotle's citizen is free to engage in cultural labor, the work of ruling and philosophy. His rule demands his alienation from nature even as it fulfills the natural end of humanity.

Cicero shares Aristotle's belief in the natural predilection for political associations (*Leg.* 1.23, 33, 62).[29] "The republic (*res publica*) is the affair of the people (*res populi*)," who are not "herded together somehow"—here the word *congregatio* implies the relations of beasts, not humans—but joined by reason and common belief, "allied by consensus about justice and in a partnership of utility" (*iuris consensu et utilitatis communione sociatus*, *Rep.* 1.39). Far from treating blood as the basis of or a barrier to citizenship, Cicero points out that the custom from the city's founding had been to open the borders to new blood, beginning with Romulus's city-inaugurating acts of kidnapping, rape, and military conquest (*Rep.* 2.12). In the course of authorizing the republic in a philosophical text that justifies it as the best possible regime, he does not conceal Rome's original identity as a state of the stateless, an association founded by a man whose birth and early nurture spans the human and animal worlds, while the protodynastic regime of the last monarch, Tarquin, brings oppression and slavery (*Rep.* 2.4, 44). But his account leaves out Aristotle's crucial teleological framework. His view is rather that men are naturally sociable beings who require some external stimulus to transform impulse into action (*Inv.* 1.5, *Off.* 1.11–12).[30] The gap between innate impulse and action, which Cicero leaves unexplained, is symptomatic of his larger failure to reconcile the natural impulse toward political association with other natural drives, such as self-preservation, allegiance to family, and the desire for glory.[31] Though social practices of mutual support like laws, customs, and so on eventually receive the stamp of nature (*Off.* 1.21, 51), caring about others' well-being remains a perpetual challenge for individual men concerned with their own lives and reputations (*Off.* 1.30). And when Cicero represents the republic as

---

notes the gendered tensions in Aristotle's citizen construct, *Manhood and Politics* (32–50), as does Pocock, "The ideal of citizenship since classical times," 32, and Okin, *Women in Western Political Thought*, 73, 277. Miller focuses on the Aristotelian citizen as a social being in "Naturalism."

[29] Wood, *Cicero's Social and Political Thought*, a book dedicated to characterizing Cicero as the first thinker to conceive the state as primarily the defender of private property, and as the inspirer of European conservative thought, remarks briefly on the aims of the republic and civic virtue (100–103, 120–131, 176–184).

[30] Nederman, "Nature, sin, and the origins of society," distinguishes Cicero's view from that of Augustine and Aristotle (7–9).

[31] For Frede, "Constitution and citizenship," this is evidence that Cicero did not know Aristotle's *Politics* but relied instead on an intermediate Peripatetic source for *de Republica* (83–84, 92–94).

advancing toward a condition of perfection by natural means (*progredientem rem publicam atque in optimum statum naturali quodam itinere et cursu venientem videris, Rep.* 2.30), what appears here as a "natural" process turns out to rest on the collective choice of citizens to imitate the model of civic virtue held up for them in the mirror-like life of the wise man (*Rep.* 2.69), who is often destroyed by the very communities he seeks to redeem (*Rep.* 1.6) and whose virtues, in any case, are unsettlingly similar to those of the tyrant.[32] Rather than take these examples as evidence of Cicero's philosophical limitations, we should consider that the contradictions in the text emerge out of a deep, unresolved conflict in his thinking. On the one hand, he cherishes the philosophy-driven desire to ground the republic in a natural order; but this is a troubled awareness, since it casts nature, the source of human impulse, as deficient, thus starkly underscoring the nature of virtuous life as a painful struggle—an insight Lucretius makes the centerpiece of his critical comparison of political life with the tortures of Sisyphus (*DRN* 3.995–1002).[33] On the other hand, this desire stands at odds with Rome's historical experience. The Social War and the conquests of Caesar in the 50s had brought about changes in citizenship laws and very likely attitudes toward citizenship—developments that challenge the Aristotelian notion of a virtuous, homogeneous citizenry intimately linked by geographic proximity and the shared experience of living together.

In his discussion of the Social War, P. A. Brunt observes that the senate's refusal to grant citizenship to the Italians before 90, though difficult to explain, is highly unlikely to have been due to a settled belief that an additional increase in the numbers of citizens and in their geographic distribution would "break the bounds of a city-state"; such thinking was "alien to the practical Roman mentality" and inconsistent with the reality of citizen rolls that already included more than 400,000 men, many settled hundreds of miles from Rome.[34] Whatever the cause of senatorial

---

[32] On the last point, with a pointed reference to Caesar (whose assassination precedes the composition of *de Officiis* by several months): "this is very troublesome, that in this exaltation and greatness of spirit a rash and excessive lust for domination tends to grow . . . the more a man excels in greatness of spirit, the more he wishes to be the first man over everyone, or rather, even the sole ruler (*illud odiosum est, quod in hac elatione et magnitudine animi facillime pertinacia et nimia cupiditas principatus innascitur . . . ut quisque animi magnitudine maxime excellet, ita maxime vult princeps omnium vel potius solus esse, Off.* 1.64)

[33] Derrida, ". . . that dangerous supplement . . .": deficient nature "cannot by definition be anything but an accident and a deviation from Nature . . . through the sequence of supplements a necessity is announced: that of an infinite chain, uneluctably multiplying the supplementary mediations that produce the sense of the very thing they defer: the mirage of the thing itself, of immediate presence, of originary perception" (84, 100).

[34] Brunt, "Fall of the Roman republic," 71.

reluctance and its relationship to Italian ambitions, the shift in Rome's self-definition from a geographically contiguous to an imperial republic leaves traces of an anxious sense of displacement from tradition, a sense that Roman customs and texts sought to mitigate by appealing to nature and natural virtue. The regular appropriation of foreign religious rituals bound conquests at the periphery to the Roman center in the context of a communally shared, divinely sanctioned order. The new Roman citizen was bidden to consider himself a "son" of the Roman fatherland (Diodorus Siculus 37.11). In a speech delivered in 56, Cicero deploys the rhetoric of virtue used in the citizenship law itself, which authorized commanders to grant the franchise to soldiers "for the sake of manly virtue" (*virtutis causa*), in a broad new view of Roman citizenship as a moral state that applies to all Italy (*Sest.* 97–99). Redefining in the course of a single paragraph "good citizens," *optimi*, as *optimates*, a label connoting senatorial faction, Cicero transformed their diverse ethnic, class, and social identities into a unified moral regime of "right thinking" under the law (97). Politicians at Rome, businessmen, residents of Italian municipalities, even freedmen compose this new *natio*, a word etymologically related to *natura* and the blood-kin terminology of *gens* and *gnatus* (*principes, municipales rusticique Romani, negoti gerentes, etiam libertini*). Cicero's strategy seems designed to answer the uncertainty about the new, expanded body politic implied by Sallust in his report that the Catilinarian conspiracy of 63 found strong support in regions that took a leading role in prosecuting the Social War, especially Etruria, and that now wanted greater power and influence at Rome (*Cat.* 17.4, 28.4). The conflicted desire to define the republic according to the static terms nature ostensibly offers while opportunistically claiming (in the face of middle republican historical realities) that generous flexibility is characteristic of Roman attitudes toward citizenship explains a constitutive tension in Cicero's rhetorical and political writings, which seek to represent civic bonds as rooted in nature but activated and reinforced through human acts and their memorialization in text.

INTRODUCING THE PROBLEM: THE CICERONIAN PREFACE

The prefaces and introductory exchanges of Cicero's dialogues on rhetoric, politics, and law cast the interpenetration of nature and its supplements in the political arts, cultural refinement, and education as a central theme.[35] The preface to the second book of *de Legibus* famously describes

---

[35] Habinek, "Ideology for an empire," demonstrates the significance of prefatory material in his analysis of the expropriation of Greek culture as a guiding theme of *Tusculans, de Oratore,* and *de Officiis*—a methodological model I have followed here.

Roman citizenship as a matter of dual identity arising from the pulls of two *patriae*, "one nature's, the other the political community's" (*duas esse censeo patrias, unam naturae, alteram civitatis*, 2.5). But this is a tactical misreading of the situation on Cicero's part, both because most Roman readers (as opposed to *novi homines*) would not have perceived civic identity in this way and because he nowhere follows up his playful characterization of membership in the town of Arpinum as "natural." The phrasing rather highlights the link between the nature of civic attachment and his earlier discussion of law and justice, which "brought everything back to nature"—an appropriate move, "since nature is master" of pursuits like relaxation (*ad naturam referens omnia . . . natura dominetur*, 2.1).

The conversation, itself an interplay of perfectly pitched compliments, occurs on a lovely island in Cicero's Arpinate estate that gives physical expression to its owner's interest in nature's harmonies. Cicero's companion Atticus, praising the setting, expresses surprise at its rugged beauty (*saxa et montes*, 2.1). But his allegiance rests finally with the products of urban culture—specifically, the Greek pursuits of athletics and philosophy. The approving contrast he initially draws between Cicero's island and the fashionable artifices of ornamental streams and marble-tiled walks he has seen elsewhere (2.1) is quickly tempered by his comparison of the site to a wrestling ground, his revelation that the surroundings spark the memory of a text, Plato's *Phaedrus* (2.6), and his subtle reminder of his choice to reside in Greece, the ultimate source of civilized refinements, embodied in buildings, artworks, and philosophers' tombs (2.4, 7). Lacking the essential supplement of the physical and intellectual arts, the natural landscape cannot hold Atticus in his ancestral fatherland.

The limitations of nature's role in the formation of knowledge have already been raised in the first book, where a gnarled oak tree prompts questions of whether knowledge of a thing is better conveyed by its living presence in nature or by its immortalization in writing (1.1–6). The written word extends its metaphorical power even over the natural world, causing trees to grow where none grew before (1.3); the visible presence of trees and streams turns out to present an obstacle to knowledge by limiting the horizons of the imagination to the material and perceptible (1.4). The preface closes with a final variation on the theme of nature, Atticus's request that Cicero write history, redressing the styles of earlier historians who were either too crude (*ieiunius, agrestis, horridus, inscitiam*, 1.6) or too artful (*erudita, ineptias*, 1.7).[36] The preface of the third and final

---

[36] So in the later *Brutus*, for example, Sisenna is compared to Cleitarchus, a Greek historian of melodramatic, highly ornamented style (43).

book closes the theme with praise of Cicero's achievement of the "exceedingly difficult balance between stern dignity and cultivation" in his life and writing (*difficillimam illam societatem gravitatis cum humanitate*, 3.1), an image that captures in a single body Atticus's praise of the perfect correspondence of Roman political power (*imperium*) and the law and principle of nature (*aptum ad ius condicionemque naturae*, 3.3). The prefaces to all three books of *de Legibus* place signs of the natural, prior, and original (scenery, biologically alive things, primitive simplicity) against signs of the cultural, the belated, and the displaced (memory, the written text, ornate style) in ever more complex relations of scale: artful *versus* natural virtue, the refined *versus* the raw, that which is remembered in text *versus* that which lives in the present. Cicero himself resolves the opposition in his writings, deeds, and deportment, precisely as his ideal orator will be imagined to do in *de Oratore*. This resolution, of course, can only be temporary. Cicero's later dialogue *Brutus* makes explicit the suggestion here that Cicero's climactic position in Roman literary and political history signifies the final peak in the empire's fortunes, before the final slide into decline: "Hortensius's voice was extinguished by his death, my voice, by the death of the republic" (*sic Q. Hortensi vox exstincta fato suo est, nostra publico, Brut.* 328).

Similar preoccupations structure the prefaces to Cicero's earlier dialogues. *De Republica*, composed between 54 and 51 BCE, survives in fragmentary form. What remains of its first preface addresses the love of virtue implanted in men by nature, which manifests itself as the desire to defend the commonwealth through the practices of political life, as opposed to a life devoted to philosophical contemplation (1.2, 1.8). Cicero's admission that virtuous men are often reviled by their fellow citizens opens the unanswered and perhaps unanswerable question of nature's apparent idiosyncrasies (why are some citizens more naturally virtuous than others?) and allows him to introduce the main thematic trajectory of the dialogue: political life as training in virtue. That philosophers (Epicureans in particular) scornfully dismiss politics as "mere exercise" (Cicero's word: *exercitatis*, 1.10) proves their fundamental failure to grasp the nature of the virtuous life: constant exercise of the political arts. Succeeding paragraphs probe the competing roles of different kinds of knowledge (anticipating *de Legibus* 1), articulating a perpetual matter of concern for Cicero, the relationship between contemplation and the active life (cf. Aristotle, *Pol.* 7.3), in the frame of a discussion about natural phenomena.[37] The discoursing politicians, Scipio Aemilianus,

---

[37] On Cicero's insistence on the practical value of intellectual pursuits, Seneca *Ep.* 49.5, discussed with other texts by Zetzel, "Plato with pillows," 135, and Asmis, "A new kind of model," 388–91.

Laelius, Scipio's nephew Tubero, and assorted friends, are at leisure (*otiose*), enjoying the break from the business of politics at Scipio's country villa.[38] Tubero questions his host about a strange sight recently witnessed at Rome: two suns appearing in the sky instead of one. Scipio reminds Tubero of Socrates' preference for investigating human affairs (1.15), a chiding response reinforced by Laelius's charge that the two suns are distracting Tubero from the current political crisis (1.19). Discord is resolved in the interlocutors' demonstration that the suns' significance lies in their political rather than natural context. When Laelius teasingly invites a legal expert to issue an edict on the suns' dual ownership of the sky, he is rebuked for ridiculing the art (*ars*) that orders the world (1.20). Furius Philus, whose Stoic role here is to defend abstract knowledge, then uses the exemplum of the learned Sulpicius Gallus (*doctissimum*) to suggest that the harmonious system of the cosmos (household, state, universe) must be studied as a marvelously unified whole (1.21–22)—a point reversed when, with a story about Gallus's calm handling of an army terrified by an eclipse, Scipio recasts the exemplum to emphasize the practical results of Gallus's knowledge (1.23). As astronomy is constructed as proper study only insofar that it affects the human spheres of military and political activity, so human action is constructed as subject to nature's law (*communi lege naturae*, 1.27). The unnatural natural phenomenon of the double suns is refigured as the unnatural political phenomenon of a single Rome split into two Romes, the senate *versus* the people (1.31–33). We are reminded of the dramatic date of the dialogue, 129 BCE, the period of urban upheaval in the wake of the Gracchan reforms. Rome's crisis may not be essentially natural, but to solve it, the text implies, Rome's leading men will bridge the gap between (knowledge of) the natural and its supplements.

The preface's astronomical thematization of the natural carries into the body of book 1, with Scipio's explanation of the cause of political associations. Like his subsequent discussion of regime types and their corrupt counterparts, it draws on Plato's *Republic* and Peripatetic theory: human associations are engendered not by weakness (*imbecillitas*), as Glaucon had intimated in Plato's *Republic*, but by "something natural to men, something like a herd instinct" (*naturalis quaedam hominum quasi congregatio*). Members of the human race are naturally inclined toward association with one another.[39] This is the doctrine of natural sociability that Cicero identifies as the Stoic view in *de Finibus*:

> The community of men, a sort of society and partnership of interests, and the
> actual love of the human race, which, from the moment of birth, given that

[38] On the philosophical allegiances of the characters, see Rawson, "Scipio, Laelius, Furius."

[39] This is an Aristotelian notion (*Pol.* 1.1–2), but Cicero may not have been aware of its implications, as Frede shows in her analysis of the heavy influence of Peripatetic thought

children are loved by their parents and the entire family is bound by marriage and parenthood, gradually creeps out of doors, first by blood relations, then by alliances of marriage, later by friendships, afterwards by neighborly relations, then by fellow-citizens and political allies and friends, and finally by embracing the whole human race. . . . Human nature is so constituted at birth as to possess an innate element of civic and national feeling, called in Greek *politikon*.

coniunctio inter homines hominum et quasi quaedam societas et communicatio utilitatum et ipsa caritas generis humani. Quae nata a primo satu, quod a procreatoribus nati diliguntur et tota domus coniugio et stirpe coniungitur, serpit sensim foras, cognationibus primum, tum adfinitatibus, deinde amicitiis, post vicinitatibus, tum civibus et iis qui publice socii atque amici sunt, deinde totius complexu gentis humanae . . . nam cum sic hominis natura generata sit ut habeat quiddam ingenitum quasi civile atque populare, quod Graeci politikón vocant (Fin. 5.65–6; cf. Off. 1.12, 1.157–58)

By these lights, human beings *cultivate* ways in which to live well together. The Stoic Chrysippus had argued that the nature of man (*natura hominis*) is such that a kind of civil code exists between the individual man and the human race (*Fin.* 3.67). Since man is born to protect and defend his fellows, it follows that the wise man should wish to pursue a political career, and so that he may live in accordance with nature, he will want a family (*Fin.* 3.68). Natural bonds of blood relationships are intentionally confused with civic bonds, as Cicero argues that a complex of intermingled virtues (*coniunctio confusioque virtutum*) links friends, brothers, relations, acquaintances, fellow citizens, and the human race (*Fin.* 5.67; cf. *Off.* 3.28).[40] Parental love is a natural attribute (*natura tributum*), as the Peripatetics were the first philosophers to teach, and "that which is older in the order of time, that the formal union of husbands and wives is conjoined by nature, out of which root kin-friendships are born" (*Fin.* 4.17). This natural love leads to the establishment of societies and even to the supreme self-sacrifice of death for the *res publica* (3.62–64). Republican citizens are members of a civic partnership, not a family or other organic unit, but as these passages suggest, it is republicans who like to represent themselves as a parts of a body, as Menenius Agrippa does in his speech to the seceding plebs in 494 BCE (Livy 2.32).

Cicero's history of the republic in *De Republica* 2, echoed in many respects by Livy, smuggles the innate pulls of blood and belonging into

---

(especially Theophrastus, in her view) in Cicero's arguments in defense of a life of active politics, "Constitution and citizenship," esp. 79–81, 88–94): she notes the difficulty of source criticism created by Cicero's claims (e.g.) that there is "really only verbal disagreement" between the Peripatetics and Academics, and that the Stoics have appropriated Peripatetic doctrine "wholesale," only changing the labels (81).

[40] The blurred degrees of relation are laid out in *Off.* 1.53–58.

the script of Rome's civic evolution. The preface identifies Cicero's main source as the *Origines* of the elder Cato, who anticipates Cicero's exemplary balance of the active and contemplative life and his blend of severity and charm (*gravitate mixtus lepos*, 2.1)—which figure the republic itself, a perfect compound of human labor exerted over time (2.2) and, we will soon be reminded, an ideally mixed regime (2.65). The narrative that follows presents the founders and early kings of Rome as dramatically externalizing the internal balance fully realized by Cato, Cicero, and the mature republic. After a rough upbringing in the natural world of the wolf and the shepherd, Romulus and Remus found a new city on the exact site of their own abandonment in the wilds (*Rep.* 2.4; cf. Livy 1.6), a place with perfect natural defenses (*nativa*, *Rep.* 2.10).[41] Romulus's heirs, the kings of Rome, who are notably not blood-kin but elevated by aristocratic choice and popular acclaim, weave a pattern of balanced forces, civilizing and wild: Numa Pompilius refines the Romans' brutish violence with rituals and games (*revocavit animos hominum studiis bellandi iam inmanis ac feros*, *Rep.* 2.26–27); his successor Tullus reverses Numa's policies by inciting war (*Rep.* 2.27, 31; cf. Livy 1.17). After Graeco-Etruscan culture is brought to Rome by the cultivated Tanaquil and her husband Lucumo (Tarquinius Priscus), their heir, the lawgiver Servius Tullius, is murdered by the lawless Tarquinius Superbus, a figure of natural appetites gone wild who surpasses the biggest beasts in terrifying power (*inmanitate vastissimas vincit beluas*, *Rep.* 1.48; cf. Livy 1.49).

This dynamic cites Cicero's earlier account of the founding of civilization. In the preface to *de Inventione*, Cicero ties the debate over oratory's status as an art, a study, an exercise, or a natural faculty (*ars, studium, exercitatio, facultas a natura profecta*) to the natural origins of political associations, attributing the founding of civilization to a "great and wise man" who combined reason with eloquence to persuade his fellow men to live in peace (*Inv.* 1.2). The distinction between this "great man" and the persuaded mass draws a final distinction between Cicero's and Aristotle's account of civic virtue and the origins of the polity. According to Aristotle, citizens "in the unqualified sense" are men who think and act for the state, those "who have a share in decision making and in offices" (*Pol.* 3.1). Good birth is not insignificant in Aristotle's views about civic identity, but it takes on importance in the context of class organization within the state rather than in defining who may be a citizen and who may not.[42] Property ownership and the possession of a

---

[41] The passage recaps Plato, *Laws* 704a–705b, and Aristotle, *Pol.* 7.6.

[42] Throughout *Politics*, Aristotle gradually tightens the standards for citizenship from "those who share in the administration of justice, and in offices" (*Pol.* 3.1), but in the best state this group excludes laborers, artisans, and of course women, children, and natural slaves (3.5).

certain gentlemanly air are qualities Aristotle associates with noble blood, but increasingly through the *Politics*, the free man is defined as one who, possessing sufficient external and internal goods for autonomy's sake, has been educated properly (*Pol.* 7.1–2; compare 3.12–13, 17).[43] In *de Republica*, Cicero's "best state" preserves the hierarchies of the Servian arrangements described in the second book, but the privilege of leadership it grants to the traditional power-holders in the senate is balanced by the power he grants to the people (1.69). Aristotle's notion that the *polis* is organized on the principle of the universal quest for excellence (*Pol.* 3.8) is transformed in Cicero's account to a spectacular order in which a few leading men (*auctores, gubernatores,* and so on) act as models of virtue for everyone else.[44] Yet Cicero's model republic, organized around the common pursuit of universal virtue, implies that virtue is a suitable goal for each citizen to pursue in practice (even if not in the fully active mode of the statesman). Elizabeth Asmis builds a compelling picture of the nature of Cicero's best (mixed) constitution, especially its "equilibrium" (*aequabilitas,* 1.69), which the statesman represents, both internally and publicly, "fostering harmony among all three parts," the senators and *equites,* the middle class, and the multitude.[45] The catalyst of virtue is eloquence. If rhetoric in *de Inventione* was the binding agent of civic identity, in the hierarchical model of *de Republica,* the movement from prehuman, solitary life to political experience occurs through a dialectic of subjection in which consent and coercion emerge concomitantly and naturally, with oratory as its driving force.[46]

[43] As Frede, "Constitution and citizenship" (98 n.54), notes, there is also the problem of the outstanding man who deserves kingship (3.13, 7.3).

[44] Critics are divided over the nature of the balance of power in Cicero's ideal republic and the significance of his references to a single *gubernator* or *moderator* (complicated, for some readers, by Scipio's admission that the best constitution, in his view, is monarchy, 1.46, 54, 69). To some (e.g., Reitzenstein, "*Die Idee des Principats*" cited in Asmis [see below]), the *gubernator* prefigures Augustus; to others (Lepore, *Il princeps Ciceroniano*), he is not an individual *princeps*-style leader but a type of republican statesman; Lintott, *Constitution of the Roman Republic,* suggests that Cicero had himself or Pompey in mind (224). Ferrary, "The statesman and the law," 91–93, and Asmis, "A new kind of model" 400–13, underscore the dialogue's stress on the need for aristocratic consensus. Note that *de Legibus* stresses the need to sustain the *appearance* of popular power while insisting on the senate's mastery of politics (3.24–27); Asmis points out the differences between the dialogues (404). Fox, "Dialogue and irony," is a "deliberately open-ended" essay worth reading along more traditional explications: it explores irony in *de Republica* as a sign of the dialogue's ultimate failure to determine what form power will take (286). Though its emphasis on the counteraction of univocality and construction of the project of Roman history as "radical instability" is overstated, it effectively draws out the ambiguities in Cicero's thought.

[45] Asmis, "A new kind of model" esp. 406, 412, drawing on *Cat.* 4.16 and *Sest.* 97 for the composition of the three groups.

[46] I owe this formulation to Wingrove, who finds a circularity in Rousseau's representation of nature in *Confessions* and *Discourse on Inequality* (*Rousseau's Republican Romance,* 26).

Is eloquence an artful skill or a natural talent? Asked and briefly
answered in the beginning of *de Inventione*, the question arises repeatedly
in the elaborate prefaces to the three books of *de Oratore*. Framing each
book in this way announces the text's role as a response to *Gorgias* and
Phaedrus, the two famous Platonic critiques of rhetoric that also interrogate rhetoric's status as something natural or acquired.[47] Also informing
the text is the debate over the source of language, nature (*physis*) or law
(or "convention," *nomos*). Arguing that language was derived from
physis, the Stoics pursued the study of etymology with the purpose of
showing that words are descended from a finite set of basic utterances
(*primagenia*) that were supposed to imitate things, or more precisely, the
impression things make on the mind. By this view, language is full of
irregularities, having grown in adaptive response to human usage, a view
supposed to have been adopted by the Stoic Crates of Pergamon.[48] In the
dedication to his brother Quintus, Cicero identifies a disagreement the
brothers had over the art versus nature question as the cause for his
decision to write *de Oratore*. Cicero views eloquence as contained within
the realm of art (*artibus eloquentiam contineri*, 1.5), something learned
in both senses of the word, the highest achievement of human culture:
a judgment recalling passage in Isocrates and elsewhere in Cicero
(*Antidosis* 253; *Inv.* 2.1, *ND* 2.148, *Tusc.* 5.5). His brother, by contrast,
considers it the product of natural talent and diligence, set apart from
learning (*in quodam ingenii atque exercitationis genere*, 1.5). From this
simple opposition, elaborating a pattern by now familiar, the prefaces

[47] Cicero's letter *Att.* 13.19.4, written in 45 BCE, praises *de Oratore* (*vehementer
probati*), lists its personae, and distinguishes this dialogue from Cicero's later work, in
which he plays a role in the conversation "in the Aristotelian fashion" (*Aristotelium
morem*). Cicero identifies himself as an Academic of the New Old Academy represented by
the Stoicizing Antiochus: he calls Plato *noster Plato* or *princeps* (*Epist. ad Quint.* 1.10.29,
Ep. Fam. 1.9.12; cf. Leeman and Pinkster *ad loc.* Goerler, "From Athens to Tusculum,"
analyzes the influence of Plato's *Phaedrus* on *de Oratore* (215ff.). On the issue of *ars* and
the acquisition of rhetorical skill, Rawson, "Logical organization," usefully discusses *de
Oratore* in the context of other handbooks or *artes* by Cato and Varro, as well as Scaevola's
lost work on law and the Mishna (334–51). The surveys by Corbeill ("Rhetorical education")
and Wisse ("Intellectual background of Cicero's rhetorical works") are invaluable.

[48] This difference of opinion in turn affects the so-called analogy-anomaly controversy.
The analogists believed that language develops according to a logical system, which led
them to encourage reforms like that proposed by the historian Sisenna, who used the word
adsentio instead of the normal deponent form *adsentior* (Varro, L.8.5). The anomalists,
with whom Cicero was allied, claimed that analogical emendations were artificial, and that
traditional Roman usage sanctioned changes like contraction (*deum* for *deorum*, *nosse* for
novisse). See Rawson, *Intellectual Life in the Late Roman Republic*, 118–123. Sinclair,
"Political declensions," argues that Caesar's promotion of analogy (in his treatise *de
Analogia*, written while he was engaged in the conquest of Gaul) was designed with an eye
on the anxious provincial elite, eager to learn a formal, systematized language that would
give them entry to imperial politics (92–95).

map *natura* and *ars* onto Roman difference from Greece, a opposition of culture buttressed by beliefs about ethnic, blood-based difference.[49] The dedication disarmingly presents the author's privileging of *ars* as the weaker, Greek view, with Quintus standing as the modern representative of ancient values. His is the attitude of the early Romans who longed for glory through eloquence despite their complete ignorance of method (*praeceptum artis*, 1.14). Once Greek rhetorical expertise finally arrives in their city, the Romans' desire to master it expresses itself in hyperbolical bodily terms: they burn with enthusiasm (*flagraverunt, excitabat*). Such is the power of their hard work and native character (*ingenia*, echoing Quintus' position in 1.5) that they defeat their Greek teachers (*superaret*, 1.15).

That victory is important. From the moment in the narrative that the *ars eloquentiae* enters Roman space it is identified as a Greek subject in every sense of the phrase: a formalized topic of study, foreign, defeated. Rather than obliterating Greek rhetoric, however, Roman victory assimilates it through the strong, young, burning bodies of the middle republic. *Ars*, a term referring not only to the theory and techniques of oratory but also to the professional handbooks circulated by rhetoricians elaborating them—and in contrast to the *practice* of speaking, which Cicero claims as an old Roman habit (*Brut.* 52–53)—is transformed by a labor and desire that Cicero, evoking national ethos and the historical fact of Roman conquest, treats as essentially *Roman* characteristics. If framing eloquence as a fraternal debate over art and nature had at first threatened to place Cicero in an uncomfortable alliance with Greece, this historical sketch redescribes his position as the defender of an art that has already been naturalized by Roman use. His personal disavowal of Greek influence and a statement of preference for Roman expertise defensively asserts his authority as a writer of the *res publica* for the *res publica*. The images of Roman potency and Greek weakness evoked here foreshadow the trajectory of the three books to come, as layers of associative prejudice link Roman republican identity with nature and natural law, art and culture with Greek decline.[50]

As we might expect, having witnessed the central place of bodies in the elite-mass encounters discussed in the first chapter, Cicero's body has a role to play in the reception of his text. The relationship he enjoys with his brother (stressed in the invocation of shared childhood memories and the repeated apostrophe *frater*, 1.1, 4, 23) uses embodied identity—the fraternal connection of blood—to underscore his essential difference

---

[49] Balsdon, *Romans and Aliens*, Edwards, *The Politics of Immorality*, and Vasaly, *Representations*, show how Roman prejudice against Greeks and other groups derives from a blurred conception of the relationship between cultural and ethnic (biological) difference.

[50] See, for example, *de Orat.* 3.131. Note, however, that Greek decline is represented in terms of natural law, part of the human cycle of social progress and failure.

from the Greeks whose arts he defends, just as it heals the breach between Cicero and Quintus, a breach to be exacerbated over the next ten years by Quintus's loyalty to Julius Caesar. The dedication proclaims that Cicero's work is not a professional book available for sale, alienated from the naturally reciprocating relations of family and close friends; it undergoes a pure transmission from writer to reader by way of the blood bond that links the brothers.[51] Implicitly drawn in to the fraternal relationship by the apostrophe *frater Quintus*, the reader is the beneficiary of a purely Roman rhetoric: eloquence produced, so to speak, in a Roman bubble. Dedicatee and interlocutors are carefully introduced to underscore their Romanness, as Cicero excuses himself to his brother Quintus for placing the authority of famous Romans before that of Greeks (*auctoritas*, 1.23). The choice to write in the voices of Roman orators active a generation earlier is partly a product of Cicero's desire to canonize a national tradition of orators comparable to the classical Greek masters, a project developed at greater length in the *Brutus*. These particular Romans, who provide the model for the stylish courtiers of Castiglione's *Il libro del cortegiano* and other Renaissance handbooks, are important for Cicero in two other ways: they are connected to him by emotional memory and social bonds, and they are neither Greek rhetoricians ("learned fabricators of speech," *dicendi artifices et doctores*, 1.23) nor philosophers.[52] All seven are active participants in the civil struggles of the early first century BCE, like Cicero's exemplum of the primeval founder-orator in *de Inventione* and himself in the *de Oratore* preface: the celebrated orators Licinius Crassus and Marcus Antonius, the old jurist Mucius Scaevola, two juniors, Sulpicius Rufus and Aurelius Cotta, and the last arrivals, Lutatius Catulus and Julius Caesar Strabo, one famous for his public career and literary interests, the other for his speechmaking wit. Down to each detail of the dialogue's dramatic frame, the narrative underscores the interlocutors' sense of belonging in Roman society, their affective relations with each other and with the *res publica* itself.

The dramatic date is crucial: September, 91 BCE, during the festival days of the Ludi Romani, immediately before the crisis that would ultimately lead to the Social War, which would begin the following year, as the Italians' support in the senate crumbled in the wake of the death of Crassus, *de Oratore*'s central character.[53] The interlocutors are placed

---

[51] See Hall's analysis of aristocratic give-and-take in "Social erosion and aristocratic manners."

[52] Dugan, *Making a New Man*, persuasively argues that Cicero's choice of figures is an integral part of his goal of creating networks of filiation connecting Cicero with a generation of well-known "elder statesmen."

[53] In 95, Crassus put his name to the *lex L. Mucia* expelling Italians from Rome and ordering a purge of the citizen rolls of Italians who had illegally gained a place there (an

at the center of the crisis over the Italians' demand for full citizen rights, the failure of the senatorial order to agree about the nature and extent of citizenship, and the imminent break with Roman tradition (1.24–27). Reminders of this context hover behind the opening argument over the nature and extent of the proper field of oratory and its nature as the vehicle of or break with Roman tradition. Of the two main interlocutors, Crassus and Marcus Antonius, Crassus seems the more ambitious: the first major speech in the dialogue belongs to him, a wide-ranging account of the orator's duties and advantages (1.32–34). Mucius Scaevola, an older man known for his legal learning, criticizes Crassus's stance with a reminder that the security of the republic rests not in eloquence (quite the opposite, as the example of the Gracchi shows) but in ancient laws, religion, and custom (*leges veteres, moresque maiorum, auspicia, religiones et caerimoniae, iura civilia*, 1.39). Crassus's dismissal of Scaevola's pragmatic position quickly distinguishes *de Oratore* from Cicero's *de Inventione*, which (as we saw in chapter 1) represented rhetoric as a rationalizing discourse subject to the systematization of law.

The dramatic setting of the discussion, the garden of Crassus's villa, clarifies Crassus's role as host and senior statesman and Cicero's relationship to his philosophical forebears.[54] The first exchange occurs in a charming glade beneath the shade of a plane tree—a setting straight out of the *Phaedrus* ("let us talk just as Socrates did," Scaevola remarks, 1.28). A difference between the Platonic and Ciceronian projects announces itself in Crassus's call for cushions to be placed on the benches beneath the plane tree. Literally softening the environment's natural beauty, the cushions give material form to the forthcoming debate over the relationship

---

action "ill-considered and probably soon regretted," Rawson, "L. Crassus and Cicero," 28). On the complicated chain of events see Sherwin-White, *Roman Citizenship*, and Brunt, "Italian aims at the time of the Social War," the latter of which surveys the background and argues that the Italians sought political influence at Rome, *contra* Gabba and Carcopino (cited in Brunt), who respectively stress the Italians' commercial aims and property rights concerns, and Mouritsen, *Italian Unification* (see note 20 above). The Social War did not definitively end until 88.

[54] Rawson, "L. Crassus and Cicero," concisely lays out the historical connection between the two men; Dugan, *Making a New Man* emphasizes the networks of filiation Cicero constructs between himself and Crassus and the other figures (esp. 40–43). For a fine-grained discussion of the relationship between Cicero and his philosophical sources, see Zetzel, "Plato and Pillows." Staffhorst, "Helen in jedem Weibe?" addresses the role of aesthetics in the nature/culture matrix in *de Inventione* 2, arguing that Cicero is putting Platonic form into practice in a literal sense, leading his aesthetic philosophy to evolve into a philosophy of eclecticism, an attempt at a "*Zusammenhang*" of nature and culture (200). Fantham, *Roman World*, also discusses the prefatory material with reference to Plato and Isocrates (49–77).

of eloquence to nature and art. Crassus's transformation of the uncomfortable natural loveliness of Socrates' glade into a wellappointed outdoor *triclinium* signals that the Platonic critique of eloquence—indeed, the Greek philosophical tradition as a whole—does not sit well, so to speak, with the speakers' urban and urbane context: like the marble benches, eloquence must be made more convenient for Rome (*commodius*, 1.29). Crassus here lays the foundation for his initial defense of rhetoric as a product of *cultus* rather than *natura* or *ingenium* (the latter view, shared by Quintus Cicero, will be upheld by Crassus's rival Antonius).

The nature/art debate moves in several new directions in the preface to book 2, set on the following day. The opening question is again *ars*, in this case, the exposure of the main interlocutors to formal education. That written records are a necessary supplement to the oral practice of oratory is ironically underlined in Cicero's note that anecdotes about Antonius and Crassus, which have been transmitted orally, are inconsistent and uncertain (2.1). According to popular opinion, the historical Crassus scorned formal learning—a position that diverges radically from his strong support of an ambitious pedagogical program for the budding orator, which had occupied most of book 1. Antonius opens book 2's debate with a surprise adoption of this position, reversing his own arguments in book 1 on behalf of eloquence-as-nature and articulating a vigorous, culturally oriented defense of eloquence that relies heavily on the Greek rhetorical tradition. Yet he, like Crassus, Cicero comments, pretended he had no education at all (2.1, 4). In their self-advertised "raw" state, the two men play out the scene of Roman victory recalled in book 1, competing with Greek philosophers in debate but judging Roman practical wisdom better than the Greek (*nostrorum hominum in omni genere prudentiam Graecis anteferre*, 2.4). Their disingenuous self-presentation as untrained, natural beings glosses the discussion of eloquence that immediately follows, where the pretense of naturalness stands in for nature, and art must be hidden in order to work its effects. An important political angle emerges in Antonius's contention that artlessness best appeals to the Roman people, who are by nature alienated by philosophical disputation (2.4).[55] If the orator is to pursue the life of Roman political action, the life Cicero elsewhere claims is the fulfillment of nature's designs for humanity, he must make a pretense of naturalness before the watchful eyes of the *res publica*.

This paradox makes an ironic transition to the arrival of the final additions to the group, Caesar Strabo and Lutatius Catulus. Excuses for their presence, late and *sans* invitation, leads into a discussion of tactlessness

---

[55] This is a common claim in Greek oratory as well: see Hesk's discussion of the Athenian orators' manipulation of their audience's suspicion of learned tricks in "The rhetoric of anti-rhetoric."

(*ineptus*, 2.16), in which Crassus deftly makes their apology his own, by way of reiterating the Roman *versus* non-Roman opposition that has already been set up in book 1: just as the Greeks are notorious for impolitely stringing out long arguments about obscure arts, so Crassus was forced to do the day before (*inviti, coacti*, 2.18). His apology both confesses to the similarity between his arguments and Greek views in the first book—which, as we will see, casts Crassus/Cicero as a voice "speaking Greek"—and tries to purify the similarity by redescribing the arguments as artless. Crassus turns next to the marble colonnade where the group has agreed to sit that day. By his interpretation, the Romans have returned the rows of columns and seats, the site of Greek philosophical disputation in Plato and later philosophers, to their original function as the site of physical exercise, a discipline that refines the body's raw strength (2.21).[56] This image is exploited in a later treatise on the best type of orator, where the best speakers seek "strength, muscles, and an attractive tan" (*Opt. Gen.* 8). By associating their rhetorical debate with exercise, the group replays the bodily assimilation of Greek eloquence by the early Romans in the book 1 preface. Here, however, assimilation is more clearly identified as improvement. Cicero will return to this theme in book 3, with Catulus's observation that the Greeks have failed to preserve their cultural heritage, to which Crassus responds with a claim for global intellectual hegemony that links Roman military *imperium* (and the strong martial bodies that sustain it) to Latin oratory and jurisprudence (3.131).[57]

For Catulus, the cause for Greek decline is *otium*, or leisure. The Romans in book 2 are also indulging in *otium*, defined as mental relaxation (*otii fructus est, non contentio animi, sed relaxatio*, 2.22). As though anticipating Catulus's equation of relaxation and decline, Crassus argues that their enjoyment is quintessentially "free" (*liber*, 2.24). For purposes of comparison he invokes a surprising image: Scipio Aemilianus and Laelius on holiday, when, even in their maturity, they liked to fly (*evolavissent*) from the city to search for seashells on the beach (2.22). The loose freedom of their bodies reflects their civic status, which here mirors their psychological state. What can be more free and natural than this childlike pleasure, so evocatively described? But it is also a flashpoint of acute social embarrassment for the discussants. Crassus reveals his

---

[56] Cicero does not say that the palaestra was run by expert professionals—an interesting omission, given Socrates' discussion of physical training in the parallel passage in *Gorgias*. Crassus argues that modern Greeks still prefer to use the space for physical exercise rather than philosophy (2.21). Note too that Sulpicius Rufus has expressed his preference for Crassus's "suburban gymnasium" over the Academy or the Lyceum (1.98).

[57] Crassus on the Greeks: *otio vero diffluentes, non modo nihil acquisierint sed ne relictum quidem et traditum et suum conservaverint.*

discomfort with Scipio's and Laelius's act of freedom by disavowing
direct knowledge of it: "I hesitate to say this of such men, but Scaevola
likes to tell the story," he says of their shell collecting (2.22). This admission
leads to further expressions of anxiety arising from the need to establish
a suitable audience for their discussion of eloquence (1.25), and finally
the debate itself becomes a direct cause of tension, as Crassus's invitation
to the two late arrivals instigates a small war of courtesies (2.26–28).[58]
Crassus's proleptic claim that *otium* offers proof of true freedom is thus
undermined by the social constraints *otium* introduces in the text. One
effect of this carefully constructed framework is to transfer anxiety from
the troubling topic of eloquence itself to the arena of social interchange—
a useful strategy in a society where professionalized learning is the product
of foreign and often enslaved labor. Here and throughout the dialogue,
Cicero (in his own voice and in Crassus's and Antonius's) will apologize
repeatedly for the impropriety of his own ~~professionalized~~, ~~artful~~,
~~unmanly~~, ~~slavish~~ text, at once acknowledging and denying the need for
specialized art in eloquence. On the other hand, the suspicion of Scipio's
and Laelius's holiday version of freedom manifest in this passage hints
at the unsettling need for unfreedom, or at least a robust self-restraint,
in a "truly" virtuous Roman free man of leisure. The physical dispositions of the free elite may enact their freedom according to certain social
rules, but instinct and artless, "natural" behavior have no role to play in
this performance.

The third and final preface develops the theme of nature and art vis-à-
vis the oratorical body with a close look at the bodies of the interlocutors
at the moments of their death. Crassus dies, tellingly, after praising the
deliberative virtues of the senate in a glorious speech (his "swansong,"
cycnea). Here his tongue and breath serve as metonyms of freedom (*libertas*, 3.4), reinforcing the notion of the eloquent orator as a man whose
body is truly free.[59] Antonius and Caesar Strabo die close to the scene of
their speech-making: on the very Rostra on which Antonius "as consul
had steadily defended the *res publica*" was placed, "that head by which
the heads of so many citizens had been saved; and not far away from it
the head of G. Julius lay with the head of his brother, L. Julius" (3.10).[60]
Like Crassus's organs of speech, the severed heads are synecdoches of
republican freedom. The image also advances the logic of amateurism

---

[58] It is, notably, a conflict between brothers, Catulus and Caesar.

[59] *Haec tibi est excidenda lingua: qua vel evulsa spiritu ipso libidinem tuam libertas mea refutabit.*

[60] *Iam M. Antoni in eis ipsis rostris, in quibus ille rem publicam constantissime consul defenderat quaeque censor imperatoriis manubiis ornarat, positum caput illud fuit a quo erant multorum civium capita servata; neque vero longe ab eo C. Iuli caput . . . cum L. Iuli fratris capite iacuit.*

framed in book 2. Such a life-destroying force must logically transcend the arts transmitted and sold in a handbook: the talents described here promise to be more than tricks. Yet, given that they are the exemplars of Cicero's ideal of the naturally best life, the active life of politics, the interlocutors' violent ends contradict what, in many Stoicizing moments in his corpus, Cicero takes to be the fundamental purpose of any living thing: self-preservation. If eloquence is the force of nature that these passages represent it to be, it is a force perversely capable of interfering with the body's drive to preserve itself, and of stopping the body's natural processes. The array of corpses lying in the open air affords an unsettling visual transition to the third day's debate, set in a shady wooded area offering protection from the withering heat of the sun. But the thematic line stressing the power of nature stays true. Now the natural properties of the trees alone are sufficient to mitigate nature's harshness, replacing material made by human hands, like the cushions and colonnade of books 1 and 2. This trajectory tracks Crassus's shift of position from book 1, where he argued that eloquence requires native physical talent but finds its apex in the arts of culture, to his robust assimilation in book 3 of Antonius' claim that eloquence is ultimately a matter of nature.

Let me summarize the programmatic themes in de Oratore's prefaces. First, the art/nature debate is framed in terms of ethnic difference and set in tension with the main characters' artful disavowal of art. Amateurism is praised, professionalism attacked. Second, the Roman body is identified as material that purifies the transmission of the ars eloquentia. Third, though eloquence is treated as an accidental talent polished in moments of leisure—in time that is literally "free"—the otium of free men appears to be as carefully fashioned as a speech, to such a degree that the freedom from which it derives no longer appears to be freedom. This is not a new observation about Roman attitudes toward otium, but it takes on special significance in the context of Cicero's definition of the republic as a free state, and eloquence as the mark of a free people (1.30). True freedom as constituted through continual acts of self-discipline is a notion in tension that will be drawn to a breaking point later in the dialogue. Finally, the prefaces embed the art/nature question, and more broadly the topic of eloquence, in the Italian struggle for Roman citizenship that threatens the res publica. The shift I will trace in the body of the dialogue, from privileging eloquence's status as an art to its identity as a product of nature, is like Aeneas's moment of decision in Aeneid 12: not so much a matter of wholesale transformation as a hybridization of the categories ars and natura. As the interlocutors align the natural assimilation of learned arts with Rome, art for art's nonnatural (perverted) sake with Greece, eloquence-as-art, the tainted half of the binary opposition that the interlocutors cannot resolve, is disavowed and exiled, while eloquence-as-nature, purified, naturalized, and Romanized, is held up to the admiration of all. Philosophers and rhetoricians, as symbols of the training in *ars* that orators must not need, are demasculinized, showing that the republican order is shot through by antagonisms of sex, gender, and class—the difference between Roman men, who are eligible for full participatory citizenship, and women, slaves, and foreigners, who are not. In this move the essentially political implications of the nature of eloquence reveal themselves.

ROME, NATURALLY

De Oratore repeatedly reminds us that for Cicero, political theory and rhetoric are intertwined.[61] Antonius criticizes Greek and Roman rhetoricians for ignoring politics in their writings (*de Orat.* 1.86). Crassus, the host and leader of the dialogue, opens the debate with a polemical choice to discuss eloquence not in the philosophical terms that the setting seems to invite but in political terms, as the mark of every free people (*in omni libero populo*, 1.30). In an irregular traverse of the "concentric circles" of affective relationships that characterize Cicero's theory of the origins of the state, which begin with self-love and move outward to embrace the cosmopolitan community of the human species (*Off.* 1.49), Crassus's next characterization moves from the strictly political to human relations defined more broadly. Eloquence now appears as the mark of a good man in all interactions with others (*nulla in re rudis*, 1.31). From these local advantages, the speech moves to the universal benefits of eloquence, with a word play on the uniquely human capacities of *oratio* and *ratio* (1.33). The ideal orator that the dialogue seeks to shape emerges in Crassus's speech as a subject with three avatars, three sets of allegiances and identities: he is autonomous, embedded in networks of friends and family, and a republican citizen. This tricolon identifies the three levels on which the interlocutors will treat the arts of speech: the self, his affective relationships, and the *res publica*.

The debate proper cites Plato's *Republic* as its authorizing text, with the jurist Scaevola replaying the role of Cephalus: both are old men who disappear after the first book has ended. Objecting to the unusually broad field of knowledge that Crassus has just sketched as the proper responsibility of the good orator, he expresses the conventional opinion (as Cephalus does) that Romulus founded Roman law, custom, and religion not on words but deeds: oratory's power has more destructive than

---

[61] Büchner, *Cicero*, argues that *de Oratore* is as much a political as a rhetorical work (203). Now see Fantham, *Roman World*, especially 305–19, on the orator as ideal statesman.

sustaining force (1.39). Crassus dismisses the link Scaevola goes on to draw between Greeks and words, Romans and deeds, by likening the older man's critique of eloquence to the opinion of pedantic Greeks (1.45). Having cast Scaevola as the Greek intruder, Crassus then undertakes a metaphorical rescue with a hyperbolic attack on "men who quibble in corners"—code for logic-chopping Greek philosophers (1.56). If attacks on eloquence are the typical tactic of Greeks, then eloquence itself cannot be a Greek practice; it has become Roman (1.58).[62] Scaevola and Crassus resolve their disagreement in joint expressions of contempt at the Greeks' "constant, useless garrulity" and "sing-song babbling" in their schools (*quotidianam loquacitatem sine usu . . . ex scholis cantilenam*, 1.105). Crassus is now free to equivocate regarding the still uncertain status of eloquence: "whether it is an art, or something like an art, eloquence must not be neglected" (*sed sive est ars, sive artis quaedam similitudo, non est quidem ea neglegenda*, 1.109). Cicero draws here on a long-established tradition of Roman prejudice against Greek learning, but for a book embedded in the Greek rhetorical tradition, the suspicion with which *de Oratore* views *institutionalized* intellectual activity is striking. This prejudice trumps linguistic and cultural identity, affecting even teachers who speak Latin (3.94).[63] "Go to the Romans for virtue, the Greeks for learning" (*de Orat.* 2.28). Laziness, restlessness, and pedantry are repeatedly invoked as signs of the Greek professionalizing corruption of education (*Brut.* 247, 224; *de Orat.* 3.127–28). Yet Crassus's defense of learned eloquence is impossible to distinguish from any Greek rhetorician's. In book 1 he offers two definitions of eloquence and the good orator: first, a broad account that inserts the study of public affairs (*multa pertractatione omnium rerum republicarum*), law, and ethics (*natura hominum*) into oratorical training (1.48). This evolves into the second, more ambitious definition:

> if anyone wants to define the complete and proper meaning of "orator," he will be an orator, I take it, worthy of such a distinguished name, who, whatever the subject arises that must be unfolded in speech, will speak about it wisely, with polish, ornament, and using his good memory, along with a certain dignity of delivery. (1.63–64)[64]

---

[62] For a discussion of Roman attitudes toward technical terminology, see Bell, 83–92.

[63] The more orators know of Greek, the more worthless their characters: so Cicero's father (2.265). Lutatius Catulus agrees: "I don't need some Greek scholar to drone at me what everybody knows" (2.75). Greek-speaking areas are where the corruption of "Asiatic" oratory first arose (*Brut.* 51, *Orat.* 230–31). Petrochilos analyzes the language of *volubilitas, ineptia, impudentia* and *levitas, Roman Attitudes to the Greeks*, 35–43.

[64] *Quam ob rem, si quis universam et propriam oratoris vim definire complectique vult, is orator erit mea sententia hoc tam gravi dignus nomine, qui, quaecumque res inciderit, quae sit dictione explicanda, prudenter et composite et ornate et memoriter dicet cum quadam etiam actionis dignitate.*

As one interlocutor later observes (3.228), this is precisely the account of
rhetoric offered by the sophist Gorgias (Plato, *Gorg.* 447c) and Isocrates
(esp. *Antidosis* 194–98, 270–75, 291).

The rest of *de Oratore* is devoted to using Crassus's claim to transform
the rhetorical handbook into a guide for ethical formation in the Roman
republican context. The first attack comes from Antonius, who points
out that Crassus's definition blurs the ethical and political boundaries
between Romans and Greeks (1.50ff.): his project is "typical of the
palaestra and its oil rather than the civic crowds of the law court"
(*palestrae magis et olei, quam huius civilis turbae et fori,* 1.81–2). To
avoid the trap Crassus set for Scaevola, Antonius holds himself at a distance from the Greek philosophical arguments he employs, describing his
knowledge of Greek as the product of chance encounter (1.82, 85) and
saying of Tisias, one of the legendary Greek founders of rhetoric, "I don't
really know his name" (*nescio,* 1.91). The second step in Antonius's
critique is his assertion that the *ars dicendi* is inborn and innate, with
techniques natural even to children (1.89–90). Pressed by Antonius to
develop a definition of eloquence that transcends art (1.111), Crassus
articulates a second position that reverses the first:

> Then, Crassus replied, my opinion is this, that nature above all, and natural
> talent, contributes by far the most to oratory; and as for those rhetoricians
> about whom Antonius spoke a little while ago, they did not lack knowledge
> or method of oratory, but nature. For there ought to be quick movement
> of wit and talent, which are sharp in analysis, rich in explaining and orna-
> menting, and solid and steadfast in memory. And if there is anyone who
> thinks these things can be bestowed by art, that is false—for it would be an
> amazing thing, if these things could be set alight and awakened by art: but
> indeed, they cannot be grafted or granted by art; for they are gifts of
> nature.[65] (1.113–14)

Antonius's pleasure at Crassus's capitulation is temporary. When
Sulpicius Rufus twice probes for more information—is natural talent really
all the orator requires? (1.131, 133)—Crassus embarks on a long
description of a demanding course of formal learning that stresses
the detailed rules and refinements of oratory, ironically introduced as
"not learned, not very challenging, not impressive, not serious" (*non aut*

---

[65] *Sic igitur, inquit Crassus, sentio naturam primum, atque ingenium ad dicendum vim
adferre maximam; neque vero istis, de quibus paulo ante dixit Antonius, scriptoribus artis
rationem dicendi et viam, sed naturam defuisse; nam et animi atque ingeni celeres quidam
motus esse debent, qui et ad excogitandum acuti et ad explicandum ornandumque sint
uberes, et ad memoriam firmi atque diuturni; et si quis est, qui haec putet arte accipi posse,
quod falsum est—praeclare enim res se habeat, si haec accendi aut commoveri arte possint:
inseri quidem et donari ab arte non possunt; omnia sunt enim illa dona naturae . . . .*

perreconditam, aut valde difficilem, aut magnificam, aut gravem rationem,
1.135), which occupies the rest of book 1—once more reversing his position
(136–207). Antonius is forced to reintroduce his earlier objection. But
just as Crassus has shifted in response to Antonius, so Antonius adapts
to Crassus, with a new definition of the orator that sidesteps specifics in
favor of claiming that general facility with language, familiarity with
suitable arguments, effective delivery, and charm are all the products of
training (1.213). What Antonius does not abandon is his criticism of
professionalized philosophical and legal studies and his skepticism
regarding Crassus's representation of the orator's broad field of expertise
(1.221, 248–49). His final admission that training of *gestus* and *vox* is
necessary (1.252) comes with an important proviso: that these skills be
"shut up" within the senate and the courts (*concludatur*, 1.260). If the
sphere of eloquence shrinks as a result, then there is more space for
"lovely leisure" (*bellissimum otium*, 1.254)—a subtle corrective to
Crassus's earlier, Greekish claim that *otium* is best devoted to rhetorical
study. Antonius's critique exposes the manner in which Crassus's ideal
Roman orator—a man for whom eloquence is the guiding force in education, ethics, and personal identity—risks losing those characteristics that
make him Roman. Meanwhile, Antonius redescribes the well-read, philosophical, and scholarly man as essentially unnatural—the opposite of the
naturalness that he is busy defining as Romanness. His own ideal orator,
by contrast, is a communicator so skillful that his listeners are barely
aware of his skill (1.221–22).

   Antonius's reasoning rests on the twin insights that Crassus's *eloquentia*
cannot be separated from *ars* and that training in the performance of
artful (Greek) speech and the (philosophical) knowledge that sustains it
transgresses the ideals and conventions of his own class, gender, ethnic
identity, and civic ideology. Oratory is a subject "mixed with falsehood
(*mendacio mixta sit*), which does not often attain knowledge (*scientia*),
which sets traps (*aucupetur*) for men's opinions and, often, their
misguided beliefs" (*errores*, 2.30). Formal training distracts and enfeebles
the Roman citizen, whose attention is best turned to the active life.
Antonius's criticism of Greek rhetorical studies simultaneously seeks to
limit the most refined incarnations of eloquence within the forum and to
naturalize it.[66] His redescription of oratory as a product of nature belonging exclusively to the courtroom and senate house reflects his desire to keep
what he has named as a Greek and problematic practice under control,
subject to a natural law that mimics and glosses Roman *mos maiorum*.

---

[66] Note that Catulus later praises Crassus for his attempt to broaden the scope of oratory,
"just like the ancient Greeks did" For a discussion of the similarity between Crassus and
the sophists, see Schütrumpf, "Cicero's *De Orat.* 1," 249.

What Antonius articulates here is a rhetoric of naturalization, a discourse that appeals to nature as its root and sustenance in nature's own language. Practical experience emerges as the replacement of learning and the savior of eloquence: Antonius's own knowledge derives from life rather than books (1.208). Rooting speech in empirical knowledge not only purifies the act of persuasion, in Antonius's view; experience actually adorns speech. The orator with a wide experience of life will cultivate a style that is pleasingly variegated, decorated with his multicolored impressions of the world. Sight, taste, feel, and sound are invoked as empirical partners in a purification of eloquence that is also its assimilation to nature: "Since ability to speak should not starve and go naked but be besprinkled (*aspersa*) and adorned (*distincta*) with a kind of charming variety in many details, it is the part of a good orator to have heard and seen much . . . , not acquiring all this as his own possession, but tasting what belongs to others" (*sed ut aliena libasse*, 1.218). "A good orator ought to feel the pulses of every class, time of life and degree, and to taste the thoughts and feelings of those before whom he is pleading . . . any cause" (1.223–24).[67] Once again, the body—now evocatively imagined as speaking, moving, and soaking up sensations among the diverse crowds of the law courts and the assembly— is the endpoint and exemplum of Antonius's vision of a redeemed rhetorical practice.[68]

Once again, the reader faces artifice within artifice. As various characters in the dialogue point out, Antonius's theory is inconsistent with his practice. His long and elaborate opening speech in book 2 contends that eloquence has "only a little to do with art" (*arte mediocris*, 2.30), and that oratory is a matter of "common sense" drawn from the experience of public life (2.31, 55ff.), but Cicero portrays him as a figure who cannot resist the seduction of unbridled speech (32ff.). His encomium of oratory is ironically praised as a masterwork of refinement, fluency, and polish (*subtiliter, copiosissime, expolivit*, 2.39–40). Catulus comments ironically on the excess of Antonius's performance (2.39), and Crassus agrees, complimenting Antonius on his new-found "polish" (2.40). Antonius's change of heart has made him the very type of hypocrite he is trying to attack: "what of countless other cases, in which it was not that singularly sharp wit (*acumen quoddam singulare*), which everyone grants to you, that shone out the most brilliantly, but that very capacity which you now want to delegate to me, which has always been exceptional and preeminent?" (2.125). To Crassus's attack on his ability to speak artfully

---

[67] *Teneat oportet venas cuiusque generis, aetatis, ordinis, et eorum, apud quos aliquid aget, mentes sensus degustet.*

[68] I explore the implications of Antonius's representation of the body in the next chapter.

Antonius opposes his simple familiarity with commonplaces (*loci communes*), his habit of listening to others, composition exercises, and above all practice (2.130ff.). When he ripped the toga off the shoulders of Manlius Aquillius, exposing a torso scarred by the campaigns of a long military career, Antonius says, "it was not by means of art; about that I don't know what to say" (*non arte, de qua quid loquar nescio*, 2.195). His emotional defense of Norbanus was equally bare of technique (2.198).[69] Antonius reiterates Quintus's and the archaic Romans' view: "between native talent (*ingenium*) and hard work (*diligentia*) there is little room for art (*ars*)" (2.150).

How can the orator to learn the arts of speech, when his speech is supposed to be spontaneous and natural? In book 3, Cicero roughly assimilates the two views. Developing the line sketched out at the beginning of the dialogue, Crassus argues that only the natural *ingenium* of the Roman orator can absorb the best aspects of Greek learning without succumbing to the artifices of that culture; indeed, the orator can improve upon Greek learning by infusing it with Roman strength. Refuting Antonius's argument that formal training in philosophy has no place in rhetoric (2.157ff.), in book 3 Crassus blends the two into a putatively organic whole (3.57). Attacking that "foolish, useless, reprehensible split between tongue and brain" that creates split selves by dividing education in two (3.61), he blames Socrates for the original separation, when "in fact they cohere" (*re cohaerentes*, 3.60). He praises the pre-Socratics, whose study of philosophy, particularly ethics, and eloquence paid heed to the biological link binding body and mind together (3.72). Unifying these two flows in his voice and physical motions, Cicero's orator literally embodies learning, giving vitality to philosophical discourse and its "thin and bloodless style" (*tenui quodam exsanguique sermone*, 1.56). His eloquence exhibits a charm of coloring owed not to cosmetics but to blood (*non fuco sed sanguine diffusus debet color*, 3.199). A wholly whole, this speaking body is a microinstance of eloquence itself, a single

---

[69] But a scant few paragraphs later Antonius warns his younger listeners on the pitfalls of emotional appeals. "My own practice is to begin by reflecting whether the case calls for such treatment . . . you must not bound all of a sudden into that emotional style . . . and once you have assumed it, you must not be in a hurry to change it" (2.205, 213) Antonius offers advice on precisely which emotions the speaker must incite in his audience, having considered the matter of the case, the atmosphere of the courtroom, and his own performative capabilities (2.206–12). Crassus, too, gives advice on the self-conscious manipulation of emotional effects, using poetry to demonstrate his points (3.216ff.). "But all these emotions must be accompanied by gesture," he advises, "not stagy ones, borrowed from theaters, but from the parade ground, or the palaestra" (3.220). The paradox behind Antonius's and Crassus's defense—that their practice was in fact an artificial act—is surely what drives Cicero's anxiety in the first place: see below and chapter 5.

unitary virtue (*una est . . . eloquentia*, 3.22; cf. 3.55). Not only can there
be no rhetoric without virtue, this formulation implies, but there can be no
virtue without rhetoric. This, finally, is the endpoint of the dialogue, but it
should not be confused with a fixed position on the conflict of nature and
acquired artfulness. In Crassus's discourse on style and delivery, the complex rhetorical strategies of apology and attack involved in his original
defense of *ars* are rearticulated in terms of naturalization. The natural
endowments praised by Antonius become the touchstone of *ars*, and training disappears into subordinate clauses: "Nature itself, *if it has been
trained a little*, given a plentiful supply of matter, will, without any leader,
easily find an abundance of things for the ornamentation of a speech" (my
emphasis, 3.125).[70] *Ars* is now the barred term, but by the logic of the bar,
~~ars~~ remains as the symptom of the thing purporting to replace it. And style
and delivery become discursively subordinate to Roman law as the sine
qua non of the orator's education. Back in the first book, when asked how
a budding orator might be expected to learn everything on his ideal
syllabus, Crassus had praised law, second only to philosophy (1.195).[71]

In fact, in the third book, eloquence itself turns out to be governed by
law—the laws of nature. Though Crassus tries to forestall criticism of
the professionalized topic of meter and rhythm with careful apologies,
the real defense of his treatment is its substance: that the good speaker
should avoid codifying eloquence in terms of cases, codes, and rules—
that is, in the Greek fashion, as the dialogue has previously defined such
an approach—but rather to view it as "so potent a force that it embraces
the origin and operation and developments of all things, all the virtues
and duties" (3.76).[72] Good speeches are compared to the beauty of the
unadorned human body and the sublimity of nature, even the splendor
of jewels (3.96). The language of *cultus* and *ars* is replaced by a naturalized aesthetic of proportion and taste (3.102, 103). "In oratory, as in
most matters," he concludes, "nature has contrived with incredible skill
that the thing possessing most utility also have the greatest amount of
dignity, and indeed usually of beauty also" (3.178).[73] The universe, the

---

[70] *Ita facile in rerum abundantia ad orationis ornamenta sine duce natura ipsa, si modo
est exercitata, delabitur.*

[71] By comparison, Greek law is disordered and absurd (*inconditum ac paene ridiculum*,
2.197); Roman ancients are said to be more prudent than Lycurgus, Draco, and Solon.

[72] *Illa vis autem eloquentiae tanta est ut omnium rerum, virtutum, officiorum omnisque
naturae, quae mores hominum, quae animos, quae vitam continet, originem, vim mutationesque teneat, eadem mores, leges, iura describat, rem publicam regat.* This is not, I
should stress again, a new solution; it draws heavily on Isocrates. The point of the prefaces
was to inscribe the Isocratean text in the Roman republican context.

[73] *Sed ut in plerisque rebus incredibiliter hoc natura est ipsa fabricata, sic in oratione, ut
ea, quae maximam utilitatem in se continerent, eadem haberent plurimum vel dignitatis vel
saepe etiam venustatis.*

fine arts, physical nature, trees: form follows function, and beauty is the natural aesthetic result (3.178–80). Book 3 also emphasizes the importance of experience in public life: his *magister*, as Crassus calls it (3.74), and his advice against excessive complexity recalls Antonius—"so successful is your eloquence!" Antonius wryly remarks (3.51). As one analysis of *de Oratore* concludes, "There is, in the end, no contradiction between Antonius's and Crassus's views."[74] The collapse of the categories *ars* and *natura* exorcises the specter of artificiality from the practice of oratory. Now the solution is nature itself, which the dialogue has already established holds a unique relation to Roman character (by virtue of being Roman). Potency, physical power, and a sense of propriety, generated out of experience, nature, and the *tirocinium fori* rather than the suspiciously passive speculations of academic theory, preserves the Roman republican orator as a natural entity free from the need of training and thus *free* in the fullest sense, free for the active pursuit of civic participation. Cicero's strong rejection of Greek and philosophical authority in favor of Roman is not a simple expression of nationalism or defensiveness born from a sense of cultural inferiority but part of an attempt to transform oratory, at the deepest level, into a Roman practice rooted in Roman nature, and hence to make Rome the best, and most natural, polity, linked by the quintessentially natural bonds of speech.

To transform the complex rules of rhetorical persuasion into a matter of natural law is, Roland Barthes believed, one of the most important functions of Western rhetoric: that it appears to codify language, to code the uncodable, to exert mastery over the power of speech.[75] Part of the reason that we have come to view language as a code, he argues, is the influence of ancient and medieval rhetoricians, who succeeded in presenting language as an ordered system that could best be comprehended in terms of natural categories. Once these categories appear to be natural, one who knows them seems to have a special and unassailable control over language and its uses. This reminds us that Antonius's naturalization of rhetoric amounts to a claim of natural domination in terms of class and ethnicity. If language is naturally accessible to those of common sense and inborn talent, in the broader context of Roman structures of oppression, this group must be Roman, male, well-educated, and wealthy. Rooting eloquence in the essentials of natural law makes it inaccessible to those without the natural *ingenium* that now emerges as the special property of the elite Roman man.

So teachers must be banished from the republic's public spaces—an act that Cicero carries out in the text, and that the historical Crassus decreed

---

[74] Wisse, *Ethos and Pathos*, 197.
[75] Barthes, "The old rhetoric," passim.

during his censorship.[76] For learning does not only demystify the process through which a man becomes a master; it is a supplement to eloquence in the Derridean sense: a dangerous supplement that affects the orator in ways he cannot control.[77] Once absorbed, learning visibly and irretrievably marks the body, communicating itself through gestures and mannerisms that reveal the contamination of acquisition itself. The suspicion of artifice about which Antonius complains (2.156) is more than the audience's concern that it is being deceived: it threatens to cast the orator's speech as unnatural and hence deracinated from the discursive operations of the *res publica*. Teachers are living proof of the failure of the putatively naturally dominant classes to wield the powers given to them "naturally," without the aid and assistance of training.[78] Teachers thus demystify the naturalness of propertied men's essentializing claims to rule, and they threaten to destabilize the political order by promising rule to anyone who can acquire the supplement of learning. In the classroom, essence, such as high birth, can seem not to matter. A troubled acknowledgment of this lies behind the Ciceronian, and indeed the modern, suspicion of teaching. Cicero's ironically self-cancelling silencing of rhetoricians and philosophers derives from his belief that republican oratory must anchor itself in nature. So language craftsmen languish "in corners" (1.30), while the virtue of the orator grows great from the performance of speech in the public eye (cf. *Rep.* 1.2). In the final analysis, the orator fulfills his virtuous potential in a way that no one else can because he lives his natural superiority in his very body, a manly and authoritative Roman body.[79] He will not need makeup, oil, the curling iron, or other false instruments of adornment; he will fight the good fight, a warrior in the hot and dusty battlefield of the forum (*Brut.* 36, 158; *de Orat.* 1.81, 3.100; *Orat.* 228–29).

Roman culture placed a high value on the virtues of justice, courage, self-discipline, and a kind of blunt sincerity singled out by Cicero as a peculiar characteristic of the Roman, as opposed to Greek or barbarian, character (1.102).[80] But *de Oratore* ends as it began, with equivocation,

[76] His attempt extended to the teaching of Latin rhetoric in public (*de Orat.* 3.93): Rawson, "L. Crassus and Cicero," 27.

[77] Leeman traces "l'hyperbole et l'ironie chez les Romains en tant que mécanismes de défense et d'assimilation a l'égard de la culture grecque" in an article by that name, 347–55.

[78] For further discussion of this point, see Connolly, "Like the labors of Heracles" and "Problems of the past."

[79] Women, the private others rarely mentioned in Cicero's rhetorical texts, must emerge as the silent negatives of the ideal (cf. *Orat.* 59–60).

[80] Leeman, *Orationis Ratio*, 20–21, discusses the stereotype behind *Curc.* 288–92; also Guite, "Cicero's attitude to the Greeks"; Balsdon, *Romans and Aliens*, 30–54; Vasaly, *Representations*, 198–204.

as Crassus warns the younger men to hone their skills with study and hard work (3.230). Despite Cicero's efforts, eloquence remains an art, relying for effect on supplementary language (*ornatus*) and deception.[81] As it turns out to be another version of concealment, the rhetoric of naturalization engenders instability and paradox at the heart of the rhetoric of naturalization. Rhetorical training may be a system intended to invest and enforce a social code valorizing the manly republican values of restraint and sincerity, but in practice it exposes its students to a very different sensibility, training them to express themselves using the techniques of artful, soft, flexible, politically disempowered, foreign subjects. This account of eloquence as a stability born of instability and contradiction returns us to Cicero's view of the *res publica*.

HYBRIDITY

Eloquence is the tipping point between nature and culture: it is a practice of hybridity. But treating the orator as a hybrid mixture requires careful handling. In *de Oratore* (and, very likely, the missing parts of *de Republica*), the ideal citizen who is the mirror of the people subject(ivize)s himself through a perpetual process of *refining natural talent*. The move to collapse nature into culture in the formation of the orator underscores the tension between the perceived authenticity of nature and the contingent status of culture, a tension Cicero seeks to resolve by representing each in the language of the other. The ideal self of Cicero's ethical treatises is both naturally and artfully himself: "We must study what we ourselves are, in order to keep ourselves true to our proper character" (*Fin.* 4.25). So with the citizen, who "should never leave off from improving and examining himself, so that he may call others to imitate himself, so that he may offer himself in his glory of spirit and life to his fellow citizens just like a mirror" (*Rep.* 2.69–70). As Cicero closes the gap between eloquence and virtue, the orator's speaking body becomes the virtuous body of the citizen, and by extension a microcosm of the virtuous body politic: eloquence emerges as a performative ethics that embodies and enacts the common good for the instruction and pleasure of the republic. In *de Oratore,* civic identity stands exposed as a learned, artificial performance even as it uses the language of ethnic purity and authenticity in its claim to produce a citizen who is the incarnation of nature and nature's law.

---

[81] Robert Kaster suggests to me that the best translation for *ornatus* is "outfit" rather than the common "ornament," since the idea is connected with the means ("equipment") used to give shape to a speech rather than something merely ornamental (private communication).

This is a performative view of selfhood whose gestures toward spectacle, mutability, embodiment, and what I will later call "interdiscursivity" (all matter for subsequent chapters) must convey their radical meaning in the language of naturalization. This is why a handbook on the arts of rhetoric persistently calls *natura* as a witness in its own defense, despite the fact that the very repetition of that call reveals that its object is merely naturalness pretending to be nature. Nor is Cicero talking only about training for talking in the senate or the Forum. Because he views the *vir bonus* shaped by and for oratory as a perfect man, an agent of performative ethics in the context of communal relations—of politics—to be an orator turns out to be both a self and a citizen. It is to practice an art profoundly anxious about its origins and status in the world.

As political ideology shapes the questions privileged by rhetorical discourse, so rhetoric illuminates hidden corners of political theory. Cicero's presentation of the ideal orator as a nature-culture hybrid, in possession of an eloquence that is at once an innate capacity and a learned art, reflects his understanding of the citizen as a nature-culture hybrid. Orator and citizen alike are creatures born from nature but fashioned into subjects by a cultural process whose power to make the self "from the ground up" ends up calling into question what role nature plays in shaping it at all. As Cicero represents it, nature's role in framing character and individuality is both essential and supplementary (for the latter, *ipsi iudicio nostro accommodamus*, *Off.* 1.115). Does the self become virtuous by its obedience to natural law or cultural convention? What is the difference between the two?

Cicero's desire to figure political identity as a natural identity in his political writings is the touchstone for the nature-culture debate in his rhetorical work. Like eloquence, living in a community—living a political life—demands an artfulness that does not "come naturally," but at the same time it is natural, the defining characteristic of humanity and the instrument of basic human affectivity. When Cicero naturalizes the social world in which his readers and ideal characters move, "describing" a *societas hominum* that in his story is ordained by nature, he tells us of a complex and more demanding relationship than that established in Aristotle's *Politics*, where Aristotle denatures the citizen by branding the family natural and apolitical and base, and imagining relations between free men as exchanges of domination untainted by domestic concerns or obligations. That citizen's participation in the public sphere, however it might be defined, depends on his emancipation from the chains of material things—the incessant demands of the household, physical labor, bodily weakness (hence Aristotle's careful discussion of gymnastics as a part of citizen education, *Pol.* 8.4)—and his entry into a polis life that operates on a necessarily small scale.[82] By contrast, Cicero links all men in a relation of *societas* that is at once of nature and of culture: it is not natural, but emerges when men restrain their natural desires; yet they have a natural desire to do just that. Rather than defining *agora* against *oikos*, Cicero embarks on the project of making the whole world a male family of citizens (like his collections of interlocutors).[83]

In *de Legibus*, Cicero suggests that appeals to justice that sidestep nature and tradition and treat communal opinion as the basis for law make justice irremediably arbitrary (1.42–47). Hoisting law outside the realm of nature makes it vulnerable to the forces of culture, where nature's putatively transparent legitimacy legitimates its offspring. In the preface to *de Republica*, Cicero claims that contemporary notions of civic virtue have been handed down "from those men who confirmed them, already shaped by training, some by custom, others in laws" (1.2). But where does this "already" come from? Here nature seems to take shape under the same laws that govern the formation of culture.[84]

In the debate over the status of rhetoric in *de Oratore* lies Cicero's central insight into the republic itself (which has since early modernity been viewed as a particular symptom of republicanism): that it is a marriage of artificiality and natural impulse, a performative, dramatic, visible, temporally finite order that must speak the language of naturalness in order to conceal its own contingent and spectacular qualities. This places Cicero's insistence on the virtues of stylish speech in a different light: not only as a response to Plato's hypocritical condemnation of style (which Crassus views as evidence of the philosopher's grasp of the need for persuasion, 1.47, 49), but as an admission that, if the orator *represents* the citizen body in any meaningful sense, he captures its artificial nature

---

[82] Aristotle, *Pol.* 7.2, cites Hippodamus's plan for a polis of 10,000 citizens with approval; his own view (much less clear) is "that which suffices for the purposes of life and can be taken at a single view" (7.4). On the intervening, influential views of the Stoics, which I have scanted here due to my focus on the rhetorical tradition: Baldry, "Zeno's ideal state," Schofield, *The Stoic Idea of the City*, esp. 57–91.

[83] This is, as several readers have reminded me, a position adopted by Cicero in his most heavily Stoicizing moments. It is worth comparing to his evolving views on *concordia ordinum* and *consensus omnium*: the best place to start would be the *Pro Sestio* 96 ff., where Cicero defines the *optimates* to be all good men in Italy (insightfully discussed by Wirszubski, "Cicero's *cum dignitate otium*," and Brunt, *Fall of the Roman Republic*, 54–56. On *concordia*, see Lepore, *Il princeps Ciceroniano*, 183–95.

[84] Ferrary, "The statesman and the law," points out that laws in Cicero's *de Republica* and *de Legibus* are not based on natural moral law or on any strict interpretation of Stoic thought but belong to the *ius naturae* as "the expression of a *ratio prudentis*," the reason of a wise man, who is not the perhaps unrealizable Stoic *sapiens* but the traditional leading men of Rome (69–70). I examine this issue in greater detail in chapter 4.

as a political association as well as its natural nature as a product of human desire to live together.

Cicero's *de Oratore* is not a formal treatise about citizenship. In its presentation of the ideal orator as the amalgam of an ethical and civic ideal, however, it is negotiating broader shifts in thought and practice related to the granting of citizenship and the activities of citizens in first century Rome. The breakdown of that community, as it appeared to Cicero in the middle of the 50s, haunts the dialogue. Here is the rhetoric of naturalization rewritten, in a letter of October 54: "We have lost, my dear Pomponius, not only every drop of the blood of the state (*sucum ac sanguinem*), but even its former color and appearance (*colorem et speciem pristinam*); there is no republic I can take pleasure in (*nulla est res publica quae delectet*), where I can rest" (4.18.2). *De Oratore's* two central questions, dramatically posed in its prologues and opening scenes—"Is eloquence an art?" and "Is the good orator a product of nature or culture?"—mean more than they have generally been taken to mean: more than a debate over the epistemological and ethical status of the *ars dicendi*; more than an answer to Plato's critique of rhetoric in *Gorgias*, *Republic*, and other dialogues; more than a carefully slanted contrast between Roman intellectual discourse and the pseudo philosophies of the Greeks. I have focused here on how these questions relate to the explicit goal of Ciceronian rhetorical theory, the training of men for the political arena, which means taking into consideration Cicero's beliefs about the nature of the speaker not merely as "a good man skilled in speaking," in the famous words of the elder Cato, nor as an ethnic Roman, nor as a manly man, but as a citizen of the Roman *res publica*, which Cicero's equation of virtue with eloquence redefines as a state of speech.

This chapter has argued that in the debate he stages over eloquence's connection to art and to nature, Cicero raises difficult questions about civic performance and inauthenticity, epistemological concerns about the status of the orator's knowledge, and social concerns about the role of the artful professional in oratorical pedagogy. More detailed discussion about these issues follows in subsequent chapters. My goal here was to argue that all of them elaborate what is primarily a political problem: the nature—or the culture?—of the republican citizen. To Cicero, training in the arts of eloquence allows the self to reveal and express its natural state as a self in community with other selves. But because this logic reveals the artificial and internally divided nature of the self, a state that stands in tension with civic and conventional beliefs about selfhood and truth, Cicero disavows the *ars* and tries to link speaking well with nature and the natural good. The way he carries out this project reveals the ambiguity at the heart of the enterprise, because he chooses to hang his defense of rhetoric on Roman nature. But his dialogue forces us to ask, what is Roman nature? Claiming to purify speech by linking it to Roman nature simply redraws the circles, for Cicero is simultaneously committed to a vision of citizenship that is not biological or blood-based. What finally emerges from *de Oratore* is a view of civic virtue that, like eloquence, is a fusion of the natural and the cultural.[85] What is new here is Cicero's effort to resolve its contradictions.

[85] Analogues: Isocrates, *Soph.* 10, 17; Quintilian 1.1.1–2; Ps.-Plutarch, *Lib. Educ.* 4a–c.

Chapter Three

THE BODY POLITIC

Restore your selues unto your temper, Fathers;
And, without perturbation, heare me speake:
Remember who I am, and of what place
What petty fellow this is, that opposes;
One, that hath exercis'd his eloquence,
Still to the bane of the Nobility:
A boasting, insolent tongue-man.
—Ben Jonson, *Catiline*

THESE LINES ARE SPOKEN BY Jonson's rebel protagonist, who seeks to undermine the "tongue-man," his rival Cicero, by linking his powers of persuasion to his low birth and envious ambition. "Peace leud Traitor or wash thy Mouth," the younger Cato retorts, setting the stage for Cicero's counterattack on Catiline's vicious habits of speech and lifestyle. Like much Renaissance drama, the play draws on a tradition of skepticism about eloquence two thousand years in the making, a tradition that revolves around the question, what is the relationship between virtue and the ability to persuade? We shall see in this chapter that Catiline's rhetorical strategy—his powerful *redescriptio* of Cicero as a man reduced to the slippery muscle behind his teeth—presses on the most vulnerable spot in Cicero's representation of republican subjectivity in performative terms, the body.[1] The speaking bodies of the senatorial elite had always played a vital role in Roman politics, making traditional structures of power transcendent through constant restagings of authority in competition with one another before the people. As we saw in chapter 1, the Hellenistic systematization of rhetoric in the *Rhetorica* and *De Inventione* had presented a reason-privileging alternative to the charismatic appropriation of argument in republican oratory. In Cicero's later writings, the body returns to center stage as the embodied proof of republican virtue—but not quite in the mode of the charismatic bodies memorialized in Valerius Maximus or Aulus Gellius. Now the body is represented as the prime instrument of the communication of the *communis sensus*, the common sensibility, and he emphasizes the body

---

[1] Jonson here rewrites Sallust's account of Catiline's attack on Cicero as a "serf-citizen" (*inquilinus civis*), an invective term singling out issues of class and municipal origins (*BC* 31.7).

as a point of commonality between speaker and audience—a site at which republican virtue may begin to replicate itself.

Cicero's idea of embodied excellence, like much of his rhetorical and political thought, is not new. Aristotle included gymnastics, music, and other modes of instruction for the senses in civic education (*Pol.* 7–8); Aristotle's student Theophrastus wrote a lost treatise on proper delivery; and Isocrates defended his project of training in embodied virtue in the *Antidosis*—all authors known to Cicero.[2] Two things distinguish Cicero's representation of the virtuous speaker from his Greek predecessors. The first is his handling of the unequal balance of power or status between speaker and audience. Cicero's virtuous body cracks open the traditional model of political communication: if the orator is the embodiment of senatorial authority, his embodied virtue, as Cicero represents it, is also exemplary (and therefore learnable), responsive, demonstrative, and common, the special property of the human race and the vessel of the passions that sustain and constitute the republic. No populist, Cicero tries to balance these two competing impulses, making the speaking body itself figure his notion of *concordia ordinum*. The second is his revelation (made explicit through various expressions of anxiety) of the body's fragility. The body is vulnerable, changeable, mortal matter, with weaknesses associated with the female, enslaved, and poor; the impossibility of its perfect management undermines Roman ideals of self-mastery, which are themselves rooted in assumptions about masculinity and class. This fragility, in light of Cicero's equation between the virtuous body and the republic in his articulation of a model of political subjectivity, figures the fragility of the republic.

In his early lectures on rhetoric, given at Basel in the early 1870s, Nietzsche slapped a harsh judgment on Cicero: "Cicero considers the book he wrote much later in life, *de Oratore*, to be very important, as far as form and content are concerned. . . . But he never understood the opposition of the true philosophers and the orators. His book is crude

---

[2] Crassus warns against total immersion in books, saying that "if a man cannot learn something quickly, he will never be able to learn it at all" (*de Orat.* 3.89; cf. 87–88)—a remark that may reflect Cicero's study of Greek rhetoric (I do not refer to his philosophical studies). The questions of when and how closely Cicero studied the Greek tradition are vexed: Solmsen, "The Aristotelian tradition in ancient rhetoric," argues that the early *de Inventione* displays signs of confusion between various Greek authorities, while *de Oratore* and *Orator* reflect deeper familiarity with (or greater interest in) Aristotle, as evidenced by Cicero's appropriation of the tripartite Aristotelian division of rhetoric into logos, ethos, and pathos (178). Wisse defends the depth of Cicero's knowledge in "*De Oratore*: Rhetoric, philosophy, and the making of the ideal orator"; on the other side, Fortenbaugh skeptically (but judiciously) examines the issue with special attention to prose rhythm, "Cicero's knowledge of the rhetorical treatises of Aristotle and Theophrastus" (with useful further references).

and distasteful compared to Aristotle's."[3] On the contrary, examining
the body in Ciceronian rhetorical discourse unlocks his contribution to
ancient and early modern virtue theory, the investigation into the
nature of the man who lives well: an agent-based concept as opposed
to an act-based code. It also responds to a powerful strand in the
Western philosophical tradition, one that problematizes the body and
the very notion of embodiment. And it resonates with poststructuralist
and especially feminist thought about the nature of subjectivity—
specifically, the challenge of conceptualizing embodied subjectivity in
political terms.

Picking up from the last chapter's arguments about nature, I argue that
Cicero constructs a contest over the communication of knowledge
between the Roman orator and the Greek philosopher that turns on the
way the orator embodies, emotionalizes, and contextualizes what he
knows—making it *natural* by making it a product of the body, taking
philosophical themes and giving them flesh and blood (*de Orat.* 1.56).
We have seen how Crassus's appropriation of Socrates' characterization
of sophistic orators in *Gorgias* dialogically and intertextually inverts
conventional associations between philosophy and rhetoric, Greek and
Roman. The orator's body, not hidden in dark corners like the bodies of
philosophers (*de Orat.* 1.29) or conspirators but visible and audible in
senate and Forum, overcomes the potentially unnatural, unmanning
effects of specialized training. In this chapter I explore further how the
speaking citizen is imagined to negotiate republican politics, and specifically how his communicative act cleanses him of the Greekish taint of
ars. What Plato had taken to be one of the most corrupt and corrupting
links in the chain of communication, performance before a receptive
crowd, Cicero renames as a purifying (and quintessentially natural)
moment of oratorical practice.

I begin with Cicero's response to Plato's critique of rhetoric, summarized in his claim that virtue lies within the reach of the orator alone, precisely because his knowledge and management of his body offers him
robust resources that philosophy is imagined to destroy. The rest of the
chapter reads Cicero against Jürgen Habermas and feminist theorists of
subjectivity to explore this challenging question: What are the consequences of defining the virtuous self as a communicator, someone whose
virtues rest not in adherence to absolute standards or goods but in responsiveness to communal norms during a life of active, embodied engagement
in the affairs of the republic? If Cicero writes about the orator in exalted
terms, it is because in the action of his speaking body he glimpses both the
high promise of virtue and the danger of corrupting vice.

[3] Translation slightly adapted from Blair, "Nietzsche's lecture notes on rhetoric," 102–3.

THE PROBLEM WITH PHILOSOPHERS

The education of the ancient man customarily culminates in
rhetoric: it is the highest spiritual activity of the well-educated
political man—an odd notion for us!
—Nietzsche, "Lectures on Rhetoric"

The main historical source for Jonson's *Catiline* and the terms in which he
expresses his suspicion of eloquence is Sallust, who censures the aristocratic conspirator as having *satis eloquentiae, sapientiae parum* (BC 5).
But the critique of rhetoric runs deep in the Western intellectual tradition,
finding its origins in Plato's *Apology*, *Phaedrus*, *Gorgias*, and *Republic*.[4]
Cicero uses Plato as an entry point, and in his tendency to use "Plato" as
a shorthand for "philosophers" (and vice versa), he is above all concerned
to stress rhetoric's superiority to philosophy.[5] Philosophical knowledge is
essential—"without philosophy, that eloquent man whom we seek cannot
exist"—but it is categorically subordinate, aiding the orator just as ath-
letic exercise helps the actor (*sic adiuvet ut palaestra histrionem*, Orat. 14;
cf. *de Orat.* 3.80–81). Cicero exploits Plato's representation of Socratic
dialectic (knowledge-acquiring dialogue) as the opposite of rhetoric
(opinion-spreading speech) and as a model of pure communication, cleansed
of the falsities and passions clouding democratic and sophistic oratory. If
we find this interpretation of Plato impoverished, it is worth remembering
that Plato's critique and the tradition it engendered are sufficiently influential that one historian of rhetoric recently opened the revised edition of his
influential study of the rhetorical tradition with the words, "The goal of
this book is to remove the misapprehensions and prejudices that still affect
our appreciation of rhetoric."[6] Though Brian Vickers carries out his
salvage duties in his *In Defence of Rhetoric* with perspicuity, characterizing
rhetoric as a discourse in need of redemption from philosophy's assault
leads to problematic consequences. In his attempt to defend rhetoric at
what he takes as its weakest points, which are mostly defined by philosophers, Vickers loses sight of the ways in which philosophy misreads rhetoric,
and rhetoric in turn misreads philosophy. Rhetoric does this by taking
altogether different paths, exploring modes of subjectivity and conceptualizations of knowledge that diverge from the philosophical tradition.

[4] For Cicero's response to the philosophers and especially Plato, see Gaines, "Cicero's
response," and Schütrumpf, "Platonic elements."

[5] Grilli, "Cicerone tra retorica e filosofia," 55–65, tracks Cicero's treatment of philosophy
in a range of writings spanning his career.

[6] Vickers, *In Defence of Rhetoric*, vii. Ober's reading of Plato in *Political Dissent* in
Democratic Athens (156–240) provocatively transforms Plato, critic-of-rhetoric, into Plato,
constructive critic-of-democratic knowledge.

Cicero's tendentious representation in *de Oratore* of the contest between eloquence and philosophy opens with a reference to Plato's *Gorgias* (1.46), and it is worth surveying that dialogue with Cicero's project in mind.[7] In the first scene, Socrates cannily opens the argument with what is intended to stand as a dramatic proof of rhetoric's central weakness, its epistemology: specifically, its unrigorous approach to the classic philosophical problem of definition. "What exactly is your profession?" he asks Gorgias and Polus, and when he is told "Rhetoric," he seeks to define the precise areas of expertise with which Gorgias's art of speaking concerns itself (447d–53a).[8] Gorgias flounders, first praising instead of defining the power of persuasion (451d), next admitting that the rhetor convinces, but does not instruct, his audience on matters of justice (454b–55a) and all manner of things of which they themselves are entirely ignorant (459b–60a). From this Socrates concludes that effective rhetoric relies on the speaker's willful deception of his audience, whom he convinces he has "more knowledge than the expert" (459b). Plato's dramatization of the sophist's incapacity to answer Socrates constructs a sharp dichotomy between rhetoric, "the persuasion from which belief comes without knowing," and dialectic, "the persuasion from which knowing comes" (454e), and it introduces the main issues to be debated later in the dialogue: the relativism of sophistic knowledge, persuasion's role in democratic politics, the relationship between knowledge, speech, and virtue, and the sophists' use of ornament and other techniques that Socrates casts as extraneous or obstructive to communication and the acquisition of knowledge. Within the dramatic space of the dialogue, however, Socrates' primary concern is to convince his interlocutors that these different-sounding problems are essentially one and the same. Without a firm epistemological foundation, all the elaborate speech techniques taught by the sophists are falsities and tricks: as not-knowledge, and therefore not-virtue, they float free from moral constraints of all kinds, whether socially constructed or philosophically defined. Socrates concludes that rhetoric is a knack and a form of flattery: because rhetoricians cannot build their

---

[7] Plato's *Phaedrus*, especially as it is surveyed by Cooper, "Plato, Isocrates, and Cicero," is worth comparing to *Gorgias*.

[8] Plato introduces several important philosophical problems in his "stage directions" to the dialogue: the difference between knowledge and belief, and the integrity of the speaker who speaks for others rather than himself are dramatized in this scene when Socrates becomes Chaerephon's ventriloquist (447c), just as Polus, and then Callicles, speak for Gorgias (448a, 481b). For further readings that probe Plato with an eye on his own use of rhetoric, his characterization, plot, and style, and his debt to democratic practices and language, see Monoson, *Plato's Democratic Entanglements*, especially. the overview of 3–18, and Blondell, *The Play of Character*, especially 165–67, which deftly analyzes internal signs of Plato's criticism of his own methodology. On Socrates as a democratic thinker in *Gorgias*, see Euben, "Reading democracy," with Barber's skeptical response, "Misreading democracy."

arguments on truth, their only anchor is the ignorant desires of those they wish to convince. When Callicles, the angry latecomer to the dialogue, points out that Socrates' dismissal of democratic knowledge and speech will get him killed, the point is underscored that the true philosopher has no place in the democratic polis (486b; cf. 515a).[9]

In *Gorgias*'s dismissal of knowledge gained or communicated in ways other than philosophical dialectic, from emotional or stylistic effect to social custom or opinion, the body functions as the sign of taint. Socrates' first argument, that rhetors persuade without teaching real knowledge, leads to his denunciation of rhetoric as a kind of verbal cookery or facial makeup.[10] As fancy cookery is to good nourishment, so rhetoric is to the administration of justice (463d, 465c). Persuasion outside the bounds of dialectic seduces like a material object that is beautiful on the outside and corrupt within: the listeners who are seduced fall victim to their bodies' insatiable greed. Second, Socrates points out, pleasure is a key part of rhetoric's appeal—a problem, since pleasure unmoors the rational capacity to assess truth and goodness. Pain, pleasure's opposite, presents similar obstacles to reason, which Socrates analyzes and Plato dramatizes by linking the collapse of Polus's and Callicles' arguments to their loss of self-control. The sputtering Polus shoulders his way into the conversation to defend Gorgias (461b), and Callicles quits the debate in a sullen rage (505d). Socrates warns the group from the beginning that they are embarking on a discussion that is likely to anger them, but his ironic, provoking warnings fail, and he alone remains in command of his emotions and his reason at the end of the dialogue. This dramatic development deepens Plato's account of oratorical persuasion as a form of slavery to passion. Here, in a move replayed in other dialogues, Plato links rhetoric's vices to the vulnerabilities of the body: ornament and stylistic figures, expressed in the text through analogies with sensual desire, emerge as obstacles to knowledge's realization.[11] And the corrupt body of rhetoric is a sexed entity that draws on deep associations in the Greek

---

[9] But the dialogue concludes with Socrates encouraging Callicles to join him in completing his training in virtue, at which time they will turn together to the political life (527d)—an ending Cicero does not discuss.

[10] Cole, *The Origins of Rhetoric*, 9: "Since Plato sees dialectic as the philosopher's supreme means of discovering the true nature of reality, it follows that the dialectically accomplished rhetorician has absolute mastery both of the facts of any case he pleads and all that can be correctly inferred from them." Further discussion in Vickers, *In Defence of Rhetoric*, 83, 88, 147; Halliwell, "Philosophy and rhetoric," 224–34; Swearingen, *Rhetoric and Irony*, 56–73; and duBois, "Violence, apathy, and the rhetoric of philosophy," 122–30.

[11] In *Phaedrus*, Socrates takes the position that the rhetor should be able to deceive his audience—which, he acknowledges, demands mastery of the knowledge of arousing passion—and by this *psychagogia* to lead them ultimately to the good (260a). This idea reappears in a cruder form in *Statesman*, where Socrates links teaching to telling myths

cultural imaginary between femininity and pleasure, emotion, and frailty. Rhetoric unmans the unwary listener.[12]

This limited reading of Plato lies behind Cicero's accusation that Socrates is to blame for the violence he did to knowledge by ripping the common name away from wisdom and eloquence and separating them into two disciplines (de Orat. 3.60).[13] Good philosophers, it turns out, are also orators (de Orat. 1.49), modeled on Aristotle and Isocrates. Pointing out that Philip II of Macedon placed Aristotle in charge of educating his son, the future king—a move that locates Aristotle in the world of political rule—Crassus declares that the name "orator" may be applied to the philosopher "who conveys to us a full range of topics and of speech," just as the name "philosopher" may be given to the man who possesses "wisdom conjoined with eloquence" (de Orat. 3.141–42; cf. 2.18, 2.154). Oratory, by contrast, is by definition a fully accessible pursuit. Its tools are available to all and its field is, in every sense of the phrase, common knowledge: the worst vice for those who wish to speak effectively "is to shrink away from the common mode of speech, and from the custom derived from communal sensibility" (in dicendo autem vitium vel maximum sit a vulgari genere orationis, atque a consuetudine communis sensus abhorrere, 1.12). A talented persuader like Plato might be a summus orator in denial of his own dependence on enticing

---

to mobs (304c). But the case of Phaedrus is notably complicated by Plato's subtle representation of the erotic interplay between Socrates and Phaedrus, which (as in Symposium) is assimilated to the acquisition of philosophical knowledge. Socrates' strategy of representation in these dialogues recalls Hesiod's dream of a world without women in Theogony and Hippolytus's aggressive lament about the necessity of female bodies for procreation. See the rich discussion and references in Arthur, "Dream of a world without women"; Zeitlin, "The power of Aphrodite"; and Irigaray's analysis of the cave in Plato's Republic as a claustrophobic, dirty womb from which philosophers emerge, Speculum of the Other Woman.

[12] On the contest of philosophy and rhetoric, see Oravec and Salvador, "The duality of rhetoric," 173, who point out that Plato's disallowance of the tropes of rhetoric from his texts, which self-consciously (even if ironically) identify as antirhetorical, belies dialectic's reliance on rhetoric as the contrast by which dialectic defines itself. This is one of the paradoxes in which all confrontations with rhetoric, particularly critical ones, become entangled. Like writing, which Plato describes as a pharmakon, a drug that heals and destroys, rhetoric exerts pressure on the very texts that purport to attack it (the contradiction at the heart of Derrida's essay on the Phaedrus, "Plato's pharmacy"). The Platonic text is embroiled in what Oravec and Salvador call the "distinctive duality" of rhetoric: its simultaneous existence as theory and practice, a discourse that itself describes or codifies discourse. The all-encompassing universality of rhetoric, which makes it impossible to view it from the outside, is precisely what Plato finds both fruitful and troublesome and what, by its own nature, he cannot escape.

[13] Fantham, The Roman World, critically discusses Cicero's dodging of Gorgias's indictment of eloquence in the hands of the unjust (59–64).

words, as Crassus ironically notes, but just as they reject the language that creates community through emotion, instruction, and delight (the traditional three aims of eloquence), they also refuse to participate in the life of the state—the life, implicitly, of emotion, instruction, and delight (de Orat. 1.47). Philosophers dispute with one another "in corners, for the sake of filling up spare time," and where the orator develops themes "with gravity and exuberance," their talk is "thin and bloodless" (de Orat. 1.56, 3.122), and the philosopher's beautiful thoughts become repulsive (squalidiora, Orat. 115), especially the Stoics, with their "compressed and retracted" style (Brut. 309; cf. 118–19).[14]

This is not to say that Ciceronian eloquence is a universal property: his interlocutors and addresses are all leading men, wealthy and well-born.[15] This is a good opportunity to join those like Ettore Lepore who argue that, just as the rector or gubernator he discusses in de Republica should be understood as an ideal model or type, Cicero's broader discussion of civic identity—particularly by the middle 50s—encompasses a more generous circle than the traditional senatorial order and its allies.[16] In the philosophical treatises, though political and economic inequality is acknowledged and indeed defended (e.g., Rep. 1.69; cf 1.43, 53, 2.42; Leg. 3.27), Cicero also defends the legal rights that the Romans "most explicitly and commonly subsumed" under libertas: "immunity from arbitrary coercion and punishment by magistrates, and some degree of participation in political power."[17] In de Republica, where Cicero defends the mixed constitution as best, his leading speaker Scipio promotes agreement or harmony (consensus) to three blended "orders," highest, lowest, and middle (ex summis et infimis et mediis interiectis ordinibus, 2.69). As Elizabeth Asmis points out, Cicero's Platonic language here does not involve a wholesale appropriation of Plato's ideal republic but instead a conspicuous act of substitution: for Plato's tripartite division of philosophers, guardian-soldiers, and workers, Cicero alludes to the ordines of Roman society, whose upper (though not top) ranks in the Pro Sestio include Italian farmers and freedmen.[18] Though Cicero may not expect his ideal citizen to arise from every class and corner of Italy, and though he repeatedly stresses the role of the senate in providing the ultimate authority for the government (auctoritas, Rep. 2.57), his universalizing language of (male) embodiment resists a reading that would limit his notion of citizen identity to the topmost sliver of Roman society.

---

[14] ... in angulis, consumendi otii causa, disserant ... de quibys illi tenui quodam exsanguique sermone disputant, hic cum omni gravitate et iucunditate explicet.

[15] Intelligently discussed by Hall, "Social evasion and aristocratic manners in Cicero's de Oratore," 117–18.

[16] So Lepore, Il princeps Ciceroniano, 185–90.

[17] Brunt, "Libertas in the republic," 297.

[18] Asmis, "A new kind of model," 405–6.

To Cicero, eloquence is a more vast and all-encompassing enterprise than is commonly realized (*de Orat.* 1.16). Criticizing the "completely ridiculous" scholars who eviscerate rhetoric with ever-proliferating rules and categorizations (*perridiculi, de Orat.* 1.86), he builds on the more ambitious view that Isocrates explored in the speeches *Against the Sophists, Helen, Antidosis*, and *Nicocles*: that to study the art of speech is to study all things human, ethical and political.[19] "The force of eloquence (*illa vis eloquentiae*) is so great," Crassus observes, "that it holds the origin, essential force, and changes of all things, of all virtues, duties, and the entire natural law that embraces human customs, spirit, and life; it inscribes traditions, legislation, and laws (*mores, leges, iura*); it rules the republic (*rem publicam regat*); and to every relevant situation it speaks in an ornate and flowing way" (*de Orat.* 3.76).[20] A crucial point in this articulation is the emphasis on the accommodations oratory makes to the minds and senses of men (*oratio . . . hominum sensibus ac mentibus accommodata, de Orat.* 1.54). The *communis sensus* operates on several levels—the rational, the linguistic, the emotional, and the aesthetic—all of which rest on communal observation of the orator's body and the passions it expresses.[21]

At the same time, key elements in rhetoric, from the concept of tact to proper Latinity, are impossible to express in words (*decorum, apte*). Rhetoric is thus figured as a discourse of contradiction: a common pursuit limited to the few, an expertise whose appeal must be popular, an art that must conceal itself, a goal that cannot be represented or fulfilled—and, most important for my purposes here, an embodied performance of passion that mysteriously transforms reason into will.[22] This representation draws on the rhetoric of traditional republican *auctoritas*—such as Scipio's greeting of the people as moral judges (Livy 38.51, Gel. 4.18), or Crassus's characterization of the senate as the people's slaves (*de Orat.* 1.225)—to reinvent the elite body as the site of political unification and emotional identification. This body had always been, and indeed sought to be, the target of the people's gaze in the contest for noble *dignitas* and *auctoritas*; what Cicero seeks to do is theorize the body as the living embodiment of the particular *auctoritas* that governs the *concordia ordinum* of his political

[19] On Isocrates' views, see Jaeger, *Paideia*, vol. 3, 56–70, 132–55. Fantham, *The Roman World of Cicero's de Oratore*, discusses Cicero's debt to Isocrates (23).

[20] In full: *Illa vis autem eloquentiae tanta est ut omnium rerum, virtutum, officiorum omnisque naturae, quae mores hominum, quae animos, quae vitam continet, originem, vim mutationesque teneat, eadem mores, leges, iura, describat, rem publicam regat, omniaque ad quamcumque rem pertineantque ornate copioseque dicat.* De Inventione, as we have seen, identifies persuasive speech as the defining characteristic of humanity and the capacity that engendered the first political associations (*De Inv.* 1.1–3; cf. *de Orat.* 1.32–33).

[21] Compare Isocrates, *Panegyricus* 48–50, *Nicocles* 6, and *Antidosis* 180–81.

[22] A selection of passages about concealment and mystification: *Orat.* 145, 197; Quintilian, *Inst. Orat.* 9.4.143–47, 12.9.5–6.

philosophy. This body, like the harmonious harps and flutes he praises in *de Republica*, must charm its audience while also holding itself up to them as a mirror of the good life (*sese splendore animi et vitae suae sicut speculum praebeat civibus*, 2.69). The "citizens" here are not mere passive admirers of elite power; they are invited to judge, like trained listeners of music (*aures eruditae*), and their role as judges implies the orator's willingness to hold himself accountable before them.

When Cicero claims (in the voice of Crassus) that the good orator must study the workings of his body as well as his mind, emotion as well as reason, conventional belief and philosophical definition, and further, that he must combine passionate inspiration with knowledge born of the close study of law, logic, and history, he is responding directly to the limits that what he calls "philosophy" tries to place on rhetoric. Unlike "philosophy," rhetoric has a fundamentally political orientation: the origins and the safety of the republic lie with the orator alone (*de Orat.* 1.33–34), the "friend of peace and a well-built state" (*Brut.* 45). The instrument of republican politics and the sum, purpose, and organizing principle of aesthetics and intellectual life, the *ars dicendi* becomes the chain that links all the arts and sciences (*de Orat.* 2.33, 3.132). We have already seen Cicero using the (putatively) unified organicism of rhetoric to prove its (putatively) natural roots, and this is reflected in Cicero's representation of the orator: he is actor, common man, storyteller, judge, and philosopher rolled into one, and nature is his guide (*de Orat.* 1.128, 3.143).

The extravagant claims that Cicero makes on rhetoric's behalf have led critics to conclude that he is simply being "rhetorical," like Gorgias at the beginning of his conversation with Socrates—sidestepping the serious matter of philosophical critique in favor of a hyperbolic reiteration of his own views.[23] Quentin Skinner, whose study of the relationship between the *ars oratoria* and the *ars civilis* in Roman and early modern thought offers a sympathetic reading of rhetoric's aims, suggests that Cicero evades the philosophical critique by permitting his characters in *de Oratore* to express contradicting opinions on the topic of rhetoric's ethical utility.[24] More troubling for some readers, especially philosophically oriented ones, is the shaky basis for Cicero's own theory of knowledge. John Cooper, for example, sets out in a sympathetic but rigorous article to test whether sophists (represented

---

[23] Vickers calls Cicero's response to Plato "unfortunate" because it claims too much for the orator, on which see below (*In Defence of Rhetoric*, 164–66); Kennedy summarizes Cicero's views without explaining them (*The Art of Rhetoric in the Roman World*). Schütrümpf argues that Cicero's position parrots Peripatetic beliefs in "Cicero's *de Orat.* 1 and the Greek philosophical tradition."

[24] Skinner, *Reason and Rhetoric in the Philosophy of Hobbes*, 100–4.

by Isocrates) or Hellenistic and Roman rhetoricians (represented by Cicero) have a distinctive theory of what constitutes sound argument to which they could appeal in defense of their practice and against the claims of the philosophers.[25] His answer (for both) is negative, on the grounds, in Cicero's case, that his skeptical brand of Academicism leaves Cicero accepting "the philosophers' idea of the truth of things" but denying that anyone knows the truth about what (for example) justice is: in *de Natura Deorum*, for example, Cicero is content with a Stoic view that is "closer to resembling the truth" (*ad veritatis similitudinem propensior*, 3.95). This is a weak epistemology, Cooper concludes, "if oratory is to stand on its own and not be subordinate to dogmatic philosophy."[26]

My own aims here, as I see it, do not cross with Cooper's concerns. What I seek to explain are the particular figures and images by which Cicero attacks what he understands to be the philosophers' criticism of rhetoric and the comparative virtues, as he sees them, of the orator's pursuits. So far I follow the promising tack of Robert Gaines and Emanuele Narducci, who argue that Cicero's rhetorical writings constitute not a manual but a philosophy of rhetoric. This philosophy, Gaines believes, innovatively conceives rhetoric as more than a discipline (*disciplina, ars*): it aims ultimately to "particularize the orator as a principal object of theoretical investigation" by defining the orator as an entity whose state of knowledge is constituted through his rhetorical activity.[27] Hence the title *de Oratore*, or *On the Orator*, for Cicero's most important work on rhetoric, instead of the discipline-oriented title *de Oratoria*. Tracing the dialogue's claims on their own terms shows that Cicero is primarily concerned with the application of a rhetorical ethics that embraces precisely those aspects of the political that Plato problematizes.

Cicero's claims for the virtuous orator rests on two points: first, rhetoric's status as an ethical discourse of dynamic reach and effectivity that treats the body as its literally material concern, and second, its role in perpetuating the *vita activa*, the active life of republican politics,

---

[25] Cooper, "Plato, Isocrates, and Cicero," 65–66.

[26] Ibid., 79–80.

[27] Gaines, "Cicero's response to the philosophers in *de Oratore*, Book 1," 56. He rightly disputes Leeman and Pinkster's proposal that Cicero's presentation of the debate over rhetoric's status as an *ars*, and its relationship to philosophy, is a *disputatio in utramque partem* disclosing a skeptical (because Academic) "suspension of judgment" (43). Baumlin, "Positioning ethos," also suggestively explores the ethical possibilities in rhetorical theory. In "Beredsamkeit und Weisheit," Etienne Gilson examines Cicero's argument for the identification between the good orator and the good man, and between reason and speech; Narducci, *Cicerone e l'eloquenza Romana*, analyzes Cicero's criticism of the split between rhetoric and philosophy, influenced by the Academic philosoper Philo of Larissa (70ff.).

formed by a collection of emotive bodies constituted and moved by the good man.[28] If, as imitators from Quintilian to Castiglione recognized, *de Oratore* is a courtesy manual for the Roman elite, and if, as the last chapter suggested, it is a sophisticated exploration into the hybrid nature of Roman citizenship, it is also a source of thinking about the self that is, unexpectedly, most fruitfully read in the light of postmodern conceptualizations of subjectivity, agency, and political communication. Cicero's perfect orator is an ideal man, but, unlike the ethical agent praised by Socrates in *Gorgias*, he is a man formed by his knowledge of public life and his will to shape it.

Writing in 54 BCE, just after finishing *de Oratore*, Cicero describes his project in the just begun *de Republica* as "concerned with the best condition of the state and the best citizen" (*de optimo statu civitatis, de optimo cive, Q. fr.* 3.5.1). That *de Oratore* rehearses the lost discussions of the citizen in this dialogue is suggested by its treatment of the breakdown of civic order (*Rep.* 1.31, 6.1) and his references to eloquent men active in politcs: "When Scipio had spoken, Mummius agreed, for he was saturated with a kind of hatred for rhetoricians" (*Rep.* 5.11). Rather than a philosophy of rhetoric, Cicero outlines a performative ethics—a virtue theory organized around the human ability to communicate in the context of the political community.[29] Rhetoric emerges in Cicero as a discourse within which the self is shaped from childhood through maturity in a never-ending, circular process of self-fashioning, communal response, and self-reevaluation. This is what Richard Lanham, following the psychological model of G. H. Mead, calls the creation of the *homo rhetoricus*: a model that is "dynamic not static," generating "process not entity," an ethics that grows "with the self rather than against it."[30] The theory is a strongly normative one, and my discussion explores the ways in which the text acts to guard and discipline itself, both articulating and suppressing the theoretical possibilities it raises—a pattern that creates tension and sometimes a state of outright contradiction of views. As a senator writing for members of his own class, Cicero seeks to discipline or deny the political possibilities opened up by his own text's link between speech and virtue, but those possibilities are irreducibly inherent in his formulation of what it means to live well in a just, thriving republic.

[28] Both positions respond vigorously to Plato's attack on rhetoric as an embodied, pleasurable, passionate practice based in opinion rather than knowledge. In this, they are most comparable to Isocrates (*Antidosis*, esp. 284ff.).

[29] For this view, see also Grilli, "Cicerone tra retorica e filosofia," who rightly takes Cicero's use of the word "orator" to mean "political man." Note I do not say "communicative ethics," the theory associated with Jürgen Habermas: I do this to stay true to Cicero's tight focus on the performing body, with all the excesses and failings involved in performance.

[30] Lanham, *The Motives of Eloquence*, 4, 156.

The corporeal citizen

"This is a day we have long hoped for," exclaims Sulpicius to Cotta when the two senior interlocutors of *de Oratore* begin their debate over the nature of rhetoric (1.136). But Cotta can barely follow the conversation:

> just as though I had entered some opulent, well-furnished home (*in aliquam locupletem ac refertam domum*), where the tapestries were not unrolled, the silver was not displayed, and neither paintings nor statues were arranged in open view, but all these many magnificent things were piled up and packed away, just so in Crassus's speech I could glimpse the riches and adornments of his talent (*divitias atque ornamenta eius ingenii*), through wrappings and coverings (*per quaedam involucra atque integumenta*), as it were; but although I wanted to gaze at them, I had barely the power to peek. (*de Orat.* 1.161)

Cotta's bewildered desire to grasp the source and meaning of Crassus's eloquence leads him on a journey into a sumptuous mansion that is Crassus himself—much like the so-called memory house, which is packed with mental objects prompting the orator's recall in the middle of a performance. The indirect invocation of the memory house recalls Plato's argument in *Meno* and elsewhere that knowledge of the good does not derive from a source external to the soul but from memory. But here Crassus, the good orator personified (though he denies this status, imitating Socrates), is both object of desire and the trigger of memory for his listeners, as Scaevola acknowledges when he compares Crassus to Socrates, both "stimulants" of desire for knowledge in their followers (*de Orat.* 1.204).

The group's longing for Crassus, crucially described here as the embodiment of material luxuries, hints at the underlying goal of *de Oratore*: to present the good orator as a magnetic *exemplum* that prompts the memory of and the desire for virtue. At the same time, the confusion voiced by the group functions as a trace of a different, troubling suppressed memory—the memory of the gap between eloquence and goodness. "I can't follow, this can't be right," "I'm amazed," the interlocutors say: Crassus is impossible to imitate, yet beckons imitation—a prefiguring of the endless quality of rhetorical self-fashioning in a republican regime built on the endless quest to live well.[31] Built into the system of rhetorical training that Crassus and Antonius ultimately advocate is the

---

[31] On the benefits and risks of imitation, and Cicero's emphasis on variety and flexibility in the student's choice of model, see Fantham, *Roman World*, 98–101.

simultaneous exhortation toward perfection and the recognition of perfection's unattainability at the level of the particular and the general: precisely what we would expect of a text that is aimed at the formation of the republican subject-citizen rather than simply the good public speaker or the good (private) man.

Cicero's project has roots in the Greek rhetorical tradition. Gorgias, according to Plato, touted oratory as a kind of ethical training. Aristotle emphasizes the importance of ethics in oratorical education in his *Rhetoric*, arguing that rhetoric is an offshoot of ethical studies (1356a25). Isocrates vigorously defended his system of rhetorical *paideia*, whose goal was embodied excellence, as the best education for the government of the self and others (*Antidosis* 253–54). What makes Cicero's ideal rhetorical training such an effective means of forming *civic* subjectivity is the body, the target-site for rhetoric's training and refinement of the self. To borrow the term made popular by Pierre Bourdieu, it was the bodily *hexis* of the elite Roman—his idiosyncratic assemblage of habits of posture, gesture, dress, facial expression, and vocal range structured by ideologies of gender, class, and civic identity—that literally embodies political mythology, confirming and proclaiming his place in the social order to himself and to his fellow citizens.[32] According to this theory of social logic, beliefs about the innate characteristics of any type or class undergo a complex process of enactment on the levels of self-conceptualization and of social practice through the minutiae of bodily *hexis*. The spoken word is useless without bodily accompaniment (*de Orat.* 1.114; cf. *Brutus* 110). As Erik Gunderson perceptively notes of Quintilian, "Bodily excellence cites and performs the authority of the good man ... the orator's body will be good precisely as it reveals the goodness of the orator himself," and though Quintilian derives his judgments of virtue and vice from the anterior principle of the good soul, we readers "can see instead a body that is shot through with the effects of the matrix of knowledge/power, a matrix that allows for the transcription of the meanings onto bodily surfaces."[33] Bodies "in action" have an eloquence all their own (*actio quasi corporis quaedam eloquentia, Orat. 55*).[34]

In the political context of the Roman republic, where the republic is constituted in encounters between elites, or between elite speakers and the people, oratory is more than an instrument of personal self-fashioning and social apprenticeship—more than a means by which members of

[32] Bourdieu, *The Logic of Practice*, 69; cf. his discussion of *habitus*, 52–65.

[33] Gunderson, *Staging Masculinity*, 62. His perceptive treatment of the representation of the speaking body in Roman rhetorical discourse runs parallel to my discussion at several points.

[34] Literally, "Delivery is, as it were, a kind of eloquence of the body."

Roman elite fashioned themselves according to elite ideals. The particular calibration of Cicero's treatment of the body refigures the body's political significance as a sign of republican virtue. He treats speech as the basis of the process by which the orator comes to know himself as a subject and as a citizen. Self-knowledge begins in the body, for rhetorical training offers a quasi-military order of mastery over the slack and sluggish body: "speaking must be brought out of exercise in the home, in the shade, straight into the middle of the battle line, into the dust, the noise, the camp, the battle action of the lawcourt" (de Orat. 1.157). The body is the basis for the orator's talent (linguae solutio, vocis sonus, latera, vires, conformatio quaedam et figura totius oris et corporis, de Orat. 1.114).

When Cicero maps and polices the body of the orator, literally submitting it to disciplina, he is both giving the orator the tools by which he can prove his ability to control himself and, in political terms, he is presenting the elite body as something in need of control, lest it exercise its authority arbitrarily. Hence the attention to gesture, posture, and appearance throughout Ciceronian rhetoric—a markedly heavier emphasis than Aristotle lays on the action of the speaker in his Rhetoric.[35] Out of the interplay among the rational, the emotional, and the physical arises the republican self. Cicero's account of it transforms what had been solely a sign of traditional elite hegemony, the body that speaks traditional authority, into a sign of tempered domination, of connection to the listeners (senate, jury, or people) and even accountability to them.

Where to Socrates in Gorgias the rational part of the soul governs the desires and impulses of the body, Cicero sees a more complex interaction governing the relations between animus and corpus. His critical descriptions of virtuous speaking bodies in Brutus prefigure the elder Seneca's pictures of his favorite declaimers in the prologues to his books of Controversiae as well as the letters of the younger Seneca, the younger Pliny, and Fronto. In all these texts, analysis of speaking style is interwoven with analysis of the speaker's body—and not only his actio or delivery, the fifth official part of oratory (after inventio, dispositio, elocutio, and memoria), but his habits of movement and gesture in everyday life. L. Appuleius Saturninus, a violent demagogue killed by a gang of senatorial vigilantes in 100 BCE after his attempt to hold a third tribunate, was said to owe his success rather more to his fashionable appearance and gestures than to his powers of speech making or his character.[36]

---

[35] Another influence on Cicero (now lost) was surely Aristotle's student Theophrastus's work on style.

[36] Magis specie tamen et motu atque ipso amictu capiebat homines quam aut dicendi copia aut mediocritate prudentiae (Brut. 224). Bodily motion is the source of several jokes in Brutus, such as Caesar Strabo's query of an orator who constantly paced and swayed his body from side to side as to why he was speaking "from a little boat" (Brut. 216).

The description of Cicero's son-in-law G. Calpurnius Piso's diction and deportment shifts seamlessly into praise of his character:

> his choice of words was elegant, his compositional style both compact and rounded, as it were; not only were his arguments varied and grounded in proof, but his ideas were logical and sharp; his movements were naturally so graceful, that they gave the impression of artfulness, though that was not so (*gestusque natura ita venustus ut ars etiam, quae non erat*) ... with regard to self-restraint, respectful devotion, or other type of virtue (*nec continentia nec pietate nec ullo genere virtutis*) I think no one of his age is comparable. (*Brut.* 272)

Cicero himself benefited from training with Molon of Rhodes, in habits of speech, body, and disposition: "the straining of my voice was relaxed, along with my style of speaking, which had been, as it were, feverish; my lungs and fairly weak body gained strength" (*Brut.* 316). The *Brutus* represents rhetoric itself with corporeal imagery. Demetrius rendered language "soft and pliable" (*mollem et teneram*), by contrast to Lysias, whose "powerful sinews" (*lacerti*) do not balance his generally "shriveled" style (*strigiosior, Brut.* 38, 64). Good style "requires no rouge" (*Brut.* 36). This means, of course, that the body limits as well as enables. Cicero distinguishes carefully between the kinds of faults of diction and pronunciation that have to do with trainable affectation and those deriving from nature: voices that are from childhood very soft, reedy, high-pitched, grating, toneless, or effeminate (*de Orat.* 3.41).

Cicero's articulation frames the ideal orator within a way of life, a set of technologies, and a theoretical project, constituted through specific practices of discipline and self-knowledge. He fashions himself through dialogue within himself (embodied in his pen and his own gaze), and the watching eyes and ears of others: "such is the kind of sensation and order of speaking, that the speech seems to represent, as it were, the character of the speaker himself; for by adopting a certain mode of thought and expression, united with physical action that is gentle and signifies ease and affability, such an effect is produced that we speakers seem to be noble, of good habits, and virtuous" (*de Orat.* 2.184).[37] Faults of character or sheer deceitfulness—a possibility implied by the language of "seeming" in this sentence—Cicero imagines the audience discovering in the speaker's performance, just as the budding orator, closely observing the body of whomever he has chosen as a model, practices his movements until he has perfectly captured the other man's habits without mimicking his vices

---

[37] *Tantum autem efficitur sensu quodam ac ratione dicendi, ut quasi mores oratoris effingat oratio; genere enim quodam sententiarum et genere verborum, adhibita etiam actione leni facilitatemque significante efficitur, ut probi, ut bene morati, ut boni viri esse videamtur.*

(*de Orat.* 2.90). This scrutiny identifies the body as the privileged site of ethical imagination and improvement. Even the impermanent temporality of speech performance becomes a virtue rather than a vice, and the written text gives pride of precedence to live performance: Cicero praises speakers whose speeches are not recorded in many texts, since their emotion and drive makes capturing their effect in written text impossible (*Brut.* 82–86).[38]

Two themes emerge here: the first epistemological—where the orator gains his knowledge—and the second ethical: the status of his knowledge vis-à-vis philosophy. The climax of Antonius' argument about the natural sources of oratory answers both questions by representing the good orator as a man defined by his human capacity to evaluate physical sensations and experiences with his reason. To speak—to act in the world—he gathers information about the world via hearing, taste, and feel:

> For the faculty of speaking should not be plain and bare (*dicendi facultas non debeat esse ieiuna atque nuda*) but sprinkled and adorned with a certain pleasurable variety of things (*aspersa atque distincta multarum rerum iucunda quadam varietate*). It should be the good orator's part to have heard much, to have seen much, to have gone over many subjects in his spirit and mind and still others in his reading; though not so as to have taken possession of them as his own but rather to have taken sips of them, like things belonging to others (*neque ea, ut sua, possedisse; sed, ut aliena, libasse*). . . . He ought to penetrate the very veins (*oportet venas*) of each type, age, and class, and of those before whom he speaks or is going to speak; he must taste their minds and senses (*mentes sensusque degustet*). (*de Orat.* 1.218, 222–23)

Cicero's representation of a complex, dynamic interrelation between the body and the mind of the good orator rewrites Plato's Orphic image of the *soma* as *sema*, the body as the soul's tomb (*Crat.* 400c). Plato had imagined matter itself to be an imperfect reflection of the reality of the Forms, judging empirical observation and physical sensation as automatically suspect modes of knowledge apprehension. In Plato's view, the body is a "conceptual blind spot": it is what is not mind, what the mind must master in order to control itself.[39] To Cicero, embodied experience

---

[38] Here I read the significance of writing rather differently from Gunderson, *Staging Masculinity*, who plays the ephemerality of the performance off the different instability of the text, or Dugan, *Making a New Man*, who stresses the immortality the fixed text promises (though whether it offers it in practice is a different story). Vasaly points out that in Ciceronian oratory, "both verbal and nonverbal signs are ubiquitous; the study of how meaning is conveyed takes in a far wider field of signification than previously considered" (*Representations*, 11).

[39] Grosz, *Volatile Bodies*, 3.

is the part of human communication that philosophy forgets. The orator's knowledge of his body and the bodies of his listeners places him in a position of epistemological and ethical privilege compared to the philosopher, who cultivates uncommon language and dismisses bodily experience as merely the first step on the ladder of knowledge. Clearly, Cicero has Plato in mind here, and a particular reading of Plato at that; he knows that some philosophers do make the body an object of concern, such as the Stoic Chrysippus, who wrote:

> It is not true that there exists an art that we call medicine, concerned with the diseased body, but no corresponding art concerned with the diseased soul. Nor is it true that the latter is inferior than the former, in its theoretical grasp and therapeutic treatment of individual cases . . . For the correlative affinity of the two will reveal to us, I think, the similarity of therapeutic treatments and the analogical relationship of the two modes of doctoring. (SVF 3.471)

Yet the Stoics fail to persuade. The Roman Stoic Rutilius Rufus and his friends refused to use emotional appeals or ornament in his defense against a trumped-up charge of bribery, choosing instead to give a bare, factual speech "that could have been delivered in Plato's *Republic* . . . no doubt lest they be renounced by the Stoics" (*de Orat.* 1.230). In his comparison of Rutilius with Socrates, Antonius links Socrates and Rutilius in the denial of the resources of the body and its capacity to make meaning in the world through emotion like pity and sadness.

Cicero's orator abjures the narrow specialization and plain style of speaking praised by philosophers, then, not because it fails to meet his stylistic standards but because it bespeaks a way of life that is solitary, disembodied, not fully human. What makes a good man, in *de Oratore* and throughout the corpus, is his human capacity to speak, which involves active understanding and control of his body and the extent to which it shapes his relation to the world. "Who is the speaking man whom stupefied audiences gaze at in astonishment . . . whom they consider a god, as it were, among men?" (*de Orat.* 3.53). The man who can arouse their passions through the directed arousal of his own bodily performance, who has "sought into, listened, read, debated, handled, and experienced the material" of human life, and who stages that knowledge in a meaningful way in the public sphere (1.61–63, 3.54). This entails a certain ethical fluidity, a capacity to think himself into another's subject position. Cicero's *vir perfectus* develops not out of abstract standards of virtue but out of the traditions, sensibilities, and passions of his community.

We have seen that the good orator is a corporeal self, both because his accounts of it are filled with body language and because it partakes of Stoic theories of selfhood. Now, Cicero is not a strict Stoic materialist who believes that the soul or *animus* is corporeal in nature, though it has a different nature from our corporeal arms and legs.[40] Rather, he conceives in Academic fashion of an immaterial and immortal soul inhabiting a body that enjoys an interactive relationship with the soul. It is a messy and inconsistent picture, but for Cicero, rhetoric differs from philosophy precisely because it embraces messy inconsistency.[41] Philosophical dialectic is about pinpointing the meanings of words and concepts; rhetoric is about naming the many ways in which words can be twisted to mean different things. The corporeal self is not a product of rigorous philosophy. For in the rhetorical works Cicero never claims that he is actually doing philosophy; he seeks to explore the model of communication that rhetoric offers in the context of republican politics.[42] We shall see later how Cicero's position that communication involves the whole self, body and mind, for both speaker and audience derives directly from his vision of *res publica*.

Rephrasing Josiah Ober, who refers to the epistemological basis of Athenian democratic speech making as "democratic knowledge," we might call what Cicero is dealing in "republican knowledge."[43] The significance of philosophy for such knowledge cannot be denied: in *de Oratore* in particular, Crassus voices the need for the orator to master the basics of logical argumentation. The knowledge that matters to the interlocutors, however, is that which Cicero describes in *De Amicitia*, "We ought to examine those things which exist in daily use and the communal life, not those which are imagined or hoped for" (*nos autem ea quae sunt in usu vitaque communi, non ea quae finguntur aut optantur, spectare debemus*, 18). In the face of the tension between body knowledge and philosophical knowledge, Cicero tries to claim both, by arguing that the body is actually a control on deceit. As I discuss in the next section, this theory of the subject that is corporeal and communal (for knowledge is a matter of communal agreement rather than essence) is also a theory of political communication: it links the orator to the community and makes him responsible for his words. And it evokes the republic as a collective of living bodies, in whose presence and passion the state is literally constituted.

---

[40] Fortenbaugh comments that Cicero's view of emotion and its performance is "vaguely Stoic," "*Benevolentiam conciliare*," 272.

[41] Compare Isocrates' view of knowledge (esp. *Antidosis* 270–71).

[42] More on the relationship between rhetoric and philosophy in Grilli, "Cicerone tra retorica e filosofia."

[43] Ober, *Political Dissent*, 33–36.

A THEORY OF POLITICAL COMMUNICATION

Some feminist theorists challenge the liberal notion that democratic citizenship may be sufficiently broadly conceived, despite its long history of exclusion, as to welcome women as full citizens. They point as evidence to the ideological and practical role played by military service in Western civilization's Whiggish narratives of its own history—a key aspect of critiques of republican theory as well. Liberal feminists seeking equal rights ask whether the ongoing political and cultural significance of the military, a phenomenon visible on every movie marquee, is compatible with the current exclusion of women from combat by most governments. Maternalist feminists argue that women's nature as nurturers and caretakers (whether it is innate or culturally constructed) demands the total rejection of martial values from the ideology of democratic citizenship. Others question whether a liberal citizenship that is, historically, closely bound up with the birth of modern market capitalism, can ever be so conceptually open as to embrace nonpublic agents outside the market— that is, women who primarily identify (or are identified by others) as wives and mothers—as full citizens.[44] Writing inclusive stories of democratic civic identity involves a daunting array of challenges for observers seeking to foster a variety of paths to full citizenship.[45]

The most far-reaching feminist critique—and the one most suggestively linked with Cicero's interest in the bonds that link the *res publica*—contends that the individualistic, atomistic concept of the subject endorsed by classical liberal theory fails to take into account the importance of issues that have left their mark on women's experiences, historically speaking: family and community, affective relations, and reciprocal obligations. Liberalism's deracinated association of self-interested persons, by this view, cannot be considered a political community in any meaningful sense. Nonfeminist theorists share this concern. Alastair MacIntyre, for instance, decries the moral complacency of liberalism's moral pluralism, which leaves citizens adrift to decide important moral questions on a purely subjective basis and with irrational methods. Michael Sandel, a communitarian, worries that the liberal citizen ideal is a personality insufficiently situated in a "commonality" of shared views and values. Pragmatists like Richard Rorty and Michael Walzer appeal, along Ciceronian lines, to common norms of justice and morality agreed

---

[44] Feminist criticism of liberal citizenship is far too extensive to survey in detail here. To begin, see Susan Moller Okin, *Women in Western Political Thought*; Jean Bethke Elshtain, *Public Man, Private Woman*; and Mary Dietz, "Context is all: Feminism and theories of citizenship."

[45] Tully discusses the role of narrative and recognition in identity politics in "The challenge of reimagining citizenship and belonging in multicultural and multinational societies."

on in any given community—a stance whose appeal is lessened by the fact that it tends to enable moral and political tyranny, at the hands of either the majority or a powerful minority.[46]

In their critique of claims that subjectivity is generated out of external influences or material causes, feminist theorists have explored the ways that the self's subjective engagement in local practices, institutions, and communities lends coherence to that self and meaning to the events of the world.[47] By their view, subjectivity is determined by experience, a complex of habits resulting from the semiotic interaction of "outer world" and "inner world," the continuous engagement of a self or subject in social reality. The influential work of Teresa de Lauretis argues that we identify ourselves by and through our subject positions within networks of relations involving others. Flexible, mutable things, subject to change over time and responsive to their environment, bodies are key to her theory. She struggles to articulate a view of virtue that grants epistemological dignity to the body while not reducing women to their bodies alone.[48]

Elizabeth Grosz draws on Merleau-Ponty's work on phenomenology in her attempt to accord the body, memory, and emotion primacy in feminist political experience—that is, she seeks to expose the links between the ways in which subjectivity has been conceived in the mainstream philosophical tradition as disembodied, atemporal, and dispassionate and the ways in which the politically oppressed group "women" has been associated with the body and strong emotion.[49] From a different critical perspective, but with similar goals, Iris Marion Young, a political scientist concerned with individuals' sense of membership in the democratic community, has called on theorists to reconsider the rhetorical tradition, and particularly its sophisticated treatment of emotion, memory, and civility. All the "affective, embodied, and stylistic aspects of communication, finally, involve attention to the particular audience of one's communication, and orienting one's claims and arguments to the particular assumptions, history, and idioms of that audience," she writes. "In all of these ways, rhetoric constitutes the flesh and blood of any political communication."[50]

In his rhetorical writings, Cicero represents the republican subject as engendered from the context in which he comes to know himself, the community. Recall his account of the origins of civilization, where the first civilization was the invention of the first orator (de Inv. 1.1–3, de Orat.

---

[46] A useful survey of these and other views: Macedo, *Liberal Virtues*, 9–38.

[47] See, for example, de Lauretis, *Technologies of Gender*; Flax, *Disputed Subjects*; Grosz, *Volatile Bodies*, Probyn, *Sexing the Self*.

[48] Grimshaw, "Practices of freedom," judiciously summarizes this struggle (69).

[49] Grosz, *Volatile Bodies*, 100, 109.

[50] Young, *Inclusion and Democracy*, 65. See now Tambornino's exploration of embodiment in Arendt, Taylor, Nietzsche, and Hampshire in *The Corporeal Turn*, with a helpful introductory discussion (1–15).

1.30; cf. Hobbes, *Elements* 1.5). Nature devises and designates human beings for communal life; the community is the framework within which virtue may be maximized. In this sense the orator is nature's supplement, since it is he who activates natural impulses toward community and creates the polity. To become a good speaker is thus to maximize what is best about human nature in particular, and it is to partake of the virtue that enables communal life, the telos of human existence. By this view the orator is the exemplum of the best life—the point of Crassus's repeated contrast between orators and philosophers and his claim that the orator replaces the philosopher as a model for virtue. Viewed in this light, Cicero's representation of the *orator perfectus* takes on significance as an intervention in ethical theory that reinvents the process of conceptualizing the good life in terms of communication in the civic or political context and the passions that enable and energize those acts of communication. Consequently, he must configure his self not in binarist terms, as an order of rule, mind over body or reason over passion, but as a cohesion of these dualities. All the effects of depth and interiority (or what we are accustomed to calling depth and interiority) he explains in terms of the inscriptions and transformations of the corporeal surfaces of the speaker and the community. This is the proper context for reading Cicero's repeated calls for orators to speak a common language that will not alienate or anger audiences (*oratio hominum sensibus ac mentibus accommodata*, de Orat. 1.54; cf. 1.260; 2.108, 185–86). Like Iris Young, Cicero insists that the orator use his body to welcome citizens into the arena of public discourse from the very start of the speech, to incorporate the audience as such (2.315).

To read the body as encoding identity is to read the body like a narrative. The orator Cicero describes has a body that is literally the stuff of interpretation; this is the real meaning of *actio quasi corporis eloquentia* (*Orat.* 55).[51] The body is read like an inscription, the object of codes and rules, just like spoken language. And like a text, the body proffers an almost inexhaustible series of significations that operate on both rational and emotional grounds. This is the reason behind Antonius's display of Manlius Aquilius, whose scarred body he strips in public, to the astonishment and

---

[51] The specific nature of Cicero's debt to Stoicism in his rhetorical writings, and particularly what Cicero understands as Zeno's contribution to epistemology, is difficult to assess. There are unquestionably provocative connections. Cicero cites Zeno's use of the hand as a metaphor in both his epistemological and rhetorical contexts: Zeno compares the open palm to an impression, assent to an impression to a hand curled in a fist, *katalepsis* (an impression that is true and such that it cannot be false) to a clenched fist, and knowledge to that fist gripped tightly by the other hand (*Acad.* 2.145, discussed in Hankinson, "Stoic epistemology," 65); Cicero also says that Zeno compared dialectic to the clenched fist, rhetoric to the open palm (*Orat.* 113). Cicero's claim that virtue is essentially one (e.g., de Orat. 3.22) is certainly Stoic in nature. Nowhere, however, do the Stoics treat rhetoric as an ethical therapy. See the rich discussion of the hand metaphor in Atherton, "Hand over fist." Useful general studies of Stoic ethics are Long, *Hellenistic Philosophy*, and Nussbaum, *The Therapy of Desire*.

sympathy of the crowd. In the same way, the orator's body in motion creates meaning as an actor does, with the crucial difference that he feels the emotion himself as he speaks. His body becomes, literally, the carrier of the narrative, narrativized. But if the orator's body is an inscribed text, who is doing the writing? The complexity of this process is explored in feminist scholarship that treats the body as a surface to be read, as layers of interwoven surfaces, inscribed by social meanings by a stylus, a tattoo, the ingestion or refusal of food, or plastic surgery. Cicero's text similarly understands the body as the site of the intermingling of mind and culture: it can also be seen as the mode of expression of hidden depths. Cicero's text oscillates between treating the body as a social object, to be lifted, twisted, written upon by various disciplines, and the body as rendered meaningful as it is experienced, enmeshed as it is in networks of significations.[52] This is, in the words of Nietzsche, "the subject as multiplicity."[53]

In the course of their training, in declamation and other exercises, Roman orators literally speak in the voices of others, even in the language of others (de Orat. 1.149–50). Though the orator's practices of discipline are institutionalized by tradition, they are not static. His exercises limber the voice and limbs and prepare him to mount a multitude of personae in which he might best appeal to his audience. As Antonius comments, "All by myself I play three characters with equanimity of soul: myself, my adversary [in court], and my judge" (tris personas unus sustineo summa animi aequitate, meam, adversari, iudicis, de Orat. 2.102). More than a century later, Quintilian looks back at Cicero himself, saying, "I regard impersonation as my most difficult of tasks. . . . For the same speaker has at one time to impersonate Caesar, at another Cicero or Cato. . . . Do you suppose Cicero thought in the same way or assumed the same character when he wrote for Titus Ampius and the rest? Did he not bear in mind the fortune, rank, and achievements of each single individual and represent the character of all to whom he gave a voice?" (3.8.50–51). He constantly positions and repositions himself, making meaning meaningful in the public sphere and responding to the responses of the crowd (de Orat. 1.60–62, 2.185–86). Ironically, this is Antonius's argument for oratory not being an art, since it is impossible to systematize even forensic oratory alone in rigid and unchanging categories (sunt enim varia et ad vulgarem popularemque sensum accommodata omnia genera huius forensis nostrae dictionis, de Orat. 1.108).[54]

[52] Grosz, Volatile Bodies, 116.

[53] Nietzsche, The Will to Power (New York, 1968), 270.

[54] Bek, Toward Paradise on Earth, 168–70, discusses the active participation of the visitor to the Roman domus "through visually taking possession" of a room in carrying out the physical behavior appropriate to their social roles, which differed from place to place and from time to time.

The orator alters his pleading according to the circumstances; and we know the importance of altering one's style from the heavy significance Cicero ascribes to the wrong kind of gesture or vocal trill, which brands the offending orator as a Greekling or an effeminate.

In keeping with Peripatetic and Stoic thought about the passions, Cicero treats them as bodily conditions, and in his text, the passions and related topics attract bodily metaphors.[55] Crassus, when giving an emotional performance, seems to be on fire (2.188), and what attracts imitators is his characteristic body language: a stamp of the foot and gestures that accompany certain phrasings—which Sulpicius, for one, tries hard to mimic in his own performances (de Orat. 3.47). Of the best style of eloquence—ornamental, emotion-produced, and emotion-inducing–Crassus declares that it is "embellished first of all by a kind of color and flavor (colore, sapore), as it were, so that it may be solemn, urbane, and erudite, gentlemanly, appealing, and polished, so that it may have the necessary feelings and sufferings. This is not a matter of individual details: these things are visible in the whole body" (de Orat. 3.96). The use of the word corpus in the final phrase holds two meanings: the structure of the speech taken as a whole, but also the performing body of the speaker. As Crassus goes on to say, it is difficult to say why our senses (sensus) are affected by oratorical performance, but it is clear that like pictures, music, perfume, things that are soft or smooth to the touch, and food and drink, eloquent language reaches and transforms the physical senses (de Orat. 3.98–100).

We have already seen Cicero define the good citizen as a mirror:

> Then Laelius said, "Now I see what, by way of duty and responsibility (officio et muneri), you would assign to the man I was seeking for." "Clearly," Scipio said, "to this one thing, almost by itself (for in it alone stands everything else): that he should never cease from training and examining himself, that he should call on others to imitate him (ut numquam a se ipso instituendo contemplandoque discedat, ut ad imitationem sui vocet alios), and that with the glorious spectacle of his mind and his life (sese splendore animi et vitae suae) he should present himself, a mirror (speculum), as it were, to his fellow-citizens." (2.69)

Contrast the elder Cato, who risks being literally unfinished because he avoids the "polish of learning" (politissimam doctrinam, de Orat. 3.135).

---

[55] Braund and Gill, introduction, The Passions in Roman Thought and Literature. Mind and body are both material things for the materialist Peripatetics and Stoics; the Stoics define the passions as diseased conditions of the animus. See also the helpful discussions of Kaster, Emotion, Restraint, and Community in Ancient Rome, and Flory, "Stoic psychology, classical rhetoric, and theories of imagination in Western philosophy."

Though a self inexorably in process, he fights to remain in a static state—by contrast to Cicero's injunction to his readers that "we must decide who we want to be, what kind of man we want to be, and what sort of life we want to lead," writing those decisions on our bodies through our comportment in public and private (*Off.* 1.117ff.).

This is why, in response to the Frankfurt School's and especially Jürgen Habermas's work on intersubjectivity and communicative rationality, I call the Ciceronian subject the "interdiscursive" subject. Habermas writes in response to three different philosophical traditions and competing conceptualizations of knowledge: the Kantian (broadly conceived), the materialist, and the postmodern. The last, he thinks, is a destructive critique that, having concluded against its opponents that the subject is not and cannot become master in his own house, seeks the sources of subjectivity elsewhere—in the Heideggerian dispensation of Being, the accidental systems of structuralism, or Foucauldian discourse formation.[56] But what if, he asks, reason itself were reconceived as contingent and embodied, the product of intersubjective understanding and reciprocal recognition? In his strong claims for the importance of speech training in the ethical formation of the self, Cicero shares Habermas's intention to reconceive rationality in terms of social practice and oral communication.

This embodied subject Cicero treats in terms of a fairly strict version of the Stoic claim that human beings have a natural tendency to live together in communities, and he implies, in fact, that they cannot partake fully in the virtues natural to the species unless they live in community with one another. Thus Cicero's rhetorical theory develops Stoic arguments for natural sociability in several important directions. His is a peculiarly communal vision of the body in action in the public view. The Platonic concern with the internal state of the soul expressed by the word *sophrosune* is supplemented with an emphasis on how the whole self appears to others, captured in the concept of *decorum*. As the index of virtue to other viewers, it is the object of a public, scrutinizing, self-creating gaze. For the self must watch the reactions of others in order to monitor itself, and this reaction is more than an act, even if, as we will see in chapter 5, the text reveals great anxiety on this score. Habitually undertaken, the move in reaction to others' reactions affects the makeup of the self, externally and internally.

The physicality of the body also enables the self to perceive his or her own status and responsibilities in the community. This implies that Cicero views the *vir bonus* as essentially located in the community, as a civic entity. The citizen is a body among other bodies, who originally

---

[56] Habermas, *Philosophical Discourse of Modernity*, 310.

formed political associations by communicating with one another through speech. The vision of the perfect orator adumbrated here and throughout *de Oratore* is key to Cicero's beliefs about republican citizenship and its relationship to ethical self-formation. Republican citizenship, like eloquence, is the practice of spectacular virtue in the course of an active life in the setting of a political community—which, like Aristotle, Cicero treats as the natural end of human existence.[57]

In *de Officiis*, a treatise on moral duty written in the form of a letter to his son, Cicero describes the active life as the "full glory of virtue" (*virtutis laus omnis, Off.* 1.19), and later he places the active life firmly in the forum (*gerenda res publica est*, 1.72). Like Aristotle, Cicero faces the challenge of explaining how the life of study is consistent with his definition of the life of action. Unlike Aristotle, who suggests in *Politics* 7 that doing philosophy is the best sort of active life, Cicero carefully distinguishes between the general learning necessary for the virtuous life and the professional study of a career philosopher. To allow oneself to be tugged away from the life of active practice, even by the pursuit of knowledge, is against the moral duty laid down by nature. Nature demands philosophical amateurism from its citizens precisely in the service of communal good; like eloquence, moral duty is virtuous because of its active presence in and for the community.

For Habermas, too, human society exists through and in the interactions of subjects: it is a network or web of intersubjectivity.[58] From this claim, he develops a notion of communicative competency. Successful acts of communication between subjects, he argues, involve the listener's agreement to five assumptions: that the utterance is true, that the speaker is sincere, that the utterance functions within an appropriate and mutually comprehensible framework of values, that it suits the relation between speaker and listener, and that, conceptually speaking, it is understandable. Since they imply a noise-free communicative process liberated from domination, violence, or ignorance, Habermas treats these assumptions as the communicative foundation of the essential political project of modernity, the effort to sustain and improve democracy. By his lights, successful acts of communication are acutely sensitive to their social situationality; they are subject to self-reflection and critique from others; and ideally, they place value on all forms and styles of discourse—for example, by accepting popular or emotional forms as well as rational, dispassionate debate. Intersubjective agreement is a negotiated assent

[57] Aristotle's famous view of men as political animals: *Pol.* 1.2; Cicero elaborates in *de Officiis* 1.50.

[58] I summarize here views expressed in Habermas, *Philosophical Discourse of Modernity*; see useful relevant readings of his thought in Benhabib, *Situating the Self*, especially "Models of public space," and Dews, "Communicative paradigms and subjectivity."

among autonomous selves engaged in dialogues that are and must be the foundation for critical social thought. Like moral duty, eloquence resides at the intersection of knowledge and action. Like *decorum*, the virtue at the heart of moral duty, eloquence demands knowledge of and control over the workings of the self—a self molded by the communal setting in which it exists.

Cicero's representation of the virtuous orator, then, can profitably be interpreted in terms of Habermas's criteria for communicative competency in the context of Frankfurt School intersubjectivity. My choice of the word "interdiscursive" is meant to signal two important differences between them. First, I want to underline the Ciceronian sensitivity to communication's resonance with alienation, tradition, and the passage of time, to the layers of experience, emotion, gossip, rumor, and memory that we call history. His is not a psychological theory of communication that focuses solely on the interaction of two or more rational-minded subjects outside time. Cicero offers instead an account of virtue that takes into account the embedded quality of the communicators' location in the sediments of history and tradition, and the awareness that the self arising out of those sediments is constructed and staged. When his imaginary orator speaks, he speaks always from the tense awareness that his beliefs and practices are not fully his own, insofar as they are the products of historical tradition and, more confusingly, the perceptions of others. The ideal self wants "to seem to be what he wants to seem" to others, but he does not exactly choose that subjectivity; it is, in a sense, given to him by the troika of nature, his education, and the community in which he lives (*de Orat.* 2.176).[59]

Second, Cicero identifies communication—"discourse," in the more mundane sense of the word—as the practice through which the virtuous self is constituted. The subjects in the interdiscursive relationship are not always already there in the first place, at least not as fully virtuous subjects; it is precisely the moment of encounter that produces virtue. What was there before—an embodied cluster of beliefs, assumptions, allegiances, and so on—is a potentiality that becomes an identifiably good self only in the process of contact with other human beings. Recall the scenes of the founding of civilization through speech in *de Inventione* and *de Oratore*, which were discussed in chapter 1, and the main interlocutors' disavowal of knowledge that is gained from books in favor of the knowledge that comes from the experience of the active life. As Cicero says in *de Officiis*, "All the glory of virtue stands in action" (*virtutis enim laus omnis in actione constitit*, 1.19). Though the word *actio* refers here to the opposition

---

[59] Consider the importance of Cicero's *persona* theory in *de Officiis* 1; this is a topic for chapter 4.

of relaxation, its other meaning hovers in the background: the action of oratorical delivery. *Actio* is the first, second, and third most important part of oratorical performance, as Demosthenes famously said (*de Orat.* 3.213). Even barbarians can understand the body talk, or *eloquentia corporis*, of *actio* (*de Orat.* 3.221–3), and the orator's virtue derives from this act of persuasion, not the weak kind conveyed in a written text. The most effective performers will not even bother to record their speeches, which are imagined to live on in the civic memory (*Brut.* 91).

The virtue of eloquence as Cicero describes it in *de Oratore* is twofold. First, it requires knowledge both topical and general, without which words are simply prolix foolishness, and this knowledge must be coupled with the oral and cultural skills appropriate for the subtle, winningly urbane man (1.17). Now, this alone cannot make rhetoric a virtuous practice, because knowledge may be put to evil uses in the absence of certain constraints (about which I will say more later), and further, because knowledge and skills that are not proclaimed in public do not partake of virtue in its fullest sense. Hence the second, and crucial, aspect of eloquence as a virtue: the authentic *vir bonus dicendi peritus* is capable of activating his array of knowledge and rational argument, bringing it to bear both in his ethical life and in the political life of his community. And the very process of conveying knowledge, in Cicero's view, helps mold the speaker into a virtuous agent. That which is at once the instrument of ethical discipline and its object is the living link between self and community: the body, which, after an ironic *praeteritio* (*de Orat.* 1.18), Cicero describes in the third book of the dialogue.

The *orator perfectus* represented in Cicero's rhetorical writings is no less than the perfect citizen—in fact, the perfect (masculine) self. This self knows itself and its community, and it organizes itself according to the laws of the community, written and unwritten; it seeks to move, not dominate, its fellow citizens; and its virtue makes itself known through appearance, or more precisely performance, like an actor on stage (*histrionum*, 1.18). As Thomas Jefferson told his nephew Peter Carr, paraphrasing Cicero, "Whenever you are to do a thing, ask yourself how you would act if all the world were looking at you and act accordingly."[60] Cicero's meditation on the scarcity of eloquent men at the beginning of the dialogue may now be explained as a recognition of the demanding nature of his vision of the ideal speaker-citizen-self, a self who brings moral virtue to life in performance, both in his private and in his public roles or "masks"—*personae*, as Cicero calls them in the later treatise *de Officiis* (1.107ff.).

The conception of a citizen-self whose identity rests in the natural performance of speech makes for a provocative answer to those who

---

[60] Cited in Fliegelman, *Declaring Independence*, 115.

wish to reconceive citizenship outside the modern mold of nation-states. If we follow Cicero in treating his eloquent speaker as the glue of the republic, we see that the state is made up of republican subjects linked by shared values, above all the value of *oratio/ratio*, talk and reason. And by insisting that rhetoricians examine the naturally persuasive ways this talk might work, relying on emotion and embodied situationality, Cicero offers a corrective to the disembodied Habermasian view of communicative rationality. Aristotle's extensive comments on the use of emotion in oratory (*Rhet.* 1377b22ff.) provide the basis for Cicero's claim that "Nothing in oratory is more important than to win for the orator the favor of his hearer, and to have the latter so affected as to be swayed by something resembling a mental impulse or emotion, rather than by judgment or deliberation. For men decide far more problems by hate, love, lust, rage, sorrow, joy, hope, fear, illusion, or some other inward emotion than by reality, or authority, or any legal standard, or judicial precedent, or statute" (*de Orat.* 2.178). But Aristotle does not elaborate a theory of the eloquent speaker as the best man and ideal citizen. Philosophers and Atticist orators, because they cultivate a communicative style that steers clear of strong emotion, tend to fail in their attempts to persuade. Cicero thus finds their speech literally impoverished: its incomprehensibility makes their knowledge illegitimate in the public sphere. When Cicero accuses the language adopted by philosophers of being incomprehensible to the general public, and therefore without strength or bearing in the world, this is not simple polemic but the core of Cicero's objection to language that is untethered from social practice, and the implication that such speech risks floating loose of its moral tethers. Without the diverse forest of eyes and ears that supervises the orator and compels him to supervise himself, breaches of common comprehensibility and courtesy become the norm. Amid the decline of civility, the rules of discourse itself, including the criteria for truth-telling, begin to erode.

Here Socrates' original objection in *Gorgias* intrudes. Free from the constraints of proof and "true" knowledge, what constraints are capable of binding the eloquent man? Is he not free to say whatever he likes, whether direct lies or matters of speculation, and to present them as truth? Cicero acknowledges this problem in the first sentence of *de Inventione*, where he admits that "often I have pondered within myself, whether more good or evil has come to men and to politics from our habit of speechmaking and great enthusiasm for eloquence."[61] His answer is that the orator who devotes himself thoughtfully to public life and the

---

[61] *Saepe et multum hoc mecum cogitavi, bonine an mali plus attulerit hominibus et civitatibus copia dicendi ac summum eloquentiae studium.*

service of his fellow citizens will not act as a force for evil and destruction (*Inv.* 1.1). Cicero has in mind an ongoing process of communal observation and supervision that will rein in the orator by making him answer to the communal will. Just as the good orator welcomes the audience with his gaze (3.221), and his eloquent body appeals to the audience, giving pleasure to it (*Brut.* 38), so the community provides the crucial setting for the orator's virtue. Cicero recalls an anecdote about the epic poet Antimachus, who gave a reading of his poem and watched the entire audience walk out, with the exception of Plato: "'I shall continue,' Antimachus said, 'for Plato alone is worth a hundred thousand others.'" Such may not be the case for the orator, however: if Demosthenes were deserted by all but one listener, his powers of speech would fall away (*Brut.* 191). If Elizabeth Asmis is right, as I think she is, to interpret Cicero's view of the republic as a partnership of "pooled contributions," where each element is bound not to alienate the others, we are able to see the orator's role in strengthening that partnership through speech.[62]

Cicero's comment to Quintus in *de Oratore* that the orator's worst vice is deviation from customary usage is the precursor to the theory of communication that he will flesh out throughout the dialogue. Speaking in terms an audience cannot easily understand is not merely a matter of giving offense or showing off. It drains meaning from the speech—which implies in turn that the community's ears are necessary preconditions for a speech to have meaning at all. The significance of the listener's horizon of expectations reveals itself more clearly in Cicero's elaboration of the four traditional virtues of oratory, derived from rhetorical studies by Aristotle, Theophrastus, and Hermagoras (1.144; cf. 3.37). Purity of Latin (*pure et Latine*) and crystal clarity (*plane et dilucide*) are necessary to convey ideas clearly; embellished style (*ornate*) and propriety, or rather decorum (*apte et quasi decore*), shape speech to the audience's tastes—not extra seasoning, but a crucial step in the communication of ideas.

These four virtues promote a set of values belonging to a group narrowly defined by nationality, gender, and social status. Like all virtues embraced by a dominant class, they carry with them a heavy burden of negative prejudice. In Cicero's attacks on bad Latin, cloudy thinking, garrulity, rustic phrases, and obscenity, echoes of his contempt for the talk of immigrants, women, slaves, and the ill-educated are plainly heard. Against this class and gender bias, however, lies the promise of the persuasive process. If his consummate orator tries to command the people, his enterprise is not without a certain demand on his own will to power: the

---

[62] Asmis, "The state as a partnership," 589 (full discussion of Cicero's argument in *de Republica*, 583–91).

speech must sway his audience, using arguments and strategies that are meaningful in the context of community belief and practice. In other words, good orators are highly attuned to the ideologies and customs of the communities in which they communicate. Empathy, emotion, and reason are all necessary ingredients. If they fall into inequal balance, the allure and logic of the act of persuasion decline. The speech loses meaning and, of course, fails to persuade.[63]

The orator's character as others perceive it must not be flexible "like an actor's, who simply mimics reality"; rather, it must shape the discourse of the real, becoming an "agent of reality" (actor veritatis vs. histrio veritatis, de Orat. 3.214). In doing so it follows the example of the body, with its changes in growth and age. Bodily senses are the guides to the orator, who watches and listens to the audience and modifies his speech accordingly. When highly colored language is called for, or restraint, he does so, responding to the situation and refashioning himself. As Seyla Benhabib remarks, "to be and to become a self is to insert oneself into webs of interlocution; it is to know how to answer when one is addressed and to know how to address others."[64] This recalls the Althusserian account of the interpellation of the subject, who in the process of being hailed by others enters into the regime of the Real, or the Heideggerian sense of being "thrown" into webs of narrative and remembered experience. The interdiscursive aspect of the virtuous Ciceronian orator bespeaks his awareness of the web and his sense of critical responsibility to the conventions that bind it. Cicero's corporeal self is not abstractly defined, nor does it act autonomously; rather, it emerges in the context of communal belief and practice. It cannot be separated from its own staging, the encounter with others. This is Cicero's final answer to Socrates's critique of rhetoric and its epistemological grounding in Gorgias.

An alternative history of the self

That rhetoric treats the body as the very stuff of virtue holds obvious implications for beliefs about gender and its role in the construction of

---

[63] Given the communal emphasis Cicero lays on the self's perception and rule of itself, I have been asked, does Cicero therefore believe that a person abandoned on a desert island loses the capacity to think, to reach conclusions, or to construct logical arguments with herself? No, but without companions the castaway's reason is incomplete; it holds a different status from reason that functions through dialogue in society. As Habermas suggests, arguments worked through in the safety and silence of the subject's internal consciousness are no substitute for real discourse.

[64] Benhabib, Claims of Culture, 15.

the self in social practice. In a seminal text of feminist epistemology, Evelyn Fox Keller argues that a longstanding association between men and mind, women and nature, plagues Western thought, a "deeply rooted popular mythology" that cases reason and mind as male and feeling and the body as female. "In this division of emotional and intellectual labor, women have been the guarantors and protectors of the personal, the emotional, the particular, whereas science—the province par excellence of the impersonal, the rational, and the general—has been the preserve of men."[65] This is not true of Ciceronian rhetorical discourse, which resists philosophy's tendencies to dualism, to split subjectivity into two different, mutually exclusive but emphatically unequal domains. On the contrary, when he rewrites the values and practices of the properly masculine man in terms that do not perfectly cohere with conventional *mores* of Roman republican masculinity, Cicero problematizes the cultural and intellectual imperative toward gender determinacy.

This establishes Cicero as a historical ally for theoretical work on the self done by feminist thinkers who posit subjectivity as process, by which the self is shaped by the forces of cultural ideology at the twin levels of belief system and practice. Feminists theorize a self that is liberated from the external disciplines of traditional power structures but at the same time true to the acts of internal discipline that are produced from personal and political belief. Feminist theory continues to call for new approaches to thinking the self, new visions of subjectivity, and in particular concepts of selfhood that allow for conscious self-development and empowerment without reenacting the repressive disciplines of the past. Such new theory of subjectivity will first of all avoid the philosophical impasse posed by what Cicero calls "absurd" dichotomies (*de Orat.* 3.60–61): conceptualizations of the subject that divide it into the mutually exclusive categories of mind and body. A new theory of the self requires a notion of embodied subjectivity, which will reconfigure the mental and the physical, the biological and the psychological, underscoring the interactivity of each. Second, it will refuse models of selfhood based in ideals of singularity and consistency, using instead multiplicity and flexibility as its templates. Third, the self will be viewed as attuned (not enslaved) to constantly shiftingsocial, political, geographic, and cultural inscriptions: although society does not master the self, the self cannot float free from society and its practices.

Let me summarize. I began with Plato's critique of sophistic teaching and democratic knowledge in the *Gorgias*, pointing out that his ideal discourse (*logos*) is detached from the shifting contingencies of custom,

---

[65] Keller, *Reflections on Gender and Science* (New Haven, 1996), 6–7.

religion, and even law.[66] This is the line of argument that Cicero signals he is trying to unseat in *de Oratore*, though Cicero tends to flatten Plato's critique in his attempt to clear the ground. At the beginning of the third and last book, we remember that Crassus tells the younger men who have been pestering him to discuss rhetorical style and ornament that he should not have agreed to talk about it in isolation from the content and structure of a speech. Such a division artificially separates matters that are integrally related to one another, comparable to cutting the soul from the body (3.24). This move brings the capacity to communicate into the communal context, where style is necessary to make sense. Communally oriented, eloquence calls into question both the notion of the autonomous subject and dominant philosophical beliefs about truth. The passions elicited through speech, derived from the bodily senses of hearing and seeing, are common and inclusive, opening the field of republican politics to the vulgar commonality and mortality. Yet eloquence makes meaning in the public sphere and it is learnable, thus offering another answer to the question often asked in ancient ethics, "Can virtue be taught?" And eloquence civilizes, as the characters in *de Oratore* show by their own civil interaction. This is a problem, however, insofar as speaking in a true voices opens the horizons of experience, offering an opportunity for men temporarily to become the judge, the jury, the position, the peoples, or the disenfranchised. As a continual experiment in the expansion of the orator's image repertoire, it holds out the threat and the promise of inhabiting the person of one other than oneself.

In focusing on the possibilities as well as the silences and erasures in Cicero's text, I am heeding Lois McNay's call for feminists to rethink the scholarly tendency to read ethical normativity in terms of negativity, discipline, and repression—what she calls "subjectification as subjection"—not because the constraints and oppressions examined in the negative approach are insignificant but because they offer only an etiolated understanding of the self, and particularly of subjective individuality and agency.[67] As a practice of ethical self-fashioning, rhetoric opens up a view of subjectification that is usually overlooked in examinations of the Western tradition: the positive moments of subject construction, as opposed

---

[66] I borrow the useful term "democratic knowledge" from Josiah Ober, who defines it in *Political Dissent in Democratic Athens* as the demos's "socially and political constructed 'regime of truth," an "integrated set of assumptions about what is regarded as right, proper, and true" (34).

[67] McNay, *Gender and Agency*, 3. Contrast, for instance, Gunderson's *Staging Masculinity*, whose fine analyses suffer from their relentless focus on the psychic "wounds" caused by the open-ended nature of the orator's project (though exception must be made for ch. 6, "Love," which examines *de Oratore* as a text where the interaction of the interlocutors virtuously enacts the homosocial pleasures of rhetoric—though not without carefully defensive styling on Cicero's part, 187ff.).

to purely negative practices of subjection. However, Cicero's own text belies the constructive meaning I have so far untangled here.

FRAGILITY

At first glance, the conversations that open de Oratore, Brutus, and Orator both embrace and resist the pull of the political.[68] The latter two works are framed by laments of exile from politics. In de Oratore, the Roman statesmen celebrate the Ludi Romani, in Crassus's country villa, his place of refuge from city life. Here, both time and place help broaden the scope of the discussion from the forum to other, nonpublic aspects of Roman life. As the exemplary practitioners of Cicero's rhetoricoethical system in the context of aristocratic leisure, Crassus and his interlocutors pull down the walls separating public from private, civis from vir. Their refusal to compartmentalize public and private takes shape along with their refusal to compartmentalize knowledge: beginning with Crassus's opening speech in book 1, rhetoric stands for discursive interconnection between subjects. Correspondingly, the spaces in which the self may withdraw into itself—where it may take part in the reflection that nourishes and shapes itself—are exposed to the readerly (public) gaze.

This is an intentional move on Cicero's part, for he explicitly positions himself against the withdrawal from society that accompanies the self-reflection of the Epicureans, his favorite target in this respect. His representation of republican ethos rests rather on the collapse of the public and the private sphere in a republic constituted through discourse itself—ideally, the speech of bodies in the public eye, but also other, less formal types of intercourse among citizens. In de Oratore's dialogue form, and in the epistolary or dedicatory form of Brutus, de Officiis, and most of Cicero's other works, the definition of the vir bonus must be reached not through philosophical disputation but in civil conversation among friends, which mimics and practices more formal performances of public talk. Their civility ultimately extends beyond manners and the personal exchanges of respect that define aristocratic homosociality, since civil conversation and its pleasures are figured as essentially constitutive of the workings of republican politics.[69] This, Robert Hariman points out, is certainly Cicero's attitude in the letters written from exile or moments of withdrawal from politics: the epistles must adopt a style

[68] Robert Kaster reminds me that this tension is reflected in a letter written to Lentulus Spinther during the composition of de Oratore (Fam. 1.8.3), where Cicero laments the incompatibility of withdrawal into intellectual contemplation with his obligations to Pompey.

[69] McKinnon, "Civil citizens," discusses the significance of civility in the contemporary context, emphasizing the key role of self-respect in acquiring civility's "skills" (145).

of "intensified orality" precisely in order to recreate the conditions of the public arena where Cicero must, in practice, be silent.[70]

In a normative sense, Ciceronian performative ethics may be seen as a technology of civility, which he sees as the necessary ground for rational communication among political agents. It imagines and constructs citizens as possessing personalities adequate to participation in self-rule, positing that they learn those techniques internally through their control of their bodies, and they prove them in the public eye in performance after performance, whether orations or conversations, *orationes aut sermones*. It has long been a criticism of liberalism that because it defined the individual as rights-bearer and proprietor, it avoided matters of personality, emotion, and character.[71] By contrast, Ciceronian rhetorical republicanism defines the self as a virtuous agent on whose virtuous corporeality the republic and its well-being are balanced.

But bodies are not perfectly controllable: they evade rational, self-conscious mastery every day. Cicero addresses this in a memorable passage in *de Oratore*, where Crassus confesses to stage fright:

> "To be sure, I often notice this among you, too, and I experience it myself all the time (*in me ipso saepissime experior*), that I turn white at the beginning of my speech, and I quake from the bottom of my soul and in every limb. As a young man, in fact, I was so terrified at the start of a prosecution, that I owe Quintus Maximus an enormous favor, because he quickly dismissed the hearing the moment he saw me shattered and fainting with fear (*me fractum ac debilitatum metu viderit*)." Then everyone began to nod in agreement, and to glance significantly at one another, and they all started to talk at once. (1.120–21)

The virtuous performance is demanding, and every performance opens up the possibility of failure. A related problem involves the orator's memory: as he fashions himself through the memory of performances, a memory prompted by reading or observation, the process keeps virtue alive through the new performance, but it also opens up virtue to another cycle of misreading and misremembering. And will the performance itself be remembered? This is the failure against which Cicero struggles in *Brutus*, which memorializes the orators of the Roman past at a time (45 BCE) when memory of the republic seemed to be failing (*de Rep.* 5.2). The potential of bodies to perform virtue is also a potential to exceed the very boundaries of virtue, to transgress the very system they are

---

[70] Hariman, *Political Style*, 109.
[71] Pocock, "Virtues, rights, and manners," 45.

imagined to sustain. The mortal beastliness of the body is underscored in anecdotes about pedagogical technique where teachers metaphorically animalize the bodies of their students when they "rein in" their uncontrolled energies: to take one example, Isocrates' teachings are described as having "whipped" Ephorus and "bridled" Theopompus (*de Orat.* 3.36).

To these causes of failure must be added the problem of pleasure:

> If only I could express these things to you to the degree that they reveal themselves, as I seem to myself to see them right now, in the forum and the lawcourts! . . . There is nothing more glorious than the perfect orator. For to pass over the actual practice of eloquence, that governing force in every tranquil and free community, there is such charm about the mere power to deliver a set speech, that no impression more delightful than this can be received by the ear or the intelligence of man. Can any music be composed that is sweeter than a well-balanced speech? (*de Orat.* 2.33–34)

With his wish that he could use his powers of speech to induce a literally physical vision before the eyes of his listeners, moving them bodily from Crassus's holiday villa to the Roman forum, Antonius exposes the problematic attractions of locating oratory's powers in the body. Here the morally and socially redemptive powers of persuasion—its ability to lead the city-state responsibly and well—coincide with its corporeal aspect: the orator appeals to his listeners in this passage precisely because of the charm of his voice (*oblectatio*), which wraps the cognitive content of the speech in pleasure. The political community that Antonius describes is truly a body politic, convened and guided by its bodily capacities (hearing, vision, and the like) and their corresponding pleasures. Antonius's praise enacts its own stress on the body in its wish to affect the physical sight of his listeners: he literally wants to move them (*movere*, one of the three goals of rhetoric) into the public space of the law court. But the pleasures offered there are experienced in the context of submission (*dominatur*). And the submission occurs not only on the part of the listening crowd but also on the part of the orator, who must change his tune according to the desires of the crowd (*de Orat.* 1.54, 108, 2.185–86). The decisions that the community makes thus seem embedded in a double act of pleasurable submission—a problem for the reclamation of rhetoric as performative ethics, since indulgence in pleasure is a central part of the story of Rome's decline (Sallust, *Cat.* 1–6, *Jug.* 1–2). How reliable is the body as a performer of republican virtue? And how is its power related to the charismatic authority claimed by Roman orators of earlier republican history, an authority Cicero seeks to bridle in his earlier work, *de Inventione*?

Cicero represents his orator's body as embedded in republican networks that anchor communicative practices in the political sphere, and
as the site of connection for elite and mass. The speakers of *de Oratore*
represent the speaking self and its audience as members of a community linked and reified through the senses (*sensus*) of sight, hearing, smell,
touch, and taste, as Crassus points out in his analogy between the
power of eloquence and the power of the visual arts, music, perfume,
objects of a certain texture, and good food and drink (3.100). Their
common bodies make possible the common experiences that the process
of casual conversation or oratory transforms into political identity and
political will. This powerful formulation is precisely what Hobbes
rejects in *Elements of Law*, in his dismissal of the classical and humanist value of prudence, which he defines as "nothing else but Conjecture
from Experience"—a quality in which even "brute Beasts also participate" (16, 26).[72] Since bodies that can be made through technologies of
rhetorical training can also be unmade, constant practice and supervision is the rhetorician's answer: this is part of the point of *de Oratore*'s
setting in a private villa, where the elegant arts of persuasion that the
interlocutors make central to public eloquence are clearly shown to be
equally powerful as the engine of "private" conversation. Performative
ethics offers an endless challenge to the practitioner, a challenge that,
precisely because it holds out the promise of failure, is the source of
anxiety as well as inspiration. The roots of this anxiety lie in republican
political ideology, which shares with and drives rhetorical discourse's
preoccupation with the performing body.

Cicero's acknowledgment of the frailties of the performing body,
even his own well-trained one, resonates with, and may be explained
by, his preoccupation with the frailties of the republican body politic.
His account of the republic is haunted by the nearness of its failure and
collapse—which looms precisely because of the republic's reliance on
the maintenance of virtue in the citizen body, both individually and collectively. If the most obvious cause of failure in 55 BCE is the ongoing
breakdown of political order and the fracturing of the senatorial order
into the camps of Caesar, Pompey, and their critics in the senate, Cicero
is also concerned with theoretical instabilities in the republic. Just as
the republic grows like a child into manhood (*Rep.* 2.45), so it can
decay like an old man; its embodied nature promises its own death.
Even the *populus* can create a "not unstable state," he writes in the
voice of Scipio, "so long as no injustices and strong desires" appear
(*nullis interiectis iniquitatibus aut cupiditatibus, de Rep.* 1.42; cf. 2.68).
An elegiac tone colors his view of republican antiquity in book 5,

---

[72] Cited in Skinner, *Reason and Rhetoric*, 262.

where he meditates on a line from Ennius's *Annales*, "the Roman state stands in its ancient customs and its men" (*moribus antiquis res stat Romana virisque*):

> which verse he [Ennius] either in brevity or truth-value seems to me to have communicated from an oracle. For neither men, unless the polity (*civitas*) has been endowed with customs, nor customs (*mores*), if these men had not been there to support them, would be able to found or maintain for very long such a great republic, one ruling so far and wide (*fuse lateque imperantem rem publicam*). Before our own time, then, paternal custom itself produced outstanding men, and outstanding men retained the old customs and institutions of their ancestors. Though when our age received the republic, like a painting (*picturam*), a beautiful painting, but in fact already fading with old age, it not only neglected to renew its colors to their earlier state but also took no care at all to preserve even its shapes and their external outlines (*liniamenta*), so to speak . . . And what remains from the old customs, in which, the poet said, the Roman state stood? . . . And what shall I say about our men? For our customs themselves have died off because of our lack of men, for which great evil we must not only offer an explanation but must try ourselves in, so to speak, a capital case. For by our faults, not by some chance or fate, we hold the republic in name only, but in fact we lost the thing itself long ago. (5.3)

Like a picture, the republic is a physical entity open to public gaze that requires constant supervision and care (*curavit*) to keep (the virtue of) its shape.

It is to shore up against this vision of failure that Cicero conceives of the embodied citizen-subject as a dynamic normative control, the source of political stability through the constant adjustment of subjective machinery. The (speaking) body is the site of reflection and discipline, the object of intensive labor that anchors and sustains the community through performance and observation. For as this passage shows, with its preoccupation with the fatally corrupting passage of time, the republic—unlike the perfectly stable state theorized by Aristotle and Polybius and indeed Cicero, in the defense of monarchy that plays such a surprisingly central role in *de Republica*—exists in finite and localized time, with all the problems of particularity and potential failure that this vision incurs. As Pocock writes in his analysis of the revolution in temporality involved in the republican revival of the Italian Renaissance, the republic is not timeless: "it existed in time, not eternity, and was therefore transitory and doomed to impermanence. . . . Only as a partnership in virtue among all citizens could the republic persist; if virtue were less than universal, its failure at one point must in time corrode its existence in all others. The aim of politics is to escape from time; time is the dimension of imperfection and change must necessarily be degenerate."[73]

To battle the effects of time, Cicero mounts a demanding, self-perpetuating performative ethics of visible virtue centered in the body of the orator—and in the collectivity of orators who represent the *populus*, in the civic body as well. The problem is that the very vehicle of performance of virtue is vulnerable, not only to the seductions of luxury and pleasure that Sallust and the rest of the Roman moralistic tradition lament, but also to the weakness and excess of the body itself—and the very nature of the body as mortal matter. After all, women, noncitizens, slaves, even animals possess bodies, so it is common matter in the fullest sense, a fact that undermines even as it enables the putative autonomy of the ideal citizen-man-subject. Cicero elaborates an ethical theory of the embodied self, setting up oratorical training as that which begins from nature but which manages its excesses and pleasures, bolstering it with a laudatory defense of embodiment in the face of philosophical critique. Linked by common bodily practices, the republic stands and falls by the body and its virtues. But the awareness of finitude and fatality underlying this passage persists. The nature of the republic, we recall, is essentially suprarational, beyond the scope or reach of reason (*vincit ipsa rerum publicarum natura saepe rationem*, *de Rep.* 2.57). Like bodies, republics have no mind, and like bodies, they die. This is the power of the text, which preserves a replica of republican performative ethics, ready for revival even when the republic has suffered its inevitable end.

I have argued in this chapter that Ciceronian rhetorical discourse offers a psychology of an embodied, communal subject. This psychology is rooted in and responds to a problem in republican political thought: the immanent fragility of the *res publica* as a political association sustained by the visible virtue of citizen bodies. Cicero's effort to develop a performative definition of virtue resonates with contemporary projects by feminists and political theorists. To different degrees, these thinkers share Cicero's critical reaction against his understanding of Plato's rejection of the body and bodily performance, and Aristotle's theory of an autonomous self whose aim is mastery, not knowledge, of the body. But Cicero's views are laden with internal contradiction. Though his system valorizes popular communication, he is no *popularis*; though it relies heavily on specialized knowledge of the body, he habitually disavows both specialization and the body; though the arousal of emotion is central to his vision of a political community, he stresses its rational and refined elements (while acknowledging the ultimate insufficiency of rational persuasion). In the context of oratorical performance, for both

---

[73] Pocock, *The Machiavellian Moment*, 53.

speaker and audience, the experience of the senses arouses passion, whether pity or fury, resentment or sympathy. This is why philosophers, even Stoics, along with mendacious or shallow orators, must fail to persuade: the operations of speech are meaningless without the accompanying presence of authentically felt passion. This passion may not fly free, however; it must be directed, and the sum of Cicero's project in his rhetorical writings is to construct a self that may instruct the direction of passion in public once it has done so within itself. From the object of supervision, passions emerge as the source of civic obligation. To this, then, I turn in the next two chapters.

Chapter Four

THE AESTHETICS OF VIRTUE

The strongest form of law . . . is not graven on tablets of
marble or brass, but on the hearts of the citizens. This forms
the real constitution of the State, takes on every day new
powers, when other laws decay or die out, restores them or
takes their place, keeps a people in the ways it was meant to
go, and insensibly replaces authority by force of habit. I am
speaking of morality, of custom, above all of public opinion;
a power unknown to political thinkers, on which nonetheless
success in everything else depends.
—Rousseau, Social Contract

THE PROBLEM OF LIBERTY

THE STANDARD ACCOUNT OF POLITICAL liberty conforms to an opposition
laid out by Benjamin Constant in postrevolutionary France and elaborated
by Isaiah Berlin in 1958. Negative liberty, or "freedom from," is so
called because it involves the absence of interference in the operations of
individual free choice.[1] Positive liberty, or "freedom to," demands the
individual take action in reining in the self, with the object of achieving
mastery over it. Broadly associated in political philosophy with the
Greco-Roman tradition and especially Sparta and Rome, positive liberty
is often taken to mean the freedom to participate in politics; in Berlin's
presentation, it also takes the form of subordinating individual desires to
the common interest, and conceiving the self as a cog in a greater
machine, the machine of the centralized society. Berlin effectively links
negative liberty with the heroic tradition of Anglo-American classical
liberalism, making positive liberty the ominous symbol of classical com-
munalism and the quasi-religious harbinger of modern totalitarianism.[2]
Though it was an ideological milestone in the context of the cold war,

---

[1] Berlin, *Four Concepts of Liberty*, 7. Standard references are Wirszubski, *Libertas*
(pre-Berlin) and Brunt, "*Libertas*," whose useful surveys of the evidence are marred by the
influence of the positive-negative binary (so, rightly, Roller, *Constructing Autocracy*, 219, 232).

[2] Pettit, *Republicanism*, 18–20. For a helpful overview of the debate in light of its relevance
to postmodern thought about identity: Sidorsky, "The third concept of liberty," 536–43.

Berlin's framework is of limited use in understanding the history of Western notions of liberty, especially as it developed in Rome.

The binary at work in Roman *libertas* is not presence versus absence but master versus slave: the liberty prized by both patrician and plebs was the liberty of the free. "Liberty is to live upon one's own Terms; Slavery is, to live at the mere Mercy of another; and a Life of Slavery is, to those who can bear it, a continual State of Uncertainty and Wretchedness, often an Apprehension of Violence, often the lingering Dread of a violent Death": the late seventeenth-century republican language in Trenchard and Gordon's *Cato's Letters* echoes the well-documented Roman dread of the slave's vulnerability, especially the enforced pain and humiliation of physical punishment. Cicero anticipated the terror of arbitrary rule in early modern antimonarchist republicanism when he described liberty as that which "a people under a king lack," since subjects must obey the royal will regardless of whether it is just or unjust (*Rep.* 2.43). Sallust, Livy, Seneca, and later republican thinkers such as Machiavelli joined Cicero in speaking of liberty in primarily negative terms, as defined by the absence of interference guaranteed by law, especially the interference of a magistrate in the free (legal) actions of a citizen.

The cultural historian Matthew Roller, who defends the primacy of the negative aspect of ancient *libertas*, argues that we should not understand the word as a fully fledged concept in Roman society but as a metaphor, a term of social description (the quality of not-slavery) that has been imported into the political domain, to be made available for use (as Ronald Syme complains) by *optimates* and *populares* alike. While we should not be misled by this flexibility to believe that the term is without meaning, Roller concludes, we must also guard against retrojecting modern meanings into it by forgetting the original derivation of *libertas* in the context of slavery.[3] That historical derivation is precisely what encourages Philip Pettit in his influential reformulation of republican liberty as nondomination, the right to be free even of the possibility of arbitrary mastery at the hands of a boss, spouse, or landlord.

The distorted equation between ancient liberty and participation in politics derives from yet another modern misreading of context, in this case the various conditions under which the Romans discussed what we now understand as political ideas. When Cicero praises popular *libertas* in his *contiones* on Rullus's proposal for agrarian reform, he responds to the demands of the Rostra, which had long cultivated a discourse and

---

[3] Roller, *Constructing Autocracy*, 227–33 (and see his fine discussion of the master-slave relation, 214–26).

style that memorialized the founding republican antagonism between elite and mass, and his speeches refer accordingly to "the few" (*pauci*), "the tyranny of the few," and the defense of the people's traditional liberty (*traditam libertatem, Leg. Agr.* 2.16, 25, 3.13). His comments regarding *libertas* in his philosophical works are another matter. In a well-known passage in *de Legibus*, after voicing aristocratic criticism of the tribunate and popular liberty through the persona of his brother Quintus, Cicero presents himself as the advocate of compromise between elite and mass (*temperamentum*, 3.24), stipulating that the people's liberty must be authentic, not merely word play (*re non verbo danda libertas*)—which Cicero interprets as meaning that they will be led to yield to the authority of leading men (*adduceretur ut auctoritati principum cederet*, 3.25). His remarks before the senate and to his friends and social equals must be distinguished from these. When Cicero speaks among equals, he represents political participation, especially the freedom to say what one thinks, as key to the accrual of standing (*dignitas*), and this *dignitas* he associates with *libertas*. In a letter to Lentulus Spinther (55 BCE), for instance, Cicero laments the overthrow of the republic by the tyrannical machinations of Pompey and Caesar: "The entire system of the senate, the law courts, the whole republic, has been changed" (*commutata tota ratio est senatus, iudiciorum, rei totius publicae, Fam.* 1.8.3–4). He explains that the members of the senate have lost the *dignitas* of deliberation (*dignitas in sententiis dicendis*) and the *libertas* they enjoyed in running political affairs (*libertas in re publica*).[4] To eighteenth- and nineteenth-century readers of Cicero's letters, whose experience encompassed the lively debate of the coffeehouse, the growth of the press, and, most important, the spread of electoral representative government in theory and practice, the link connecting participation in political affairs (primarily the right to vote) to antityrannical notions of liberty must have seemed obvious. Cicero's original claims for senatorial *libertas* were thus appropriated as part of the advocacy of universal "freedom to" suffrage reform.

Dignitas rests not on the simple declaration of one's opinion but on being heard and seeing that opinion put into practice. But if it was clear to Cicero that wielding political influence was the key to senatorial *libertas*, he could and did argue precisely from this point that the desire for influence over others could swiftly mutate into the quest for tyranni- cal domination (*Off.* 1.64). Others suggested that tyranny was built into the elite conception and practice of republican politics. This is the claim of two *popularis* tribunes in Sallust's histories, Memmius and

---

[4] Other identifications of *libertas* with senatorial *dignitas* (and *auctoritas*) in Brunt, "Libertas," 323, 328: see esp. *Leg. Agr.* 1.22, *Phil.* 3.19, *Dom.* 130, *Phil.* 4.5, 13.33.

Macer: that the political activity of the nobles amounts to an eternal bid for *dominatio*. "They want to be tyrants; you want to be free" (*Jug* 31.23; cf. Macer's account of senatorial tyranny, Sal., *Hist.* 8–13). Such talk fuels Quintus Cicero's criticism of the post-Gracchan tribunate in the passage from *de Legibus* mentioned earlier (3.19–22). Looking closely at Cicero's reply, we see that his emphasis on popular obedience to senatorial authority is tempered by acknowledgment of the substance of Sallust's accusation: the tendency of the senatorial class to yield to violent ambition (exemplified by his rival Clodius) and *invidia*, a word that means not only jealousy but the self-interested desire to deny another a good.[5] Cicero's subsequent criticism of the secret ballot returns to this theme: he treats the risk it poses to the senate's *auctoritas* as equivalent to the danger of its abuse by real or potential tyrants (*dominatu ac potentia principum. . . . potentissimis hominibus*, 3.34). His aim in transforming the vote into a form of civic dialogue is the amelioration of conflict between *senatus* and *populus* (*contentionis causa*, 3.39). If these passages indicate the depth of Cicero's aristocratic bias, it is important to note the emphasis they place on the crucial role of elite self-mastery in consolidating civic harmony.

Cicero's rhetorical writings elaborate this line of thought. In chapter 3, concentrating on Cicero's recovery of the body for ethical discourse, I sought to explain his place in the history of the self and his relevance for contemporary debates over the nature of political communication. Here I examine in more detail the way Cicero addresses the dialectical relationship between *libertas* and *dignitas*—between the maintenance of a society governed by law and the aggressive self-assertion demanded by the give-and-take contest of elite social relations—by underscoring the importance of law in the formation of the ideal orator, what he calls in the letter to Spinther a "courageous and constant senator" (*fortis et constantis senatoris*, 4). He transposes the leading citizen's entrapment in this dialectic in miniature, we might say, in his portrayal of the internal relations of the speaking self. In his effort to resolve the potentially contradictory impulses of the elite man and the demands of republican politics, Cicero envisages a process of individual self-rule that reflects and enacts self-abnegation in the political context of consensus and consent, through oratorical training and performance, with a view to achieving of the label of *vir bonus*, or "good (elite) man."

If the Roman citizen must, in the republican run of things, allow himself to be "recruited to other identities," to repress (to a degree) his natural *amour-propre* in favor of the communal good, Cicero redeems that

---

[5] I owe this particular definition of *invidia* to Kaster, *Emotion, Restraint, and Community*, 98–103.

sacrifice by building it up as a cornerstone of the virtuous, manly orator, whom, as we have already seen, he describes as the ideal Roman self.[6] Cicero's elaboration of a republican style is a different kind of negotiation of self-interest and communal good from that which characterizes the heroic actions of many Roman exempla, such as Horatius Cocles, Mucius Scaevola, and the Decii. In the course of his training and career, the orator engages in an ongoing process of internal, willed submission to laws of reason and propriety, a submission that derives from the self's love of himself and others. Cicero's rhetorical writings may in fact be interpreted as a long elaboration of the republican attempt to negotiate the competing attractions of self-aggrandizement and communal responsibility—crudely, of power and its abuse—through the policing of speech and the speaking body.

The role of emotion, the feelings of the eloquent man and his listeners, is key to Cicero's solution of the problem. Rhetoric disciplines the self that it trains by the law of love, in a repetitive, performative process I call republican patriotism. This patriotism involves more than a simple series of acts of self-observation and restraint (if such a process can ever be called simple). When the orator proves his self-mastery in his performances—whether in the formal context of a speech or under the informal circumstances of conversation and general social practice—with the visible evidence of his emotive, physical body, which he shapes and directs according to a corresponding internal, literally self-perpetuating law, he brings relations of power into the realm of aesthetics. In more ways than one, power lies in his look and the feelings behind it.

The intersection of power, love, and art in Cicero's thought leads me, in the second half of the chapter, to read him against one of his contemporaries, the poet Catullus. Catullus represents his reading community as similarly bound by a dual law of shared aesthetic tastes and the affective bonds of shared emotion, and in doing so, he helps illuminate the gaps and fissures in Cicero's attempt to suture self and community. His poetry maps and explores the measures of distance that Cicero seeks to erase between autonomy and interdependence, the protection of property and the praise of poverty, self-restraint and passion, reason and sentiment, civil manners and manly courage, transparency and theatricality, the rule of law and the magnetic pull of custom.

---

[6] The conception of "identity recruitment" is Pettit's: "[W]hile each of us is a personal self in this sense—in this sense of owning a personal heritage—it is also true of each of us that we often suspend the hold that that self has and allow ourselves to be recruited to other identities. We find ourselves responding in a way that owns, not a personal heritage, but a heritage that is shared with others," *Republicanism*, 257.

THE REPUBLIC OF PASSIONS

Roman oratory was an agonistic exercise in the expression of individual identity, a contest for symbolic capital.[7] "The industry of Scipio Africanus brought him virtue; his virtue brought him glory; his glory brought him rivals" (*Rhet. Her.* 4.25.34). Carlin Barton vividly documents the Romans' pleasure in undergoing and spectating ordeals in the forum, on the battlefield, and in the arena, where a real man (*vir*) "willed himself to be expendable."[8] In a letter to Lupercus, the younger Pliny compares the successful orator to a tightrope walker, and later to a helmsman in a storm (*Ep.* 9.26.3–4). "In fact," he says at first, "the orator ought to be excited and elevated, at times even to the point where he boils over, and almost to approach the precipice . . . It may be safer to travel through the flat plain, but it is also humbler and less exalted" (9.26.2). Part of the performance's thrill was observing the lengths to which the orator might go, the degree to which he would push the envelope of convention in his effort to gather his listeners under his sway. "As with certain skills, which gain more from risks than from anything else, so with eloquence," Pliny continues. "You've seen tightrope walkers, and the applause they win as they move, every minute looking as though they are about to fall. For those things which are the most unexpected and the most dangerous are also the most applauded" (3–4).[9] The orating body was a site of dramatic and unpredictable change: from a calm picture of serene authority, the speaker might lash himself into a passionate frenzy, weeping, dripping with sweat, stalking up and down the rostrum, his hair disordered, his toga falling off one shoulder, and his breath coming in short gasps (cf. *de Orat.* 2.196, 6.2.27, 11.3.147).

Animated speech-making offered men the opportunity to draw attention to themselves, to gain a place in the public eye. At the same time, however, the orator had always to be aware of the boundaries of propriety—especially because the republican audience seemed to enjoy performances that stretched the rules of convention. In Rome, owing to "the violent

---

[7] Gleason, *Making Men*, furnishes a useful introduction to the concept of symbolic capital and concomitant ideas (xxi and passim), using it as a model with which to explore the implications of rhetoric's agonistic aspects in the second sophistic (esp. 131–58). Bourdieu defines the term "symbolic capital" in *Outline of a Theory of Practice* (183–97), and later refines it in *The Logic of Practice* (118–25).

[8] Barton, *Roman Honor*, 40 (more on the same topic, 38–87 passim).

[9] *Debet enim orator erigi attolli, interdum etiam effervescere ecferri, ac saepe accedere ad praeceps; nam plerumque altis et excelsis adiacent abrupta. Tutius per plana sed humilius et depressius iter . . . Nam ut quasdam artes ita eloquentiam nihil magis quam ancipitia commendant. Vides qui per funem in summa nituntur, quantos soleant excitare clamores, cum iam iamque casuri videntur. Sunt enim maxime mirabilia quae maxime insperata, maxime periculosa. . . .*

passions of the crowd" (*maximi motus populi*), Antonius comments in
de Oratore, "it would seem that an oratorical style rather more grand
and brilliant must be pursued, and often the greatest part of a speech must
be directed to arousing the emotions of the audience, by means of exhortation or act of summoning memory, in the state of hope or fear, or
toward desire or longing for glory. . . . But because the orator's greatest
stage, it appears, is the public meeting, we are provoked by nature itself
to use the more ornate kind of oratory" (2.337–38).[10]

The intensity Cicero brings to his call for oratorical self-government
arises from the particular way he imagines speech and its reception to
constitute the political dynamic of the republic. Salient here is Cicero's
portrayal of the contrast between accepted practices of public speech
in Greece and Rome, in which he says the Greeks pass legislation and
engage in other public business while sitting down, implying that
Romans remain standing throughout their meetings (*Flacc.* 16–17).[11]
His condemnation of the Greeks reflects his general interest in the
mimetic importance of the orderly citizen body for the well-ordered
body politic. Standing up was only one aspect of the physical rules that
simultaneously constrained public speech acts and embodied social
hierarchies at Rome. If it is in the nature of a Roman audience to enjoy
a spectacle, the virtuous orator must control and moderate the audience's desire—which he can do only by feeling their desire, which he
must then at once repress and redirect. His dialogue *Brutus* evaluates
orators principally according to this capacity. Antonius's delivery was
exemplary: "he controlled everything by purpose and something like
deliberate art" (*ad rationem et tamquam ad artem dirigebat*); his
conscious use of embellishment complemented his outstanding delivery
(*Brut.* 140–42). Cicero compares him to a general with cavalry, infantry,
and skirmishers, who knows how to place his forces in the most effective
place (139). The dynamic relationship between orator and audience
means that transgressive behaviors on the part of the orator respond to
the transgressive desire of the audience eager for entertainment and
scandal—the display of the obscene side of official authority.[12] The
orator Gaius Staienus "cultivated an intense, fretful, violent style of
speaking" which was greeted so favorably that "he would have achieved

---

[10] *Genus quoque dicendi grandius quoddam et illustrius esse adhibendum videtur;
maximaque pars orationis admovenda est ad animorum motus non numquam aut cohor-
tatione aut commemoratione aliqua aut in spem aut in metum aut ad cupiditatem aut ad
gloriam concitandos. . . . Fit autem ut, quia maxima quasi oratoris scaena videatur contion-
is esse, natura ipsa ad ornatius dicendi genus excitemur.*

[11] Appian ascribes the senate's refusal to allow permanent theaters in Rome to the
Roman preference of standing during public gatherings (*BC* 1.28).

[12] See my discussion of power and obscenity in chapter 1.

higher honors if he had not been caught in open crime" (*Brut.* 241).[13] Cicero underscores the moral deficiencies of such scandalous performers and vividly evokes the bad ends they eventually met. Of the sedition-mongers who followed the Gracchi, for instance, he judges Saturninus to have been the most effective orator, but the seditious tribune's success talent turns out to rely on his delivery and style of clothing (*Brut.* 224). Gaius Titius, an admirer of Saturninus and a conspicuously effeminate gesticulator, became the model for a scandalously fashionable dance step (*Brut.* 225).

Cicero's ideal orator absorbs contemporary conventions of taste from his observation of Roman society and its habits. As he proceeds to advertise those conventions to his audience, he makes his self-mastery a symbol of *concordia*: he becomes a walking lesson in self-government and proof against the accusation of self-aggrandizing tyranny. Here is the "great citizen," a man "nearly divine" (*magni cuiusdam civis et divini paene viri, Rep.* 1.45), whose gifts of persuasion make him the proper leader of the republic—not alone, like a tyrant, but in company with the people.[14] He embodies the notion of *consensus* prevailing in Cicero's philosophical writing and appearing in his speech *pro Sestio*, a union that is a "hierarchical blending of wills," in which the senators and the knights lead the rest of the people in the formation of opinion and policy.[15] In the forum, his self-mastery would ameliorate the terror of the ever-dominating nobles; in the senate and the law courts, it would take the form of symbolic assurance of recognition and respect for political and social equals. Aristotle had suggested in his extensive discussion of emotions (*Rhet.* 2.1–11), that the good speaker become an expert in emotion and its control. As Cicero's orator throws out his arm and lets it drop, adopts a facial expression that expresses intensity but avoids a pop-eyed stare, and stops his eyes from rolling or glaring, he becomes a vehicle of self-created, embodied passions that he controls with a tight rein (*Orat.* 59–60) in a perpetual process of self-policing through which he enacts continual consent to the laws of propriety.

---

[13] *Fervido quodam et petulanti et furioso genere dicendi; quod quia multis gratum erat et probabatur, ascendisset ad honores, nisi in facinore manifesto deprehensus.*

[14] Ferrary, "The Statesman and the law," rightly notes the paternalistic flavor of Cicero's language in this passage (62–63).

[15] I use the phrase of Asmis, "A new kind of model," 406; she rightly emphasizes the contrast (likely due to performance context) between the tendency toward hierarchization in *de Republica* with *pro Sestio*'s opening up of consensus to "the whole people," and she argues convincingly (following Lepore, Büchner, and Heinze) that *de Republica* aims to articulate, in its discussion of the single leader (*rector, gubernator, prudens*), a type or philosophical ideal rather than a historical individual such as Pompey or even Cicero himself.

The ultimate source of the laws of propriety that will guide him, however, is not obvious. That this is a problem involving political identity as well as rhetorical technique is clarified by Cicero's work on civic ethics in his last written work, *de Officiis*. Here, the passions are more than instruments in the persuasion of the crowd: they form the basis of the connections that form the republic itself; and the virtue of *decorum* in managing the passions emerges as the foundation without which the other three virtues discussed there—wisdom, justice, and courage—are useless.

To understand the theoretical impact of Cicero's treatment of *decorum*, it is necessary to begin from a viewpoint on high, examining its place in his vision of the origins of political associations. Where, in Cicero's view, do political associations come from? From *ratio* and *oratio*, reason and speech. These, the gifts of nature, exist to enable men to come together to form towns and cities: "By the power of reason nature links together man with man for the partnership of speech and life," he says in *de Officiis*; "it instills in him a kind of *amor* for his children, and it drives him to desire that assemblies and crowds should meet, and that he should join them" (1.12; cf. *vinculum est ratio et oratio*, 1.50). The same opinion is articulated in *de Republica*: "I claim this alone, that nature has given to the human race such a great compulsion toward virtue and such a great desire to protect the common well-being, that this power conquers all the temptations of pleasure and leisure" (*Rep.* 1.1). This is a Stoic notion: as Athenaeus tells us, it was a fundamental claim of Zeno's *Republic* that love is a god who brings about friendship, freedom, concord, and nothing else (*Deipnos.* 561c).[16] In *Republic* 1, Cicero asserts that all the blandishments of pleasure and leisure have been "conquered" by the common need for virtue (*necessitas virtutis*) and the desire to defend the republic. *Amor* is what makes the citizen passionate for the state (*Rep.* 1.1).

We have seen this before: the innate love of human beings for one other, which compels them to want to live together in ordered communities rather than in caves like the Cyclops. It becomes a staple of Anglo-American and French Enlightenment thought. In the early eighteenth

---

[16] Schofield, *The Stoic Idea of the City*, 49; he points out that "it is striking, and presumably due ultimately to Zeno's influence, that *eros* is the only state of mind ordinarily conceived of as a passion or desire (*epithumia*) that is not invariably defined as such in standard Stoic lists of desires" (30 n. 17). This makes room, as I see it, for Cicero's discussion of *amor* as the foundation of human politics. Cf. *de Oratore*: "What other power than speech could have been strong enough to gather scattered humanity into one place, or to lead it out of its wild and rustic existence to this humane and civil state of culture, or, once states were established, what else could lay out laws, judgments, rights?" Cicero asks (*quae vis alia potuit aut dispersos homines unum in locum congregare, aut a fera agrestique vita ad hunc humanum cultum civilemque deducere aut iam constitutis civitatibus leges iudicia, iura describere?*, 1.33).

century, a rebellious student of Locke commented, "if any Appetite or Sense be natural, the Sense of Fellowship is the same"—and the essential sameness of minds that arises from natural sociability is expressed most sublimely in passionate language: "this was the spirit [God] allotted to Heroes, Statesmen, Poets, Orators, Musicians, and even Philosophers." The Earl of Shaftesbury saw the world as a hierarchy, from the men who gained fame from the valorous actions of the body down the ladder of language experts—from those whose passion was allied with reason and eloquence (Statesmen), past musicians, to the philosophers whose reliance on reason and denial of passion, Shaftesbury complained (though an ardent Platonist), led them to "unnatural" thoughts like those of Hobbes's.[17] Adam Smith agreed: "Man, who can subsist only in society, was fitted by nature to that situation for which he was made. All the members of human society stand in need of each others' assistance, and are likewise exposed to mutual injuries. . . . All the different members of it are bound together by the agreeable bands of love and affection, and are, as it were, thereby drawn to one common center of mutual good offices. . . . Society cannot subsist among those who are at all times ready to hurt and injure one another" (*The Theory of Moral Sentiments* 2.ii.3). Hobbes's rejection of this theory is the basic strategy of *Leviathan*, where in the state of nature the impulse toward natural sociability is not sufficiently powerful to defeat mutual suspicion and aggression among men, and where, in his most famous words, "every man is an enemy to every man," and their lives are "solitary, poor, nasty, brutish, and short" (1.13.9).

Love, to Cicero, underpins the law of propriety that in turn sustains concord. In *de Officiis*, he argues that the strongest compulsion laid on citizens to obey legally sanctioned power and authority (*imperium, potestas*) is not fear but love (*diligere*, 2.23). Suggestively, he draws an implicit contrast between the liberty sustained by obedience to authority and the tyrant's exercise of brute force—Cicero has Caesar in mind— which leads to the slow growth of hatred, the snake that eventually bites the tyrant (2.24). "Let us cast away fear, and hold tight to love" (*ut metus absit, caritas retineatur*, 24; cf. 2.29). He repeatedly refers to civic love in his letters, which, functioning as performative texts, stage the affective relations in the private sphere as a model for the public one.[18] Deliberative oratory, too, is an opportunity to perform, through speech,

---

[17] "Essay on the freedom of wit and humour," 99; "Essay on enthusiasm," 54, both included in Shaftesbury's *Characteristicks*.

[18] Similarly, the rhetorical and philosophical treatises stage the interaction between characters as a model for the ethical views aired in the conversations on the significance of dramatory *de Oratore*, see Hall, "Social evasion and aristocratic manners."

the affection that Cicero sees as literally constituting the state. Compare this passage from a postexile speech with the jumble of affections described in *de Officiis*:

> When I have been torn away from so many and different things, which I pass over because I cannot recall them without tears, can I deny that I am a human being, can I repudiate the common sensibility of nature? I would say that I offered not one praiseworthy or beneficial thing to the *res publica*, if for its sake I had lost what I lost with serenity, and I would have considered such toughness of mind, just like that of a body which does not realize that it is being burned, to be stupidity rather than virtue . . . [having suffered for the state] you would not grieve as a wise man (*sapiens*) does, like those who care for nothing, but as a man who loves (*amans*) your people and possessions as common humanity (*communis humanitas*) demands, there is glory and divine fame . . . (*Dom.* 97–98)

> But of all social bonds (*societatum*), none is more noble, none more hardy, than good men similar in mores joined by friendship (*familiaritas*) . . . But when you survey the matter with a reasoned spirit, of all social bonds, none is more serious, none more dear, than that with links each one of us with the *res publica* . . . our fatherland embraces all our loves of everything (*omnes omnium caritate patria una complexa est*). (*Off.* 1.56, 58)

Though Cicero elsewhere disavows and exiles the pleasures of sensual love (e.g., *Tusc.* 3–4), in passages like these, love generates the very existence of civilized humanity. As Crassus tells Cotta, what the young man seeking training in oratory needs is "a desire like of that of love" (*quid censes, Cotta, nisi studium, et ardorem quendam amoris?*, *de Orat.* 1.134). In the first book of *de Natura Deorum*, Cotta condemns the Epicureans for promoting utilitarianism in human relations. *Amicitia*, he reminds his interlocutors, is derived from *amor*, and a so-called friendship made for the purpose of profit is not a friendship at all but a "buying and selling of personal advantages" (*mercatura quaedam utilitatum suarum*, 1.122). Cicero's encomium of friendship in *De Amicitia* also stresses its cognate relation with *amor* and *amare* (26, 100) and links the general importance of emotion with the relations of affection (48).[19] Although it is instilled by nature, this love is not always felt to come naturally. Quoting Terence's famous line from the *Heauton Timoroumenos*, "I think that nothing concerned with humanity is not my concern," Cicero notes, "but indeed it is difficult to be concerned with others' affairs" (*Off.* 1.30). As elsewhere in the Ciceronian view of ethical formation, nature requires

---

[19] Skinner, *Catullus in Verona*, persuasively suggests that "by insisting so frankly upon the affective component of friendship, Cicero appears to acknowledge that the positive overtones of the word had suffered impairment during his lifetime" (76).

the supplementation of culture: civic affections must be cultivated and enhanced by repetitive practice. The virtue that governs affection for Cicero, the virtue in whose analysis he generates an index of those practices that reinforce communal affection and civility, is the visually oriented, performative virtue of *decorum*.

Decorum: Enactment of civic love

The discussion of *decorum* is the climax of the first book of Cicero's *Officiis*, just as it underpins the entire discussion of style in *Oratore*. It is the last of the four canonical virtues that make up *honestas*, or honorableness, as Cicero modifies them from Greek moral philosophy: wisdom, justice, courage, and *decorum*. Cicero's Latin version of the Stoic Panaetius's *to prepon*, "the fitting," or "the proper," broadens, reconfigures, and makes external and visual the internally oriented *sophrosune* or "self-restraint" of Plato and the Greek moralists.[20] *Decorum* is a special virtue. Three times in the introductory paragraphs he notes that it is inseparable from the other three virtues and indeed from *honestas* itself (1.93–95). Is his lack of certainty the result of carelessness or a failure of philosophical rigor? No: Cicero's release of strict control over the concept of *decorum* arises rather from a belief, influenced by his work on oratorical performance and political theory, that because society finds its primordial ordering principle in the human interaction of speech, the proper regulation of speech (and its attendant bodily behaviors) is the original and essential virtue of civil life.

Decorum arises directly from natural sociability. Cicero compares it to *reverentia*, the quality of respect for men, not only the elite but "the rest" (*optimi cuiusque et reliquorum, Off.* 1.99). It is the vehicle by which men express their affection and regard for one another in the practices of everyday life, and those who do not possess it are "not only arrogant, but completely depraved" (*nam neglegere, quid de se quisque sentiat, non solum arrogantis, sed etiam omnino dissoluti, Off.* 1.99). *Decorum* is what sustains those assemblies and gatherings originally ordained by nature. *Decorum* is a two-edged virtue, inspired by love but restraining love's immense force. It governs rational and somatic acts without distinction: "*decorum* ... is discerned in every deed, every word, in short, in every movement and attitude of the body" (*Off.* 1.126). Repeated similes comparing *decorum* and physical health suggest that,

---

[20] Dyck's commentary examines Cicero's choice of the word in detail (241–50), and comments helpfully on the Panaetian modification of the Platonic and Aristotelian *sophrosune*; it should be assumed that I rely on his work throughout.

conceptually speaking, it overlaps with the visible beauties of the body (1.95). At the end of his introductory remarks, Cicero stresses *decorum's* enactment in communal observation and applause: "*decorum* shines out in life (*elucet*), it arouses the applause of those we live with, by the order, consistency, and restraint of all words and deeds" (1.98). As Cicero's frequent references to theater and literary criticism suggest—ten times in roughly sixty paragraphs—*decorum* is primarily an aesthetic quality apperceived by vision and hearing.[21] The ethicocivic goals articulated at the beginning of the treatise, in Cicero's address to his son, are given material form at the end of book 1 in a performative index of acts of the body and the tongue, that is, the social practices and styles of speech, which by the observation and judgment of others mark the virtuous man. Internal self-composure, the Greek *sophrosune*, appears briefly (100–101) but is abandoned after four sentences that revive the language of display and visuality, with *elucere* again the governing verb: "*elucebit omnis constantia omnisque moderatio*" (102). And Cicero ends that section of the argument with a discussion of that quintessentially social act, telling jokes (*in ipso ioco aliquod probi ingenii lumen eluceat*, 104).

Possessing the virtue of *decorum* entails following strict rules that Cicero patterns on dramatic performance. Liberty does not mean "you do as you please" (*Part.* 34). As poets follow rules set by tradition and the audience's expectation in creating their characters—putting the proprieties of theatrical tradition on visual display—so nature gives humans their "roles" (*partes*) in life, which they must fulfill by adopting the proper modes of speaking, dressing, walking, and house decorating (1.98). Here *de Officiis* repeats and reiterates key passages in *de Oratore*, especially Crassus's discussion in book 3, on the fifth and crucial part of oratory: *actio*, delivery. As the rhetorical dialogue does, *de Officiis* 1 replaces the dual model of the self posited in Plato—a model in which, in the body (*soma*) is a tomb (*sema*) and the mind proper is master of the slave-body—with a more fluid, conversible relation between body and mind. Where justice restrains men from violating one another's bodies and property, *decorum* guards against the violation of sensibility (*Off.* 1.99). Without *decorum*—the habits of speech and manner ordered by "concord, propriety, moderation . . . beauty, loveliness, harmony" (*Off.* 1.14)—the acts of rational communication necessary for the survival of the *res publica* cannot occur, which means that constitutions and laws cannot be invented in the first place. To reverse the point, what makes each one of us human is the possession of a rational sensorium governed by a dual law: *decorum* in speech and behavior, which itself is

---

[21] Similes: "Just as grace and physical beauty cannot be separated from health, so with this which we are discussing, *decorum* is completely blended with *virtus*."

underwritten by the natural law of civil sentiment. *Decorum* governs oratorical performance, of course—this remains Cicero's special interest, derived from his belief that the polity originates in public speech—but also the most trivial social acts, from laughing to striding along the street, from wrapping one's toga to giving gifts: in all these things, "nature is our special teacher and guide" (*praesertim natura ipsa magistra et duce, Off.* 1.129, cf. 100, 146). "Nature is so constructed that the things possessing most utility also have the greatest amount of dignity and, indeed, of charm too."[22]

Where do the laws of *decorum* come from? Nowhere in *de Oratore* or in *de Officiis* does Cicero derive them from atemporal, immutable standards.[23] Performed *decorum* rather neatly harmonizes with *natura* in such a way "that it manifests itself in the attitude of a free man" (*cum specie quadam liberali, Off.* 1.96, cf. 104). As a category rooted in nature, *decorum* essentializes class status, making the rules adhered to by elite male Romans the most perfectly mimetic of natural law. Cicero does not deny that these rules are contingent on the social *mores* of any given time or event; on the contrary, he reminds the reader of the real circumstances under which the rules of *decorum* alter over time: styles of oratory, conversation, and wit (133, cf. 144). If the virtue of *decorum* appears at any given point in time to derive from mutable and unstable social conventions (say, in the performance of civil manners), and the rules of social convention change over time, how can Cicero meaningfully claim that it is derived from nature? *Decorum* finds its essential roots in human sociability, which is implanted by and subject to the law of nature. The rules constraining bodily behavior—modesty, for example—are natural per se. "Nature seems to have conceived a great system for our bodies . . . their honorable parts it has placed in front, while the ugly and base parts it has covered up and hidden away" (1.126). This is not a new idea, of course: in Xenophon's *Memorabilia*, Socrates points out that our mouths, which we use to eat, are conveniently situated near the eyes and nose, whose senses contribute to our enjoyment of a good meal, while unpleasant excreta exit the body through a duct turned away from our organs of perception and placed as far as reasonably possible from the nose. The mechanics of defecation provide evidence of the gods' beneficent and intelligent craftsmanship (I.iv.7).[24] But there is a deeper and more

---

[22] *[N]atura est ipsa fabricata . . . ut ea quam maximam utilitatem in se continerent eadem haberent plurimum vel dignitatis vel saepe etiam venustatis* (*de Orat.* 3.178).

[23] "The notion that the laws of Cicero drew their legitimacy from the fact that they were based on, or were a reflection of, a natural moral law" is persuasively rejected by Ferrary, "The statesman and the law," 68 (and see 68–73).

[24] I owe this reference to Daniel McLean.

complex justification at work. Like Michel Foucault, Cicero tends to use the passive voice to describe the self-policing of ethical formation: "Two things must be avoided, that there be nothing effeminate or soft on the one hand, nor anything coarse and crude on the other"; "Guard must be kept, lest we employ a dawdling sashay in our gait," and so forth (*Off.* 1.121, 130). The force behind these passives is what, along with reason, Cicero says separates men from beasts: an aesthetic sensibility bestowed by nature that allows men to perceive the beautiful, the ordered, and the tasteful (1.126, cf. 146). This capacity is the sine qua non of human civility, whether one is making laws or making conversation. And both these acts, it turns out, are also instilled by nature.

To argue that *decorum* is a carefully calibrated expression of natural sociability does not perfectly solve the problem of its different incarnations in time and space: certainly Cicero believes that Roman *mores* are superior—more in line with natural law, in fact—than those of, say, the Greeks. The preface to *de Republica* comes face to face with this paradoxical state of affairs. "Where does the *ius gentium* come from, and civil law, justice, fidelity, fairness, modesty, self-restraint, hatred of vice, love of glory, honor, and bravery in the face of hard work and danger?" They arise from men of the distant Roman past, "men who established these things (*haec*) by custom and enforced them by law, once they had been instilled by training" (*de Rep.* 1.2). *Informata* is a mysterious passive: who or what does the *disciplina*, precisely, is not clear. Cicero deepens the mystery with his allusion to a remark by the Academic Xenocrates, who was once asked, as Socrates asked Gorgias, "what exactly do your students (*discipuli*) learn?" He answered, "to do spontaneously (*sua sponte*) that which they are compelled to do by law" (1.2). Virtue is now revealed in its ideal form as a law always already inscribed in the self. Or as we can now say more precisely, having uncovered the role of sentiment in Cicero's conception of *decorum*, virtue emerges as what Rousseau would call a law of the heart.

The question "where does virtue come from?" raises serious questions about the nature of moral agency in Ciceronian virtue theory; it seems to up a paradoxical model of active self-cultivation and passive naturalization. In *de Republica*, Cicero heals the breach with the vision of a self who discovers the civil law, virtue, and duty through a process of training whose ultimate origins remain unexplained. In *de Officiis* 1, the virtuous self is at once a product of nature and of culture, a bundle of spontaneous impulses that are already scripted from a social code that itself is conceived as the expression of natural law. This is not only a fantasy of a self-governing self but also a fantasy of self-government ruled by sentiment, itself subject to the ineffable authority of nature. In other words, one loves one's fellow citizens with and through natural law, and it not only exists as, but is sensed to be, an internalized part of the soul, a *regula vitae*.[25] To conceive of natural sentiment as the basis and source of social practice compels the temporal and cultural contingencies of *decorum* to assume the force of essence.

In the epigraph to this chapter, drawn from his *Social Contract*, Jean-Jacques Rousseau observes that the most important form of law is that "which is not graven on tablets of marble or brass, but on the hearts of the citizens. This forms the real constitution of the State, and it takes on every day new powers," he says; "it keeps a people in the ways it was meant to go, and insensibly replaces authority by the force of habit." As Terry Eagleton observes, Rousseau presents a law "at one with the body's spontaneous impulses, entwined with sensibility and its affections, lived out in unreflective custom."[26] We can see that Cicero's solution is one to which republican theorists return again and again. It is nonetheless a paradoxical solution. On the one hand, natural sentiment promises the freedom of an autonomous choice, but sentiment's grounding in natural law simultaneously implies the suppression of choice.[27] We might think in this context about Cicero's high praise of carefully cultivated friendships between virtuous men, not only in *de Officiis* but also in the treatise *de Amicitia*, written at roughly the same time. If we are shaped by nature to fulfill certain roles, what independent part does our own desire play in forging emotional bonds? In a famous passage near the end of *The Theory of Moral Sentiments*, Adam Smith declares that "human society, when we contemplate it in a certain abstract and philosophical light, appears like a great, an immense machine, whose regular and harmonious movements produce a thousand agreeable effects" (Part 7.iii.1). Smith's vision develops to its logical conclusion the antisubjective, even antihumanist automaticity of Cicero's self, which eerily feels sentiments that in a sense are not originally its own. There is a touch of the oppressive in Cicero's representation of natural sociability, and indeed of friendships between men.[28]

As in *de Officiis*, the affective bonds of friends in *de Amicitia* are both independently willed and the subject of a natural law that directs virtuous men to associate with one another, which is to say that it is somehow alienated from the self. Virtue creates and preserves friendship, and friendship but it is something we must search for throughout our lives. Yet we do not really discover it; it finds us (*Amic.* 100).

---

[25] "The duties that emerge from sociability," Cicero says, "conform more to nature than those that emerge from learning" (*placet igitur aptiora esse naturae ea officia quae ex communitate quam ea quae ex cognitione ducantur, Off.* 1.153).

[26] Eagleton, *Ideology of the Aesthetic*, 19, 20.

[27] Dolar, "At first sight," 131–32.

[28] Smith includes a discussion of how to escape from friendship that is drawn from Cato's dictum to let problematic friendships "be unraveled, rather than torn apart" (76).

Help in understanding Cicero's representation of automatic love may be found in the work of the Lacanian theorist Mladen Dolar, who suggests that love can best be formulated as a paradox: "the junction of a contingent exterior with the most intimate interior."[29] By his reading, we might see love as a three-step process of subjectivation: first, the instant or gradual conversion of the contingent exterior of the beloved into an object of the lover's or friend's inner desire; second, a purely formal change where the beloved remains the same but the lover's or friend's position as a desiring self reconfigures itself around the idea of the beloved; and finally, the point of no return, at which love is no longer a matter of choice but inevitability, what Roland Barthes calls the "tautology" of love, when "the adorable is what is adorable."[30] The pure chance of love at first sight—whether the friendship of truly virtuous men described in de Amicitia or the erotic love of Catullus 51 (ille mi par esse deo uidetur)—is transformed into an inexorable, automatic experience from which the lover cannot escape—a kind of machine that, once in operation, is impossible to bring to a stop. As Catullus notes in poem 72, "great injury forces a lover to love more, but to want to love less" (7–8). Hence Cicero's overdetermined insistence on the authenticity of feeling. In his praise of visible sentiment, the civic sphere emerges as a libidinal order where, we might say, feeling makes it real. In fact, the civic order of the real cannot exist apart from feeling. "A humane and polished people, who have more sensibility to the passions of others," Adam Smith remarks in Theory of Moral Sentiments, "can more readily enter into an animated and passionate behavior, and can more easily pardon some little excess. Cicero, in the times of the highest Roman politeness, could, without degrading himself, weep with all the bitterness of sorrow in the sight of the whole senate and the whole people; as it is evidence he must have done in the whole of every oration" (Part 5.ii).

Here Catullus helps us read Cicero with a more critical eye. For where Cicero is eager to suture together the fissures in his virtuous man, fissures created by paradoxes of nature and culture, honesty that is inscribed on the heart and the space between the heart and the act, temporal contingency and cosmic immutability, Catullus is preoccupied with fissures and gaps. His poems about the inescapable automation of passion, the misery that results from the breakdown of a friendship or love affair that felt authentic and natural, emerges from the same cultural frame as Cicero's ethical and rhetorical writing. He is not an apolitical poet, an author whose interest in sentiment disbars him from engaging with the political discourse of his time. On the contrary, Catullus's preoccupation with sentiment places him at the center of republican concerns.

---

[29] Dolar, "At first sight," 129.
[30] Barthes, "Adorable!" A Lover's Discourse, 21.

To put Catullus in perspective, we may recall Cicero's habit of relating his literary education to his public *persona*.[31] In his speech *Pro Archia*, delivered the year after he was consul, Cicero claims that Archias "supplies me with the means by which my spirit (*animus*) is restored (*reficiatur*, a word whose other meaning, interestingly, is "reelected" or "restored to office") from the uproar of the lawcourt, and by which my ears, exhausted by noise, relax" (12). Archias's work cultivates and broadens the soul (*animos nostros doctrina excolamus, relaxemus*). Far from seducing Cicero away from legal and governmental affairs, poems are instrumental in fulfilling them: "From these studies my oratory grows," he says:

> that faculty which, as far as my abilities go, has never deserted my friends in times of danger. Though it seems rather frivolous (*levior*) to some, I know from what source I draw the things that are the most important of all. For if it had not been for the precepts of many men and many works of literature, I would never have persuaded myself that nothing was worth seeking in life except fame and honor, and that in pursuing those things every bodily agony, every risk of death and exile must be counted as nothing. (13–14)[32]

Within a few paragraphs his argument broadens to embrace the emotional pathos in poetry and theater that affects virtuous men (*instituti optimis rebus non poetarum voce moveamur?* 19). This anticipates Adam Smith's claim in his *Theory of Moral Sentiments* that imagination fired by direct observation, literature, or theater is the quality peculiar to humans that is the source of our moral virtue. "This is the source of our fellow-feeling for the misery of others," he writes, "it is by changing places in fancy with the sufferer, we come either to conceive or to be affected by what he feels. . . . Neither is it those circumstances only, which create pain or sorrow, that call forth our fellow-feeling" (1.1).[33]

CATULLUS'S REPUBLICAN RHETORIC

A number of scholars have considered Catullus in his historical context—David Ross, T. P. Wiseman, Amy Richlin, William Fitzgerald, David Wray, Brian Krostenko, Marilyn Skinner, and Daniel Selden, to

---

[31] G. B. Conte argues that intertextuality is "the very condition of literary legibility" in *Genres and Readers*, 137.

[32] He continues, "nor would I have thrown myself into so many great struggles and daily battles with desperate men . . . [The images of great men represented in literature] I always hold up before myself as I help govern the republic, and by meditating on great men I shape my mind and soul."

[33] Smith's term "sentiment" needs to be distinguished from sentimentality: to Smith, human sentiments have a cognitive aspect and are subject to contemplation and modification.

name a few—and I owe a debt to Fitzgerald and Selden, in particular, for their provocative discussions of aristocratic language in Catullus's drama of textual self-fashioning.[34] The standard approach has been to treat Catullus as a countercultural voice speaking out against Roman political conventions as well as the hoary old social and sexual values of the *seueriores* in poem 5 (5.2) or the *stulti* in poem 68 (68.137). So Paul Allen Miller presents a common view when he writes that Catullus "had to perform a feat of linguistic and ideological engineering unprecedented in the history of Western poetry," the creation of "a radically new subjective and lyric space within a preexisting ideological environment fundamentally hostile to his intent."[35] Involved in what Miller calls the "radical" redefinition of the traditional values of Catullus' equestrian class is the total repudiation of legal and governmental responsibilities, the rejection of Roman civic life.[36]

Catullus's Renaissance editor Pierio Valeriano approached the matter rather differently.

> Since Catullus expresses the emotions of love, since in his lamentation for his brother he concedes to nature the magnitude of his grief and does his duty to piety, since he recognizes the gods whose rites he sings, since he celebrates men worthy of praise, since he sets a limit to pleasure, since, emerging from the whirling depths of the passions, he pulls himself together at times and prudently embraces fortitude, justice, and temperance . . .[37]

So, Valeriano declares, Catullus's poetry falls under the rubric of moral philosophy and is therefore directly relevant to the education of young men in the kingdoms and small republics of early modern Italy. As Hume would say three centuries later, theories of abstract philosophy prevail and are exploded in turn, but expressions of passion "maintain a universal, undisputed empire over the minds of men."[38] So for Valeriano, Catullan passion and its readerly allure make him the ideal teacher of republican citizens.

It is his view that I am developing here. Did Catullus consciously write "to teach as well as to delight," *prodesse et delectare*, as the orators were supposed to do?[39] I am not primarily concerned with the poet's authorial intention or the interpretations adopted by his Roman audience in the

---

[34] Selden, "Ceveat lector," esp. 496–97.

[35] Miller, *Lyric Texts and Lyric Consciousness*, 130.

[36] Ibid., 135, 133.

[37] Text and translation (slightly adapted) from Julia Haig Gaisser, *Catullus and His Renaissance Readers*, 117.

[38] Hume, "Of the standard of taste," 220.

[39] Selden powerfully argues that Catullus's text is concerned to show the mutual incompatibility of teaching, moving, and delighting in "Ceveat lector," 479–89.

mid-first century BCE; what I want to unpack are the conditions of poetic legibility, the ideological circumstances under which Catullus's text could make sense to its readers, the patterns that express, in Jameson's words, "ideological dilemmas that are ultimately rooted in social and political structures" of Roman society itself.[40] Being moved is precisely the story told by many of Catullus's poems, and *carmen* 68 in particular. This elegy is the longest expression of Catullan sentiment in all its variety, from the close male friendship that frames the poem to its inset tales of heterosexual erotic passion and brotherly love. At the heart of 68, echoing a pattern in the corpus as a whole, lies a self who discovers in sentimental experience the polar absolutes of death and life. I will focus on the rules that structure his experience—the double law of aesthetics and sentiment that shapes his authorial "I".

Poem 68 notoriously falls into two or three distinct parts. The first forty lines respond to a plea from a friend named Manius or Mallius, claiming that Catullus cannot write poetry because of his grief for his own dead brother. The next hundred lines reverse the opening *recusatio* by offering an inset poem anyway, addressed to a man named Allius who may or may not be the initial addressee. The final five or six couplets, though textual problems abound, appear to return to the scene of the introduction.

The first couplet sets out the central theme:

> *Quod mihi fortuna casuque oppressus acerbo*
> *conscriptum hoc lacrimis mittis epistolium.* . . .

> As for the fact that to me in my bitterness, you, taxed by fortune
>   and chance,
> send a little note written with tears. . . .

The opening salutation is thus a greeting that is also a response. Mallius has sent Catullus a little note written with tears, a text that appropriates a subject position, the miserable lover, from Catullus's own work and anticipates words and images from Catullus's following inset poem (incessant tears, 55–6; shipwreck, 63). From the start, the two men's friendship is embedded in their literary relationship, and more specifically in their writerly style. Mallius's text is more than a demonstration of shared literary values, however; it is a textual dunning, a calling in of accounts. Mallius calls on Catullus to take his turn in the obligatory exchange of amicable duties that the poet calls *officium* (12; repeated in the inset text, 42), and in doing so he casts *amicitia* explicitly as a social economy governed by a law, a law that has to do with sentiment, to be sure, but that is a law all the same.

---

[40] Jameson, *The Political Unconscious*, 81.

There is a long pause between *quod* (the fact of the sending) and *epistolium* (the note itself): Mallius's original text is the opening and closing referent in the first couplet. What occupies Catullus in the space between those two words is the texture of his relationship with Mallius: he emphasizes the way in which the note has successfully conveyed Mallius's misery not only in its content, which has presented an author *oppressus fortuna casuque*, but in the materiality of its ink, *conscriptum lacrimis*. The following lines build on the connection between writing and a particular sentiment, the healing comfort that Mallius seeks from Catullus's poems. The contemporaneity of the scene, solidly established with a reference to the *ueteres scriptores* of the past whose work fails to console the mourner (7), is enhanced by the textual intertwining of references to Catullus and his friend: "*id gratum est mihi, me quoniam tibi dicis amicum*" and further reminders of their exchanges in the past, present and future, *munera et Musarum et Veneris* (10). Some readers have argued that the line refers literally to Catullus's dual function as Mallius's poet and his pimp, but even if we avoid that interpretation it is clear that the lines blur literary appreciation with physical experience, line with limb, text and life.[41] The poem's beginning underlines that the strong aesthetic bond—the context of Mallius's call for a poetic lifeline—is activated through sentiment, which is itself embedded in the lived system of *amicitia*. Oppressed by evil fortune (1), Mallius resembles a shipwrecked sailor close to death on foamy waves (3–4). His bodily functions are interrupted (*somno*, 5) and his tormented mind cannot enjoy his usual comforts (*anxia*, 8). The aid he requires comes in the shape of a modern text, one whose shared temporal location and aesthetic values can supplement Mallius's self-insufficiency.[42] More than aesthetic salve, the poem requested from Catullus's appears to promise support (*subleuem*, 4) and restoration (*restituam*, 4) of a more serious kind. But Catullus's response at lines 15ff. implies that Mallius expects a poem that recalls their happy youth, their love and games (*iucundum cum aetas florida uer ageret, multa satis lusi; non est dea nescia nostri*, 16–7). That is, Mallius joins Cornelius Nepos, the addressee of poem 1, in thinking Catullus's *nugae* worth something (*aliquid*, 1.4) more than its subject may at first suggest.

---

[41] Prescott, "The unity of Catullus lxviii" (499), reviews the case and claims ambiguity. Hubbard persuasively argues that the impact "is precisely our hesitation between the literal and the figural. . . The text substitutes for experience on both sides of the literary phenomenon" in "Catullus 68: The text as self-demystification" (40).

[42] Compare the effect of Archias's poetry, which restores Cicero after a trying day in the law courts.

The picture of a critical readership is important. In his fine study of Cicero and Catullus, Brian Krostenko has shown that aesthetic terms like *bellus, elegans, lepidus*, and *venustus* are the signal markers of aristocratic Roman social codes, whether they appear in Cicero's *Philippics* or in Catullus's epigrams. Poem 1 programmatically inaugurates the practical cycle of reading and writing, giving and receiving to which the poet will refer again and again throughout his corpus. "To whom shall I give this new booklet, buffed just now with the dry pumice? To you, Cornelius." Why does Nepos get the book? What are the membership criteria in the Catullan circle? In poem 1 and in many others, the solidarity of Catullus's implicitly exclusive social group rests in the members' possession of the common aesthetic standards described by these words. So Nepos is not only the "only Italian to have explained every age of history in learned and carefully composed books" (5–7), he is the one who appreciates Catullus's *lepidae nugae* for what they are.

The nexus of poetic style, social decorum, and emotion is set up as a major Catullan theme from the very start of the polymetrics. Poem 1 enacts the spare Callimachean aesthetic of self-conscious thinness even in its personal dedication: its understated style both sets the tone of the book and jokes about its stylistic distance from the conventions of poetic composition. But if Catullus presents the relationship between himself and his addressee as a matter of bare judgment—"you used to think my oddments were something" (*solebas . . . esse aliquid putare*, 3–4)—the poem itself colors the Catullus-Nepos connection with sentiment in an comic or pathetic mode. The series of q's in *quare-quidquid-qualecumque-quod*—again, whether we treat them as jokey or querulous—display an author seeking acknowledgment from a reader, and manipulating his emotional reaction to achieve it. Aesthetic assessment stands revealed as implicated in a relation of sentiment: Nepos's feel for Catullus's poetry is related to his feeling for the poet himself.

Krostenko analyzes what he calls the "language of social performance" with great sensitivity. What I wish to add to his account is analysis of the crucial role of passion, which activates the pull of community and makes its connections crackle with dynamic tension, offering the prospect of betrayal as well as the assertion of eternal faith. Catullus binds the knowledge of the social codes implied in words like *uenustus* and *lepidus* with a certain emotional sensibility, a sentiment that is also a code of behavior and belief. To refuse Mallius's request in poem 68 is to break the law of their literary and social community, as Catullus recognizes with those anxious words *amicum, officium*, and *dona* (9, 12, 14), but it is also to offend Mallius as a self, to break the law of sentiment that governs their friendship. The world in which Catullus and

Cornelius move is tightly structured and kept in line by laws of taste that are also rules of emotion.[43] The way people look, the way they talk and dress, what they read and what they believe, is one of the poet's most obvious concerns. What emerges in the polymetrics and the elegiacs is no less than a *pathaesthetics* in which three aspects of life are interlocked: literary preference, personal manners, and sentimental experience. Laws of social and literary decorum intersect and overlap with emotional sensation. To gain membership in the Catullan community is not just a matter of following rules and behavior; it is a matter of feeling, and further, of feeling the same emotions. Catullan poetics binds together, we might say, notional education in literary taste with a sentimental education. The men of Catullus's circle gain membership in it because they meet a double standard of law, one part based in *decorum*, one part based other in passion.

The first poem in Catullus's corpus devoted to representing the first person Ego's love begins, famously, "Let us live, and let us love" (5.1). The poem has a teasing tone, produced by its repetitive call for kisses (*da mi basia mille, deinde centum, dein mille altera, dein secunda centum*, etc., 7–8), but its main theme is the spectacularity of love. Catullus for the first time "reveals" his lover's name, Lesbia; and he invites her into the open, so to speak, where they will disdain "the rumors of the too severe old men" (2). We recall that it is the moment of unimpeded observation of his beloved in the Sapphic poem 51 that Catullus uses as the frame for his description of the many physical effects of love. In poem 5, eternal night will come all too soon, when the lovers will be invisible to everyone's sight, including their own (6). But their daytime revelation must not be too complete; the kisses must be jumbled up to ward off the evil eye (12; cf. *poem 7*). One can, it seems, reveal too much. And this reminds us that the "revelation" of a name that is really a pseudonym is a joke on the reader. We cannot immediately see or know the nature of Catullus's passion.

But in fact, "observing" the actions, and from that inferring the nature of others, turns out to be the common theme of a large number of Catullus's poems about relations of the heart. From the polymetrics to the elegiacs, what attracts Catullus to his loves and likes is their common ability to perform in accordance with his particular standards of *decorum*—a rule he sets by fusing programmatic Callimachean language with the social language of Roman manners. In poem 86,

---

[43] In poem 12, Marrucinus Asinius is attacked for napkin stealing. Egnatius drinks urine, to the horror of all, in 37, and Quintia is revealed as a figure of ersatz *venustas* in 86. The list goes on.

Lesbia's allure is a process in action, a performance of charm and wit that meets or even surpasses Catullus's own:

> Quintia is beautiful, in the vulgar sense. To me she is fair, tall,
> she stands up straight: these details, yes, I allow,
> but "beautiful"? I deny it. For there is no charm,
> not a single speck of salt in that grand figure.
> Lesbia is beautiful, who is not only the most fair,
> but she steals all the gifts of Venus from everyone else.

> *Quintia formosa est multis. mihi candida, longa,*
> *recta est: haec ego sic singula confiteor,*
> *totum illud formosa nego. nam nulla uenustas,*
> *nulla in tam magno est corpore mica salis.*
> *Lesbia formosa est, quae cum pulcherrima tota est,*
> *tum omnibus una omnes surripuit Veneres.*

Contrast the lover of Flavius in poem 6, a text that develops the theme of erotic revelation introduced in poem 5:

> Flavius, your loves,
> unless they were dim-witted and inelegant,
> you would want to tell to Catullus, nor could you hold back.

> *Flavi, delicias tuas Catullo,*
> *ni sint illepidae atque inelegantes,*
> *uelles dicere nec tacere posses.*

Here the tables are turned, and Flavius, saddled with an apparently *illepida* and *inelegans* lover who does not meet Catullus's exacting standards of taste, refuses to discuss her. That is, he refuses to participate in the proper performative exchange of talk that is the bedrock of Catullus's relationship with his friends and lovers.[44] Poems 5, 6, and 86 are models of what Krostenko calls Catullus's "language of social performance." This is the index of social practices and literary tastes marked by programmatic words such as *uenustas*, *lepos*, *bellus*, and *elegans*, which signify the solidarity of Catullus's elite circle, comprising himself and "like-minded persons."[45]

Catullus's vivid description of Lesbia's charms, and his demands to see visible evidence of the charms of his friends' lovers, is matched only by his preoccupation with the visible signs of his friends' membership in his

---

[44] Contrast the way poem 1 treats the dedication to Nepos as a literary and sentimental exchange.

[45] Krostenko, *Cicero, Catullus, and the Language of Social Performance*, 244.

circle (e.g., *tuo lepore incensus, Licini*, 50.7–8). This is the keystone of
the Catullan poetics of exclusivity, which marks out some addressees and
readers as members of the circle and others just as emphatically not.
Failure to meet these standards of performance is an invitation to invective,
as in poem 10:

> My dear Varus led me out to his love,
> having caught sight of me lazing in the forum,
> a little tart, or so she struck me at first sight,
> not entirely unappealing, nor uncharming . . .
> "But you are entirely lacking in taste! you go through life
>   offending others,
> a woman who does not allow a man a moment's slip."

> *Varus me meus ad suos amores*
> *uisum duxerat e foro otiosum*
> *scortillum, ut mihi tum repente uisum est,*
> *non sane illepidum neque inuenustum . . .*
> *"sed tu insulsa male et molesta uiuis,*
> *per quam non licet esse neglegentem."*

Here, caught out in a false boast by Varus's girlfriend, Catullus turns
on her, casting her rudeness not only as a sign of low taste also but also
as the mark of an actively offensive stain on the city: she is worse than a
cinaedus (24). As Lesbia's active revelation of charismatic wit draws
Catullus inexorably to her, so this woman actively repulses him. (We
recall that when their love affair turns sour, Lesbia makes herself a spectacle of impropriety comparable to Varus's girlfriend and others attacked
in the corpus for being *insulsa* or *ineptus* by indulging her lust in public
places, inns, and streetcorners (11, 75); Catullus, by contrast, withdraws
from sight, a fallen flower (11), a sight for the gods alone (76.19).)

Let me take stock of the sensibility of manners and taste that Catullus's
friends and his objects of erotic desire are imagined to share. The language
of *decorum* is not a social end in and of itself, a matter of securing a place
in a literary elite; it is the performative means to a subjective end. In other
words, for Catullus, it is never solely a matter of looking the right way, but
of looking *and loving* the right way. The spectacular dynamics of his
passions and friendships are represented as cutting below the surface of the
performance to the subjective sensibilities connecting performer and audience: more than dots and dashes signaling neoteric belonging, they pro-
claim the possession of shared erotic, poetic, and social sentiments. Take
poem 12, an invective against a man who steals napkins at fancy dinner
parties: the theft is not simply a matter of potential legal action or even a
trampling of strictly social rules; it is a transgression of the *style* of a
circle—a sensibility that is all-important precisely because it is bound only

by independent affections. The napkin is worth nothing in cash terms; its value is only sentimental. But in Catullus's representation, what matters is what the napkin represents, the ties of affection that bind its members.

So with all the specific gestures of their exclusivist social performances: the performances are expressions of a deeper subjective order. Every reader early learns to notice how Catullus's addressees form a closed circle, and this is indeed a central aspect of Catullan poetics: the construction of a cultural collectivity that is maintained through acts of exchange, some willing, some not: reading and writing, invitations and acceptances, rivalries in love. From Cornelius to the unnamed woman who spurns Catullus in the closing poem of the polymetrics (*supplicis*, 60.4) to the Gellius described in the whole collection's final poem, who also spurns Catullus and will pay for it (*supplicium*, 116.8), these relationships are structured in a dual law that is the central theme of a majority of poems: a law of *decorum* that spans literary taste and social practice, and a law of sentiment generated by the emotional relationship that connects Catullus to his community. We recall Dolar's description of falling in love: the contingent exterior—or in this case, the contingent social practices of manners—is internalized, worshipped; it becomes impossible to live without: a *regula vitae*.

In poem 68, however, it is Catullus who fails, Catullus who is *insulsus*. As he recognizes with those anxious words *amicum, officium*, and *dona* (9, 12, 14), to refuse Mallius's request in poem 68 is to break the law of their literary and social community, but it is also to offend Mallius as a self, to break the law of sentiment that governs their friendship. Grief for his dead brother has overwhelmed the poet, and with the loss of control over his emotional *decorum* Catullus loses the ability to write poetry. To beg forgiveness, Catullus offers a brief sentimental autobiography that moves from his first taste of love and heartbreak (15–18) to the sudden onslaught of grief that put all other feelings to flight (*cuius ego interitu tota de mente fugaui/haec studia*, 25–6). As his brother's death fractures Catullus' sentimental experience, it also affects his social and literary habits; he underlines his new aloofness from Mallius's small erotic jokes (28–30) and his own lack of books (33–6). But the laws of friendship and aesthetics that link the two men draw Catullus back to Mallius's request, and with the prosaic phrase *quod cum ita sint* he offers to speak: "This being the case, I would not wish you to think that I do this from a brutish disposition, or an insufficiently delicate sensibility" And after one final protest, the "real" poem begins. But of course it is not a "real" poem. Every one of the opening forty lines marks the inset poem as a text born of compulsion, what Catullus forces himself to write: not the product of the putatively natural inspiration born of passionate friendship that drives Catullus from his bed in poem 50 (*hoc, iucunde, tibi poema feci*, 16) or the love poems, but a kind of automatic, mechanically produced text that seems doomed to fail in its stated goal. And so it does, as the ostensible motivation for poetry composition—Mallius's loss and trauma—becomes totally subordinated to the poet's own preoccupation with loss.

We have already seen that Mallius himself figures poetry as the site of failure. In the *ueteres scriptores'* inability to comfort him lies the possibility that Catullus too will fall short. The inset text speaks now to a slightly different addressee, Allius instead of Mallius, which suggests that this poem is not the real thing but a ghost or phantasm of the poem he would, under different circumstances, send to his friend. This embedded poem retains traces of the earlier *recusatio*, as Catullus uses *litotes* to invoke the social obligation that has driven him to write: "I am unable to keep silent, goddess, about the way Allius has aided me, with how many services (*officia*) he has aided me" (41–42)—and then, after describing the weight of his debt, he turns immediately to the ephemerality of his payment, suggesting that the passage of time may destroy the poem (43–44). Here shared sentiment, and the rule of exchange it invokes, produces only artificial comfort. The frightening specters of old age, black night, and death—warded off by confidence in other texts concerned with poetic immortality—are supported here by the lack of consolation provided by the old poetry that has survived, and by Catullus's own yielding to grief a few lines earlier.[46] He has promised Mallius in the strongest of terms that he cannot write—he has neither the will nor the material with which to do so. While that promise recognizes the high standard Mallius has set for the Catullan text, it amounts to a denial of textual authenticity for what will come. What Catullus will write is not his own voice, but merely the socially derivative product of Mallius's demand and Catullus's sense of obligation (*ultro ego deferrem, copia siqua foret*, 40). What Mallius receives is a poem of impossibility at best, of falsity at worst. In fact, both alternatives are realized by the inset poem, which represents a series of emotional connections that turn out to be false or flawed.

In a famous study of Thomas More that helped inaugurate the New Historicism, Stephen Greenblatt laid bare the competing tensions of public and private, court, church, and council in and through which More produced his writings. More used irony to mystify the presentation of identity, especially his own enigmatic textual ego, Greenblatt argued, precisely because the legitimacy of identity presented a central social and political problem in the Tudor court.[47] More's textual "I"—in a double inscription of cultural forces and authorial response—reveals the pressure points and weak spots in the social "I" that produced it. As Ellen Oliensis has written of Horace, if his subjection to the old witch Canidia perverts the proper

---

[46] Hubbard, "Catullus 68," suggestively observes that "there is a silence in his voice . . . assertion and plenitude are inextricably linked with negation and void" (33).

[47] Greenblatt, *Renaissance Self-Fashioning*, 11–20.

order of things, his subordination to Maecenas is an instance of the kind of coupling that holds Roman society together; but "the opposition between Maecenas and Canidia is tempered by a certain resemblance."[48]

Recent work on imperial Roman literature has explored in some depth how autocracy transformed the conditions of cultural production at large. We can see, for instance, how the impact of imperial benefaction led poets like Juvenal or Statius to conceive poetry writing as a competitive, consumer-driven economy. Readers from Ronald Syme to Shadi Bartsch have shown how worries about the real power of the senate under autocracy helped create a widespread authorial preoccupation with the theme of pretense, appearance, and spectacle. Can we read Catullus—or any second- or first-century Roman poet, for that matter—as a republican poet in the same way that we are accustomed to reading Ovid as Augustan and Valerius Flaccus as Flavian? My answer here is yes, and further, that *precisely* what we are used to calling an "imperial" concern with spectacularity, with emotion and its staging, is in fact a central element of Catullan poetics. It is usual to suppose that the play of identity is one that occurs only on the dramatic stage or the poetic performance, and to cast the self-conscious self-styling of the literary writer in opposition to Cicero's world, the world of politics (or Realpolitik). The complex staging of the self visible in Catullus's poetry, in its embrace of erotic passion, its obsession with double language, and its studied critique of the political scene, seems to reject the ethics and ideology of the forum in favor of the private world of *otium*: "I care nothing for you, Caesar." I have argued that no simple opposition exists between the fashionings of the self in Roman poetry and in Roman politics. Just as Catullus's poetry exposes the inauthenticity or potential instability of the performed self in social practice, despite the compulsion of the natural law of the heart, so Cicero's rhetorical and political writings try and fail to paper over the infringements on elite freedom "freely to run political affairs" (*Fam.* 1.8.3) through his preoccupation with the laws of social performance.

ORATORY AND LIBERTY, *DECORUM* AND CONSENT

To practice rhetoric at Rome is to train habits of speech and bodily movement according to the standards by which elite masculine dignity and authority are measured, to imitate the statues that adorned the Forum and other public spaces in the city. The Roman orator is not a ponderous character, however, heavy with the consciousness of his high responsibilities and status. On the contrary, he should be encouraged to

[48] Oliensis, "Canidia, Canicula," 135.

possess that ineffable quality that Catullus and Cicero describe with words like *lepos* or *suavitas*, Baldesar Castiglione *sprezzatura*, and the third earl of Shaftesbury "wit." This, Caesar Strabo says in his long discussion of humor in book 2 of *de Oratore*, is one of the many aspects of oratorical performance that are impossible to teach (2.215ff.).[49] Above all, it requires certain "liberties" of mind and character, since it rests on the orator's willingness to speak freely before the civic community and thus to risk offending the target of his joke. Strabo takes particular delight in the following exchange between Servius Galba, who keeps trying to influence law court tribunals by filling them with his friends, and Lucius Scribonius, a tribune with a reputation for philandering. When, Scribonius asks, will Galba leave his own dining room when he seeks candidates for the court? "As soon as you leave other people's bedrooms," Galba replies, amid general laughter (*de Orat.* 2.263). But for Cicero there is a deeper significance to the orator's wit. Not only is it proof of his years of immersion in the "liberal arts," the learning suitable for a free man (*eruditio libero digna*, *de Orat.* 1.17), but in an almost ontological sense, his agility of mind and the graceful gestures that express it are heralds of his civic liberty, his citizenship in a free state.[50]

Teachers of the art of jokes face what comedians call a tough crowd: they succeed only in arousing laughter at their own expense (*de Orat.* 2.217). This is true not only because the sources of laughter are dimly understood and resistant to analysis, but because wit rests on the appearance of effortlessness. Jokes planned ahead of time, that sound labored or contrived, fall flat. This is a perfect illustration of the paradoxical role of oratorical training: evidence of its influence undoes its effects. The goal of the orator's polished effortlessness is to hide his labors. The same applies to rhythmical effect: "the orator's effort to please, and the industry he put into polishing his speech, will scarcely be noticed" is the ideal outcome, but possible only if he takes enough care to conceal his arts (*Orat.* 197). Through the voice of the joke-teller Caesar Strabo, Cicero suggests that among the many reasons driving the concealment and mystification of rhetorical labor is the imperative of seeming free. Rhetoric "alone has always flourished among every free people," he says, "always dominating" the rest of the arts (*haec una res in omni libero populo . . . praecipue semper floruit, semperque dominata est*, *de Orat.* 1.30). The orator wants "to look like the kind of man he wants to seem to be" (*de Orat.* 2.176)—that is, he wants to appear to be *free*.

When the most obvious techniques of training and self-mastery vanish—mechanical obedience to the rules of composition, the visible

---

[49] Dugan, *Making a New Man*, overreaches when he concludes that the impossibility of Strabo's lessons is a sign of his transgressive aesthetic (117–33), but his discussion is valuable.

[50] Rebhorn, "Baldesar Castiglione," speaks of the supple courtly body in Castiglione's Renaissance treatise *Il libro del cortigiano* as "free in a social and even ontological way" (247).

struggle for memory, robotic gestures (the most telling sign that the "natural" enhancement of the speech is artificial)—when these vanish, and the orator produces a effortlessly masterful performance, it means that his self-mastery has reached such an advanced stage as to suggest his freedom from the need to master himself in the first place.

This is the essence of rhetoric's paradoxical nature as a discipline of - liberty. The only master that is allowed into the arena of oratory is theself, and the self's command over itself is so complete as to go unnoticed—even, perhaps, by the self. From this point is derived the early modern emphasis on civility and manners so ably analyzed by J.G.A. Pocock, who concludes, "The social psychology of the age declared that encounters with things and persons evoked passions and refined them into manners; it was preeminently the function of commerce to refine the passions and polish the manners; and the social ethos of the age of enlightenment was built upon the concept of close encounters of the third kind ... This defense of commercial society, no less than the vindication of classical virtue, was carried out with the weapons of humanism."[51] This humanism, though Pocock does not say this in so many words here, is Ciceronian and rhetorical in nature.

The Roman conception of liberty has been contrasted to Greek *eleutheria* on the Berlinian grounds that it is limited and highly demanding, and further, that notions of limit and restraint are themselves inherent in *libertas*. *Libertas* is not so much the right to act on one's own spontaneous initiative, Chaim Wirszubski suggests, but the freedom to choose a conventional authority—an augur, senator, or patron—with manifest *auctoritas*.[52] Along with *auctoritas* and *dignitas*, a special Roman commitment to *officium*, especially of a militaristic nature, is sometimes invoked to explain the limits of *libertas*, such as that apparently expressed in this fragment of an Ennian tragedy (fr. 300–303 V):

> It befits a man to live in true virtue
> And to stand bravely, secure, against his adversaries;
> This is liberty, he who preserves a pure and staunch heart;
> Other ways, slavish ways, hide in night-shadows

> *Sed virum virtute vera animatum addecet*
> *Fortiterque innoxium stare adversus adversarios;*
> *Ea libertas est, qui pectus purum et firmum gestitat;*
> *Aliae res obnoxiosae nocte in obscura latent*

Ennius's sentiments express a familiar view, one that Cicero takes in the *Paradoxa Stoicorum*: "What is liberty, then? The power of living as you

---

[51] Pocock, "Virtues, rights, and manners," 49, 50.
[52] Wirszubski, *Libertas*, 35.

like. But," he goes on to say in a mode perhaps derived from his teacher Philo of Larissa, a Stoicizing Academic, "who lives as he likes, except the man who pursues the good, who rejoices in doing his duty, for whom the road of life is carefully thought through and mapped out beforehand?" (34–35).[53] Wirszubski's emphasis on external authorities overlooks the way obedience to the law is figured by Cicero as consent to one's own passions, and the subjects of the *res publica* are imagined as binding themselves rather than submitting to any purely external coercion.[54]

Just as rhetoric's repressive force liberates the self, permitting it to speak in the only style that is, putatively, truly free, so the speaking self advertises the conditions of liberty for the citizens at large. We saw at the beginning of this chapter that Cicero, along with Sallust, Livy, and Seneca, understands republican *libertas* as freedom from domination from a single ruler or a faction: "*libertas* consists not in having a just master, but in having no master at all" (*libertas, quae non in eo est, ut iusto utamur domino, sed ut nullo, Rep.* 2.43).[55] Sallust's Catiline complains that "ever since our republic submitted to the jurisdiction and control of a few powerful men, the rest of us have been abjectly servile (*obnoxii*) toward them" (*Cat.* 20.6–7).[56] Though it is not correct that the Romans conceived themselves as free only insofar as they were "all slaves to the law" (*legum idcirco omnes servi sumus ut liberi esse possimus, Cluent.* 146), Cicero's vivid metaphor and its claim to apply universally capture the sensibility of republican *libertas* for both the people and the senate. From the perspective of the first group, the word "slaves" figures the law's strong positive restraint of elite efforts to dominate as well as the fear of elite manipulation of the law in order to enslave the people (as Cicero suggests in his discussion of the secret ballot, *Leg.* 3.34). For the political class, the imagery of slavery acknowledges the

---

[53] *Quid est enim libertas? Potestas vivendi ut velis. Quis igitur vivit ut vult nisi qui recta sequitur, qui gaudent officio, cui vivendi via considerata atque provisa est . . .*

[54] I modify this phrasing from Kahn's work on the subject of early modern contract theory in "The duty to love," 86.

[55] Pettit, *Republicanism*, makes an ambitious claim for the significance of the republican definition of *libertas* as nondomination for contemporary political thought (51–79). Brunt provides a lucid discussion in "*Libertas*" (281–350), developing the argument of Wirszubski, *Libertas*. Both aim with limited success to refine the distinctions drawn by Benjamin Constant between active and passive freedom, ("Liberty of the ancients") and by Isaiah Berlin between negative and positive liberty (*Four Essays on Liberty*).

[56] *Postquam res publica in paucorum potentium ius atque dicionem concessit . . . ceteri omnes . . . eis obnoxii.* Seneca describes slaves as "bodies enslaved and signed over to their masters" (*corpora obnoxia sunt et adscripta dominis, Ben.* 3.20). Further discussion in light of neo-Roman theories of freedom appears in Skinner, *Liberty Before Liberalism*, 36–47.

law's necessary frustration of the elite will to power, which must go about its business without stirring up factionalism or the suspicion of tyranny. Precisely because formal legislation circumscribing Roman private life and its affective relations was minimal (though Cicero suggests their regulation by law, *Marc.* 23), the social conventions that regulated ethics, behavior, and deportment played a correspondingly important role. Better, in keeping with Xenocrates' answer, that the self spontaneously regulate itself.

Dangerous territory remains. The Stoics asserted that every living creature holds itself in esteem (*intellegamus omne animal se ipsum diligere, Fin.* 5.27). As the regulated self turns all the energies of its ambition, its will to power, back onto itself, the power of his commitment—which is also a self-dedication to the republic—is sufficiently great that it may lead to unnatural contempt for others. When the good man in *de Officiis* looks down (*despiciens*) on human concerns, his disposition seems incompatible with the ideal of civility Cicero has just laid out (1.61ff.). Alternatively, the performances that train the audiences and the speaker's eyes on himself create a self-obsession that threatens to undermine the communal ethic of republican politics. Sallust complains of the line crossed when Romans' virtuous acts, intended as bids for the honor of communal approval, are transformed into games of ambition designed to accrue wealth and power for their owner's sake (*Cat.* 1.7). The awareness of others' gaze arouses both the desire to show off, to exploit the spectacularity of the self, and the desire to hide from it, through the masks of personae that both reveal and dissimulate the self to the world.

A third possibility is that the self may be diminished, even destroyed. As Cicero translates the Platonic *Epistle 9*: "He recalled that man was not born for himself alone, but for his fatherland and for his family and friends, so that only a tiny part is left over for himself" (*non sibi se soli natum meminerit sed patriae, sed suis, ut perexigua pars ipsi relinquatur, Fin.* 2.45). His attack on the Epicureans' inability to explain patriotic self-sacrifice in this treatise on the ends of *life* is an implicit admission that self-mastery can lead to acts of sacrifice that violently exceed the natural order of things. This is borne out in his accounts of famous heroes: Regulus endures torture in Carthage, a man who "seems wretched to us listeners, but [the deed] was more pleasurable to him as he suffered" (*qui nobis miserabilis videtur audientibus, illi perpetienti voluptarius, Fin.* 2.65). Burning enthusiasm drove Decius to give his life for the republic, with a stronger desire than that which Epicurus thinks pleasure should be sought (*ardentiore studio, Fin.* 2.61). Other examples include Lucretia, who killed herself after her rape by Tarquin, and Lucius Verginius, who killed his own daughter. Violence, narcissism, and alienation are close neighbors to heroic patriotism.[57]

Finally, the passions of Cicero's self-governed orator threaten to shatter his sense of self. His power and virtue lie in his capacity to move his listeners, to bring them to feel the emotions he stages for them in his speech; this is why the ornate style of speaking is the most effective (*de Orat.* 3.96ff.).[58] We have seen that, though he draws on modes of disputation and logical argument from philosophy, his knowledge of emotion and the many aspects of eloquence that trigger it—tropes and figures, dramatic gestures and vocal expression—must transcend the unattractive dryness and abstraction of philosophical knowledge (*Orat.* 115). The audience will not experience emotions of anger, fear, grief, hatred, or pity, Antonius says in *de Oratore*, "unless all these emotions (*motus*), which the orator wishes to arouse in the judge, seem to be stamped and burned into the orator himself" (*in ipso oratore impressi esse atque inusti videbuntur*, 2.189). Antonius's account of the embodied oratorical performance assumes that the audience will not be drawn to feel emotions until the orator does so with the proof of his body, the signals (*signa*) expressed in open pain, a voice shot through with passion, an expression twisted with feeling, even tears—arising from emotions that "affect the speaker even more than his audience" (*de Orat.* 2.190–91). As Cicero remarks of the spare and concise "Attic" style of oratory, "the burning of the soul is not always present, and when it subsides, all that power and, as it were, the flame of the orator goes out" (*Brut.* 93).[59] The orator is like the poet, "on fire in his soul, with a certain inspiration that is something like madness" (*inflammatione animorum . . . quodam afflatu quasi furoris, de Orat.* 2.194).

The risks involved in the orator's staging of passion match its power. If the strict restraint of the Atticist means that his passions are not in play, and his oratory consequently suffers, the Asianist may yield himself up entirely to those passions. The Roman audience does not always respond positively to this kind of passionate performance (*de Orat.* 3.100–101). They are repulsed by the loss of balanced grace that is

---

[57] Many examples of the excessive expenditure of energy and life are cited in Barton, *Roman Honor*, 34–87.

[58] "Therefore one must make use of this type of oratory (the high, ornamented style), which grips the audience . . . the highest glory of eloquence is the amplification of the matter by means of ornamentation" (*Genus igitur dicendi est eligendum quod maxime teneat eos qui audiant . . . summa autem laus eloquentiae est amplificare rem ornando, de Orat.* 3.97, 102).

[59] *Ardor animi non semper adest, isque cum consedit, omnis illa vis et quasi flamma oratoris exstinguitur*, (*Brut.* 93). Here I am quoting Cicero's account of Asianism and Atticism, but I do not mean to imply that "schools" of style existed; see the properly judicious historical account of Wisse, "Intellectual background," 364–68.

characteristic of the free man, his revelation of a self that is awkward and gross—*ineptus*, a word that *de Oratore*'s interlocutors use to describe Greeks and philosophers (2.17–18). More important, loss of control visibly destabilizes the authenticity of his emotions and the integrity of his self-government.

FALLING IN LOVE WITH THE LAW

Recognition of the role passion plays in Ciceronian self-government should modify a persistent fable in the history of political thought. In her pathbreaking work on the relations of humanist philology, republican theory, and the exile of the feminine, Stephanie Jed argues that the figure of M. Junius Brutus, the avenger of Lucretia and the founder of the Roman republic, acts as a "cue to the Romans to subordinate their emotions to the cause of liberty."[60] Brutus's sons would agree, at least in Livy's account: where the monarchy had given free rein to their desires (*libido solutior fuerat*), the new liberty feels to them like slavery (2.3.2). As they see it, kingly rule is a humanized and even participatory governmental system. The king and his subjects are bound together in their common experience of emotion—anger, pity, love, and hate. By exploiting those emotions in the person of the king, his subjects are capable of modifying monarchical politics. The republican rule of law, by contrast, is relentless, literally deaf (*surdam*), with nothing of the king's mellowness or indulgence (2.3.3–4). It is brutish, self-annihilating, and dehumanizing. So Brutus's sons believe, and their stubborn adherence to the libidinal order of monarchy leads them to their deaths by the order of their own father.

By one reading, this primal scene of Livian republican history establishes Brutus's dispassionate masculinity, exemplified by his consent to his sons' execution, as the model of civic ethos, which severs virtue from sentiment and the just rule of law from the passions. This is a view commonly found in scholarship on early modern and Enlightenment revivals of republicanism, which suggests that modern views of the republican citizen as a man of sentimental feeling mark an abrupt break from the Roman tradition. They claim, in short, that Roman republican liberty rests on the successful containment of civic passions. Brutus, the *castigator lacrimarum*, represents a dispassionate masculinity that is specifically Roman, cut off from the sensual and sentimental attachments that shape and nourish citizens in the work of Rousseau and other early modern theorists. The Roman citizen's consent is represented as the subjugation

---

[60] Jed, *Chaste Thinking*, 10.

or erasure of feeling in obedience to the overriding compulsion of the communal good, the "fruit of a masculine reason divorced by pathos," in sharp contrast to Romantic political virility born of desire. So Jed concludes, and Elizabeth Wingrove agrees: "the moral detachment, despotic brutality, slavish reserve . . . the stoicism associated with an earlier republican tradition contrasts sharply with the sensuous and sentimental appeal of [Rousseau's] moral experience."[61]

Historians of political thought are not alone in reconsidering the place of passion in republican citizenship. At this moment in the early twenty-first century, we are undergoing another republican revival of sorts. Political theorists confronting central, pervasive problems of liberalism, especially widespread civic disengagement and the fragmentation effect of identity politics, are seeking to articulate a model politics that is at once more inclusive and more demanding, more tolerant of difference and more proactive in condemning intolerance. Only the citizens who deliberate together stay together, many of these theorists say: so the job of political theory is to imagine under what kinds of conditions and in what institutions political deliberation might best proceed. Quentin Skinner, Cass Sunstein, and others invoke the eighteenth-century ideal of the "republic of reason" in their improved model of liberal democracy. Skinner has argued that the classical belief in dialogic reason underpins the republican vision of government, and he finds support in early American and French revolutionary-era speeches and treatises. At the first meeting of the U.S. Congress, Connecticut representative Roger Sherman declared:

> when the people have chosen a representative, it is his duty to meet others from the different parts of the Union, and consult, and agree with them to such acts as are for the general benefit of the whole community. If they were to be guided by instructions, there would be no use in deliberation.[62]

"The appropriate model will always be that of a dialogue," Skinner says, "the appropriate stance a willingness to negotiate over rival intuitions. . . . We strive to reach understanding in a conversational way."[63] Philip Pettit writes persuasively in defense of the public practice of civil speech, saying "The democracy must be, not just deliberative, but inclusive"; he believes that the fostering of liberal civility is key to the republicanist attempt to repair the fracturing of democratic political discourse.[64] The concept of communicative reason developed by Jürgen Habermas has aided efforts to imagine what a deliberating republic would look like.

---

[61] Wingrove, *Rousseau's Republican Romance*, 14. The quoted phrase in the preceding sentence is also hers.

[62] Sherman, cited in Pettit, *Republicanism*, 189.

[63] Skinner, *Reason and Rhetoric*, 16.

[64] Pettit, *Republicanism*, 190.

But in what sense might we take historical polities that privileged public discourse as models? Iris Marion Young warns against the ancient ideal, revived with particular force during the Enlightenment, of a citizenry that "excludes women and other groups defined as different, because its rational and universal status derives only from its opposition to affectivity, particularity, and the body . . . in practice republican politicians enforced homogeneity by excluding from citizenship all those defined as different, and associated with the body, desire or need influences that might veer citizens away from the standpoint of pure reason."[65] Instead, she concludes, we must seek models for "affective, embodied, and stylistic aspects of communication" and for "orienting one's claims and arguments to the particular assumptions, history, and idioms of that audience."[66] Seyla Benhabib joins in the call for rethinking the practices of communicative reason when she criticizes John Rawls, for one, for denying "all contestatory, rhetorical, affective, impassioned elements of public discourse, with all their excesses and virtues."[67]

My argument in this chapter is intended to suggest that the Roman rhetorical tradition provides a model.[68] What that tradition tells us, above all, is that speech is married to the learned, learnable techniques of emotion control. If liberal political theorists wish to revive republicanist ideals of public deliberation, then their revival should learn from ancient rhetoricians' preoccupation with the emotions and their regulation. The rhetoricians offer a corrective to the image of the ideal Roman citizen predominant in contemporary studies of the history of political thought—an image of dispassionate, even self-annihilating masculinity, a civic subjectivity that replaces humane sentiment with just rule, sensual experience with the erasure of desire. It is true that the image alluded to by Jed, Wingrove, and others is present in Roman texts—we might say that it constitutes the history of the fantasy of Rome as (the fantasy of) Sparta, a state based in stoic self-denial—but in Cicero, we have seen, the community of citizens finds its origins and its law in the emotions of *caritas* and *amor*, which complicate and

---

[65] Young, *Justice and the Politics of Difference*, 117.

[66] Young, *Inclusion and Democracy*, 65.

[67] Benhabib, "Toward a deliberative model," 76.

[68] Among others who have considered rhetoric as an option for democratic politics, Benjamin Barber treats talk as a "mediator of affection and affiliation as well as interest and identity," *Strong Democracy*, 177. Robert Hariman describes Vaclav Havel as an example of a republican advocate who embodies a Ciceronian (conversational and epistolary) model of liberal democratic civility, *Political Style*, 125. Also depending primarily on Cicero's accounts of aristocratic conversation, Remer argues that his "conception of conversation anticipates the ideal of conversation upheld by today's advocates of deliberative democracy," "Political oratory and conversation" (39).

undermine this fantasy. In fact, even texts imagined to be canonical sources of the dispassionate Roman citizen do not present an unproblematic version of the fantasy. Consider again Livy's account of the execution of Brutus's sons:

> They flogged the stripped men with switches and beheaded them with an axe, while the whole time their father, his face and expression, was the real spectacle, since his paternal feeling was conspicuous throughout the administration of the public punishment.

> *nudatos uirgis caedunt securique feriunt, cum inter omne tempus pater uoltusque et os eius spectaculo esset, eminente animo patrio inter publicae poenae ministerium* (2.5.8)

Brutus, the primordial republican hero, is a man defined by his choice of self-denial and harsh action over the sentimental ties of family and friendship. In this passage he oversees the execution of his two sons, captured in a vain attempt to restore the monarchy. At the moment of the sons' death, Livy's text is poised between description and silence: it carefully represents and does not represent Brutus. In his public role as consul and *pater*, and then, by swift synecdoche, in his face and expression, he becomes the spectacular object of public gaze, the focus of attention who is also paying attention: "it is by identifying themselves with the consul," Andrew Feldherr notes, "that his fellow citizens can perceive the tension between civic duty and private loss as their own."[69] But—though this in no way undermines Feldherr's reading—we do not see exactly what the crowd sees: Livy obscures our vision with the ambiguous words *eminente animo patrio*, especially *animus* (sensibility, passion, wrath). Is Brutus displaying a *paterfamilias's* fury or a father's grief? Is his expression so unrestrained that it is impossible not to notice, or is it conspicuous only from the perspective of the spectacle-greedy crowd (*spectaculo*)?

The ambiguity of the passage recalls Brutus's moment of self-revelation when Lucretia kills herself for shame after her rape by Tarquin.[70] He tugs the dagger from her breast, swears revenge, and in his new role as *castigator lacrimarum* attacks the men who show signs of sorrow, including Lucretia's father and husband (1.59.1–4). He turns next to harangue the crowd, recalling the terrors of tyranny. "With these atrocities, I think," Livy remarks, "and with others, which his active sense of injustice suggested, but by no means easy for historians to relate, he urged the

[69] Feldherr, *Spectacle and Society*, 202.

[70] On the spectacular nature of Lucretia's death, Matthes insightfully concludes that "she inaugurates a political community founded on seeing and being seen" (*Rape of Lucretia*, 6).

crowd on" (1.59.11). To push the crowd to revolt, Brutus gives an emotional, even sensational speech—about rape, murder, the exploitation of Roman workers, and Tullia in her blood-spattered carriage—but, as in the execution scene, Livy closes down the readers' view of Brutus's passion with a puzzling editorial aside. Why should the kings' tyrannical acts be difficult for Livy to relate? Isn't this precisely what he has been describing throughout book 1? What we see at work here again is Livy's ambivalent authorial hand, which leaves behind just a few traces of the passionate sensibility of the republic's founder even as it draws him in the outline of the silent stoic hero.[71]

As Americans know from experience, republics are difficult places to live in. Cicero's *de Officiis* and Catullus's poems, I have argued, arise from the republican invention of the natural citizen bound by aesthetic and sentimental laws of nature that make the community possible— which is an attempt to foreclose anxiety about what might happen when those laws are broken: falsity, inauthenticity, failure, loss, misery. But in the context of Roman republicanism, renaming the laws of *decorum* as natural laws—trying to suture together the cultural rupture by invoking nature—can never work. Why? Slavoj Žižek, in a Lacanian reading of political theory, argues that ideology exists precisely to fill in a lack, "as an effort to cover over a constitutive void in the subject." His view of ideology as an answer to loss, or the fear of loss, is provocative, but I suggest that the answer lies closer to home, in the very nature of the *res publica*.

Or rather the non-nature: for as we have seen already republics are never natural. From Aristotle onward, republics are not made up of citizens bound together by the blood ties of kin or ethnicity. On the contrary, they are artificially constructed entities, yoked by common belief, as we have seen, a shared agreement about justice and the common good. The point of republicanism is not, as Lactantius would have it, that men are related all by the same blood (*consanguineos, Inst. Div.* 5.8), but that they are not. Ennius, on the other hand, had it right, in the line that we saw in the last chapter: *moribus antiquis res stat Romana virisque* (*Rep.* 5.1; cf. *Rep.* 1.25). As Derrida says of the Declaration of Independence, the "'we' of the declaration speaks 'in the name of the people.' But [at the time of signing] this people does not yet exist. [A]t the instant in which they invent for themselves a signing identity . . . they sign in

---

[71] The setting of Lucretia's rape and suicide, the *domus*, illuminates the competing tugs of allegiance: the family is the testing ground for the republic, but it must also be abandoned for the republic. Yet unlike Aristotle, whose citizens reject the household except in their capacity as rulers over it (*Pol.* 1.1–3), Roman writers do not prescribe the abandonment of the family. On the contrary, the family's sensual and emotive experiences shape the citizen self and must be exported to the political community.

the name of nature and in the name of God. They *pose* or *posit* their institutional laws on the foundation of natural laws."[72]

These are fragile bonds, demanding strong support from ideological inculcation and repetitions of social practice. As Alexander Hamilton wrote to John Jay, "It is not safe to trust to the virtue of any people. Such proceedings will serve to produce and encourage a spirit of encroachment and arrogance in them."[73] But I am following not Derrida but Hannah Arendt in arguing that rhetorical texts reveal an important truth: that it is in constant repetitive performance, from physical participation in assemblies to exhaustive rules about bodily *decorum*, that the republic is instantiated. Hence the grand importance of communal spectacle in the republican context, from Rome to Florence to revolutionary France to the United States: communal acts and witnessings of character are pivotal in the constant self-reminding of identity and sentiment that citizens must perform in order to strengthen and reconstitute civic ties. Hence the elaboration of genres focused on virtue, taste, and sentiment: a central topic of Rousseau's *Émile*, Flaubert's *Sentimental Education*, American soap operas—and, I would add, Catullus's poetry and Ciceronian rhetoric. Though the passions threaten to escape the control of the self, the constant reiteration of them guarantees the temporal order of the republic as atemporal and eternal. We recall Pierio Valeriano's praise of Catullan sentiment: "since Catullus expresses the emotions of love" For Valeriano, we recall, passion makes Catullus the ideal teacher of republican citizens, at least for the passionate citizen that we discover in Cicero. In Cicero, republican ideology presents itself as a system rooted in purely natural impulses, from communal sociability to personal decorum.

In this chapter I have argued that republicanism carries out ideological field surgery on a set of antithetical ideas. The man engaged in political affairs—the model of the ideal republican citizen—is exhorted to pursue the exalted quest for fame on the one hand and self-restraint on the other. Ideals of individual autonomy vie with fantasies of harmonious communal interdependence. He must collapse the law of nature with the rules of social custom. He comes to view cultural *mores* as the formal, essentialized expression of natural law: he internalizes social custom, literary taste, and political law as the idiom of the natural order. He is paradoxically fully and naturally himself only when he surrenders himself to the natural law of civic sentiment and the social practices of *decorum* that breathe life into the law. His liberty derives from self-scrutiny, the desire to ameliorate political fear, and obedience to social *mores*—all

---

[72] Derrida, "Declarations of independence," 10.
[73] Alexander Hamilton, letter to John Jay, 26 November 1775, in *Writings*.

underwritten by a law of love that he discovers automatically in himself, an automaticity that calls the self's autonomy into question. The implications of these conflicted relations for the continuity of the republic make for a tragic undertone to Ciceronian ethical and rhetorical writings. Decorous acts make the state possible and secure, but Cicero's attempt to ground *decorum* in natural law offers only self-mastery as a response to the tyrannical project of a Caesar. The republican order of things is a tough, thin tissue of passionate performance: in this contradiction lie the promise of republican ideology and the roots of its despair.

Chapter Five

REPUBLICAN THEATER

Truth has no such way of prevailing, as when strong Arguments
and good Reason, are joined with the softness of Civility and
good usage.
—Locke, *A Letter Concerning Toleration*

On the other hand, in a republic such as America, one is forced
to bore oneself the whole day long by paying serious court to
the shopkeepers in the street, and become as dull and stupid as
they are; and over there, one has no Opera.
—Stendhal, *The Charterhouse of Parma*

He described someone who sounded remarkably like Iago—a
confidence-man, a cheater and betrayer and liar, who tries to
tell everyone what he imagines they want to hear in order to
maintain his own game and get what he's after. Colonel
Dr. Joseph Karemera . . . told me there is a Kinyarawanda word
for such behavior: "We call it ikinamucho—that if you want to
do something you are deceitful and not straight." Shortly after
our meeting, I learned that ikinamucho means "theater."
—Philip Gourevitch, *We Wish to Inform You That Tomorrow
We Will Be Killed with Our Families*

"THE TONGUE IS SUSPECT," Cicero complains, and talk about training the
tongue lacks *dignitas*; even his friends question his detailed treatment of
the arts of speech (*artificium*, Orat. 140, 145–46; cf. *de Orat.* 1.91, 2.28,
2.156). Part of his defensiveness derives from his awareness of the
second-tier status of the rhetorical text itself, which may be seen as "acting"
the good orator's part, with all the anxieties about mimesis that this
entails.[1] Roland Barthes believed that the rhetorician's tendency to apologize
for his profession arose out of his awareness of its essential futility, his
knowledge that the *ars rhetorica* is trying to master the unmasterable in
its attempt to freeze language, a necessarily dynamic system.[2] Cicero's

[1] Gunderson, *Staging Masculinity*, fully explores the secondary nature of the rhetorical
text, which "lacks confidence in itself" (31; cf. 29–57).
[2] Barthes, "The old rhetoric," 85.

choice of the word *artificium* also acknowledges the philosophical critique of style, from Socrates' complaints about rhetoric's cosmetic-like properties in *Gorgias* to the Stoic quest to close the gap between rhetoric and dialectic, as well as the Roman characterization of technical arts as a Greek domain and the low social status of those professional masters of *artificium*, teachers and actors.[3]

Contemporary scholarship on rhetoric and literature often casts rhetorical artifice as a problem of gender. Beginning from the assumption that masculinity is an "artificial state that boys must win against powerful odds," in the words of one anthropologist, a wave of current scholarship has explored rhetorical education as training in "staging masculinity"—a trend supported by feminist and queer studies that examine the deep-seated association in Western culture between artifice and unmanliness.[4] Roman rhetoric indeed engaged in a struggle against what it liked to call "feminine" (*mollis, effeminatus*)—those monstrous acts of speech that failed to conceal, or that even drew attention to, the theatrical flourishes that exposed artfulness, when the efficacy and authority of speech rested on artfulness' concealment. In this chapter, I pursue a different explanation of rhetoric's gender panic, arguing that it arises not from anxieties about essentialized notions of masculinity and femininity per se but from anxiety about the stability and coherence of a political regime whose survival rests on the *artificium* of virtue. This anxiety intensified in response to the breakdown of republican politics that led to Julius Caesar's achievement of perpetual dictatorship in 45 BCE—a development that, as it forced Cicero to confront the reality of demagoguery that was helping to destroy the civic fabric, revealed unsettling truths about the nature of the collective formed by the oratorical performance.

Cicero is right to identify *artificium* as a problem. Style, and talk about style, evokes the realm of theatricality, which in turn summons specters of effeminacy, artificiality, inauthenticity, and the fragmentation of civic identity: hardly the "honorable defense" Cicero promises in the *Verrines*

---

[3] *Artificium* also caps Cicero's civil *apologia* for his ornate technique, in contrast to the plain "Attic" style of speech preferred by his dedicatee, Brutus. For this characterization of Stoic rhetoric, see the comprehensive account of Atherton, "Hand over fist."

[4] Gilmore, *Manhood in the Making*, cited by Richlin, "Gender and rhetoric," 91. Pathbreaking work on Greek orators under the Roman empire has been done by Brown, *Power and Persuasion*, and Gleason, *Making Men*. Gunderson, *Staging Masculinity*, is a sophisticated exploration of the relation between gender and rhetoric: his account of his theoretical touchstones (especially Butler and Lacan) is a good guide to the issues (16–28). Dugan, *Making a New Man*, argues that Cicero advocates a transgressive aesthetic that undermines conventional Roman notions of masculinity in terms I cannot accept. I argued for gender's central role in rhetorical discourse in my 1997 dissertation and a 1998 article, "Mastering corruption," but I now consider gender only one important part of the story (see below).

(*honestum praesidium*, 1.2.9). As Plato's arguments in *Gorgias* suggest, the problem is scarcely new. What concerns me here is the particular way that the orator's act, in the sense of theatrical artificiality, demands special treatment in the particular context of the late republic. It is not coincidental that, at the end of Cicero's lifetime, the collapse of republican politics was expressed in terms of artifice and its revelation as such. Caesar commented that the republic was a contentless artifact—an *imago sine re* (Suetonius, *Jul.* 77); Laberius, forced by Caesar to act as a mime artist, declared, "Quirites, we have now lost our liberty" (*porro, Quirites, libertatem perdimus*, Macrobius 2.7.4).

In the first part of the chapter, after surveying the relationship of speech and character, I turn to Cicero's views of artificial and effeminate oratory, with the aim of showing that current directions in the interpretation of gender in Roman rhetoric need to better account for its political context and orientation. Cicero's effort to distinguish between the types of ornamented or duplicitous speech that are honorable and those that are not, his careful distancing of the orator from the actor, and his characterization of certain types of eloquence as unmanly—all intended to clarify the speech by which the republic can be truly well governed—permit us to consider the place of pleasure and its anxieties in the republican order. In the second half, I explore further the hopes and anxieties expressed in the discussion of rhythm and figure in Cicero's last rhetorical treatise, *Orator*. These "last words" on rhetoric most clearly articulate the orator's role in forming collective identity. Writing at a moment in Roman history when the way the world made sense to Roman citizens was beginning to change, as words worked loose from the lock of traditional consensus (which itself likes to conceal its own mutability), Cicero is in a position to try afresh to teach citizens how to speak to each other—though, as we shall see, his prescriptions are tinged with the violence that surrounds him.

Being and seeming

It is a now much-studied truism of ancient rhetoric and ethics that speech made the man. "As a man lives, so he speaks," Quintilian writes in his *Institutio Oratoria* (*ut vivat, etiam quemque dicere*, 11.1.30). The orator should be a "manager of circumstances and personalities" (*temporum personarumque moderator*, *Orat.* 123). Expected to live through his voice, creating a persona that would broadcast his virtues and conceal his faults, the orator had to cut the proper figure, according to his circumstances: thus Demosthenes' aphorism, "delivery is first, second and third in importance" (*Orat.* 56, *Brut.* 142; Quint. 11.3.6). Cicero observes that only an abundance of styles can properly reflect the complexity of human character, so the orator should use all three styles of speaking—grand, intermediate, and plain—and every grade in between. "As for how someone walks or sits or the type of facial features and expression each person has—is there nothing in these things that we consider either worthy or unworthy of a freeborn person? Isn't it true that we consider many people worthy of our contempt who, through a certain kind of movement or posture, seem to have scorned the law and the limit of nature?" (*Fin.* 5.47).[5] The challenge rests in staging an effective, persuasive performance while obeying the rules of propriety and staying true to character. Hellenistic rhetoricians had already mapped the virtues of good speaking onto ethical virtue (*de Orat.* 3.72).[6] Theophrastus defined the four oratorical virtues as purity (*hellenismos*), clarity (*to saphes*), propriety (*to prepon*), and stylistic equipment (*kataskeue*), a list that prepared the ground for Cicero's claim that instruction in pure pronunciation, good grammar, and proper style is an important early step in the formation of virtue.[7] As the link with ethics suggests, attending to *ethos* was not a matter of "mere surfaces" but of establishing an authentic look and a sound that bound surface to soul. Cicero censures Torquatus for pretending a gravity appropriate to the Stoics and Peripatetics in public while maintaining Epicurean beliefs at home, which proves that he is "not being himself" (*non esses tui similis*). "Are you to change your thoughts with your clothes, and have one for indoor wear, another for outside, so that it is all ostentatious play-acting on the

---

[5] *Quem ad modum quis ambulet, sedeat, qui ductus oris, qui vultus in quoque sit, nihilne est in his rebus quod dignum libero aut indignum esse ducamus? Nonne odio multos dignos putamus qui quodam motu aut statu videntur naturae legem et modum contempsisse?* (*Fin.* 5.47). See Corbeill, *Controlling Laughter*, 99–104, 128–69, on the physiological aspects of Cicero's rhetoric, and particularly his humor: "To the informed orator, specific sets of externalized characteristics can offer effective material for public mockery and ridicule. . . . [T]hese signs do more than simply indicate deviance; they also provide the orator with evidence for predicting illicit behavior" (99). Rousselle, *Porneia*, explores the "èducation sensorielle" of the young Roman child, exposing the extent to which the physical molding of the body was believed to affect his or her mental development (47–62). Gleason, "The semiotics of gender," provides an account of physiognomic handbooks, which represented themselves as reliable indices to the apprehension of human character (389–402).

[6] For an analysis of post-Aristotelian Hellenistic rhetorical theory, see Solmsen, "Aristotelian tradition in ancient rhetoric," which is especially concerned with the amalgamation of the five activities of the orator and the various parts of speech (proem, narratio, etc.); on Hellenistic rhetoric's points of intersection with ethics, Enos and Schnakenberg argue that Cicero's work "latinizes" Hellenistic theory, with special attention to Cicero's treatment of "Roman" traits such as *dignitas, auctoritas, honor, and gloria* (203–6).

[7] Kennedy, *Art of Rhetoric*, 283. Long, *Hellenistic Philosophy*, discusses Cicero's and Seneca's beliefs about "what is needed if a man is to act well in all spheres at all times . . . orderliness, propriety, consistency, and harmony. To know what all of these are is to know what is good" (202).

surface, while the truth is hidden within?" (*ut in fronte ostentatio sit, intus veritas occultetur*, *Fin.* 2.77). We have already seen Cicero's over-determined insistence that the orator be "on fire" with his passions, since he cannot move a jury with an emotion he himself fails to feel (*de Orat.* 2.188–89). The belief in the ethically revelatory capacity of delivery complicates Cicero's representation of its techniques, because the notion of artful craft exists in tension with his commitment to authenticity. Acting, then, demands special attention.

After instructing and moving, charming the audience is the orator's third task. As early as Pindar, this power is described in terms of erotic concealment and revelation: "secret are the keys by which wise Persuasion unlocks the shrines of eros" (9.39).[8] Erik Gunderson eloquently describes Cicero's portrayal of the good orator in *de Oratore* as the double pairing of beauty and truth and beauty and pleasure in "flashy and sensual vocabulary" that seduces the reader (and the young characters in the dialogue).[9] His insight into the way the rhetorical text embodies many of the vices it criticizes explains another element of Cicero's defensiveness about teaching style. Ovid makes the connection explicit:

> Learn the arts of persuasion, I advise you, Roman youth,
> and not only to protect terrified plaintiffs;
> like the mob, the severe judge, or the pick of the senate,
> so will a woman be captured by eloquence.

> *Disce bonas artes, moneo, Romana iuventus,*
> *Non tantum trepidos ut tueare reos;*
> *Quam populus iudexque gravis lectusque senatus,*
> *Tam dabit eloquio victa puella manus.* (*Ars* 1.459–62)

No figure is better placed to instruct the orator in charming style and delivery than the actor, professional master of a *levis ars* (1.18).[10] The good orator possesses a logician's subtlety, a philosopher's reasoning, a poet's diction, a lawyer's memory, "a tragedian's voice, and the bearing, almost, of the best of actors" (*vox tragoedorum, gestus paene summorum actorum est requirendus*, 1.128). Through the metatheatrical device of staging speakers in *de Oratore*, as well as in what they say, Cicero

---

[8] Cited by Toohey, "Eros and eloquence," 198.

[9] Gunderson, *Staging Masculinity*, 194–5.

[10] Vasaly, "Masks of rhetoric," observes that "the court of law is a theater, the tribunal is a stage" (2). Graf, "Gestures and conventions," and Fantham, "Orator and/et actor" discuss the similarities between actors and orators. Gunderson, *Staging Masculinity*, pursues the unstable connection between oratorical performance and "playing" at being a man; see also my "Mastering corruption." Other references to acting: *theatrum ingeni* (*Brut.* 6), "stage-set of the speech" (*scaena orationis*, *de Orat.* 2.338), advice to imitate actors (*Brut.* 290, *de Orat.* 1.156, 1.254, 3.102).

acknowledges that the orator's performance of character relies upon the techniques the actor uses to gain credibility and sympathy for his parts. Like the actor, the orator must try to appear to be "such a man as he would desire to seem" (*ut talis videatur, qualem se videri velit*, 2.176). Smooth delivery of a well-chosen speech makes speakers "seem to be upright, well-bred and virtuous men" (*ut probi, ut bene morati, ut boni viri esse videamtur*, 2.184).[11] But if the orator is to resemble the actor or the poet in his arousal of emotion, performing on a "stage" (*scaena, de Orat*. 2.338; cf. 2.193), Cicero insists that it must be the stage of life itself. Dramatic actors, who are only "mimes of reality" (*imitatores veritatis histriones*), he complains, have taken over the job of orators, "those who are the actors of real life" (*qui sunt veritatis ipsius actores*, 3.214). The orator must take care not to resemble the actor. The actor who toils at the study of gesture (1.251) reminds his spectators of the counterfeit qualities of self-presentation even as his virtuoso performance obscures them. Though the actor's power to entertain and arouse emotion operates according to strict social rules—Roscius's sense of propriety was proverbial—he is not constrained by the will to communal knowledge that disciplines the orator, making him a dangerous model to emulate too closely.[12] Formally speaking, his speech inhabits an extracivic realm, even if it has political consequences.

Roscius's famous propriety is worth another look. It is tempting to see him as the object of Cicero's fascinated gaze precisely because he embodied not the citizen's opposite but his double. Cicero makes no secret of his love of comedy.[13] He collected a joke book, and devotes an entire section of *de Oratore* to humor. Why? Because comedy demands the timing and subtlety of politics; it demands a keen eye—precisely the eye the statesman requires to preserve the state. Strabo, who (we recall) dominates the discussion of jokes and humor in *de Oratore*, tells of an abusive joke he directed at Helvius Mancia that engaged precisely with these questions of authenticity. In the course of proceedings, Strabo threatened his

[11] This is a particular problem for epideictic oratory, which Cicero claims Greek orators practice more often than Romans (*de Orat*. 2.341). The epideictic orator must have some knowledge of virtue, to be sure, but in a very limited sense: he need only to speak the surface of virtue, to present its appearance, for both himself and the person he eulogizes (*de Orat*. 2.349).

[12] On Roscius: *de Orat*. 1.132, 156, 3.102; *Orat*. 109–10; *Brut*. 290. Edwards, *The Politics of Immorality*: "Roscius does seem to have been in some respects exceptional. . . . Yet the paradoxical nature of the position of Roscius, whose virtues as a man give him a dignity which could only be compromised by his skills as an actor, is symptomatic of the ambiguous status of actors in Rome" (128). See further her extended discussion of actors (98–134).

[13] *Contra* Dugan, *Making a New Man*, 117–33, who argues that comedy figures Cicero's oratorical transgressions.

opponent: "'Now I'll show what kind of person you are' (*iam ostendam cuius modi sis*). When he said, 'Go ahead,' I pointed with my finger to a Gaul painted on one of Marius's Cimbrian shields beneath the New Shops—a distorted face, with his tongue hanging out and flabby cheeks. This stirred up a general laugh; nothing seemed so much like Mancia" (*de Orat.* 2.266). As Anthony Corbeill points out in his reading of this passage, the joke's power rests in "the Roman predisposition toward associating physical appearance with moral character": what you look like and what kind of person you are can be rendered as equivalent not only in Latin but in the Latin worldview as well.[14]

Here Cicero is concerned with the joke of revelation. Elsewhere he concentrates on the revelation of salvation: his insight into the Catilinarian conspiracy, and, more to the point, his technique of attacking his targets in the law court by tearing off the masks of their visible selves. "You came in angry with everyone; this, the moment I saw you, even before you began to speak, I felt and saw ahead of time," Cicero hurls at Vatinius (*Vat.* 4; cf. *Pis.* 1). If he is to purify the republic of characters like Vatinius, his own expertise must concentrate on distortion and inversion—precisely the domain of the joke.[15] Comedy helps teach citizens how to behave in the community, especially when the competitive negotiations of social status cause pain. "You want to know how each person feels with regard to you," Cicero writes evasively in a courteous letter to Lentulus Spinther, "but it is difficult to talk about individual cases" (*Fam.* 1.7.2). The abusive wit of Cicero's second *Philippic* demonstrates that when the whole community is threatened by violence, the lessons of comedy's inversion become even more crucial to sharpening the public's grasp of the inversion of society at large.

Comedy is the genre that brings together high and low, free and slave, vice and virtue: it is a genre about contiguity, set in neighboring houses, dramatizing what happens when unlikely characters (twins) or likely (young man, young woman) come together. Contiguity is a leitmotif of sorts for Roman rhetoricians, who see distortion and corruption as the near neighbor of the highest achievements of theory and practice. Quintilian writes of a "certain resemblance between virtue and defect" (*quaedam virtutum vitiorumque vicinia*, 2.12.4; cf. 3.7.25); the elder Seneca considers certain virtues "close to faults" (*vitio tam vicina virtus*, *Contr.* 7 pref. 5). Cicero describes the proximity of virtue and vice in terms of a physical reaction, where the greatest pleasures are only narrowly distinguished from disgust (*de Orat.* 3.100). In this context, duplicity may fruitfully be seen to stand not in opposition to virtuous

---

[14] Corbeill, *Controlling Laughter*, 40; I adapt his translation.
[15] On this dynamic in Machiavelli, see Matthes, *The Rape of Lucretia*, 58.

civic speech but alongside it. Duplicity enables the health of the republic; it provides a necessary supplement to the thin civic diet of reason and philosophical truth. Indeed, when the characters in Terence's *Hecyra* agree that they must not utter the truth about the rape and temporary abandonment of a pregnant bride, "like the characters in a comedy," their acknowledgment of the boundary separating them from the spectators temporarily erases it, underlining the fitness of their action in their world outside the play: veiling one's actions is a necessary facilitator of life in the community (866–67). In another letter to Lentulus Spinther, Cicero describes how his allusion to Terence in a speech eased the fact that he had undertaken the speech under pressure from Caesar. "I said I was doing what the Parasite in the *Eunuch* recommends to the soldier: 'Give tit for tat'" (*Fam.* 1.9.19).

Surveying the acts that were played out on the stages on which the orator performs—the Rostra, the temple steps that served as courts of law, the senate floor, to name the most important—we are now in a position better to understand Cicero's ambivalence about certain stylistic flourishes, especially verbal redundancy and unnecessary versification, when a speaker inserts empty material just to fill out the meter, and above all singing (*Orat.* 70, 166, 230).[16] Some of his criticism derives from the layering of ethnic prejudice on top of style, a recent habit at Rome exemplified by the Augustan writer Dionysius of Halicarnassus. Anticipating Dionysius (perhaps under the influence of Greek rhetoricians recently arrived at Rome), Cicero associates a wild singsong style with Phrygians and Carians, who are, not incidentally, metaphorical subjects of a rhetorical master, "slaves to rhythm" (*Asiaticos maxime numero servientis, Orat.* 230; cf. 57, 163). Good rhythms are "totally unlike" the familiar meters of poetry (*dissimillimus, Orat.* 227). The virtuoso who exaggerates the artificiality of his techniques is dangerous because he draws attention to the distance of his figured language from Cato's maxim *rem tenere, verba sequentur*: by making the authenticity of his language into an open question, he undermines its rootedness in his self, and by extension, the integrity of the relation between himself and the political community. Unlike the orator whose stage fright exposes him to laughter and derision, the stagey orator exposes his arguments to suspicion (*Orat.* 57) and implicitly, the grounds of political discourse in the city to disbelief—a disbelief that must destroy the republic, since the republic is based on belief and an identification with a law and a tradition that lends ontological authenticity to the aesthetics of citizenship.

---

[16] Cicero's discussion of rhythm moves along very different paths from Plato's or Aristotle's, which focus on the moral value of music and meter (e.g., *Pol.* 1339b10).

At stake in the orator's performance and the elaborate discourse surrounding it, we remember, is not the orator alone. When Cicero returns from exile in 57, his speech to the People makes himself, his life, his relationship with his family, and his sense of well-being perfectly coterminous with the republic (*Red. Pop.* 1.2–5, 14). His sense of identification with republican government extends to the heroes of the past, such as Scipio Africanus, portrayed as belonging to the whole people (II *Verr.* 4.81; cf. *Sest.* 49). As he is at pains to claim in his speeches (a pattern followed by speakers in Livy), Cicero's health and integrity figure that of the body politic. If oratory like his is the central action of politics, as he wishes it to be (*Orat.* 7–10), its revelation of its debt to theater casts the political relations within the self and between citizen and citizen in the realm of fiction. The truth of this unspeakable fiction is articulated through the metaphorical exile of characters Cicero associates with trickery and pleasure, and paradoxically, a new type of deceit. The rhetorician's first lesson is "shame on you to speak openly of the art you practice" (*artem pudere proloqui quam factites*, *Orat.* 147).

The panic of this sentiment indicates Cicero's sensitivity to helping the orator "play" himself, teaching him how to pass for a virtuous citizen, which makes ethical and political trouble for rhetorical training.[17] That the pedagogical practice of oratory, through the repetition of "unreal" exercises, generates histrionic acts of virtue potentially undermines the ideal to which it purportedly adheres. The student of such a curriculum was in a position to learn that the authority granted by eloquence is not the manifestation of free men's natural superiority, and that its tactics are identical to those of actors and women, who exist outside the charmed circle of the political class. And the speech is more than a moment in time. Oratorical habits of mind and speech smooth the workings of the state. Cicero's expressions of anxiety about the contamination of civic persuasion by the manipulative tactics of extra- or antipolitical discourse emerge out of a recognition precisely that the republic exists in the *act*, the *show*, the display of plausible authority, the theatrical presentation of ethos. This perception introduces a certain level of panic into his prescriptions for eloquence—a panic expressed as a fear of effeminacy, servility, and merely actorly, as opposed to civil, acting.

This adds another level of irony and paradox to Cicero's aesthetics of virtue: the virtuous self who obeys cultural imperatives out of natural sentiment is engaging in learned behavior that makes space for pretense. For all Cicero's talk of nature, the act of authenticity remains a sticky problem. "In a free people, in a state of equality before the law," Cicero admits, "we must train ourselves in amiability and depth of soul" (*facilitas*

---

[17] I explore these issues further (with a focus on Quintilian) in "Mastering corruption."

et altitudo animi, Off. 1.88)—a phrase used by Tacitus to describe the inscrutability of Tiberius (*Ann.* 3.44). Sentiment, the orator Cicero knows very well, is easily faked. Without necessarily adopting a teleological view of history, Cicero sees the republic improving over time: it advances toward its best condition (*optimus status*) by a kind of natural course (*naturali quodam itinere et cursu*), "strengthened not by chance, but by good counsel and discipline" (*non fortuito Romanum populum sed consilio et disciplina confirmatum esse, Rep.* 2.30). It is significant, in this passage about virtue and improvement, that the *res publica* and the *populus Romanus* are synonymous, equated entities. In order for the republic to improve, subjective practices like civil manners—practices of theatricality and artifice—are required to help all citizens constitute themselves in social practice as free and equal.[18] Hence the importance of civility in Cicero's *de Officiis* and *de Legibus*, and in the "gentlemanly" conversations that frame his dialogues.

The pleasures of civility, however, pose a certain threat to the self's autonomy. In *de Finibus*, in response to the Epicurean claim that contentment is the end of human life, Cicero argues that the honorable is the thing intrinsically and extrinsically desirable (*Fin.* 2.44). The main difference between men and animals, he says, following a now familiar line of thought, is that nature has given men reason (*ratio*), which "makes each man desire men, and according to nature, makes him mix with them in conversation and daily life, so that, swept away by his love for his household and his friends, he creeps and insinuates himself first of all into the society of his fellow citizens, and from there into the society of all mortal men" (*Fin.* 2.45).[19] His striking choice of words to describe the citizen "creeping and insinuating" himself into the company of others (*serpat, implicat*) encourages the reader to envisage the self both as requiring the supplementation of others—implying that his autonomous state is not a fully human one—and as a supplicating self, crawling like a snake on the ground into the company of other men. The snaky man reveals two threads of anxiety in Cicero's thinking, one about the condition of lack that characterizes autonomous human life and the other about the subservience of interdependent relations.[20]

---

[18] This line of thought is inspired by Wingrove, writing about the daily life of Genevans, *Rousseau's Republican Romance*, 204.

[19] *eadem ratio fecit hominem hominum appententem cumque iis natura et sermone et usu congruentem, ut profectus a caritate domesticorum ac suorum serpat longius et se implicat primum civium, deinde omnium mortalium societate* (cf. 565–66).

[20] Hanna Pitkin, writing about Machiavellian thought, sees a "central tension" in autonomy "implying a connection and a separation"; "autonomy may be conceived either as a kind of sovereign isolation or, paradoxically, as the rightful acknowledgment of interdependence" (*Fortune Is a Woman* [Berkeley, 1984], 8).

Judith Shklar wisely observes that we may revolt against artificiality and pretense, and we may defend that revulsion with appeals to truth and authenticity, but hypocrisy is indispensable in political cultures that value freedom and equality: it softens rigidity of thought or action, and it fosters a flexible multiplicity of roles for each citizen. The public stage "collectively replays the struggles of the politics of daily life, and vice versa. In the unending game of mutual unmasking, the general level of vice rises. As each side tries to destroy the credibility of its rivals, politics becomes a treadmill of dissimulation and unmasking."[21] Cicero's recommendation of verbal "coverups" for the cosmetic of rhetorical ornament acknowledges the proximity of the performances of virtuous men with others whom he figures as foreigners or unmanly men, not only in oratory but in the practices of everyday civility as well. His claim to mark off a territory of vice is an effort to draw a line between the acts that strengthen the city and those that destroy it. The formal speech is a single expert instance of this daily civic existence, a microcosm of republican politics, just as the orator's body is a living exemplum of its social mythologies. Even the *maiores* at times accommodated themselves to face new circumstances (*accommodasse, Man.* 60). "I do not think it the sign of an inconstant man (*inconstantis*) to regulate (*moderari*) one's opinions, like a ship or a ship's course, according to the weather that might be prevailing in the republic" (*Balb.* 61). Since a politics grounded in acts of persuasion is possible only through compromise, pretense is a necessary ingredient in republican politics. Misrepresentations must be admitted into a political realm that transparently defines its object as the common good. Trickery and the common good seem linked by a "fearful interconnectedness" where vice inheres within, and is partly produced by, the virtue it is imagined to oppose.[22]

Cicero's articulation of the theatrical dynamic of republican civility has a long legacy. Writing in the early eighteenth century, the Earl of Shaftesbury comments on the relation between politics and the poetic and theatrical arts: "as for the Antients, 'tis known they deriv'd both their Religion and Polity from the *Muses* Art." The eloquent speeches and daily civil conversations that Shaftesbury considers essential to the free governing of the state derive from a mimetic representation that Shaftesbury grounds in authenticity, in a move familiar from Cicero: the "Appearance of Reality is necessary to make any Passion agreeably represented, and to be able to move others, we must first be mov'd ourselves, or at least seem to be so, upon some probable Grounds."[23] Cicero expresses

---

[21] Shklar, *Ordinary Vices*, 77–78, 67.

[22] Dollimore, *Sexual Dissidence*, 33.

[23] Shaftesbury, "Essay on enthusiasm" in *Characteristicks*, 4, 9.

the desire to erase the gap between feeling and action, and the confidence that civil speech acts can make a civil world, in a wistful comment to Atticus, when, after Cicero had mentioned to him some helpful act of Varro's, Atticus had written to Cicero expressing his pleasure. "But I would prefer you had written to *him* that I was pleased with *him*," Cicero responds, "not that this is so, but that it might become so" (*sed ego mallem ad illum scripsisses mihi illum satis facere, non quo faceret sed ut faceret, Att.* 2.25.1). Following Cicero, as we have already seen, Shaftesbury finds natural sociability the basis for political community, but he responds to his Restoration context by choosing the poet, not the orator, as the catalyst who "signifies" the common sensibility, who awakens the people into their human rights and natural equality: "They make this Common Sense of the Poet, by a Greek Derivation, to signify Sense of the Public Weal, and of the Common Interest; Love of the Community or Society, Natural Affection, Humanity, Obligingness, or that sort of Civility which rises from a just Sense of the common rights of Mankind, and the natural Equality there is amongst those of the same Species."[24] Cicero's marriage of artifice and virtue, however, is necessary in the society Shaftesbury sees around him: "There are more Wheels and Counter-Poises in this Engine than are easily imagined." He compares social conventions and legal authorities to clothing: "Magistrates" are "Dressers," with "Tire-men for helpers," which is to say, police and other enforcers of the law.

For Shaftesbury as for Cicero, delving into artifice's role in political discourse, even in jest, creates a certain discomfort. That "Civil Government and Society appear a kind of Invention, and Creature of Art, I know not."[25] Again echoing Cicero (specifically, Antonius in *de Oratore*), Shaftesbury claims "not to know" the logic of political community and deliberation that he persuasively articulates throughout his essay. This not-knowing is important: acknowledging the existence of the arts of the state is exactly like tearing down the stage curtain to expose the play's props.

If it is not at all clear that frank honesty serves politics particularly well, this does not stop hypocrisy from being called the worst possible crime in public and private. Judith Shklar quotes one Elizabethan author describing the dissembler or hypocrite as "the worse kind of player, by so much as he acts the better part, which hath also two faces, ofttimes two hearts. . . . He is the stranger's saint, the neighbor's disease, the blot of goodness, a rotten stick in a dark night, a poppy in a corn field,

[24] Shaftesbury refers here to Homer as the founder of Greek and Western literature, which Shaftesbury views as the most important tie among men in the establishment of free European states.

[25] "Essay on the freedom of wit and humour," 73, 111, 115, 104.

an ill-tempered candle with a great snuff that in going out smells ill, an angel abroad, a devil at home, and worse when an angel than a devil."[26] But what is the alternative? On the grounds that manners instantiate traditional social structures, some conservative thinkers have claimed the civil arts as their domain. In an age of revolution, when the conservative Edmund Burke answers decisively that "manners are of more importance than laws," he has in mind Cicero's emphasis on the artful civility necessary for life in an equal state.[27] An anonymous piece in the *Boston Gazette* of 1763, criticizing the violent behavior that was obstructing the meetings of the turbulent Massachusetts legislature, opens with a reminder to its readers that

> Man is distinguished from other Animals, his Fellow-Inhabitants of this Planet, by a Capacity of acquiring Knowledge and Civility more than by any Excellency, corporeal or mental, with which mere Nature has furnished his species. His erect Figure, and sublime Countenance, would give him but little Elevation above the Bear, or the Tyger: nay, notwithstanding those Advantages, he would hold an inferior Rank in the Scale of Being, and would have a worse Prospect of Happiness than those Creatures; were it not for the Capacity of uniting with others and availing himself of Arts and Inventions in social Life.

What characterizes every "Gentleman, every Man of Sense and Breeding," the critic concludes, is his "more delicate and manly way of thinking."[28] The coupling of reason and civility in the first sentence introduces a call for a perfect marriage of grace and virility. "Delicate" manliness, the arts of natural civility, the uneasy marriage of republican spectacularity and its disavowal of theatricality: these paradoxical relations of truth and artifice are the ideological pillars upon which the republic stands. So, to become civilized, men become "mannered," in both senses of that word: they invent and follow social codes of manners, and they learn how to act the part. But the arts of civil life are not limited to the conservative tradition. Locke, whom I quote in the epigraph, sees artful speech as perfectly compatible with what we now call liberal reason. His descendants in the liberal tradition, especially deliberative democrats, agree.[29]

---

[26] Bishop Joseph Hall, "The hypocrite," in *A Book of Characters*, quoted in Shklar, *Ordinary Vices*, 48–49.

[27] Burke, "Letters on a regicide peace" (1796), cited in Pocock, *Virtue, Commerce and History* (1985), 49.

[28] U. (Untitled and anonymous), *Boston Gazette*, 1 August 1763, in *American Political Writing During the Founding Era*, vol. 1, 36.

[29] I pursue the theme of liberal civility further in my conclusion.

THE CIVIC STAGE

The necessity of playing the citizen in the right way takes on new importance in the broader context of republican political culture. Republican
glory is won and displayed in the public eye. Polybius's analysis of Rome's
constitution climaxes with its national character literally on display, in
the funeral celebrations of notable men, where a speaker praises the dead
man before the assembled people in a performance that drives the young
men to suffer "for the common good" (6.53–54).[30] Delivered in the presence of an actor wearing the *imago*, the wax mask of the dead man in
whose honor the speech is given, the funeral oration holds up leading
citizens for the admiration of the audience, in the process of "public
recognition of accepted virtues and behavior patterns" on which the
republic is *imagined* to base itself.[31] The final episode of book 6, the
exemplary tale of the senate's refusal to ransom eight thousand men captured
by Hannibal after the battle of Cannae, reinforces the spectacular quality
of Roman moral discourse. The Carthaginian general turns from tri-
umphant victor to troubled spectator when "*he sees with awe* the resolute
steadfastness and noble spirit" of the members of a Roman embassy who
return, in a dramatic performance of virtue, to die alongside their fellow
soldiers (6.58). The spectacular imperative of republican politics extended
to those entering politics and to nonelites. To win office, Polybius says,
young men must spend time in the Forum, "recommending themselves to
the many" (31.29.8). Until the legislation of the secret ballot in the 130s
BCE, voting in the *comitia* was a vocal utterance performed before the
eyes of fellow citizens. The most extreme enactment of the potentially
explosive dynamism of republican politics is the terrifying spectacle of
public violence in spaces designed for the mediation of the disputes.[32]
Marius, Sulla, Caesar, and Octavian did not execute their rivals in private, but displayed the physical results of their purges in the Forum. All
these events are opportunities for the Roman community to see itself in
action, to reify, consciously or not, the abstraction of civic identity, and
to cement the common sensibility of Roman political culture through
shared practices of applause or censure—or, in times of upheaval and
civil strife, through the inversion of those practices, gang violence and
public massacres. As we have seen, Hannah Arendt drew from her reading

---

[30] Polybius's own text privileges the personal over the institutional, a phenomenon of
ancient thought broadly tied to the emphasis on individual style that is the concern of this
chapter.

[31] Flower, *Ancestor Masks and Aristocratic Power*, 31.

[32] On the shock of violence in Roman public space: Cicero, *Cluent. 93, Mil. 22, Mur.*
49–53; Sallust *BC* 38.1–2.

of Roman history that political action in republics is not merely about
the performance of a given deed, it is also "the performance of that deed
before one's fellow citizens, and their response to and narration about
that deed."[33] And Jerzy Axer concludes that "theater" is too narrow a
characterization for rhetoric's "spectacular" nature: that is, Cicero's
speeches may be interpreted in terms of "all kinds of spectacles," including the gladiatorial display.[34] This cuts both ways: Brutus confesses that
his ability to perform depends on his own spectacularity, proved by the
presence of a crowd (*si a corona relictus sim, non queam dicere*, *Brut.* 192).

From the customary sanctions against fathers bathing with sons and
sons-in-law to the stress on visible signs of virtue and vice across the literary tradition, Romans are strikingly aware of the self as a public entity,
the object of others' persistent evaluative gaze, directly or indirectly, and
equally its absence, the marked refusal to look.[35] Privacy was limited;
fama, public reputation, was paramount. Even Roman bedrooms were
open to the censor's scrutiny, Dionysius of Halicarnassus wrote, contrasting the sharper boundaries between public and private he imagines
to have characterized democratic Athens (20.13.2–3). Vitruvius
describes the town house of the powerful man, within which circulated
an assortment of people: not just family members and slaves, friends and
house guests, but morning visitors (*salutatores*), clients, and supporters.[36]
Cicero made himself accessible to everyone, abandoning the comparatively private territory of the bedroom for the public rooms of his home.
This strategy extended to Cicero's decision to buy a house on the site
previously owned by the tribune Drusus, whose architect, according to a
famous anecdote, offered him a house secreted from the public gaze, but
Drusus preferred the house to be not only easily seen but easily seen into
(Vell. Pat. 2.14.3). Visitors and goods entering the house were a matter
of public judgment (II *Verr.* 5.28), as were the sounds of music and the
cooking smells that emanated from it (*Verr.* 2.5.58, *Pis.* 13). In *de
Republica*, Cicero argues that virtue may be known in the abstract but
must be practiced publicly; he describes his own career as a series of steps

[33] Cited in Matthes, *The Rape of Lucretia*, 7.

[34] Axer, "Tribunal—stage—arena," 310–11.

[35] On bathing: *Cicero, De Off.* 1.129; a father advises his son to treat others like mirrors
in Terence (*speculas, Adelphoe* 415); Tacitus refers to Tiberius's character in terms of veils
and masks (well analyzed by O'Gorman, *Irony and Misreading in the Annals,* 78–105):
see also Suetonius's claim that the emperor's ability to hide from the public encouraged
private vices (*Tiberius* 42.1). Barton's landmark study of Roman shame stresses its visibility
(*Roman Honor*, esp. 199–215. Yavetz, "*Existimatio, fama,* and the Ides of March" examines the language of late republican character evaluations; Feldherr traces theatricalization
as a theme in Roman historiography, *Spectacle and Society in Livy's History* (esp. 4–28).

[36] Vitruvius 6.5.1–3. For this and other references in this section see Treggiari, "Home
and forum: Cicero between public and private," 1–24.

taken in public that ensure his eternal life in the public arena of men's memories (*Rep.* 1.2,13). The civic bond is safeguarded by seeing and being seen. Citizens may monitor one another's behaviors, and in turn respond to the monitoring of their own: the man who fails to care about others' opinion should not be trusted to govern them (*Off.* 1.99).

Living under constant surveillance, Cicero's model citizens display their virtue in an uneasy brotherhood of scrutiny. Exposure is a constant threat. "When I obtained the quaestorship in the province of Sicily," declares Cicero, "I realized that the eyes of all men were turned upon me alone, and I saw that I and my quaestorship were staged as though on a kind of theater of the world, so I refused everything that seemed pleasant, not only unusual desires, but even those that are natural and necessary" (II *Verr.* 5.35).[37] If the story of Roman character is a story of life made visible, Cicero's comments express an uneasy awareness of the self made raw, exposed at the core of public life. Roman history, after all, has many stories of exposure: the spectacle of Lucretia's raped body (Livy 1.50), the body of Mettius, who is torn apart as an apotropaic sign of Rome's future stability (Livy 1.28), the scarred body of the old veteran whose body becomes a diagnostic text for the city, proof of its punishing debt laws (Livy 2.23).

In its role as teacher of the laws of language and virtue—which rhetoric expresses precisely in terms of spectacle, of pleasure, of "acting" (*actio*, "delivery")—rhetoric exposes the spectacular economy of republican political theater. Under the domination of powerful figures such as Pompey and Caesar, at a time when important actors were beginning to refuse or to rewrite their traditional roles, rhetorical discourse required extra defenses to protect its ability to teach the performances necessary for the republic to continue. But its arguments silently suggest that the lived, embodied, dynamic nature of political performance is a shallow, uncertain anchorage of words, appearances, and feelings—in Catullus's troubled phrase, "written on wind and running water" (c. 70).

By the first century BCE there is another problem: the challenge empire posed to practices of political communication. We have seen that oratory is a civil art that aims at creating the spectacle of agreement (*concordia*) among its citizens (*Inv.* 1.5). In the context of a culture of public persuasion, rhetorical discourse's concerns about unmanly speech emerge as the symbolic expression of desire for a sense of sameness among speakers and listeners, a common sensibility regarding taste and convention, which arises from the heart of republican anxieties about governing a necessarily heterogeneous community. From its founding in thievery,

---

[37] *Sic obtinui quaesturam in Sicilia provincia ut omnium oculos in me unum coniectos esse arbitrer, ut me quaesturamque meam quasi in aliquo terrarum orbis theatro versari existimarem, ut semper omnia quae iucunda videntur esse, ea non modo his extraordinariis cupiditatibus, sed etiam ipsa naturae ac necessitati denegarem.*

kidnapping, and rape, as the Romans' myths constantly reminded them, Rome was never singular, never homogeneous. Despite the careful conservation of citizenship in Italy and the provinces until the Social War of the early first century BCE, the inexorable war machine that was the middle republic ensured that Rome remained forever a state of imperial heterogeneity, (in) a state of change. We shall see that femininity, the biological sign of otherness, symbolizes the difference and disagreement that were both a necessary aspect of Rome's social and political dynamism and a source of anxiety for those seeking to win elections, create agreement on legislation, and forge coalitions.

WOMEN AND SPEECH

When it comes to style, *Rhetorica ad Herennium* heralds the tone of Cicero's later rhetorical treatises. Sharp vocalization harms the speaker's voice and the listener's ears, the Auctor says, because it has a "kind of slavish quality" (*inliberale*) tending "more toward womanliness than manly dignity" (*ad muliebrem potius . . . quam ad virilem dignitatem, Rhet. Her.* 3.12.22). Gendered language is an important instrument for Cicero as he distinguishes virtuous from vicious speech.[38] Oratory must be the verbal equivalent of the manly pursuits of boxing and gladiatorial combat (*Orat.* 228); markedly rhythmic oratory can seem diseased, infecting a virile style with lush extravagance (*Brut.* 51).[39] A sidling walk and effeminate gesticulations signal flightiness (*Brut.* 225).[40]

> He will also use gestures in such a way as to avoid excess: he will maintain an erect and lofty carriage, with little pacing to and from, and never for a long distance. As for darting forward, he will keep it under control and employ it rarely. There should be no effeminate bending of the neck, no twiddling of the fingers, no marking the rhythm with the finger joint. He

[38] Richlin, "Gender and rhetoric," Gunderson, *Staging Masculinity* (esp. 132–43), and Corbeill, *Controlling Laughter* (esp. 128–73), gather and discuss additional relevant passages on gender in rhetorical and oratorical discourse.

[39] Imholz, "Gladiatorial metaphors," analyzes this language in *Pro Sexto Roscio Amerino*; Brody, *Manly Writing*, traces the impact of such metaphors on the construction of rhetoric as a discourse of masculinity through the nineteenth century (11–36). Johnson, *Luxuriance and Economy*, discusses these and other metaphors in detail.

[40] On the immorality of dance, see Corbeill, *Controlling Laughter*, 135–39. Ramage, *Urbanitas*, provides a good introduction, with references, to Cicero's critical attitude towards "hyperurbane" men like P. Clodius Pulcher, A. Gabinius, Gaius Arrius, and others, whose refinement made them vulnerable to accusations of homosexuality, foppishness, extravagance, and so on (65–67). Edwards, *Politics of Immorality*, describes how Roman discourses about moral misbehavior were deployed in the pursuit of various social and political ends (esp. 63–97).

will control himself by the pose of his whole frame and the vigorous and manly visible presence of his body, extending the arm in moments of passion, and dropping it in calmer moods. And what dignity and charm are contributed by the countenance, which has a role second only to the voice! After assuring that the expression shall not be silly or grimacing, the next point is careful control of the eyes. For as the face is the image of the soul, so are the eyes its interpreters, in respect of which the subjects under discussion will provide the proper limits for the expression of joy or grief. (*Orat.* 59–60)

Idemque motu sic utetur, nihil ut supersit: in gestu status erectus et celsus; rarus incessus nec ita longus; excursio moderata eaque rara; nulla mollitia cervicum, nullae argutiae digitorum, non ad numerum articulus cadens; trunco magis toto se ipse moderans et virili laterum flexione, bracchi proiectione in contentionibus, contractione in remissis. Voltus vero qui secundum vocem plurimum potest quantam affert tum dignitatem tum venustum. In quo cum effeceris ne quid ineptum sit aut voltuosum, tum oculorum est quaedam magna moderatio. Nam ut imago est animi voltus sic indices oculi; quorum et hilaritatis et vicissim tristitiae modum res ipsae de quibus agetur temperabunt.

Passages like these, equating perversity and vice with unmanly moves like the flounce and sashay, bespeak the special power of the feminine as a symbol of corruption.[41]

Finding the middle way is a challenge. One option is cultivating the spare style known as Attic, which furnishes the orator with muscle and eradicates his need for rouge (*Brut.* 36, 64). This style resembles that of women who are judged "more beautiful when unadorned, the very lack of ornament being most becoming to them" (*Orat.* 79). No pearls, curling irons, or artificial white or red cosmetics (*fucati medicamenta*) are needed to convey pure elegance and charm (*elegantia et munditia*).[42] Both woman and speech possess a charm that does not, cannot, must not show itself. Like the inside of the throat itself (and perhaps the vagina and womb), they symbolize that which cannot be fully grasped—a secret space, a potentiality.[43] Cicero's attempt to govern the voice's potentialities

[41] As Garry Wills brilliantly observes, "the Roman empire dreamed of John Wayne" and his apparently effortless (though in fact meticulously mounted) performances of masculinity ("John Wayne's body"). Edwards discusses the penalties of failure to meet ideals of masculinity in *Politics of Immorality*; see also Corbeill on jokes and invective, *Controlling Laughter*, and Gunderson on masculinity as a wound in the subject, *Staging Masculinity*.

[42] Cicero's wistful portrayal of language without ornament is offspring of the Greek fantasy of pure *logos* interpreted by Arthur, "The dream of a world without women," 111–12, and Irigaray, *Speculum of the Other Woman*, 311, 319ff.

[43] Koestenbaum, "The queen's throat," 211–15.

arises from his recognition that it is a natural property that is nevertheless mysterious and impossible to *know*. A double move, then: the orator must conceal his intonation, rhythm, and ornament, the products of body parts he does not himself know. Further, the Attic style must be supplemented with a touch of Demosthenic vigor and ornament, a point Cicero underscores with images of manly virility. "The prizewinners, free from all vice, are not content with, as it were, mere good health, but seek strength, muscles, blood, and even a kind of ruddy charm" (*qui, cum careant omni vitio, non sunt contenti quasi bona valetudine, sed viris, lacertos, sanguinem quaerunt, quandam etiam suavitatem coloris*, Opt. Gen. 8).

Concealing and subtly calibrating rhetorical techniques stands in tension with the free, manly self-assurance that Cicero advocates in his ideal speakers, especially since deceitfulness, the interiorized quality of holding something hidden within, is an archetypal quality in representations of women and other non-*viri* in Greek and Roman literature. When Cicero recommends that his readers adopt certain practices of deception that mimic the cosmetic concealer he criticizes, he is paradoxically encouraging the would-be manly speaker to take on certain unmanly characteristics that are, nonetheless, necessary for his performance—to position himself, that is, on the spectrum of conventional Roman social practice, in proximity to non-men. As Erik Gunderson wisely observes of the discourse of masculinity in Quintilian's *Institutio Oratoria* (itself a belated supplement to Ciceronian rhetoric): "as Quintilian labors toward knowledge of the body, he reveals a body that is more process than essence . . . while he has a vision of authentic male presence, his efforts to find and fully know this essence only expose it as unstable and chimerical."[44]

Roman rhetoric might be called the history of fantasy: a fantasy of perfect, teachable virtue, of persuasion free from coercion or the deceitfulness of speech supplemented or aided by ornament. It dreams a world where the conflict between ideals of free manliness and the arts of communal life, especially the arts of speech, is erased; but it dreams in the uneasy knowledge that the powers of speech, on which politics and law rely, are impossible fully to tame and master. Rhetoric turns out to rely in part on its own negation: the dominant, free, masculine order rests on powers which that order itself damns as the natural capacities of not-free/not-Roman/not-men. *Pace* Gunderson, however, masculinity is not the essential, central problem in Roman rhetorical discourse—at least not masculinity on its own, as a gender essence floating free from politics and lived experience. The fundamental problem facing ancient men was not to be *men* as such, but to be citizen-men—a category in which

---

[44] Gunderson, *Staging Masculinity*, 60.

gender certainly plays a basic role but whose very fluidity and change-ability present problems and anxieties that trump gender, just as they cannot be considered as prior to gender.

Civic identity, speech, and ideals of masculinity in which ideals of positive and negative liberty inhere: these three things are interdependent, and as such they create the ideological basis for laws, both judicial and social, that name some as beneficiaries of and participants in freedom, others as its slaves. This naming is neither simple nor definitive. Free Roman men may be the only figures legally rendered in this system as fully active citizens, but the qualities that make them subjects—in the sense that they are subjected to rule, whether to self-rule, the rules of rhetoric, or the rule of law—also make them share qualities imagined to be essential to the nature of women. Though women hold the legal status of *cives*, they are nonethess not fully active, free citizens possessing authority over others but rather are always subjected to forces beyond their control.[45] They inhabit eternally a civic middle ground, distinct from the waiting room briefly occupied by free (male) children and the total, if changeable, condition of unfreedom suffered by slaves.

If women have little to do with rhetoric, why are women and femininity targets of criticism, not only in Cicero, the elder and younger Senecas, and Quintilian, but throughout the European rhetorical tradition? One answer much explored in recent work is that women themselves are imagined as *embodying* the art of speech, of action through indirection, of masking, concealing, ornamenting, emoting, precisely because the troubling nature of these acts excludes them from masculinity's proper domain—men being the virtuous gender.[46] "It is this system of dissimulation," Mary Wollstonecraft complains, "that I despise. Women are always to *seem* this and that."[47] This explains the way rhetoricians use gender as a border marker: one of the most effective solutions to the problem of distinguishing the kind of eloquence that is virtuous from that which is vicious is the explicit differentiation of men's speech from women's speech, a move that permits them to conceive an ideal masculine speech cleansed of the taint that women's lies and gossipy garrulousness are imagined to carry. Norman Brown captures the power of this strategy in his comments on the distinction between body and soul in Western thought: "the external enemy is (part of) ourselves, projected; our own badness, banished. The only defense against an internal danger is to make it an external danger: then we can fight it; and we are ready to fight it, since we have succeeded in deceiving ourselves into thinking that it is

---

[45] Discussion in Gardner, *Being a Roman Citizen*, 85–109.

[46] See Jarratt, *Recreating the Sophists*, and Paxson, "Personification's gender," 157.

[47] Wollstonecraft, *A Vindication of the Rights of Woman* (New York, 2002), 124.

no longer us."[48] Scholars have long recognized Greek and Roman writers' suspicion of the inherent potential for deceit in rhetorical persuasion, which they associate with women's supposedly enhanced natural capacity to lie, act, and act up for personal ends. Hesiod's Pandora, Homer's Helen, and a host of female and effeminate characters from Athenian tragedy share a natural expertise in persuasion, an uncanny talent that enables them to serve their own vices or to put in operation their necessarily misguided visions of an ideal world.[49] In this literature, women make their livelihoods by overturning men's reason with passion and desire. Barred from "honest" labor due to the responsibilities of maternity, physical weakness, or social rules, they are thrown back on subterfuge and manipulation, and they pay a heavy ideological price for the privilege.

Transformed in the course of Athenian drama into carriers of corrupt eloquence, persuasive feminine characters are not only walking warnings about the unreliability of Athens' largest subject class, they also serve as depositories for male anxieties about rhetorical speech. In his role as teacher of the city, Aristophanes makes a habit of criticizing men of public prominence in Athens by assimilating their talents to this story of feminine eloquence. His portraits of men who make a living from their quasi-erotic powers of persuasion, using their oratorical influence to seduce the city and to amass material and symbolic capital and contributing little in the way of "real" work, reflect a set of contemporary convictions regarding the natural characteristics of women. Agathon and Euripides, Socrates and Cleon—masters of language all—appear in Aristophanes' plays in the company of women and their deceptive linguistic turns. As Praxagora observes, in her argument that women are best suited to govern Athens through the process of democratic persuasion, "the men who are fucked the most, speak the best" (*Eccl.* 112–13). In bringing into the open culturally subterranean connections between eloquence and femininity, Aristophanes exposes Athenian anxieties about the power of words in democratic politics. Philosophy, too, invokes gender in its critique of rhetoric. Gendered language in Plato's *Gorgias* collects fuel for the long tradition for and against rhetoric in the early modern tradition.[50]

Women's skillful tongues are not necessarily a sign of evil. Seeking to read the connection between women and eloquence in a way that recovers and authorizes the value of women's social contributions, and indeed their identity as wives and mothers, Joan Ferrante argues that the association between women (or Woman) and the medieval personification of

---

[48] Brown, *Love's Body*, 162.

[49] See, for example, Barish, "The antitheatrical prejudice," and Zeitlin, "Playing the other: Theater, theatricality, and the feminine in Greek drama."

[50] Vickers, *In Defense of Rhetoric*, 83–147.

'Rhetoric' is explained by the natural generative capabilities of women's bodies: women, the conceivers and nurturers of human beings, are the figures that enrich human speech, producing its significatory abundance of figures and tropes.[51] More recently, feminist critics troubled by the fixed connections Ferrante draws between biology and language have represented femininity as a social construction that signifies the possibilities of language, its uncontrollable, irrational, and seductive power. Jody Enders compares the late medieval Christian equation of theatricalization with emasculation in the context of concerns about the growing elaboration and expense of church liturgy.[52] James Paxson argues that figurative language as a whole labors under its association with the feminine: the concept of personification, in particular, thematizes the idea of "a secret inside and a self-advertising outside, an outside that hawks its exteriority— a feat achieved through cosmetic embellishment, social deceptiveness, and marked penetrability" that forces woman and personfication to "share ontological identity."[53] And Patricia Parker has explored the longstanding link between masculinity and action and women with passivity, captured in English humanist John Florio's observation in 1609 that some readers may find his book on usage and style, *Worlde of Wordes*, unsuitable for a male audience, since "*Le parole sono femine, e i fatti sono maschii*, Wordes they are women, and deeds they are men."[54] Like Greek dramatists and philosophers, and English and Italian humanists, Cicero links the unmanly, noncivic tongue with unrestraint and vice; but unlike his Greek forebears, in a move that colors the later tradition, Cicero devotes his efforts to solving the problem, to cleaning up rhetorical speech and practice for virtuous use.

But because oratorical performance is, by Cicero's idealizing account, the essence of and model for republican practice, to acknowledge the presence of the feminine or the slavish in rhetoric is to acknowledge its presence in civic experience more generally. John Pocock argues that the "austerely civic" Roman definition of citizen virtue was gradually supplanted through the eighteenth century by a new understanding of the political and social significance of manners. As the ideal of the "farmer-warrior world" of Rome yielded to the transactional world of commerce and the professionalized arts, his relationships with other social beings took on new significance in the shaping of his public and private identity. If the citizen could no longer participate directly in ruling and being ruled, Pocock writes, "he was more than compensated for his loss of

---

[51] Ferrante, *Woman as Image in Medieval Literature*, 37–64.

[52] Enders, "Delivering delivery," 272–3.

[53] Paxson, "Personification's gender," 172.

[54] Cited in Parker, "Virile style," 216; see also her "On the tongue" and *Literary Fat Ladies*, 8–35, 97–125.

antique virtue by an indefinite and perhaps infinite enrichment of his personality."[55] Pocock's portrayal of the relationship between manners and virtue, and the sense of loss that he identifies as characteristic of the shift from archaic models of citizen virtue to civil manners, shed light on Cicero's anxious representation of the civil citizen, the artificial construct necessary for the existence of the Roman republic.

This means that the rhetoric of gender in Rome must be understood as a discourse of discipline and purification in the specific political formation of republicanism. Whether we treat the warnings about women's powers of persuasion in Greek poetry and philosophy as reminders of women's inferiority or as the signs of transferred anxiety about men's talk, casting back to Greek sources, appealing to ahistorical categories of gender ideology or ancient constructions of femininity cannot fully account for the gendered aspect of the rhetoricians' concerns about language. Understanding gender in rhetorical discourse is not simply a matter of defining women's prattle as empty and prettified against the stern and authoritative speech of men. The issue here is the profoundly ambiguous nature of civic identity itself. Cicero describes Socrates in prison on the eve of his trial, refusing Lysias's offer of a prepared speech in his defense, because, just as an elegant pair of boots is "not manly," Lysias's learned oration is "neither courageous nor manly" (*non essent viriles . . . fortem et virilem non videri, de Orat.* 1.231). Socrates' emphatic dismissal of eloquence from his prison cell (filled with friends devoted to philosophy) reverberates through Western history. A recurring Hobbesian metaphor for eloquence in his writing on citizenship and the state is the "witchcraft of Medea."[56] But Socrates' refusal to memorize Lysias's speech, signified by those fancy boots, is not a simple assertion of the austerity and self-reliance proper to manly men. It leads to Socrates' condemnation to death, and in the process gender categories blur. Socrates' rejection of style as a resource for other men in democratic Athens casts the normal behavior of men in the civic sphere as unmanly; meanwhile, self-abnegating obedience, the sign of submission to the communal will, becomes the sign of a stripped-down, pure manliness.[57]

My point is not that the association between manliness and self-sacrifice is unusual (it is not), but that Socrates' remark illuminates the vulnerability of persuasive talk—the bedrock of Athenian democratic practice, by which every citizen had the right of *isegoria*, free speech—to accusations

---

[55] Pocock, *Virtue, Commerce, and History*, 49.

[56] *De Cive* 12.13.

[57] Carlin Barton, quoting anthropologist Sander Gilman that "manhood is the defeat of childhood narcissism," observes that "in Roman contest culture, to will death was not to deny life but to carve its contour" (*Roman Honor*, 43): see also her discussion of gladiatorial self-sacrifice in *The Sorrows of the Ancient Romans*, 15–46.

of femininity. This kind of critique stands in tension with the claim of Greek and Roman rhetoricians that training in oratory and the constant proving of oneself in public demanded by the political system is the sum of what makes the virtuous (manly) citizen. Exiling women outside the charmed circle of active citizenship reinforces civic identity as a natural, transparent expression of masculinity, a masculine essence tied up with and resting on men's special capacities to detach themselves from self-interest and family ties and fight to the death to defend the city—assumptions that remain a key obstacle to gender equality in late modernity.[58]

For Cicero, writing about eloquence involves confronting the republic's embrace of compromise, seduction, inauthenticity, spectacle, and passion—all as truly essential to politics as reason and war, but difficult to square with idealizing traditional fantasies of manhood. Rhetorical texts bring this incongruence front and center. Rhetorical discourse has the shape it does not because masculinity is an unstable, internally contradictory and fractured construct (though like all elements of ideological thought, masculinity is exactly unstable, contradictory and fractured) but because civic identity—the sense of belonging to a political community, what we call "citizenship"—is so. In saying this I am trying to push against the conventional approach to gender, in which we treat issues of political ideology, such as the nature of civic identity, only after establishing its "roots" in ideologies of gender. Mine is a model in which political ideology—the question of how to live in a state, being both a citizen and a subject—is the primary problematic, emerging in tandem with, shaping and being shaped by, constructs of gender that map out what are essentially civic beliefs and practices, 'civic' in the sense of being related to the political community.

In the wake of feminist and queer studies of the 1980s and 1990s, it may seem appropriate to speak of the crisis of masculinity in the ancient subject: this phenomenon carries obvious resonance with our times, and with the fracturing of longstanding and deeply rooted ideologies of gender over the past century and more. Though true equality of opportunity and the erasure of prejudice will be achieved only in the ongoing course of longlasting social change, the surprising initial swiftness of the deflation of gender prejudice in the First World in recent generations is precisely proof of the fragility and mutability of sociopolitical structures and the ideologies that underpin them. It is the interweaving of gender with political power, the instability of the threads and the contingent feel of the resulting cloth, that creates the anxieties surrounding masculinity in Roman rhetoric.

[58] Among the growing bibliography on women and Western concepts of citizenship since the 1980s, see especially Brown, *Manhood and Politics*; Pateman, *The Disorder of Women*; Di Stefano, "Autonomy in the light of difference"; Yeatman, "Feminism and citizenship"; James, "Citizenship in a woman-friendly polity."

It is worth noting that in the recent antifoundationalist current of thought about subjectivity, the language of self-construction, the concern with decentering and multiplicity for its own sake, and a certain infatuation with the conception of selves-in-process—all issues that have dominated feminist studies for the past two decades—feed on a profoundly American individualist fantasy that is not adequate to the task at hand. Explaining that masculinity is a construct and that (precisely because it is not natural) constant repetition is demanded to sustain (the illusion of) it tends to collapse into the view that there is something there in the first place, an essence that, even if it is nothing more than an ideological place-holder, functions as a goal that meaningfully orders social life and expressions. But the lived experience of politics not only drives the engine of sexual difference; political ideology and practice themselves are fractured by the very instabilities that are then mapped onto gender, in the politically dominant order's attempt to cure itself from the sicknesses of the oppressed. This, however, they cannot do, because the symptoms of oppression are mirrored in the impulses of the powerful: the very faults that cast women and other groups into political disenfranchisement and moral damnation are precisely what enable (masculine) civic structure and political order. The ideal orator of Roman rhetoric is proof that the republic rests on an economy that simultaneously institutionalizes difference, by excluding elements that it calls "feminine" or "non-Roman" or "slavish" and by idealizing the free masculine Roman, and collapses the very difference it creates, by defining the citizen as a corporeal entity that desires, obeys, feels, imagines, weeps, sways and is swayed, and above all talks: he connects. Rhetorical discourse makes visible Rome's political unconscious by illuminating not only the limits of the possible for the dominant languages of identity and power but the perverse dynamic on which those languages are based. It is a dynamic of dominant inclusion and oppressed exclusion where the excluded element (weakness, inauthenticity, self-theatricality, narcissism) haunts the dominant order, not only as the specter of dominance's demise but as the disavowed basis of dominance itself.

Hence femininity is a trope deployed to assault a range of targets. The art of eloquence finds its quasi-historical roots in a political and economic struggle of early-fifth-century BCE Sicily, where, according to later Greek testimony, the violent overthrow of the tyrants Gelon and Hieron led to the first systematic theories of the spoken word.[59] Used first of all in Sicilian public space in the defense of social, political, and economic order against tyrannical oppression, the "art of speaking" is closed off as soon as it is identified as such from those who lack the social, economic,

---

[59] Cole, *The Origins of Rhetoric*, discusses the problems of the sources.

or political standing necessary to speak in that space: women, laborers, slaves, the poor, children, non-Greeks, and, as time goes on, non-Romans. The point, again, is that women as such as are not the primary target of rhetorical criticism. It is what they represent—the lack of full freedom, independent status, authority over others. The fear and contempt of women expressed in Roman rhetorical discourse transcend the fear and contempt of women, or even of femininity, or even of the not-male or not-masculine: these attitudes express concerns about what it means to live in relative peace with others under the rule of law.

The best orator

In the course of the collapse of the rule of law through the 50s and 40s, Cicero's interest in style intensified, especially for the technical details related to *elocutio* and *actio*. *Brutus* and *Orator* are his last rhetorical works, composed in 46 BCE, when Caesar had consolidated his victory with the support of men Cicero viewed as demagogues (*Fam.* 12.18.2). These two texts are almost entirely concerned with style (and in *Brutus*, its revelation of character); *de Inventione*'s preoccupation with status theory is nowhere to be seen. A history of Roman oratory, *Brutus* quietly polemicizes against contemporary realities, where Caesar's control of legions mattered more than his oratorical talent, by assembling memories of great speakers (a textual version of the usual procession of senators through the Forum) to convey the impression that the speeches delivered by elected magistrates are the frame within which politics properly occurs. Cicero makes a point of noting that his dedicatee Brutus's personal accomplishments were made possible by the same oratorical skill that helped his ancestor establish the institutions of *libertas*: magistracies and law courts (*Brut.* 53). Cicero suffers (*angor*) because under the dictatorship of Caesar, the forum has been utterly "despoiled and widowed" of every skilled voice (*voce erudita, Brut.* 6–7).[60] His last words on the topic in *Orator* articulate the Platonic ideal of the orator, who is modeled on his own ornate style.[61]

Orator's vehement purpose is to describe the orator who is best capable of exploiting the power of the performance and thereby transforms the scattered selves of his listeners into a unified collective. This aim is reflected in the form of the treatise, which abandons the dialogue form, inviting the reader to conceive of himself not as a participant in a conversation but as

[60] Cicero counsels against losing hope and abandoning work (*non est cur . . . spes infringatur aut languescat industria, Orat.* 6).

[61] Narducci, "*Orator* and the definition of the ideal orator," surveys the structure of the work and main themes, contrasting it with *Brutus* (428–30).

a member of the audience. The case Cicero lays before this readerly audience is that the *princeps* of eloquence, the Platonic idea of "orator," is the master of the "full, flowing, weighty, ornate" style, which "has the greatest force" (*amplus, copiosus, gravis, ornatus, in quo profecto vis maxima est, Orat.* 97).

This figure derives his effects from two sources. First, he is a master of propriety. He commands all three styles of oratory, the plain, the middle, and the ornate, and he brings each to bear in the proper circumstances, when, Cicero says, "there is nothing so difficult as to know what is fitting, in life as in oratory" (*Orat.* 70).[62] Cicero's emphasis on diversity is significant. Throughout the treatise, he draws on the history of oratory and personal experience to stress the necessity for the orator to respond adeptly and flexibly to the unpredictable demands of audiences and contexts (esp. *Orat.* 102–6, 108–11, 129–33). The range of Cicero's historical allusions suggests that there is more at stake here than learning how to win over a jury. On the contrary, the orator's flexible responsiveness captures the essence of republican politics. If the republic is a shared enterprise aiming at the common good (*Rep.* 1.39), the common good is not a fixed concept but one that is always contested and changing, responding to external and internal pressures: the "project" of the republic, its very reason for existence as a political association, is by nature dynamic. Political practice "must not become so ossified or hegemonic that it thwarts the very political action that is vital to republics."[63] Mastering ornate grandeur and stripped-down purity allows the orator to prove his speech's authentic connection to his audience's sensibility; his variegated style legitimizes diversity of opinion and feeling even as it seeks to transform diversity into unity (*Orat.* 125).

Second, he is expert in three crucial areas: ornament, rhythm, and sound. Here too the key issue is propriety: Cicero stresses that the arrangement of words in the sentence must be carefully carried out so that the words fit together as "aptly as possible," and so that they fall in the proper rhythm (*apte, Orat.* 149). So far Cicero is speaking what he himself describes as Brutus's Attic language of clarity and propriety, taking care to link his representation of the effects of the best style to natural harmonies, like those of trees (*Orator* 147). Oratory, of course, is much more than musical noise; it involves the presentation of reasoned argument. And as we know from *de Oratore*, style is supposed to be regulated by its interaction with the regulating gaze of the audience.[64] In that dialogue, Cicero had recalled the case of Rutilius Rufus, a Roman

---

[62] The word *decorum* and its verbal forms, as well as *aptum* and its cognates, appear repeatedly in the subsequent discussion.

[63] Matthes, *The Rape of Lucretia*, 1.

[64] See chapter 4.

adherent to Stoic philosophy, who, when brought to trial on a politically motivated charge of extortion, demanded to be defended with dispassionate speeches, *sans* lamentation, emotional appeals to patriotism, or prayers (1.230). His defense failed, and Rutilius was exiled. When rules and reason are proved insufficient, where does legitimacy lie? In the emotional responses of the republic's citizens. *De Oratore* focuses on the formation of virtuous orators whose function is to stage and channel emotion in a way that gives life to and orders the polity. In *Orator*, however, Cicero ventures beyond the limits of persuasion that rests on reason.

There is profound political significance in the fact that instead of argument or character, *Orator* focuses exclusively on style, most of all on ornament and rhythm, the arts that speak to the most basic (even, in the case of rhythm, nonverbal) aspects of human communication.[65] We are back to basics here. Rhythm and sound exert persuasive effects, Cicero claims, because they tap into a universal human sensitivity to propriety. The ears possess a natural capacity for measuring all sounds, since nature prompts humans to grasp "the patterns and rhythms of language" (*Orat.* 177–78). Cicero had argued in *de Oratore* that the masses (*vulgus imperitorum*) understand style because of nature's "extraordinary force": for every man "by a certain silent sensibility without any knowledge of art or systematic reason (*omnes enim tacito quodam sensu sine ulla arte aut ratione*) can form judgments of what is right or wrong, not only in the case of art, but in their judgment of the rhythm and sound of words (3.195). These things are profoundly fixed in the "common sensibility" (*communibus sensibus*), so that "everyone is moved, not only by the artful disposition of words, but also by rhythms and sounds . . . there is no closer relative (*cognatum*) to our minds than rhythm and sound (*numeri et voces*), by which we are aroused, inflamed, charmed, soothed, and brought to laughter or sorrow" (3.196–97). The history of early Rome, Cicero suggests, supports the idea that rhythm and sound are

---

[65] To work his almost magical effect, the orator must be present; reading his speeches provides only a dim echo of his original performance (*Brut.* 93). This sentiment, and the emphasis on sound that I am about to discuss, undermines Dugan's claim that the treatise's main concern is with the sublime as it is expressed in textual form ("the *Orator* shows a particular preoccupation with writing," *Making a New Man*, 285). It is true that the pen (the symbol of writing, in Dugan's view) plays an important role in the self-government of the orator (e.g., *Orat.* 150), but this does not affect the treatise's concentration on the articulation of voice in performance. Cicero wrote the treatise in 46, within months of returning to public speaking (after several years' silence), with the so-called Caesarian speeches (*Pro Ligario, Pro Marcello, Pro Rege Deiotaro*). If he viewed these speeches as politically compromised, this might have been further reason for him to explore the potential of grandly passionate speaking; this is a matter for further investigation. Dugan rightly notes that "the body is the underlying metaphor that governs the *Orator's* discourse on style" (270); his discussion of body imagery is directly relevant to my argument here.

crucial players in the formation of the political collective. He associates the arts of poems and songs with the wise king Numa (*rege doctissimo*), who established the playing of instruments and speaking of verses in ritual contexts.

In view of his account of the king in the second book of *de Republica*, the reference here makes sense. Introduced by Scipio in the course of his history of early Rome, Numa symbolizes ideal *concordia*: he is the first monarch to be installed by the collective consent of the Roman people and the aristocratic curia (2.25). He establishes social practices that instill the love of peace and the advance of civilized arts (*amor otii et pacis*), which refound Rome as a harmonious polity, by contrast to the warlike proclivities of Romulus (and Numa's successor, Tullus Hostilius, who restored the balance of Rome's martial character). He enshrines that harmony in the realm of sense perception through the repetitive practice of ritual (*ardentis consuetudinis et cupiditate bellandi religionum caerimoniis mitigavit*, 2.26). The sounds that the citizens are made to learn by heart (*perdiscenda*) and perform in public ritual embody and advertise the civil peace of early Roman collective identity.[66]

The connection between rhythm and sound and the development of the early Roman collective clothes Cicero's comments on the aesthetic appeal of oratorical rhythm with political flesh. The pleasure of rhythm and sound is pleasure that is felt by all, regardless of class or education. The relationship between rhythm, sound, and rhetorical virtue expressed in Cicero's notion of *decorum* speaks to the importance of harmony, not only in the soul of the individual listener but as a sensory experience for the political community at large. Rhythm, so easily recognized even by the most inexperienced auditors, hails them and invites them into the community, creating a moment in which everyone is united in assent or critique. When orators or actors make mistakes, the crowd is quick to shout them down (*Orat.* 196). That is, rhythm provides an experience of collectivity, a recognition that aids identification, both between the orator and the listener and between listener and listener. What makes this connection special for Cicero is that it connects the world of the political assembly or the law court to the world of the aesthetic and moral, which is also the world of the natural: it bootstraps the naturally implanted aesthetic reaction of the *communis sensus* into a collective political awareness. Everyone is moved (*moventur omnes, de Orat.* 3.196).

The moment of rhetorical persuasion is thus the moment where emotion and law are put to the test. It creates a moment of questioning in every listener—not only "how do I judge, guilty or innocent?" but a

---

[66] Cf. Quintilian 9.4.143–7, 12.9.5–6.

deeper question about the meaning of sitting in judgment, reinforcing the legitimacy of the system. The listener may choose to listen, to walk away, to cheer, to riot. It is to guarantee that he will join his fellows, lost in admiration and the desire to applaud (*Orat.* 236), that Cicero advocates the ornate orator's mastery of the entire range of potentially appealing styles by contrast with the emotionally and politically impoverished approach of the "restrained and plain" self-described Atticist (*Orat.* 73). At stake, Cicero concludes in the last paragraph, is "the approval of the crowd and the pleasure of the ears" (*ad volgi assensum . . . ad aurium voluptatem*, 237). In closing, he apologizes to Brutus for his aggressive tone and promises not to fight him (*neque pugnabo*) over their difference of opinion. Nonetheless, the thrust of the treatise has left no doubt that if leading men like Brutus—the men Cicero calls *rectores, auctores, gubernatores, moderatores, conservatores, optimi cives*—hope to heal the republic, they must change their habits (*mutatio morum*) before the people (*in populo, Leg.* 3.31–32).[67]

The nature of the moment of persuasion as a crucial moment in the formation of collective identity is illuminated by Philip Pettit, who speaks in broad terms of identification with others as an essential step toward internalizing social norms of civility and civil dialogue. While each of us is a personal self, he observes—each with his or her own sense of personal heritage, memory, beliefs, plans, commitments, and failures— we are not only selves, we also "suspend" our selves' hold on us, in order to think in ways that arise from a heritage we may identify as common, and thus to enter into a dialogue (spoken or silent) with our fellow citizens.[68]

Ornament, the other necessary area of expertise for the best orator, defined here as the appropriate use of figures of thought and figures of speech, like rhythm and vocal sound, is a more complicated case. It too is a mark of innate harmony, signified by the way it is suited to internal organization in the context of the rhetorical treatise, since figures are

---

[67] Rector: *Rep.* 5.5, 5.6, 6.1; *rector rei publicae et consilii publici auctor, de Orat.* 1.211; *gubernator, Rep.* 2.51; *conservator, Rep.* 6.13; *tutor et procurator: Rep.* 2.51; *moderator, Rep.* 5.8; *civis, Rep.* 5.3, 6.1; *magnus civis, Rep.* 1.45; *optimus civis, Q. fr.* 3.5.1. References and discussion of the "originality" of Cicero's conception appear in Ferrary, "The statesman and the law," 51–53. Like Ferrary, I am persuaded by Lepore, *Il princeps Ciceroniano*, that Cicero's treatment of this ideal figure is not intended to refer protreptically to a Caesar-style *princeps*.

[68] Pettit, *Republicanism*, 257, and further: "It is a matter of owning heritages of experience and belief and intention that transcend your personal concerns," 258. Springborg criticizes Pettit's normative appropriation of the republican tradition, especially his attempt to distinguish the republican from the liberal definition of freedom, "Republicanism, freedom from domination, and the Cambridge contextual historians," 851–57. See further McCormick, "Machiavelli against republicanism."

always presented carefully identified and named. Ornament not only illumines (*lumina* is Cicero's word for ornament), it helps organize the oration into accessible units of thought; it clarifies; it brings the subject into sharper focus. Rational and rationally organized patterns of ornament sublime the speech from the inside, creating an aesthetic interplay of spirit and sense. In this sense they perform an essentially propaedeutic role, processing the raw stuff of words for use in the service of reason.[69] As with rhythm and sound, this is only half the story of ornament's impact. The peak of the best orator's talent is his ability to handle both what the Greeks call *to ethikon*, that which relates to character and habit, and *to pathetikon*, by which the spirit is "aroused and excited" (*perturbantur et concitantur, Orat.* 128). In this alone the best style of oratory "rules" (*regnat*), for it is violent, fiery, rushed, and impossible to resist (*vehemens, incensum, incitatum,* 128–89). It is just at this point in the treatise that Cicero takes up the topic of ornament, beginning with metaphor and its capacity to whirl the mind around every which way. The transport of meaning creates its own space, which Cicero treats as a space of pleasure, pleasure born of mental motion, of minds transported. Metaphor in this text functions metaphorically: it captures in one word, "metaphor," all the effects of ornate eloquence. Cicero speaks of metaphor in terms of propriety and place: *translatio* is a word "placed in a foreign place as though it were its own place" (*de Orat.* 3.157). But metaphor is also the ornament that specially distinguishes the best orator, whose style will be filled with metaphors (*frequentissimae tralationes*), which "transport the mind and carry it back and move it here and there, a rapid tumult of thought (*motus cogitationis celeriter*) that gives pleasure through its own constant motion" (*Orat.* 134).

Cicero's identification of metaphor as the quality that distinguishes the best orator contrasts with other treatments of metaphor in the rhetorical tradition. To Aristotle, metaphor consists in "giving the thing a name that belongs to something else," a trick that will save the language from seeming mean and prosaic while highlighting the clarity of ordinary words (*Poet.* 1457b6, 1458a32–34). When metaphor properly corresponds to the thing signified, it gives style clearness, charm, and distinction "as nothing else can, and it is not a thing whose use can be taught by one man to another" (*Rhet.* 1405a8–12). He classifies metaphors under the heading of words that are *xenikon*, "unusual" or literally "foreign," and points out that improper use of metaphor leads to the laughable (*Poetics* 1458b13–15, 22–23). Nowhere is metaphor identified with the best style. The sense of metaphor as a transference that is necessary for speech to be persuasive but that is vulnerable to impropriety

---

[69] The image is Eagleton's, *Ideology of the Aesthetic,* 105.

appears again in Quintilian. For Quintilian, metaphor adds to the abundance and sublimity of language by the "borrowing of what it does not have, and what is most difficult, it provides against a name lacking for any thing. . . . We do this either because it is necessary or because it is clearer or (as I have said) because it is more proper" (*decentius*, 8.6.5–6, 11). He warns that excessive use of metaphor obscures and exhausts speech, and when used continuously metaphors lead to confusing allegories and enigmas (*allegorias et aenigmata*, 8.6.14, cf. *de Orat.* 3.167, *obscuritas*, *aenigmata*). Borrowing examples of metaphorical vice quoted in Cicero's earlier work—"the state was *castrated* by the death of Africanus," "Glaucia, the *excrement* of the curia"—Quintilian emphasizes that metaphors may be harsh (*durae*), literally "far-fetched" (*ductae a longinqua similitudine*, 8.6.17).

In Greek works that composed a canon for Roman readers by Cicero's lifetime, the breakdown of the polity leads to the misuse of words, and conversely, the misuse of words can lead to the breakdown of the polity. When Socrates describes in the *Republic* how oligarchy mutates into democracy, he says that false words "run up" to take the place of true words, so that "self-discipline is called cowardice . . . insolence becomes sophistication, anarchy freedom, extravagance generosity, and shamelessness courage" (560d–e). Thucydides complains of the inversion of the meanings of courage and other virtues during the civil strife at Corcyra (3.82.4–5). In his *Antidosis*, Isocrates complains that the Athenians no longer use words in their natural sense, *kata phusin*; instead they "metaphorize," or "transfer" meanings (*metapherousin*), so that words that once described "the best actions" (*kallista pragmata*) now signify the "most corrupt activities" (*ta phaulotata*, 283; cf. Sallust *Cat.* 52.11–12). This association between corruption and the metaphorical exchange of words (and its extreme version, catachresis) dominates early modern discussions of figure, such as George Puttenham's 1589 *Arte of English Poesie* (3.17), which treats metaphor in terms of motion, and links it to violence and unnaturalness. "There is a kind of wresting of a single word from his owne right signification, to another not so naturall, but yet of some affinitie or conueniencie with it, as to say, *I cannot digest your unkinde words*, for I cannot take them in good part. . . . Or to call the top of a tree, or of a hill, the crowne of a tree or of a hill: for in deede *crowne* is the highest ornament of a Princes head, made like a close garland, or els the top of a mans head, where the haire windes about, and because such terme is not applyed *naturally* to a tree, or to a hill, but is transported from a mans head to a hill or tree, therefore it is called by *metaphore*, or the figure of *transport*." As Isocrates and Puttenham see it, the relationship between rhetorical and political instability emerges most clearly in the figure of metaphor, the transfer of signification in language such that words take on "new" and "unnatural" meanings. If the agenda of Plato, Thucydides, and Isocrates is to prevent this kind of signification change, and if Aristotle and Quintilian and Puttenham seek to regulate it, Cicero's association of metaphor with the best style of oratory rehabilitates the figure.

Cicero takes time to explain in some detail the pleasure metaphor gives, and why men use it so often when it is not necessary. Again, the language of motion plays a prominent role:

> I suppose it happens either because this is some kind of mark of talent, to leap over things placed before your feet and catch up other things found at a distance; or because he who listens is led elsewhere in his thought, and nonetheless he does not really wander, which is a very great pleasure, or because a subject and its whole likeness is captured in a single word, or because every metaphor, at least those that are chosen reasonably, is directed straight to our senses, especially the sense of sight, which is the sharpest. . . .

> *Id accidere credo vel quod ingenii specimen est quoddam transilire ante pedes posita et alia longe repetitia sumere, vel quod is qui audit alio ducitur cogitatione neque tamen aberrat, quae maxima est delectatio; vel quod singulis verbis res ac totum simile conficitur; vel quod omnis translatio, quae quidem sumpta ratione est, ad sensus ipsos admovetur, maxime oculorum, qui est sensus acerrimus. . . . (de Orat. 3.160–61)*

Metaphor, in Cicero's happy phrase, leaps; it moves minds here and there; it unmoors the mind from its accustomed paths, though in such a way that the listener does not feel lost but somehow directed. Paradoxically, the order of metaphor rests on errancy, a departure from the rational into the world of direct sense perception that brings it into close proximity to poetry.

But this is no innocent mode of transportation. Ornament, rhythm, and sounds are not natural ends in themselves, they are means, and means not just to persuade but to summon up shared passion in the audience. In those circumstances for speaking that allow the grand style, then the orator "pours himself out completely, then he rules and bends spirits, and he moves them where he wishes" (*Orat.* 125). Rhythm exerts the effect it does because of the powerful force it gives to speech, like that of boxers or gladiators, who never move (*non motus*) without grace that is married to literal impact, *ad pugnam*: so the orator seeks to land a good blow with each sentence (*plagam gravem, Orat.* 228). Rhythm and metaphor blend pleasure with force: unity in pleasure and pressure under force emerge as the instruments of *common experience* that grant the best style its power. This is the eloquence "carried along on a great and roaring course, which everyone gazes up at, which everyone admires, which everyone loses faith in being able to acquire. It is the power of this eloquence to sway spirits, to move them in every possible way. Sometimes it shatters the senses, at other times it steals into them; it grafts on new opinions, it tears out innate ones" (*Orat.* 97).[70] The violence of Cicero's language in this passage stands in tension with his emphasis elsewhere on *decorum* and its seat in nature. Ornament, rhythm, and sound, which Cicero has represented in the language of cosmic order and natural harmony, turn out to be enablers of radical, even destructive changes in the civic mind.

THE TERRORS OF COLLECTIVITY

The gap between Cicero's adorned style and Brutus's thin style poses a question that we might call a question of collective identity. What is actually happening as Cicero's best orator persuades his audience? The moment of being moved by the most powerful oratory is a moment at which the audience is driven by its deepest natural impulse to respond as such: individual rational beings are transformed into a collective of unreason, a cohesive mass linked by uncritical, helpless pleasure, led by force. "At that moment it is effective," Cicero writes, "when the listener is now occupied and held by the orator. For he does not act as though he is intent on watching the orator or trapping him, but he favors the orator and wants him to succeed, and amazed at the force of his speaking, he does not seek to criticize" (*Orat.* 210). And in *Brutus*: "The listening multitude is delighted, and it is led by the oration: it is drowned, so to speak, in pleasure. Do you disagree? It rejoices, it grieves, it laughs, it weeps, it approves, it hates, it disdains, it envies, it is brought to pity, shame, regret, it grows angry, it is amazed; it hopes, it fears; these things happen as the minds of those who are present are dragged about by words and thoughts and delivery" (188).

Like its microcosm, metaphor, eloquence brings the orator and the citizen outside themselves (*Orat.* 132). As such it is a key part of political practice—the passionate transport of the mind that both enables the orator to persuade his audience, and arouses the audience from one state of mind to another. The oscillation of thought "here and there" that metaphor accomplishes brings pleasure, but it also makes possible the crucial moment at which the minds of the orator and listener step outside themselves and their own conscious control. This transformation is also wreaked on the orator. "I seem to excel not because of my talent,

---

[70] In *de Oratore*, Cicero disciplines the figure by praising the modesty of the metaphor that does not burst violently into the sentence but comes in "as though by prayer, not force" (3.165).

but because of *dolor*, passion . . . no force of talent, but great force of spirit inflames me, so that I myself do not keep hold of myself; nor would anyone who listens be set on fire, unless the speech that reached him were on fire" (*Orat.* 130, 132). Though Cicero aims to describe the orator in rational terms as a master of his art, and a master of himself—indeed, in *de Oratore* oratory is presented as a technique of ethical self-formation and discipline second to none—the best orator turns out to possess a talent that is literally unspeakable; and not only does he move the people out of themselves, he loses control of himself as well. "I myself do not keep hold of myself," Cicero says, and these words are echoed by Antonius in *de Oratore*, who describes himself set on fire by his own passionate words.

Now we are in a position to appreciate the relationship between the rhetorical figure of metaphor and the broader political implications of eloquent speech. To Hannah Arendt, the of spirit, the unfixed self, without which the political is impossible, is expressed in the figure of metaphor. She suggests that the simple fact that we are able to draw mental analogies may be seen as a kind of 'proof' that mind and body, thinking and sense experience, the invisible and the visible, belong together, are 'made' for each other, as it were." Metaphor, to her, is "evidence of the extraordinary quality of thinking, of its being always out of order"—a necessary element if we are to escape the trap of our own individual perspective.[71] Metaphor and other figures are thus proof of the fact that we can think outside ourselves, specifically, that our minds are capable of being transported into another place. Just as Cicero has said, the rhetorical figure is an active sign of *communis sensus*, a reminder of mental commonality and shared ground in the midst of difference and dispute.

In his earliest work, *de Inventione*, the figure of transport is literally present at the birth of the political community. *Eloquentia* is what gathers people from the wild forests to the proto-urban political community. "There was a time when men wandered around in the fields in the manner of beasts, and sustained life on wild food; they did nothing by the reason of the mind, but by bodily strength" (1.2). Then a *magnus vir*, a great man, becomes aware of man's potential and he compels and gathers the men scattered in the fields in one place (*unum in locum*) by means of reason and speech. Eloquence is thus the original transporter of men; it collected them in the first political society. Without its power, politics is literally unimaginable, meaning that the violent acts of movement and reordering, expressed in verbs like *tractare* and *perfringere*, constitute necessary violence. The oscillating motion of the mind, even the shattering of the psychic structures that enable the listener to respond to the

---

[71] Arendt, *The Life of the Mind*, 109.

orator is a precondition for the establishment of a political relation to others.

The language of unity and harmony in Cicero's descriptions of the best orator's audience aestheticizes what is in fact a very unstable moment when the listening community loses itself in prerational amazement (e.g., *Orat.* 168). This emerges indirectly in Cicero's insistence that prose rhythm be carefully concealed from the audience (*Orat.* 209). Manifest obedience to a particular metrical rule makes sentences sound forced, and they lose their force. The only law of rhythm, it turns out, is to disobey law. The awareness of system ruins the effect; the appeal of rhythm and sound must swim just below the surface of rational apprehension. Woken into consciousness, the audience's awareness of the effects of sound and rhythm destroys its collective harmony: the audience breaks up into individual atoms of disgust, bored alienation, and distrust.[72] These passages refer to the site of speech with which Cicero is most concerned in his rhetorical writings throughout his career, from *de Inventione* to *Orator*: the law court. And the law court, it may be objected, is a minor venue compared to the *contio* or the curia, with only a small audience made up of senators and (at times) *equites*. Yet when we recall the significance of oratory as the spoken sign of law in *de Inventione*, as well as Crassus's claim that the orator, whose principal tasks arise in the law court, preserves the republic, it is clear that forensic speaking holds a unique place in rhetoric's performative ethics by virtue of its role in preserving republican justice. As Cicero warns his jury in the Verrine orations, the movements of its collective mind are the object of scrutiny from the rest of the citizenry (I.3.7). The jury is the republic writ small. Consequently, the orator "should master the civil law, of which court cases are in daily need; for what is more scandalous than to take responsibility for legal and civil disputes, when you do not know our statutes and civil law?" (*Orat.* 120). As Andrew Riggsby notes, the Roman courts existed not for the sake of justice in the abstract but for the good of the community as a whole; the courts are "where the community protects itself, its property, and its rights."[73]

In his insistent attempt to get at the "essence" of *eloquentia*, Cicero keeps returning to an account in which the opposition between community and individual becomes irrelevant, in which the communal emerges as the abandonment of the individual in an ecstatic moment of

---

[72] So Crassus had warned his audience (*de Orat.* 3.163–66). For helpful discussion of metaphor's risks and rewards, see Fantham, *Roman World*, 271–75.

[73] Riggsby, *Crime and Community*, 158. Gellius reports that Cicero wrote a scientific treatise on law (1.22.7); for Cicero's views on law's capacity to affect all citizens, see *de Orat.* 1.188.

passionate identification, into which the hearer is plunged when his mind is transported beyond his conscious control. If the mind-altering power of eloquence, which Cicero expresses in such violent language, involves a kind of shattering of self, Cicero's emphasis on propriety and harmony is an implicit argument on behalf of the redemptive power of that shattering: the individual is violently snatched out of himself only to find himself a part of the aesthetic and political collective. But Cicero complicates his own account by emphasizing that the speaker, too, participates in this process: he, too, loses himself briefly in the effort to drive others out of themselves. Losing oneself is part of the game: that, it seems, is politics.

Cicero's apology for style may be seen as marking and masking a recognition of the fundamental irrationality and loss of self that is the essence of persuasion, the pivot of the political process. The construction of collective identity requires, first of all, that individuals internalize values that the collective is imagined to share. As Cicero says of the *res publica*, citizens are bound together by shared ideas about justice and the common good (*Rep.* 1.39). But being a member of a collective also involves a certain degree of identification: that is, identifying with the groups whose interests are associated with those values. To Cicero, this process involves a kind of necessary violence, whereby the best and most politically effective oratory—ornamental, rhythmic speech—dislodges the mind of the speaker as well as of the listener. In this power, we have found the unspoken reason for Cicero's apology for his discussion of *elocutio*. On the one hand, his rhetorical writings pursue pedagogical ends: to identify and construct the decorous *vir bonus dicendi peritus*, the good man skilled at speaking. On the other, the orator is a master of techniques that undermine the notion of limits on and order in the self. Anxiety about style extends deeper than concern for appearing Greek or lower-class or effeminate; it has to do with the shattering effects on the speaking self, the tension between the focus on the individual and individual achievement central to contest culture and the bonds that form Roman society. This is the anxiety of the collectivity: that it defies reason (*Rep.* 2.57). By representing the best orator's talent as stemming from his capacity to arouse emotion, Cicero shows how legislation and law court proceedings—the underpinnings of the republic and its moral virtue—may yield to the fickle passions of the audience. If this scene reinforces the orator's performative power, it is also a terrifying spectacle of the republican citizenry as a collective of unreason. The solution, of course, is Cicero himself: first a living exemplar of the ideal middle way between ornamented and bare speech, then transformed into a textual memory in *Brutus*, once the republic has fallen into decline (*Brut.* 21, 328).

Cicero's last two rhetorical treatises are a frustrated acknowledgment of the warping of public speech in a republic where the rule of law was crumbling. *Moving* men in this period of republican history had become a dangerous act: Cicero himself had personally suffered at the hands of masses moved to violence by the demagogic rhetoric of a Clodius; Sallust casts Catiline's eloquence as a key instrument in his insurrection (*Cat.* 5).[74] But Cicero's apology is not a simple reaction to Caesarian politics or a defense against Socrates' complaint that eloquence can be used by bad people for bad ends. It is a powerful provocation to those interested in the collective, individual selfhood, and speech, because it poses a challenging question also asked by contemporary political theory: whether the formation of the collective is subject to rational analysis, or whether the transportations of the self into the realm of nonreason that occur at the moment of eloquent persuasion bespeak the descriptive limits that circumscribe political terminology. Ernesto Laclau argues for the sheer *impossibility* of representing the collectivity in language, a conclusion he reaches after analyzing the signifying incapacities of words like "class," "people," "nation," or "society."[75] These words, in his view, do not qualify as metaphors, but as catachreses or *abusiones* defined by Quintilian as the replacement of a word by another that does not belong. Cicero's representation of the powerful, prerational experience of collectivity similarly suggests that the collective is beyond expression.

We have seen that in Cicero's *de Republica*, a republic is an association linked by shared values about justice and the common good. *Legum servi sumus ut liberi esse possimus*, "we are all slaves to the law in order that we may be free" (*Cluent.* 146). Cicero's treatment of republican politics casts citizens as willing participants in the authorship of every law that constrains them; his system ensures that they are only ever self-coercing. But this ideal balance is troubled by unfixity and violence in Cicero's representation of the moment at which the collective comes into being, the moment of collective persuasion. Collective identity emerges in the verbal exchange between orator and audience whose efficacy seems to derive precisely from the confusion of coercion and consent, order and unreason, an ambiguous interplay of force and pleasure. Rhetoric is a dangerous toolbox: what gives it the power to create habits

---

[74] As Victoria Wohl notes in her compelling reading of the dynamic of patriotism in Pericles' funeral oration in Thucydides, Pericles' power springs from his repudiation of pleasure (*hédone*), the kind of pleasure offered by the venal and whorish politicians who lead the city to disaster after Pericles' death. Thus "pleasure and power seem to move in opposite directions, but this is not quite the case," for Pericles' oration itself enjoins the Athenians to fall in love with the city and take pleasure in its power (*Love Among the Ruins*, 65).

[75] Laclau, "Identity and hegemony," 56–59.

of trust and civic love resides in the realm of the prerational. If being recruited to other identities is a necessary part of politics, as Hannah Arendt and Philip Pettit suggest, Cicero reminds us that the process is a violent one. To constitute a republic involves not just adopting an extra layer of identity—interleaving civic concerns and investments with personal ones—but shedding the personal and the individual, to become part of a listening collective that may turn into a roaring mob in the blink of an eye.

Chapter Six

IMPERIAL REENACTMENTS

Deference was not a hierarchical but a republican
characteristic. . . . The Few are not above a kind of deference
to the judgment of the Many, even when they deem its
expression naïve; so that there is a point at which deference and
virtue become nearly identical.
—J.G.A. Pocock, *The Machiavellian Moment*

SALLUST EXPLAINS THE REPUBLIC as a regime of inexorable, desperate competition. "All men who are eager to surpass the other animals (*ceteris animalibus*) must strive with all their resources, lest they pass through life like beasts" (*Jug.* 1.1). Such a regime always falters on the edge of failure: the threat of failure is its permanent spur, and, as Sallust notes, even imperial victory brings defeat. "When the republic grew through labor and just practice (*labore atque iustitia*), when great kings were tamed in war, savage nations and powerful states conquered by armed force, when Carthage, rival of Roman imperial power, fell, and all the seas and lands lay exposed, *fortuna* first grew cruel and overturned everything" (*Jug.* 10.2). Lucretius represents men loaded down by the weight of unknown burdens, careening from villa to house to city center, in a restless, meaningless, endless rush (1053-66).[1] Republican desires for virtue and the imperial power that is understood as virtue's due, spurred by the recognition of their absent or unfinished condition, are perpetually burdened by the unsettling knowledge that perfect fulfillment is impossible.[2] Perfectability is an illusion; virtue can never fully satisfy its own insatiable demands; the striving self must always perceive itself as incomplete. The Julio-Claudians' replacement of republican government with dynastic rule did not so much confirm that republican desire would never be attained—that scarcely needed doing—but rather

---

[1] Leach, "Ciceronian 'Bi-Marcus'" discusses this passage in her Lacanian-inflected discussion of the anxiety of the transience of republican *honores* and the uncertainties of public recognition (146–47).

[2] On empire as the reward for *pietas* and *religio*: Cicero, *sed pietate ac religione atque hac una sapientia, quod deorum numine omnia regi gubernarique perspeximus, omnis gentis nationesque superavimus* (*Har. Resp.* 19).

redirected old anxieties in new directions. The artifice and theatricality of political life, the near-paranoid awareness of *constantly being watched*—topoi that we have grown used to treating as characteristically, even constitutively "imperial" (aided by the visual prompts of Rome on film)—were already central to republican political culture.[3] Essentially republican in origins and nature, they do not derive from the transition to autocracy but rather rework what had always been republican concerns. The republic died later than we think. The so-called Augustan Age is not an autocracy but another wounded iteration of the perpetually wounded and reestablished republic. So far Augustus was instinctively right to claim to lead a *res publica restituta*.

This chapter explores Roman rhetoric in the aftermath of the civil wars that claimed Cicero as a victim in 43 BCE. Having argued for rhetoric's central importance in understanding republican thought, it is essential that I acknowledge that the qualities that made rhetoric such an effective instrument of republican hegemony are precisely what allow it to retain its place at the center of pedagogical practice and political culture under autocracy. Cicero's insistent characterization of the orator's habits of self-knowledge and self-control as practices of manly virtue, as we saw in the last chapter, was a strategy designed in part to conceal the orator's points of similarity to the cosmetically enhanced woman and the eloquent actor. Under the changed conditions of autocracy, at the very moment that rhetoric's subterranean identity as a practice incorporating techniques of charming subservience fully reveals itself, a fictitiously pure version of republican oratory is memorialized as the virtuous opposite of the decayed imperial present. So Tacitus:

> Great eloquence, like fire, is nourished by fuel, and stimulated by motion, and by burning it grows bright. . . . We speak not of a leisurely and peaceable art, and one that finds pleasure in good morals and proper behavior; no, great and memorable eloquence is a foster-daughter of license, which fools used to call liberty; it is the companion of treason, a goad for an unbridled nation, without obedience, without rigor, overbearing, rash, arrogant; it does not grow in well-ordered states. (*Dial.* 36.1, 40.2)[4]

---

[3] So Haynes implies in "Tacitus' dangerous word," an insightful critique of the "empire as spectacle/theater" paradigm used by, e.g., Bartsch, *Actors in the Audience*, and Sinclair, *Tacitus the Sententious Historian*.

[4] *Magna eloquentia, sicut flamma, materia alitur et motibus excitatur et urendo clarescit . . . non de otiosa et quieta re loquimus et quae probitate et modestia gaudeat, sed est magna illa et notabilis eloquentia alumna licentiae, quam stulti libertatem vocabant, comes seditionum, effrenati populi incitamentum, sine obsequio, sine severitate, contumax, temeraria, adrogans, quae in bene constitutis civitatibus non oritur.*

Quintilian, better attuned to the nature of rhetoric, takes the pragmatic view.[5] His is a strategy of accommodation that recuperates rhetoric's original Latin articulation in *de Inventione* and *Rhetorica ad Herennium* as a rationalized system of civic healing, mediating dispute and moderating the differences of ethnicity and custom that characterized the increasingly cosmopolitan empire. Earlier in the first century, and by contrast with Quintilian, are the Augustan declaimers, who experimented with language's capacity for resistance in the face of a new regime that had already proved itself to be a deft manipulator of word and meaning.

REPLAY AND PARODY

This book has argued that the ideological structures underpinning all social manifestations, including rhetorical theory and oratorical practice, constitute a binary of inclusion and exclusion whose constant state of flux meets the eternally changing material circumstances of lived experience, and whose binary parts consequently produce within themselves a splitting of the difference by which the ruling part finds elements within itself that deviate from the ruling standard and the ruled part finds parallels and points of connection with the ruling one.[6] This dynamic process has that essential virtue of ideology, fluidity; but it also means that the dissident, the perverse, and the deviant may find their origins in the ruling order as well as the oppressed one. This view furnishes us with, if not full understanding, at least a phenomenological model of social structural change.

The republican order lays bare this activity in a peculiarly spectacular way—but then again, we have seen precisely how important the theory and practice of civic spectacle is to constituting the republic. Its fragile civic bonds are forged through obedience to social norms, an obedience displayed in constant repetition, watchfulness, and self-care; but its strictness must not be such that it thwarts the vitality and individuality of the citizens: each man must hold to his own nature in his own way (*tenenda sunt sua cuique*, *Off.* 1.110). The republic stands or falls on the visibly performed virtue of its citizens. This is the reason it chooses systems of education and political communication that enable and display the virtue of autonomous self-government. But as we have seen, the performative,

---

[5] On the relationship between Quintilian and Tacitus, with a useful overview of the debate over Tacitus's use of his characters to voice opinions on oratory's future, see Brink, "Quintilian's *de causis corruptae eloquentiae* and Tacitus' *Dialogus de Oratoribus*," esp. 497–99. Goldberg, "Appreciating Aper," and Rutledge, "Oratory and politics in the Empire," critique Tacitus's emphasis on decline.

[6] See my discussion of Gramsci in chapter 1.

though it is defined by rules—rules indeed imagined to mirror, enact, and reinforce the proper internal nature of the rulers and the ruled—must be protean and adaptable, because it is constituted through bodies in action over time, which themselves cope with a variety of changing circumstances of economy, violence, migration, and so on. Inexorable temporality in a scheme of embodied repetition is the engine that drives social change of all kinds: this is what places oratory and other discourses that distill, thematize, and codify elements of performance at the epicenter of social change.

Rhetoric's power as a political discourse lies not only in the promise of mastery over language that it offers, but in its implicit claim that the world is subject to the spectacular order that eloquence can impose upon it. To put it another way, rhetoric's peculiar capacity to articulate rules of speech as correlating to, even exchangeable with, the rules of virtue engenders an ideal of regulated political life. And rhetoric offers practical aids to making the ideal real. As a pedagogy, rhetoric's prescriptions for constant exercise, for *practice*, mirrors the republic's demand for constant readiness to serve. Pedagogy and political regime alike set standards for thought and action and require repetitive performances that others will judge in the perpetual process of evaluation (*existimatio*) that in turns reinforces those standards, like a train laying its own tracks.[7] *Virtus, dignitas, auctoritas, gravitas, severitas, gloria, laus, honor, pietas, officium, fides,* and *eloquentia*: all these values are subject to the monitoring force of the public gaze.[8] Whether Cicero and his contemporaries believe that their political machinery is actually working at any given time, their actions are always already regulated by belief in its legitimacy—a belief sustained by their subjection to this gaze.

Repetition is key to the ways both rhetoric and the republic make sense of the world. Just as the second, fifth, or hundredth time the student of rhetoric sets himself to untangle a complex thesis using the tools of status theory is another step in the inculcation of his conviction that human action and motivation may be grasped through these particular tools, so the repetitive practice of voting in elections on the Campus Martius year after year—or even hearing at a distance that elections have occurred once more—lends popular participation a place in the making of political reality.[9] As Slavoj Žižek argues, the power of ideology is not that no one knows the truth, it is that everyone knows that what passes for truth is

---

[7] The train analogy is from Bourdieu, *The Logic of Practice,* 57. On the need for constant practice and the readiness of observers to identify defects, *de Orat.* 1.129–30.

[8] See the brief but insightful discussion of Minyard, *Lucretius and the Late Republic,* 9; also Habinek's discussion of *existimatio* in Cato and Terence, *The Politics of Latin Literature,* 45–59.

[9] M. Jameson, observing that the Athenians demanded a much larger network of ritual performances than any one person could practically engage in, suggestively concludes that the communal participation actually mandated by the demands of ritual did not necessarily

fiction and yet continues to behave as though fiction were truth.[10] Ideology does not act like a mask or a curtain that, if it were ripped away, would reveal reality, "the actual state of things." On the contrary, the consensus of misrecognition is reality itself. People value money, for instance, but they also know there is nothing essentially mystical or magical about it: what they do not acknowledge is that, in the course of the choices they make through life, it is indeed the illusion of money's magic that guides them. The mass of Roman citizens might have no illusions about their influence as individuals—the weighting of votes alone would remind them of it—but this would not necessarily affect their invested belief in the legitimacy of the system as a whole.

When a performance is repeated again and again, however, the possibility of parody hovers close by. Every repetition of an act increases the distance between the act being performed at the time and the original action it imitates. Repetition entails the possibility of mistakes or reimaginings intended or not. If the original action is a rule or a law where the demand for reenactment is built in from the start—as it always is in the rule-bound discourses of politics or education—then it must also be the case that parody is constitutive of the original rule.[11] Whether the parodic component of a given act will be activated at any given moment is up to the particular articulation of the ensemble of institutionalized beliefs and practices dominant at that moment. To acknowledge the presence of parody—to invoke the gap between the repeated performance and its original—is to draw attention to what everyone knows is there but which they have repeatedly chosen not to act on.

This is why the famous observation of Caesar, made some time after he was given the newly invented constitutional status of *dictator perpetuo* in 49 (Cicero, Phil. 2.87), that the republic was nothing, was so intolerable, in conjunction with his acceptance of singular honors and his general disdain of convention. He spoke a truth known to all but admitted by none, and in doing so he bluntly interrupted the performance of republican politics: "the *res publica* was nothing, only a label without body or form."[12]

---

involve literal acts. Unfailing attendance at the rites was not expected or even possible; what mattered was "knowledge that the rites were being performed in the right time, in the right place" ("The spectacular and the obscure," 331, 333).

[10] Žižek, *The Sublime Object of Ideology*, 28, 32–33. Taking the famous phrase of Marx, "Sie wissen das nicht, aber sie tun es," he counters that rather than the original "They do not know it, but they are doing it," the more accurate formulation would be "They do know it, and they are doing it": "the illusion is therefore double: it consists in overlooking the illusion which is structuring our real, effective relationship to reality. And this overlooked, unconscious illusion is what may be called the ideological fantasy."

[11] Laclau, "Identity and hegemony," 78–79.

[12] Suetonius, *Div. Jul.* 77: *nec minoris inpotentiae uoces propalam edebat, ut Titus Ampius scribit: nihil esse rem publicam, appellationem modo sine corpore ac specie.*

Suetonius's source tellingly links Caesar's remark about the republic with his dismissal of the interpretation of entrails as meaningless without his sanction. These are declarations about the essential vulnerability of political or religious beliefs to displacement by the pressure of new attitudes. Llewellyn Morgan sets the comment in the con-text of the "indeterminacy of meaning in the crisis of the late republic," when *res publica,* along with other terms, has become nothing more than a slogan.[13] In response to Stanley Fish, for whom radical semantic indeterminacy is an inescapable function of the structures of authority that constitute human society, Morgan emphasizes the specificity of the historical conditions under which such a comment would make sense: a society in crisis. Such was the Roman republic in the 40s, after the death of Pompey and Caesar's consolidation of power. Through the utterances of Caesar and others—including Cicero, whose letters from 47 on speak of loss and collapse—the republic begins to shake loose from its foundation in speech. The breakdown points to the importance of speech in lending plausibility to the regime—the importance of the agreement not to acknowledge determining fictions as such.

Reading resistance in Augustan declamation

Active during the early first century CE, the elder Seneca (father of the Neronian philosopher and politician) produced an unusual literary work: a collection of arguments for rhetorical practice exercises called *controversiae* and *suasoriae,* first employed in classical Greece and used in Rome as assignments for adolescents attending schools of rhetoric.[14] The eleven extant books follow a pattern. First, they set out the conditions of the case proper: forensic *controversiae* that gave material for speeches of prosecution or defense include "A woman made infertile by a tyrant's tortures is later sued for divorce; she accuses her husband of maltreatment"; "On a dare, a youth dresses as a woman and goes out at night; he is raped; the attackers are convicted, but can he then speak in

---

[13] Morgan, "*Levi quidem de re,*" 32, where he also cites the concise formulation of Minyard, *Lucretius and the Late Republic,* 14–15: "Words were released from their anchor in agreement about reality . . . and it became nearly impossible to tell whether a term was being used to name the things it had originally named, was being expanded legitimately to take account of new perceptions of reality, or was simply being used . . . to disguise reality."

[14] The history of *controversiae* and *suasoriae* is covered by Fairweather (*Seneca the Elder*), Bloomer ("Schooling in persona"), Leeman (*Orationis Ratio*), and Sussman ("The elder Seneca and declamation"). The original title of of Seneca's work is unknown. It bears the unwieldy title of *Oratorum et Rhetorum Divisiones Colores et Sententiae* (Fairweather), but for the sake of brevity I call the text the *Controversiae*; these "cases" constitute the bulk of the work. When I make specific reference to the same collection's *Suasoriae,* a closely related but separate kind of exercise, I so indicate.

public?" and so on. The deliberative *suasoriae* addressed broader themes of history and myth: "Should Agamemnon sacrifice Iphigeneia?" "Should Cicero avoid execution by promising Antony to burn his writings?" Following each theme are excerpts that illustrate "approaches" to it known as *colores* (a translation of the Hellenistic term *chromata*), which Seneca reports as recalled from memory of particular performances. From the start, then, the text finds itself imitating an absent performance imitating an absent performance that Seneca laments as already (under Augustus and Tiberius) dead and gone (*Contr.* 1 pref. 11).[15] *Colores* are followed by lists of *sententiae*, or epigrams. The whole is punctuated by Seneca's comments and biographical notes on the declaimers, which often develop topics mentioned in the prefaces. The spotty quality of the *Controversiae* "narrative" evokes the droll repartee of what Seneca suggests is a typical day spent in declamation.

The men Seneca describes were known as *declamatores*, or declaimers, a group that itself overlaps with the longer-lasting tradition of *scholastici*, or schoolmen.[16] Their activity suggests how rhetoric fuels a resistant sensibility, a shift in the self's consciousness of relation to the structures of power, more subtly than the launch of a conspiracy or even the withdrawal from politics. Their practices ask us to craft a new lexicon of resistance that foregrounds language and style on the level of the individual practitioner. As Michel Foucault said in a late interview, the problem is not to dissolve relations of power, an impossible task, but "to give one's self the rules of law, the techniques of management, and the ethos" that redistribute the balance of power.[17] This redistribution is what the declaimers were about as they forged a new means of cultural production, one that fell largely outside the influence and patronage of Augustus: the exercise of verbal freedom in the context of the modified schoolroom; the transformation of declamation, originally a schoolboy exercise in rhetoric, into a series of experiments with something as basic and politically loaded as the Latin language itself; the experimentation, ultimately, in the care of the self, for the declaimers (at least in Seneca's representation) exploited the nascent links between Ciceronian performative ethics and the stylistics of the self that was emerging as the primary mode of philosophical ethics. For the declaimers, the specialized practices of the Roman rhetorical school constituted a mode of activism that could respond to the rapidly shifting political grounds of the newly established autocracy. They should be

[15] A point well made by Gunderson, *Declamation, Paternity, and Roman Identity,* 57–58.

[16] On the declaimers, see especially M. Beard, "Looking (harder) for Roman myth," and Bloomer, "A preface to the history of declamation." Introductions and discussions of the fundamentals can be found in Bonner, *Roman Declamation.*

[17] Foucault, "The ethic of care for the self as a practice of freedom,"18.

seen as the inheritors of the conceptual spaces opened up by Ciceronian
rhetorical discourse and its performative ethics of republican politics.
They transformed what had been a "practice" in the sense of "rehears-
al" into a "finished product," and in so doing, they disclosed the theatricality that had always been there in the first place, the nascent
absurdity of a politics performed in words.

Judith Butler calls for a new language of resistance in her observation
that Althusser allows for the possibility of "bad" (resistant) subjects, but
he fails to consider what kinds of disobedience might be involved in
resistance. Resistance is more than breaking the law: it might well take
the form of

> the parodic inhabiting of conformity that subtly calls into question the
> legitimacy of the command, a repetition of the law into hyperbole, a
> rearticulation of the law against the authority of the one who delivers it.
> Here the performative, the call by the law which seeks to produce a lawful
> subject, produces a set of consequences that exceed and confound what
> appears to be the disciplining intention motivating the law.[18]

The subtly parodic transformation of conformity, I will argue, describes
the declaimers' practice. Of course, Butler's formulation might also be
applied to Augustus. He enacted radical innovations in the apparatus of
political power within a carefully maintained framework of republican
ways and means.[19] To Velleius Paterculus, Augustus was a republican
leader in the tradition of the great instigators of civil war of the first
century BCE, the difference lying in the peacefulness and stability following
his victory (2.89.1–4). The *princeps*' deliberate and unprecedented
assumption of power was facilitated by his adherence to republican exempla, particularly in areas of senatorial organization and social legislation.[20]
The phenomenon of transformation within tradition is an outstanding

---

[18] Butler, *Bodies That Matter*, 122.

[19] On the political side, Eck concludes his fine article on Augustus's use of tradition and
innovation: "Daß seine Herrschaft so stabil war und immer mehr ven den verschiedenen
Gruppen im Reich akseptiert wurde, war eine nicht unwesentliche Folge dieser Art von
Politik" ("Augustus' administrative Reformen: Pragmatismus oder systematisches
Planen?", 118). See also Zanker, *The Power of Images in the Age of Augustus* (Ann Akbor,
1990); Wallace-Hadrill, "*Mutatio morum*"; Eder, "Augustus and the power of tradition:
The Augustan principate as binding link between republic and empire."

[20] Galinsky concludes: "[T]here is always some interplay between tradition and innovation.
Yet the phenomenon deserves to be singled out as a characteristic of the Augustan age. . . .
[because of] the extraordinary intensity of the exchange between old and new. . . . Both the
degree of adherence to tradition and the new departures were extraordinary and can be
seen in every aspect of Augustan culture. Extraordinary, too, was the creative tension
between them. Though intense, such changes, particularly in the areas of Augustan politics
and administration, were gradual and evolutionary, but they were all the more thorough
for it" (*Augustan Culture*, 363).

characteristic of the early imperial period, recognized by scholars of its poetry, art, and architecture and adduced by historians as one of the most significant elements of Augustus's own survival and that of the autocracy he established.[21] The declaimers echo Augustus's strategy: in following the Ciceronian exemplum, they construct a world where verbal experimentation is the norm.

On the printed page of a modern text, the material of declamation can appear abstruse and unpromising, the cases frivolous and the incessant disputations over diction and argument asinine and bizarre.[22] But we should remember the central role declamation played in cultural discourse at Rome. It was the training ground of senatorial and equestrian youth, including the young men entering Augustus's new *cursus honorum*, members of the emperor's family, and poets like Ovid, Persius, and Statius. Provincials like the elder Seneca and his circle of Corduban friends seem to have cultivated declamation as a challenging field of competition where the possession of eloquence, charisma, and an imposing physical presence could vie with the *auctoritas* endowed by ancient blood or enormous wealth.[23] One declaimer, Albucius Silus, complains: "What reason have I to speak in court? More listen to me at home than listen to anyone in court" (*Contr.* 7 pref. 8). Recent studies of the meager evidence for contemporary oratory outside of declamation suggest that this portrayal is unsound; but Albucius's remark suggests that in a culture still organized around intense competition, private homes were an obvious substitute for the dangerous arena of the courtroom in uncertain times.[24] Among the enthusiasts who listened and, through lively commentary, participated were Augustus, Maecenas, Agrippa, Asinius Pollio, and other powerful players in the new government. Their presence was something of a risk, of course, as one might imagine when a case involving tyrannicide, adoption, or book-burning was the topic of the day, but this appears to have been part of the serious game that so deeply absorbed the declaiming players.

Language was an area of expertise whose mastery offered a relatively safe means of exercising a certain degree of *libertas* before the *princeps*, as in the case of M. Pomponius Porcellus, a teacher who rebuked Tiberius for

[21] Galinsky, *Augustan Culture*, 56; cf. D. Kennedy, "'Augustan' and 'anti-Augustan.'"

[22] Gunderson laments their treatment and calls for new attention for these men "forever going on about nothing," *Declamation, Paternity, and Roman Identity*, 90, 112.

[23] Bloomer, *Latinity and Literary Society at Rome*, 124–29 and 150–53. Gleason, *Making Men*, on the epideictic performances of the Greek second sophistic, noted that declamation was the "anvil upon which the self-presentation of ambitious upper-class men was forged" (introduction, xx).

[24] Brunt, "The role of the senate in the Augustan regime," helpfully enumerates and comments on the extensive evidence for debate in the senate under Augustus and Tiberius, in Suetonius, Tacitus, and Dio. On the state of imperial oratory, see now Dominik "Tacitus and Pliny on oratory" and Rutledge "Oratory and politics in the empire."

a lapse in diction and escaped unscathed: when a certain Ateius Capito insisted that the emperor's choice of word was acceptable Latin, or that if it were not then, it certainly would be from that day onward, Porcellus retorted: "You can give citizenship to people, Caesar, but not to words" (Suet. *De Rhet. et Gramm.* 22). *Libertas* is one of several key words in the declaimers' debates over *color* and style. Several declaimers arranged politically motivated suicides. Some of the most vocal critics of Augustus appear in the *Controversiae* as the strongest enthusiasts of declamation. The historian Asinius Pollio made his suspicion of autocracy publicly known.[25] The jurist Antistius Labeo used his skills with oratory and the law in research remote from the daily action of the political world. Cassius Severus, who criticized professional declamation but nevertheless spoke like a declaimer (Tac. *Dial.* 19, 26), was outspoken, obstinate, and an enemy of Augustus.[26] He attacked allies of Augustus, including Quinctilius Varus, then the son-in-law of Agrippa, and his books were burned. So were those of his rival, the declaimer Titus Labienus: Cassius sardonically told his friends that Augustus should not have bothered, for he had all the books in his head (*Contr.* 10 pref. 8).[27] Here he follows the precedent of Gaius Trebonius, Julius Caesar's former general, who celebrated his hopes for a new *libertas* after taking part in his assassination by composing an invective in the manner of Lucilius (Cicero, *Fam.* 12.16.3).

Risk taking was the declaimers' bread and butter. Audiences agreed that Albucius's performances were far from flawless; still, "however one repented of having gone to hear him," Seneca says, "one was always glad to go again" (7 pref. 6).[28] He had a highly uneven oratorical style, which Seneca attributed to his lack of confidence and a slavish attention to *le dernier cri* (*Contr.* 7 pref. 4). Arellius Fuscus was also known for his jerky variations: his oratory ranged from a bare smoothness to wandering prolixity: neither sharp, hard or jagged (*solidum, horridum*), nor rich or sleek (*laeta*), his style was brilliant (*splendida*) and licentious (*lasciva*, 2 pref. 1). Votienus Montanus, "a man of the rarest but not faultless talent" (*homo rarissumi etiamsi non emendatissimi ingeni*, 9.5.15) and the source of "Montanian sayings" that circulated after his performances (*Montaniana*, 9.5.14), cultivated a reputation for experimenting with epigram. In his

[25] Pliny, *Nat.* 36.33; *Contr.* 4 pref. 3; Tacitus *Ann.* 4.34.

[26] Syme, *The Roman Revolution*, 486.

[27] I call Cassius and Labienus rivals from Seneca's description of Cassius as *hominis Labieno invissimi* (10 pref. 8).

[28] Born in Novaria in Cisalpine Gaul, a "very stout and stable town," according to Tacitus (*firmissima transpadanae regionis municipia*, *Hist.* 1.70), Albucius served there as an aedile before departing for Rome in his thirties. He maintained his Gaulish provincial connections throughout his life, pleading cases in Mediolanum even after his voluntary retirement from forensic practice at Rome (Suet. 30.4).

début before the centumviral court, Montanus defended a woman accused of poisoning her father to gain her inheritance prematurely. He began with a beautifully phrased *sententia*, "something very clever, that won't be forgotten through the ages, something better put than—I don't know—than *anything* ever said in this sort of case," Seneca observes, and he followed them up with three increasingly obscure *sententiae* (9.5.16). Other declaimers employed styles that tested their audiences' aesthetic taste as well as their powers of comprehension, with experiments in unevenness, repetition, and overrefinement. Otho handled the legal issues behind *controversiae* by dropping hints to his audience and intermittently falling silent (*silentium et significationem*). He spoke easily and well, deceiving his listeners into thinking that his argument was the only possible right one; but later on, Seneca writes, they would wonder why he was so allusive and difficult when there was no need (*suspiciosa*, 2 pref. 37). Otho's efforts to communicate through loaded silence and signals are clearly directed toward exploiting the average audience's love of the challenging and the unusual. Quintus Haterius used archaic words to similar effect, "out of anxiety to say nothing that was not elegant and brilliant" (*culte . . . splendide*). Haterius's experiments with diction often went too far, and his audience would respond with derision (4 pref. 7). Speed of delivery was another characteristic Haterian flaw, so pronounced that he employed a freedman to tell him when to slow down: an unimpressed but amused Augustus punned that Haterius's puffs of air needed a brake.[29] Seneca's friend and fellow Spaniard Porcius Latro was as immoderate as Haterius in both work and play, obsessively allocating one day to epigrams, another to enthymemes, the next to figures, and so on; unable to stop declaiming, he was then too lazy to begin again once he had stopped, against the advice of doctors and voice trainers (1 pref. 13–14).

Low to high, crass to elegant—the declaimers altered styles in an instant. Titus Labienus, for example, in a convoluted *controversia* that involved a rivalry between two soldiers who were also father and son, began by saying, "The same tent cannot hold a hero and a loser" (*non capit idem contubernium fortem virum et victum*, 10.2.19). This sentence, nicely alliterative but rather coarsely phrased by the standards of declamation, he followed with a striking metaphor: "You carved my humiliation into bronze" (*ignominiam meam in aes incidisti*), which, Seneca comments, broke all the rules of figural convention. It was fear of being thought a "schoolman" (*scholasticus*) that drove Albucius to declaim about "the lowest things: vinegar and flea-mint and lanterns and

---

[29] The pun lies in Augustus's conflation of the verb *sufflo*, to inflate or puff up, with *sufflamen*, a wagon bar used as a brake (*Haterius noster sufflaminandus est*). Tacitus describes Haterius in the same terms (*Ann.* 4.61).

sponges" (7 pref. 3). "The pursuit of vulgarism is one of the virtues of style that rarely works out in practice: one needs great restraint and precisely the right moment" (7 pref. 5).[30]

But why did Albucius pursue a vulgar style in the first place? And what significance did a declaimer hold for his audience that they would react so strongly to his solecisms, misquotations, and other slips of the tongue? By Seneca's account, audiences were eager to encourage the declaimers to tread ever closer to the cliff of impropriety and outrageousness, though they punished those who tumbled over the edge. Was their interest a consequence of rhetoric's increasing specialization and esotericism, or the outgrowth of a desire to regulate Latin and Latinity on behalf of national or class interests? Philosopher of art Arthur Danto asks similar questions of artworks and performances of the 1970s and 1980s, which shared the goal of startling or offending their audiences, who in turn were eager to patronize and study artists whose work parlayed the greatest shock value. Photographs of S/M scenes, paintings of terrorists and their hooded victims, and realistic sculptures of tortured bodies: these works travel, Danto argues, into a realm of art that seeks to close the distance between representation and reality by employing "obscenity, frontal nudity, blood, excrement, mutilation, real danger, actual pain, possible death."[31] His paradigmatic example is the 1972 *Deadman*, by Chris Burden, for which Burden had himself enclosed in a sack and placed in the middle of a California road: he was not killed, but he could have been, and his death, Danto says, "[would not have violated] the boundaries of the work because the work incorporated those boundaries as part of its substance."[32] This work presents itself as the defiant opposite of banality, and it dares the viewer to disagree.

"Disturbational art": Burden's self-sacrifice or Annie Sprinkle's aggressive self-revelations are ephemeral and indefinite artforms that seek to reexamine traditional limits on art as a practice, that is, as a process that is intended to affect its observers in a meaningful way. The disturbational artist puts himself or herself on the line, exposing the audience to actions or speeches that are jolting, transgressive, frightening. In Danto's view, disturbational art carries with it the threat to compromise reality in the eyes of its viewers, to force them to reconsider the ways in which daily life, including more conventional art, fails to engage with the pressing political and aesthetic issues of our world. Because the world makes space more readily for conventional art, the art at the margins retreats into ever

---

[30] *Idiotismos est inter oratorias virtutes res quae raro procedit: magno enim temperamento puos est et occasione quadam.*

[31] Danto, "Art and disturbation," in *The Philosophical Disenfranchisement of Art*, 121.

[32] Ibid., 123.

more fantastical pathways of irrationality and, sometimes, sociopathy. Perhaps, Danto says, it is for this reason that the historical response to disturbational art has been "to disarm it by cooptation, incorporating it instantaneously into the cool institutions of the artworld where it will be rendered harmless and distant."[33] To view the declaimers as practitioners of disturbational art is knowingly to press the limits of our evidence and recover the tense and vivid quality of their performances, which pushed the envelope of conventional rhetorical and social practice.

Their experiments did not always succeed. "Of course the whole thing may simply explode into giggles. With our rational minds we find [their efforts] utterly discredited."[34] As with any experimental form of discourse, the declaimers encountered problems of reception, but they refused to be satisfied with an accepted fashion, like Albucius Silus, who never ceased switching his declamatory style, despite the fact that it adversely affected his performance (7 pref. 5). Audiences took their experiments seriously, and gained gratification from observing them in action. With ever more precise refinements, abandoning the conventional adherence to a single individual style, pruning away common aphorisms and figures and inventing hitherto unheard of modes of speech, they created oratorical practice anew.

The same Cestius who, we will see, was tormented by Cassius Severus derided Albucius Silus for saying in the course of an argument, "Why is a cup broken when it falls, but a sponge, if it falls, is not broken?" (7 pref. 8). The arguments deployed in declamation deviate from the rules of logic. Montanus defended his decision to avoid declamation by saying that he wanted to avoid its bad habits, that is, the sacrifice of the best argument for the sake of ornament (9 pref. 4; cf. 2.1.26). Albucius, who declaimed for hours without a stop, piled arguments on top of arguments, and viewing none of them as based on firm ground: everything had to be proved with reference to another unprovable point (7 pref.). Albucius's irrationality extended itself to acts Seneca condemns as genuine impropriety. In a very common *controversia* involving a man who rapes two women, one of whom then demands the legal punishment of death, the other marriage, most of the Senecan declaimers focus not on the criminal nature of rape but on the immoderation of a man who would rape not one but two women in the same night. The most outrageous comments stress the humor of the topic: "I congratulate you, virgins, that dawn came so quickly." "You ask what brought an end to his rapes? Day," and Latro's contribution, "He was just preparing himself for a third—if only night had not ended!" By Seneca's standards Albucius goes too far by

[33] Ibid., 119.
[34] Ibid., 131.

recommending that the rapist turn to men to satisfy his desires. Haterius, too, said obscene things about child sexuality and other matters (4.5.9). This aspect of the declaimers' competition, which involved inventing obscene and improper ways in which to speak about obscene and improper objects and practices, transforms the republican contest into parody. Dorion said something "rather too exalted" (*elatiorem*) to suit forensic oratory, in a case involving self-cannibalism: "What longing is this, my child, to eat and drink blood? What, child, am I babbling about?" (1.8). Alfius Flavus said: "He was his own food—and his own death." "Cestius reproved him," Seneca writes, "saying, 'Obviously you read Ovid, that writer who filled our generation with erotica.' For Ovid describes a man eating himself in the *Metamorphoses*" (3.7). It is tempting to contrast these passages with those concerned with policing sexuality in the speeches of Scipio Aemilianus, surveyed in chapter 1; it seems that the discourse of supervision is being rearticulated (in the declaimers' formal language, at least) as a discourse of experimentation and laughter.

These habits did not translate effectively into courtroom practice—which is very likely the point. They staged their failures: Albucius was one of several declaimers to receive what Cicero calls the "hard knocks" of the Roman courts and Forum (*de Orat.* 1.81; cf. Quintilian 10.1.32–33). Fabianus was observed to lack toughness (*robur*) and the fighter's edge (*pugnatorius mucro*) of the law court orator (*Contr.* 2 pref. 2). The Greek-born Cestius Pius invited risk when he billed a performance as an answer to Cicero's *Pro Milone*: his crowd of devotees included Cassius Severus, a prominent orator of the Augustan period and a well-known critic (and practitioner) of declamation.[35] Seneca's account derives from Cassius's firsthand report (3 pref. 16–17). Cestius began with self-praise. When he compared himself with legendary men and animals ("If I were a Thracian, I should be Fusius; if I were a mime, I should be Bathyllus; if I were a horse, I should be Melissio"), Cassius exclaimed, "If you were a sewer, you'd be the Cloaca Maxima!" The listeners shouted with laughter; only the *scholastici*, or "schoolmen," glared at Cassius, wondering who the "fat-necked" intruder was. Cestius announced that he would not open his mouth until Cassius left the room; Cassius snapped in reply that he would not leave the public bath until he had had his wash. Cassius soon prosecuted Cestius on unspecified grounds, and found to his delight that the popular declaimer was terrified of speaking in court, tremblingly begging the praetor for an indefinite adjournment. Only after humiliating Cestius twice more on desultory charges of ingratitude and incompetence

---

[35] Composing replies to Ciceronian speeches appears to have been a common practice in the first and second centuries CE, as Quintilian attests (10.5.20). For Cassius's criticisms of declamation, see below and Suetonius, 22.1.

did he finally name his terms: Cestius must publicly swear that he was less eloquent than Cicero.[36] When Cestius refused, the orator gave up the feud: "I've told you this little story," he concludes in Seneca's account, "so that you may understand that declaimers are a completely different type of men" (3 pref. 18).[37]

In their habits of life, the declaimers of the early imperial period confirm Cassius's caustic observation that they were "different men," from the manner in which they lived their lives to the habits they cultivated in their declamatory styles. Albucius Silus engineered his own death with the theatrical sense that pervaded his declamations. At home in Spain, he summoned a *contio*, gave a lengthy speech explaining his weariness of life, and then starved himself to death (Suet. 30.5). Montanus complained of the "dangerous stupor" that gradually overwhelms declaimers (*periculosus stupor*, Contr. 9 pref. 2); the Greek rhetorician Miltiades commented that declaimers in search of an archaic word are "mad—in the right way" (*epi to dexion mainontai*, 9.2.26). The madness of some declaimers is linked to the excessive behavior and lack of control in men like Porcius Latro, Haterius, and Musa. "He had great talent, but no heart. Everything was taken to the edge of turgidity," Seneca says of Musa, "with the result that it was beyond nature as well as beyond reason."[38] His language was dreamy, fantastic, and chimerical: as he put it, siphons "rain back at the sky" (*caelo repluunt*); sprays are "perfumed rain showers" (*odoratos imbres*); a decorative spruce garden becomes an "ornamented forest" (*caelatas silvas*); and in an ecphrasis of a nature scene, the "groves swell" (*nemora surgentia*). Over and over Seneca emphasizes the genuine differences of character and practice between the declaimers and other men: Sparsus, for example, was considered sane among the *scholastici*, but among the sane he ranked as a *scholasticus*—which is to say, mad (1.7). Vibius Gallus presses the constraints of reality the furthest. This Gallus was

> once as eloquent as he was later crazed. He was the one man of my acquaintance not to have fallen into madness by chance, but to have come to it by an act of judgment. He aped the mad, thinking insanity would be a good pander to his genius—and so made a reality of what he pretended. . . .

[36] Cassius's charges are clearly intended to recall laws commonly debated in declamations of this period: for the charge of "unspecified offences," see Contr. 5.1, Decl. Min. 252, 344, 370; for ingratitude, Contr. 9.1 and 2.5, Decl. Min. 333, 368; Quint. 7.4.37–38; for the *actio dementiae*, Contr. 6.7, 10.3, 2.3, 7.6, Decl. Min. 346. An exhaustive commentary on the relation between historically attested *leges* and the legal issues of the *controversiae* appears in Bonner, *Roman Declamation*, 84–132.

[37] *Hanc, inquit, tibi fabellam rettuli ut scires in declamationibus tantum non aliud genus hominum esse.*

[38] *Multum habuit ingeni, nihil cordis; omnia usque ad ultimum tumorem perducta, ut non extra sanitatem sed extra naturam essent*, 10 pref. 9.

[In giving declamations] he would say, in a tone almost like a singer's (*paene cantantis modo*) "I wish to describe love" as though it were "I wish to rave like a bacchant." Then he would proceed. . . . but he would keep saying, "I wish to describe love." So here he kept repeating "I wish to describe wealth." I remember one thing involving a tiny bit of madness [in a case involving a son's love for his father]: "I do not like gangs of slaves whom their master does not know, slave-camps filling the countryside with their din for miles around. I love my father gratis."(2.1. 25–26)

Gallus went mad of his own volition, instead of by compulsion: courting a crazy affect in his speech, he lost his soul. His insanity suggests the disturbational artwork of Kathy Acker. "How can I learn to talk better?" one of her characters, Janey, asks an absent lover. "Teach me how to talk to you." But as it turns out, the language she must learn in order to seduce her lover and to remain herself is entirely irrational. She imagines a dialogue, saying, "Teach me a new language:

"Rock-n-roll is rock-n-roll."	"Rock-n-roll is rock-n-roll."
"The night is red."	"The night is red."
"The streets are deserted."	"The streets are deserted."
"The children in the city are going insane."	"The children in the city are going insane."

The dialogue repeats, with only a few variations, until the final line: "'The children in the city are going insane.'" At that point Janey cries, "How can I tell the difference between sanity and insanity? . . . Anyway I don't know if there are any children anymore. Maybe they went out of fashion."[39] Janey articulates the declaimers' political circumstances and their strategies when she concludes, "At this point in my life politics don't disappear but take place inside my body."

From what source does Gallus's madness come? Cicero provides an answer in *de Oratore*, in a line we have seen before, whose substance the declaimers may be seen as putting into practice. When asked by Sulpicius Cotta what the good orator requires, besides knowledge of literature, philosophy, and rhetorical technique, "What else, Cotta," Crassus says with a smile, "except zeal, and a fervor like that of love?" (1.134). Crassus's favored quality of *ardor* transformed the declaimers into what the younger Pliny joined Cassius Severus in calling "a different species of being": caught up in their passion for eloquence, their system of values altered, followed by their bodily dispositions, effectively setting them apart from their less fanatical contemporaries.[40] The peculiarities of the

[39] All quotes from *Blood and Guts in High School*, 95–97.
[40] Pliny, *Ep.* 1.5.11–13; see further Petronius, *Sat.* 3–6; Juvenal 7; Tacitus, *Dial.* 35; Lucian, "The professor of public speaking" (*Rhetoron didaskalos*).

declaimers as they are represented in the *Controversiae*'s prefaces have led to their dismissal by critics ancient and modern as eccentric pedants. In his history of rhetoric at Rome, M. L. Clarke writes, "Of Seneca's four great declaimers two, Latro and Albucius, committed suicide. Of the lesser men who appear in his pages one went mad, and several others, to judge by Seneca's comments, behaved as if they were mad. In the unreal atmosphere of the schools, with their mutual admiration and false values, it was hard to preserve one's balance, and a man who seemed sane within their walls would appear hardly normal outside."[41] Clarke puts its finger on the crux of the declaimers' singularity: their collective denial of conventional social logics, and their construction of a stimulating, if self-destructive, alternative mode of oratorical practice. Living within what Raymond Williams in his study of innovative and emergent social structures calls "the tolerances of the dominant order," the declaimers "extended the distance" between their practices, specifically the declamation and the exercises that accompanied it, and the social relations that produced the conditions under which rhetorical discourse existed.[42]

Augustus sought to present (and represent) his rule as legitimate, observing precedent and sustaining existing customs and institutions even while radically remaking the structures of governance, basing them on his *domus* and *familia*. In the first chapter of the *Res Gestae*, Augustus represents himself as a *privatus*: "At the age of nineteen, on my private initiative and at my private expense (*exercitum privato consilio et privata impensa*), I raised an army, with which I redeemed into liberty the res publica, oppressed by the tyranny of a faction." Again, in *Res Gestae*: "By new laws passed on my initiative I brought back into use many exemplary practices of our ancestors that were disappearing in our time (*multa exempla maiorum exolescentia iam ex nostro saeculo*), and in many ways I myself transmitted exemplary practices (*exempla imitanda*) to posterity for their imitation" (8.5). As Karl Galinsky observes in his study of the Augustan period, "formerly shared public concepts are fragmented into an unrestrained proliferation of private representations and values. There are disparate efforts to urge the acceptance of such individual values or 'programs' as public ones, but all this expresses only the excessive relativization of the *res publica* into a multiplicity of *res privatae*."[43] Evidence of Augustus's interest in blurring the boundaries between public and domestic is his choice to present the title *pater patriae* as the culmination of all his efforts at the climactic end of the *Res Gestae*.

The declaimers, too, observed precedent; at the same time, they probed their audiences and themselves to discover just how far they

---

[41] Clarke, *Rhetoric at Rome*, 89.

[42] Williams, *The Sociology of Culture*, 190.

[43] Galinsky, *Augustan Culture*, 61.

could press their stylistic and performative innovations. The declaimers are symptomatic of Augustus's social experimentation, his simultaneous appropriation of republican *auctoritas* and development of an indeterminate political role. If Augustus experiments with and explores the construction of a new, constantly shifting, evanescent *auctoritas*, the declaimers experiment with Ciceronian practices of political subjectivity, transforming the fashioning of the self to respond to the altered pressures of Augustan society. As Andrew Wallace-Hadrill comments, "All Augustus' reforms, the 'political' ones too, are aimed at *mores*."[44] The declaimers redefine republican definitions of *libertas* in terms of personal *licentia*, exploring new concepts of *libertas* in the wake of the demise of the old one, in response to Augustus' own redirecting of affairs from the public sphere to the private one.[45] Augustus's strategy was taken in another direction by members of the senatorial order, who, when encouraged to give aid to the state by the very material means of rebuilding roads and regulating the grain supply, thought better of supporting and refurbishing the *res publica* that Augustus had restored. Their refusal discloses a turning aside or self-distancing from Augustan public policy in favor of what we might call his "private" policy": the new emphasis on personal *auctoritas* gained primarily through morals and maintenance of propriety. These nobles and provincials invented a new kind of phantasmatic Rome, one that had more to do with the trappings of personal dignity and the upholding of intangibles such as language than the tangible *cura viarum*, the reconstruction of buildings and temples, and the *cura annonae* of the *populus Romanus*.

QUINTILIAN : A REPUBLICAN EDUCATION FOR AUTOCRACY

The desire to order language in rhetorical discourse reflects a desire to reform the order of human life. Indicative of this is the tendency for rhetorical, social, and moral lexica to overlap, as in Cicero's choice of *decorum* and its verbal cognates to frame his discussion of eloquence. His favorite question, *quid decet?* (what is fitting)?, assimilates the regulation of language to the maintenance of social hierarchy. The Latin terms for rhetoric's formal parts resonate with the language of Roman political order: *dispositio, partitio, distributio* all carry the sense of legal governance and administration. *Deminutio*, the slighting style, also means the formal financial deduction from an estate, and the deprivation of civil rights; *propositio*, the announcement of what is coming next in the argument, also refers to

---

[44] Wallace-Hadrill, "*Mutatio morum*," 9.
[45] Galinsky, *Augustan Culture*, 55.

the posting up of notices of proposed bills; *reditus*, the "return" to a topic, has the same connotation as tax return, that is, revenue; *repetitio*, or repetition, also means a legal action for reclamation of property, and *deprecatio* means a formal appeal for mercy and a plea of mitigating circumstances, as well as the orator's plea to the audience for attention. *Rogatio*, posing a question, means proposing a measure to the assembly of the people; *praeteritio* means not only saying one will not say more on a topic, but also a refusal to select candidates for office. *Coercitio*, or pausing to stop interruptions from the audience, also means the infliction of summary punishment by a magistrate; *conciliatio*, an example of which is *captatio benevolentiae*, also refers to bonds of union that link social groups.[46]

Quintilian's twelve-book *Institutio Oratoria* is a system-generating machine. His habit of categorization—the parts of speech, types of argument, figures and tropes, proper and improper gestures—compellingly models a social order reinforced through language. In the late fourth century, Libanius exhorted his neglectful students to memorize tropes and figures laid out in texts already more than seven hundred years old: "Move closer to the classic orators; purify your language!" (*Or.* 35.18).[47] Quintilian's project is the commingling of the Hellenistic codification of rhetoric with a Ciceronian emphasis on the liberty of the well-educated man. To Cicero, the orator's place is in the public gaze, the center of an event that calls citizens together for a common purpose, giving the republic a visible form—a daily, weekly, monthly, or yearly habit of spectation during which the gaze of the *populus* evaluates its leaders. In Arendt's notion of the enlarging discourse of the public sphere, spectacles induce the "thoughtful suspension of thought" in the beholder, driving the imaginative action necessary to "regenerate" political will—precisely the orator's job.[48] Quintilian does not expect his students to participate in the ruling practices of Cicero's age. In 14 CE, Augustus abolished the *contio*, the elite-mass encounter whose key role in instantiating republican *libertas* we explored in chapter 1; not long after, Tiberius transferred electoral powers to the senate. Other spectacles, such as the triumph, were legally limited to the emperor's family. The "imperial council" (*consilium principis*) was closed to the participation and indeed the gaze of many senators.[49] The senators did not lose all their traditional opportunities to compete for *dignitas*, but the political order no longer rested on that competition, as they believed, as good readers of Cicero, the republic had done—a belief whose elements of fantasy do not negate the social effects that arise from it.

[46] I am drawing here from the thirty-nine figures of thought listed in Cicero's *Orator*.

[47] Cited in Gleason, *Making Men*, 164.

[48] Coleman eloquently recounts Arendt's influential vision of the public sphere, *Rousseau's Political Imagination* (Geneva, 1984), 36–37.

[49] Crook, *Consilium Principis*, 48.

If the republic Tacitus laments was always a fantasy, it was one shared by his republican forebears—increasing, perhaps, the sense of loss among the imperial senatorial order.[50]

Quintilian responds to this loss with an act of translation: he transposes Ciceronian public performative ethics into a domestic key, and redefines the enlargement of thought encouraged by Ciceronian rhetoric as the project of becoming a *vir bonus*, a "good man." His vision should be understood as another iteration of the ethical training described by the younger Seneca:

> When I looked into myself, Seneca, certain faults appeared to me to be located on the surface, so that I could lay my hand on them; but others were more hidden away in the depths; and others still were not there all the time, but returned from time to time—and these I would call the most trouble-some, for they are like patrolling enemies who pounce on you at the first opportunity. . . . Anyway, the state I most find myself in (for why shouldn't I admit the truth to you, as to a doctor?) is that I am not really free of the faults which I fear and hate, but, on the other hand, I am not exactly subject to them either. . . . I am neither ill nor well. Now there is no need for you to say that all virtues are fragile to start with and acquire firmness and strength in time: I know that things take time to mature. (*Tranq.* 1.1)

This passage opens *de Tranquillitate Animi*, a dialogue between Seneca and his (probably fictional) friend Serenus. In their quest to live virtuously, the two are typical of men interested in philosophy in the imperial peri-od, which focused on the self's relation to itself, a relation understood and mastered via a variety of disciplines, mental and physical. Serenus tells Seneca that he is troubled and upset, but he cannot identify the source of his anxiety; all he can do is describe his symptoms. His confes-sion represents a key moment in the developing disposition of Western thinkers to view the self as a moral practitioner, an entity defined, day by day, through his ethical beliefs and practices. Subjectivity, in Seneca's view, does not simply come into existence at birth, and it is not immutable: we must labor to maintain the virtuous parts of ourselves and root out the vices that menace the self. Seneca treats the self as an embodied entity—as Serenus says, he feels that he can touch his faults with his fingers. Seneca's diagnosis brings to light another important issue. Serenus's real trouble is not some innate weakness but a flaw actu-ally *resulting* from the process of self-construction. "What you need

[50] Roller, *Constructing Autocracy*, traces the articulation of aristocratic ethics in the new and changing conditions of the principate (see esp. Seneca's rewriting of Cicero and well-known exempla, 64–126). Gowing, *Empire and Memory*, explores the construction of the idea of republican Rome in a range of early imperial authors; his discussion of Pliny is particularly relevant to my concerns (120–31).

now," Seneca says, "is not those more radical remedies which we have now finished with—blocking yourself here, being angry with yourself there, threatening yourself sternly somewhere else—but the final treatment: confidence in yourself, and the belief that you are on the right path." Serenus's problem is that he has worked so hard to develop himself that his efforts have led him to self-revulsion (*fastidium sui*) and self-dissatisfaction (*sibi displicere*).

Seneca's awareness of the complexity of the self's development, and his willingness to address the problem of how to talk about the conscious construction and situation of a self when a person is already alive, is what drew Michel Foucault to look back to classical antiquity in his *History of Sexuality*.[51] Foucault began by noticing that ancient society did not look to an institutionalized moral code for guidance, regulation, or discipline of its daily life. To say such a thing, he decided, would be putting the cart before the horse. Before the idea of regulating moral practices could come into existence, a concept of the self as primarily an ethical practitioner whose identity arises from his or her ethical disposition had to develop. Foucault finds in Seneca an aesthetics of self-care that focuses on the body, its sensations, and their interrelationship with states of mind and that takes shape in practical exercises shared among a group. Seneca perpetually discusses the shaping of character, the molding of self, as a program designed by individual men communally linked by their interest in ethical philosophy. At no time does Seneca abandon his attempt to refine himself: the divisions Cicero makes between leisure (*otium*), the time he allots to self-introspection, and business (*negotium*, *labor*) have in Seneca dissolved into a never-ending effort to build, and rebuild, the self. The letters of Pliny, Marcus Aurelius, and Fronto exhibit a similar preoccupation, and the four *Sacred Tales* of Aelius Aristides, which document his struggle with his ailing body and his never-ending effort to cure it, are typical of this period's preoccupation with bodily functions and their effect on the psyche.[52] In this context, the constraints on rhetoric in action provided an opportunity for orators to use their speeches as acts of self-constitution in the very mode of "self-intensification" that so captivates Foucault. In other words, Quintilian intensifies what was already there in Cicero: the attention to the self as the object of self-care. The self Quintilian

---

[51] This is not to deny the existence of other ethical trends: cf. Riggsby, "Self and community in the younger Pliny," for discussion of more reactionary writings.

[52] Behr, *Aelius Aristides and the Sacred Tales*, is the most thorough study of the writings in their social context; but see also Perkins, *The suffering self*, 115–16, 176–94. Rousselle, *Porneia*, devotes the bulk of her study to the analysis of the medicalization of the body in the early imperial period.

invents is less rigidly articulated, if not less strictly policed, than the
stylization of repression Foucault finds in Greek and Latin medical and
philosophical texts: Quintilian's self is Ciceronian, decidedly embodied,
taking shape through the performances of talk, gesticulation, and emotional display.[53] Its strict scrutiny of bodily *hexis* and the eradication of
behavioral elements incommensurate with conventional ideals of masculinity and Roman identity exemplify the ceaseless action on and
toward the self that Foucault calls self-fashioning.

The republican context, of course, had anchored the construction of
this self in political competition. We remember Cicero's insistence that
the eternal labor on the self that constituted the virtuous life be directed
outward, in the *vita activa* of politics (*De Rep.* 1.2). Unmoored from this
network of rewards and dangers, from a system that correlated virtue
with the survival of the republic, Quintilian's project of self-making
through rhetorical training fuels a new version of the same engine, one
that looks back to Caesar's *de Analogia*, the *Rhetorica ad Herennium*,
and Cicero's *de Inventione*: the rationalization and codification of the
educated body for (universal) imperial use. When Quintilian reclaims the
rhetorical school as a site for moral improvement, appropriating the
smallest aspects of speech and deportment, he leaves nothing to chance:
what Cicero had covered in three books, Quintilian expands to twelve.
One chapter, in the book on delivery, virtually anatomizes the good
orator's body (11.3): breathing through the nose (56), eyebrow jutting,
eyelid blinking (77–78), lip curling (81), gesticulating with the elbow
(not recommended, 93), bending the knuckle joints in just the right way
(94–102), and so on. Bodies are marked through and through by this
training. As Kafka writes in a different context:

> Our sentence does not sound very severe. Whatever commandment the con-
> demned man has disobeyed is written on his body. "Honor your superi-
> ors.". . . When the Harrow . . . finishes its first draft of the inscription on the
> back, the layer of cotton wool begins to roll and slowly turns the body over,
> to give the Harrow fresh space for writing. Meanwhile the raw part that has
> been written on lies on the cotton wool, which is especially prepared to
> staunch the bleeding and so makes all ready for a new deepening of the
> script. . . . How quiet he grows at just about the sixth hour! Enlightenment
> comes to the most dull-witted.[54]

[53] Miller, "Pedagogy and pederasty," complains of the repression and silence seductively
reenacted in Foucault's reading of ancient ethical formation. It is worth noting that rhetoric
disrupts central tenets of the Platonic tradition that so deeply preoccupies Foucault, with
its dualist hierarchy of mind and body, its critique of emotion and verbal style, and its treatment of the self as an essentially autonomous entity.

[54] Kafka, "The penal settlement."

Precisely because the nature of the gaze that had regulated republican practice had changed, because the link between the dynamism of public speech and political decision making was being worn down by the interfering presence of the emperor, it becomes all the more crucial for Quintilian to represent his good orator as the exemplum of free autonomy. In an important passage in the middle of his introduction to rhetorical theory, Quintilian objects to Cicero's characterization of eloquence as the necessary origin of law (*Inv.* 1.2): how can eloquence be the actual origin (*primam originem*) of laws or cities, he skeptically asks, when there are nomadic nations (*vagae gentes*) who have no cities or laws but who send ambassadors, accuse and defend one another, and judge one man a better speaker than another (3.2.4)? If Quintilian frays the threads with which Cicero seeks to tie oratory to politics, however, he is also exploiting a framework established by Cicero's own late rhetorical work. In a letter of 49 BCE Cicero complains that Caesar and Pompey each want power for themselves alone (*Att.* 8.11); in 46 he breaks his long silence in the senate to give three speeches before Caesar; in 44 he begins to deliver and circulate the *Philippics*, choosing the swan song of invective. Quintilian exploits the two sides of Ciceronian rhetoric exemplified by his Caesarian orations and the speeches against Antony: its potential for reifying individual identity (the self that speaks out) is preserved side by side with rhetoric's techniques of polite submission, which, through their claim to form the good man, offer a way to reclaim submission as manly, if not free.

As in Cicero, Quintilian's rhetorical education now bears the whole burden of performative ethics. The consequences of behaving like an actor, a eunuch, a slave, or a woman are correspondingly dire. "Healthy bodies, enjoying a good circulation and strengthened by exercise, acquire grace from the same source that gives them strength, but the man who attempts to enhance these physical graces by the effeminate use of depilatories and cosmetics succeeds merely in defacing them by the very care that he bestows on them ... tasteful dress lends dignity, but effeminate and luxurious apparel does not adorn the body, but merely exposes the mind" (8 pref. 19–20).[55] Ornament remains an essential part of oratory, but excessive ornament is repulsive: so it must be bold, manly, chaste, "free from all effeminate smoothness and the false hues derived from artificial dyes, glowing with health and vigor" (8.3.6–11).[56] The body that

---

[55] *Corpore sana et integri sanguinis et exercitatione firmata ex iisdem his speciem accipiunt ex quibus vires . . . ; at eadem si quis volsa atque fucata muliebriter comat, foedissima sint ipso formae labore. Et cultus concessus atque magnificus addit hominibus . . . auctoritatem; at muliebris et luxuriosus non corpus exornat, sed detegit mentem.*

[56] *Sed hic ornatus virilis et fortis et sanctus sit nec effeminatam levitatem et fuco ementitum colorem amet, sanguine et viribus niteat.* Fantham explores the limits of ornatus in "*Varietas and satietas*," 275.

was a site for experimentation for the declaimers appears in Quintilian as a Ciceronian entity of self-supervision and discipline. His vision of education upholds the natural order through the retelling of mythic paradigms in declamation: this is the conservative side of the practice in the context of an imperially sanctioned educational program, outside the sphere of the Augustan declaimers' experimentation.[57] During a Quintilianic declamatory performance, the speaker learned to manipulate his body and speech in order to position himself in self-conscious opposition to his social inferiors. And in their content, the declamations helped inculcate attitudes toward social control.

On the other hand, Quintilian directs even more attention toward rhetoric's function as a reason-based source of justice. He devotes four books to the invention and arrangement of narration and argument (3–5, 7), and his capstone account in book 12 of the *vir bonus dicendi peritus*, the "good man skilled in speaking," stresses that the laws would be useless (*leges ipsae nihil valeant*) unless defended by the voice of the advocate (12.7.1). His insistence on the orator's political role is subtle: as Teresa Morgan points out, his representation of typically uneducated or illiterate people—barbarians, peasants, slaves, children, and women—does not fit the contemporary evidence for well-educated women and slaves (as well as the children who were Quintilian's own pupils), but it does coincide with those who lacked political freedom, in republican as well as imperial Rome.[58] Quintilian's aim, expressed in the closing words of the treatise, is encouraging "goodwill" (*bona voluntas*) to be directed for the preservation of law (12.11.31). Rebuking those who suggest that oratory decayed after the death of Cicero, Quintilian recovers the value of middling eloquence (*modica eloquentia*) that produces great profits (*magnos fructus*, 12.11.29).

From Gibbon's perspective in *Decline and Fall*, the end of the first century witnessed the demise of the classical age of art and literature. Under the Flavians, he laments, "the beauties of the [earlier] poets and orators, instead of kindling a fire like their own, inspired only cold and servile imitations: or if any ventured to deviate from those models, they deviated at the same time from good sense and propriety. . . . The decline of genius was soon followed by the corruption of taste" (I.84). Gibbon uses gendered language to animate his condemnation of its aesthetic and moral values. To say that imperial orators are "servile" and lacking in "fire" is to impugn their masculine potency: the "coldness" of their speeches recalls a long tradition of Western medical representations of the female body as dank and chill, in opposition to the internal heat of the male

---

[57] Mythic paradigms: Beard, "Looking (harder) for Roman myth."

[58] Morgan, "A good man skilled in politics: Quintilian's political theory," 260–61.

body.[59] Here the historian rewrites rhetoric as weak and derivative in order to establish a literary dimension to his claim that the Roman empire declined primarily as a result of its own self-indulgence. The servile and unmanly obsequiousness of epideictic becomes an ideal representation of the effeminate languor that, in Gibbon's view, Eastern luxuries fostered in Rome: this is a view we have seen already, in Tacitus. In this chapter, I have sought to rebut the Tacitean and Gibbonian account by showing how so rhetoric reinvents Ciceronian performative ethics in imperial guise. Quintilian, confronted with the ethical challenge of living a virtuous life under autocracy, might have put it this way: to speak out while looking up at the object of one's praise is not the best of circumstances, but doing so at least forces the head to be held up, not to droop down like the head of a slave.

[59] It is true that the language of temperature is a very common term in literary criticism and thus might be expected to be on some level ideologically "free," but like so many other tropes of literary discourse, it retains traces of gender and class ideology. Hanson provides a careful discussion of the competing views on temperature of the female body in the Hippocratic corpus, Aristotle, Soranus and Galen, pointing out that Aristotle was refuting the belief that women's bodies were hotter than men's, and that his argument exerted a decisive influence on later medical and scientific writings ("The medical writers' woman," 332).

THE CICERONIAN CITIZEN IN A GLOBAL WORLD

THIS BOOK HAS ARGUED that Roman rhetoric makes a major contribution to the way the western tradition thinks about politics. It looks forward, almost in spite of itself, to liberal and communitarian theorists who want to conceive a theory of citizenship broad enough to be available to all types of citizens yet one sufficiently strong, unified, and appealing to hold its own in a sea of cultural relativism and intellectual abstraction. No liberal, Cicero uses rhetoric to think through political problems in a fashion relevant to the liberal claim that citizens have the capacity "to act as conscientious interpreters and enforcers" of the public morality, and that this capacity alone is the bedrock of a powerful, shared civic identity. As Stephen Macedo writes in his study of the civic virtues that in his compelling view, underpin liberalism:

> Liberalism stands for "self-government" in a radical sense of that term . . . and calls for critical reflectiveness on public principles, a demeanor that complements the reflective attitude of autonomous liberal agents, shaping, criticizing, revising, and pursuing their personal commitments and projects.[1]

The speaking self that rhetorical texts seek to produce is a body with passions and sentiments, and it speaks a language generated out of and generating communal and reciprocal truth; these texts insist on the importance of the style of the verbal connectives that construct us as political entities in a community. Why? Language gives the self the possession of the virtues Macedo describes: a critical self-directedness, a command of cultural ideals, a capacity to conform to impersonal rules and moral norms, and the required resolve and fortitude to act on the basis of personal deliberations.[2] Civic identity is animated by the kinetic effects of the ideal narratives we tell ourselves, and the narrative Cicero tells falls on the side of eloquence—which is to say, with community. "Can you give yourself your own evil and your own good and hang your own will over yourself as a law?" Nietzsche asks. "Can you be your own judge and avenger of your law?" Cicero answers these questions with both a yes and a no. The virtuous, eloquent man is represented as governing

---

[1] Macedo, *Liberal Virtues*, 100, 128.
[2] Modified from Macedo, *Liberal Virtues*, 225.

himself, but only under the gaze of the community—a community in which the self itself must ultimately take its place, through the human connection of language, if it is to remain human at all. Yet that connection is fueled by the drama of shared passions, whose power sutures the rifts in the republic but which, Cicero knows from experience, may also rise up to overwhelm it.

In their influential work on hegemony and social formation, Ernesto Laclau and Chantal Mouffe identify the German Romantics, and especially Hegel, as the authors of the modern conception of the social as a unity of scattered elements originally specified as fragments of an ancient "lost structural or organic totality." This is the starting point of Romantic dialectic:

> The collapse of the view of the cosmos as a meaningful order within which man occupied a precise and determined place—and the replacement of this view by a self-defining conception of the subject, as an entity maintaining relations of exteriority with the rest of the universe (the Weberian disenchantment of the world)—led the Romantic generation of the *Sturm und Drang* to an eager search for that lost unity, for a new synthesis that would permit the division to be overcome. . . . Given that the elements to be rearticulated were specified as fragments of a lost unity, it was clear that any recomposition would have an *artificial* character, as opposed to the natural *organic* unity peculiar to Greek culture.[3]

Ciceronian rhetoric and political theory expose Laclau and Mouffe's version of history as a fantasy constructed to serve modern desires to read the Greek past as natural and transparent and to erase the Roman past entirely. Roman thought has a special capacity to arouse anxiety. The conception of the social order and man's place in it that Enlightenment and Romantic thinkers found in their Latin schooltexts, and Cicero in particular, was not the "organic unity peculiar to Greek [*sic*] culture" but a tense awareness of the blurred borders between nature and self-conscious art.

In the centuries between late antiquity and the twelfth century, scholars of rhetoric focused their energies on the Latin texts most appropriate for school use: prosaic and accessible works like *de Inventione* and *Rhetorica ad Herennium*.[4] One medievalist estimates that up to two thousand copies of these two works survive, making them among the

---

[3] Laclau and Mouffe. *Hegemony and Socialist Strategy*, 93–94 (original italics). Žižek remarks on the significance of the illusory in Laclau's work in *The Ticklish Subject*, 182–84.

[4] From an immense bibliography, I have benefited most from the classic studies by Baron's *The Crisis of the Early Italian Renaissance*, Jerrold Seigel's *Rhetoric and Philosophy in Renaissance Humanism*, Pocock's *Machiavellian Moment*, esp. ch.3, "The *vita activa* and the *vivere civile*," and Skinner's *Foundations of Modern Political Thought*.

most popular Latin works of all time.[5] Easier to copy, circulate, and teach than the sophisticated dialogue *de Oratore* or Quintilian's twelve-book *Institutio Oratoria*, the compilations and digests available in this period fostered a busy industry of etymology, grammar, prosimetrics, figure, trope, and genre. But contrary to the common view still perpetuated in recent histories of rhetoric, the rise of rhetoric as a force in Renaissance political thought did not begin with the discovery and circulation of longer and more ambitious Greek and Roman texts.[6] When Poggio discovered Quintilian's *Institutio* and Asconius's commentaries on Cicero in 1416, a large group of hopeful readers was already eager to hear the romantic account of his hunt through the dusty corners of the St. Gall Monastery library. New editions of Poggio's trove, along with Aristotle's *Rhetoric* and complete manuscripts of Cicero's *de Oratore*, *Orator*, and *Brutus*, mark not the beginning of Renaissance humanism but a crest in the wave that had been building since the mid-1100s.

At that time the copying and editing of letter-writing handbooks for students and courtiers took on a distinctly political flavor, as rhetoricians mixed advice on proper modes of epistolary address with model speeches and commentary on contemporary political issues.[7] This type of handbook, the *ars dictaminis*, became the model for political pamphlets like Machiavelli's *Il Principe* and Erasmus's "mirror of princes" letter to Philip of Spain, which cast their authors in a traditional mode, as advisors to the powerful. As advice about the subject's self-presentation in a letter to a prince evolved into advice to a prince presenting himself to his subjects, the lines between actor and observer began to blur. By the end of the twelfth century, some scholars turned with new seriousness from the job of teaching princes and nobles to the problem of training non-nobles for civic service, first in the context of the late medieval courts of Europe and gradually in the less exclusive setting of the Italian republics and the English Parliament. In *The Banquet*, Dante praises one such scholar for his criticism of traditional beliefs about nobility and virtue, summarized in the opinion that high birth is no proof of goodness: "wherever virtue is, there is nobility."[8] These rhetoricians saw themselves not only as the interpreters of rhetorical manuals but as the ethical guides of their generation: in their hands, techniques of rhetorical presentation were evolving into practices of the self.

[5] Vickers, *In Defence of Rhetoric*, 216.

[6] Kennedy's work largely ignores rhetoric's contribution to civic thought in the late Middle Ages; Vickers, *In Defence of Rhetoric*, and Barthes, "The old rhetoric." complain of the aridity of medieval rhetoric.

[7] I rely here on the informative accounts of Skinner, *Foundations*, 23–48, 69–101, and Wieruszowski, *Politics and Culture*, 589–627.

[8] Skinner discusses Dante's relationship with the scholar Brunetto Latini in *Foundations*, 46.

Machiavelli's famous letter to Francesco Vettori, describing the way he read the classics, demonstrates how political ideals evolved hand in hand with the rediscovery and circulation of ancient texts, especially Cicero's rhetorical work and the closely related treatise on honorableness, *de Officiis*. When Machiavelli comes home in the evening, he tells Vettori, before he begins to read his favorite classical books, he dresses himself in formal clothing, as though to prepare himself for conversation (*parlare*) with the ancient authors. Dressing for the part, pretending that the conversation is taking place in public view, accustoms Machiavelli's imagination to the habits of active civic participation. It also contributes directly to his growing conviction that a common language and even common cultural tastes—in clothing, for instance—are necessary for citizens to live together in security and virtue.[9] Moreover, he asserts in the *Discorsi*, the language and habits of political life must be common not only in the sense that all the citizens share them; they must also be accessible to all, *volgare*, reflecting what Cicero habitually refers to as the *communis sensus*, common sensibility.

Machiavelli's letter incorporates the five core Ciceronian ideas that are repeated, mantra-like, by the Renaissance humanists responsible for this development in rhetoric.[10] First, they treat speech as that which distinguishes humans from animals, and further, as humanity's highest natural capacity. If speech is a natural human virtue, then eloquence is the sum of human existence, the means by which all other virtues are attained and—crucially—the means by which virtue is practiced in the world, in the course of the *vita activa*.

The emphasis on language as a virtue on its own terms, and more specifically on the virtue of common language, led the humanists to revive the Ciceronian claim that without eloquence, wisdom is meaningless. This is the second point: scholarship that adopts an inaccessible style, or research into topics that do not appeal to a broad audience, exile the scholar from the *vita activa* and hence from human society altogether. As Juan Luis Vives wrote in the early sixteenth century, the study of "difficult, hidden, and troublesome knowledge" bred students who ignored civic duties and family life, making them unnatural parasites on the social body.[11] The vitriol of Hobbes's critique of this position in favor of a necessarily exclusive discourse of science and philosophy in *de Cive* and *Leviathan* and the revival of Cicero's position, partly in response to

---

[9] Pocock, *The Machiavellian Moment*, 62.

[10] This is a schematic reduction of a complicated tradition of reception, but it furnishes a conceptual frame within which to understand Cicero's influence and an instrument with which to read past the prejudices that inform post-Enlightenment interpretations of rhetoric: see Fantham, *Roman World*, on the "sheer prejudice" against Cicero (185).

[11] *De Tradendis Disciplinis*, 17, translated by Foster Watson.

Hobbes, by Scottish commonsense philosophers like Francis Hutcheson and Adam Smith are indications of its profound impact on early modern thought.

Third, the humanists felt that the investigation of the emotions central to rhetorical discourse since Aristotle rendered rhetoric crucial to the knowledge of humanity, and hence to the teaching of youth and the leadership of polities. "To the will," Vives wrote in 1531, "reason and judgment are assigned as counselors, and the emotions are its torches. Further, the emotions of the mind are enflamed by the sparks of speech. So too, reason is impelled and moved by speech."[12] Speech is in fact the enabler of human community—the fourth key Ciceronian concept in the humanists' repertoire. Stefano Guazzo declared that "nature herself has given man the power of speech, but certainly not in order that he converse with himself. . . . speech is a means by which men come together and love one another."[13] As the heart of civility, the practices that enable humans to live together, eloquence formed the basis for Renaissance redefinitions of the *vita activa*, the active life, and the *vir civilis*, the civic man who took part in it. As the popularity of Castiglione's handbook *Il libro del cortegiano* suggests, Cicero's location of civility at the center of courtly life broadened the horizon of influence in Renaissance courts, and helped make possible theories of political life that substituted town hall and merchant banquet for the medieval court.

Last is the relationship between appearance and essence. Brunetto Latini, the scholar admired by Dante, asks whether the successful ruler "must actually be as he wishes to seem" (*Livre dou Tresor* 3). He affirms that they must—an answer that Machiavelli famously rejects in *Il Principe*, reading Cicero simplistically (but strategically) as the holder of the opposite view. But the origins of Machiavelli's exploration into the nature of the public leader, and the recognition that the political self was a carefully contrived and mutable persona, directly develop the insights of trecento rhetoricians whose central concern was training the student's appearance—writings derived in turn from the Ciceronian belief that bodily practice is an active instrument in shaping the self.

To the question of what Cicero's rhetorical writing offered Renaissance readers, only the briefest of answers is possible here. But the five points I have isolated in Renaissance readings of Cicero—eloquence as humanity's highest virtue, the marriage of philosophical wisdom with eloquence, the pivotal role of emotion in persuasion, speech as civic glue, and the roles of appearance and essence in subjectification—unpack his

[12] Juan Luis Vives, *The Advancement of Learning*, quoted in Vickers, *In Defence of Rhetoric*, 277.

[13] Quoted in Vickers, *In Defence of Rhetoric*, 255ff.

conceptualization of rhetoric as the pursuit of virtue. Changing the way the humanists conceived of the good life—as the *vivere civile* led by the eloquent man—Ciceronian rhetoric thus helped to enable the revival of republicanist political theory in Renaissance thought. Here is Habermas:

> Ever since Plato and Democritus, the history of philosophy has been dominated by two opposing impulses: one relentlessly elaborates the transcendent power of abstractive reason and the emancipatory unconditionality of the intelligible, whereas the other strives to unmask the imaginary purity of reason in a materialist fashion. In contrast . . . communicative rationality recalls older ideas of logos . . . it conceives of rational practice as reason concretized in history, society, body, and language.[14]

The vision of the perfect orator adumbrated in *de Oratore* cannot be separated from Cicero's beliefs about republican citizenship and its relationship to ethical self-formation. On the contrary, it shapes and is in turn shaped by those beliefs. Republican citizenship, like eloquence, is the practice of spectacular virtue in the course of an active life in the setting of a political community—which, like Aristotle, Cicero treats as the natural end of human existence.[15]

We have noted the consequences for the subject from the communal aspect of persuasion: Cicero's Crassus "sets the judge on fire with his speech," blazing with what Antonius insists is not false but true passion. In what sense can Antonius claim that his passion is authentic? As we saw in chapter 3, Cicero treats the orator's reason and feeling as, simultaneously, a reflection of and a check on common sensibility.[16] Like moral duty, eloquence resides at the intersection of knowledge and action. "Republican knowledge," the special interest of the orators, their students, and audiences, is the discourse for which Ciceronian rhetorical theory prepares its reader, as Cicero makes clear in his claim that rhetoric offers a more robust version of ethical education and a more reliable method of virtuous self-fashioning than philosophy, by its nature, is able to do.

While it makes strong claims to teach performative ethics, oratorical persuasion must also be flexible, changeable, contingent on circumstances—not promising grounds, we might say, for ethical theory. Here too Cicero gestures toward a radical alteration of the standards of truth and falsity, where what matters is what persuades. But the act of

---

[14] Habermas, *Philosophical Discourse of Modernity*, 324, 315, 317.

[15] Aristotle, *Pol.* 1:1–2.

[16] The interest in communality if identity, an interest in a theory of subjectivity that does not privilege individualism over community, is a key theme in a writing of Rosi Braidotti, a theorist of the Deleuzian school who uses the nomad as her exemplum of feminist subjectivity. For her, constant flux is *one* defining mark of namadic existence; equally important are the shifting but intense communities shaped by the journeying nomad.

persuasion has its own rules, and Cicero depends heavily on those rules to limit what an orator can or cannot say: it is the audience that supervises and judges the orator and his truth, just as the orator gauges what the crowd is prepared to hear. And these rules of persuasion extend beyond matters of logical probability in a forensic or deliberative speech to much broader areas of emotion and manners. Eloquence involves the act of emoting; and here too, we have seen, Cicero's text reclaims the target of Plato's critique.

Is it possible to envision Roman rhetoric as a model for contemporary political practice? Let me consider this briefly by taking up the problem of civility, which one might see as the cornerstone of Ciceronian performative ethics. When discussing the concept of civility in the ancient world, and specifically the Roman republic, it is easy to assume that we are moving exclusively among the elite, in that world of urbane gentility so vividly captured in the elegant poetry of Catullus or Cicero's letters to his friends, where civility is exclusively a virtue of aristocratic social practice, a synonym for *comitas*, friendship, or *urbanitas*, elegance. But I have argued in this book that the high premium Cicero placed on *decorum* in fact cannot be explained away as simple praise of an elite ideal. On the contrary: Cicero saw *decorum* as the partner of Roman republican justice, the vehicle of popular persuasion and communal trust, the bedrock of citizenship and public discourse.

It has been the scholarly habit for at least the past two centuries to dismiss Cicero's discussions of civility as a cloak for his class interests.[17] But we might also consider that anyone who wants to chart a mutually justifiable course for our unavoidably common life must take part in the quest for reasonable terms of social cooperation, setting the highest premium on effective communication and reciprocity.[18] Cicero's conception of civility is a useful place to begin that quest precisely because, while it privileges the tensions of economic and social class, it is not *essentially* bound by exclusions of class or gender: what matters is the performance. This is the significance of my insistence, in chapter 5, that gender is not a concept that we may consider a Roman essential: that oratorical training cannot be seen simply as making manly men but as making "manly" "citizens"—both concepts shaped by ideologies of power that are not essentially or necessarily linked to any biological or blood-based property of human experience. Cicero's admission of the potential for slaves, women, Greeks, actors, and professional teachers to be models of *decorum*, which he views with anxiety but cannot deny, bespeaks its availability (despite Cicero's prejudices) to those he seeks to exclude.

---

[17] See the comments of Wood, *Cicero's Social and Political Thought*, 100–115.
[18] Gutmann and Thompson, *Democracy and Disagreement*, 52–63.

We recall that in *de Officiis*, Cicero discusses the four virtues of the ideal citizen, a list drawn from Plato's *Republic*: justice, wisdom, courage, and *sophrosune*, usually translated as "self-restraint" or "self-control." This last virtue Cicero chooses to translate with the Latin word *decorum*. Latin has better equivalents for the Greek, such as *moderatio* and *modestia*; the point is that the Greek *sophrosune*, and Latin equivalents like *moderatio*, are essentially internal virtues of the well-ordered soul, and Cicero, by contrast, is concerned in this treatise on moral duties with external perception as well as internal harmony. How do we appear to others looking from the outside in? Our *decorum* (or lack of it) is what others see—and this, for Cicero, is what matters. "To neglect what others think about oneself is the mark not only of arrogance but of lack of consideration," he says (*Off.* 1.99). He proceeds to set *decorum* on a par with justice as an essential quality of citizenship, arguing that they differ only insofar as one may draw a line between physical and nonphysical violence: "the role of justice is not to do harm (*violare*) to men, the role of decorum is not to offend (*offendere*) them" (1.99). The meaning of the Latin *decorum* is not entirely dissimilar from our own English word, but as we have seen, the Latin *decorum* is a term of much greater ethical and political heft: not simply good manners or politesse, it signifies propriety produced out of self-control—very close to the English "civility."

How might Cicero's readers put this observation into action? An orator and a rhetorician, Cicero was an apostle of the ancient Greek and Roman maxim that "as a man speaks, so he is." As such, he claims that vice and virtue are bound up in, and revealed through, a man's habits of speech. And he defines speech not just as *vox*, literal voice, but as a complex of thought and behavior, opinion, argument, posture, gestures, and facial expressions ordained by nature or tradition: what he calls *eloquentia corporis*, the eloquence of the body. Regulating the motions and the passions of the speaking body, on the one hand, and emotional, passionate thoughts, on the other, go hand in hand (*Off.* 1.100).

At this stage, we may prefer to condemn Cicero for developing an elitist theory of speech that excludes those who are not already familiar with the habits of elite discourse—a common complaint of current democracy theorists like Iris Marion Young and Nancy Fraser. Indeed, Cicero habitually invokes aristocratically biased views of human nature to justify his claims for aristocratic privilege. But he does not do this in his discussion of *decorum*. What we see is a hint toward the opposite view. In *de Officiis*, Cicero argues that *decorum* is not the virtue of a robot obedient to tradition or the pressures of those around him. Instead it is defined through individual difference: "*Decorum* is that which agrees with the excellence of a man just where his nature differs from that of other creatures" (*Off.* 1.96). "Countless differences exist in natures and characters, and this is not a thing to be criticized," he continues, "everybody must resolutely hold fast to his own unique gifts" (*Off.* 1.109).

The ideal citizen is the man whose *decorum* manifests itself not in artificial stiffness or authoritarianism but in a heterogeneity of speech and manner that reflects the variety of his experiences in different social communities. "It is necessary for the orator to have seen and heard many things, to have gone over many subjects in reflection and reading," Cicero writes. The aristocratic man must be wary of appropriating a falsely populist nature, however: "he must not take possession of these things as his own property, but rather take sips of them as things belonging to others. . . . He must explore the very veins of every type, age, and class, and of those before whom he speaks or is going to speak; he must taste of their minds and senses" (*de Orat.* 1.218, 223). As Cicero sees it, the *decorum* of the good orator and the good citizen not only enables interaction with all kinds of people; more important, it censors elite arrogance and superiority. If in his treatises on rhetoric and citizenship Cicero promises to teach his aristocratic readers the easy manners they could use among their equals, he also seeks to provide the language and ceremonies of civility necessary for societies held together by ties of utility and necessity rather than aristocratic friendship.[19]

Not coincidentally, early modern writers on civility also emphasize this point. In Stefano Guazzo's summary of his treatise *La civile conversatione*, written in 1574, he says he has discussed "how to behave our selves toward others, according to the difference of estates; for that it is our hap to come in companie, sometime with the young, sometime with the olde, as soone with Gentlemen, as soone with the baser sorte, now and then with Princes, now and then with private persons, one while with the learned, another while with the ignorant, now with our owne Countriemen, then with straungers, now with the religious, now with the secular, now with men, then with women."[20] Such capacity for flexibility and shifts of perspective is not empathy; it does not entail assuming or accepting the point of view of the other. It means merely making present to oneself what the perspectives of others involved are or could be, and—if I wish to take part in a casual political conversation or in formal political deliberation—the attempt to "woo their consent" by displaying through my verbal and physical manner my equal standing with them as a free citizen.

---

[19] Like Guazzo, Justus Lipsius (*De constantia*, 1584), Montaigne (*Essais*, 1580), and other early modern writter on civility.

[20] Quoted in Vickers, *In Defence of Rhetoric*, 168.

But the natural and desirable variety of human behaviors that Cicero judges necessary for the responsible exercise of politics is only one side of *decorum*. The other is self-control. This, for ancients and moderns, is the dark side of civility: its oppressive erasure of free expression and human individuality. I have already suggested that Cicero's definition of ideal civility makes room for the variety of behaviors that are naturally produced from differences of class, nation, and political belief. But there are two additional Ciceronian reasons to reconsider civility not as a practice of self-oppression but as a part of freedom.

For the citizen to be capable of assuming the shifts in perspective that make responsible and effective politics possible, Cicero believes, the citizen must first be in control of himself. Otherwise he must be controlled by another, whether that be another person or a set of beliefs. Prejudice, the worst kind of refusal to consider multiple perspectives, is the product of a slavish mental state. Trenchard and Gordon, the early eighteenth-century radical Whig authors of *Cato's Letters*, agree: "Polite Arts and Learning are naturally produced in free States. . . . No man can shew me a bigot who is not an ignorant slave; for bigotry is a slavery of the soul to certain religious opinions, fancies, or stories, of which the bigot knows little or nothing, and damns all that do" (2.519). Modern-day conservatives like to complain that liberals have tried to make the very concept of self-governance illegitimate. But Cicero treats self-control in terms that are very congenial to the classical liberal. The issue at stake is the eradication of fear and the consolidation of social trust. In the presence of fear, as Cicero knows from years of civil war, individual citizens and the community of citizens cannot be free. Fear interferes with freedom, in the liberal sense of freedom as nondomination.[21] *Decorum* mitigates the unpredictable behaviors that increase public mistrust and arouse fear. For Cicero, these unpredictable behaviors are as much the source of trouble among elites as they are among the masses: it is the elite citizen who stalks proudly among the citizenry, alienating and enraging them.

Decorum presumes another kind of freedom: the freedom of self-construction. Anthony Appiah has explored the notion that inherent in any vision of subjectivity that views the self as constructed is, precisely, freedom.[22] Creating a self necessarily involves free choice. That is not to say our choices will be good ones, but as Cicero would point out, there are many forces arrayed against our scanting the social matrix in which our identities take shape—arrayed, that is, against bad choices. For Appiah as for Cicero, communication is the anvil on which subjectivity

---

[21] Pettit, *Republicanism*, 17–50.
[22] Appiah, *The Ethics of Identity*, 192–99.

is wrought. Seyla Benhabib argues along similar lines that the human capacity to use speech allows the emergence of a differentiated subjectivity in the life of the self, which is precisely the reason why speech must be the foundation for liberal deliberative democracy.[23] Both thinkers are working with the insight of Hannah Arendt, who observed that speech is the actualization of the human condition of plurality, that is, of living as a distinct and unique being among equals."[24]

Cicero's views on *decorum* lead him to insist that the public speaker must treat his audience of citizens as equals in an ongoing dialogue of equals—not, to be sure, because he believes that they really are his equals, but because the pretense of equality enables him to reinforce the group's sense of communal identity, and to persuade the group. In point of fact, the pretense of equality works much like the thing itself: if the elite speaker does not moderate and popularize his speech, he risks humiliating and infuriating his audience. Worse, he risks preaching to the converted, contributing to stasis and destructive factionalism. The rhetoric of *decorum*, as Cicero envisions it, literally breaks down the boundaries of class and factional interest by appealing to the common experience of speaker and listener. When policy must be articulated according to its rules, policy itself must change. As Arendt noted, "the thinking process which is active in judging something is not, like the thought process of pure reasoning, a dialogue between me and myself, but finds itself always and primarily, even if I am quite alone, in an anticipated communication with others with whom I know I must finally come to some agreement. . . . This enlarged way of thinking . . . needs the presence of others 'in whose place' it must think, whose perspective it must take into consideration, and without whom it never has the opportunity to operate at all."[25]

Having learned to control himself, to moderate behaviors that arouse fear and mistrust among his fellow citizens, Cicero's ideal citizen is in a position to assume shifting political perspectives. This experience in turn reinforces his habit of asking the central question of civility as we define it today: Does my behavior do psychic violence to my fellow citizen? To the community at large? I read Cicero against the grain not to preserve a nostalgic vision of his past reality but to provoke and to appropriate, and to explore how his views on civility speak to our present. Cicero's views focus on the need for leaders to enlist the trust of audiences by treating them as equals, and for citizens to consider their own personal behaviors in light of the mistrust they might arouse in others. What is most provocative about Cicero's thought here are the points of contact with the work of

---

[23] Benhabib, *Situating the Self*, 126.
[24] Arendt, *The Human Condition*, 178.
[25] Arendt, *Between Past and Future*, 220–21.

contemporary political theorists interested in citizenship, speech, and difference. Deliberative democracy in particular has emerged as an alternative to visions of democracy as a hyperindividualistic liberalism obsessed with individual rights, or as a market for competing special interest groups. If their theories are to be put into practice, where to begin? I would suggest that a historically enriched view of civility is a good starting point, and this is to be found in Cicero.

Roman rhetoric leaves contemporary scholars with a challenge. I end this book with a call to scholars to emphasize the fact that when we teach Roman literature, and especially the rhetorical tradition, we are teaching the evolution of the shifting perspectives, the multiple selves and professions, that are crucial to the constitution of political identity in the West. Only by understanding that history, its passions and its self-disciplines, can we do the urgent political work of the intellectual: creating citizens and subjects for a global world in which the constructs of nation, gender, and race mean less and less—while communication means everything.

> Who are you indeed who would talk or sing to America?
> Have you studied out the land, its idioms and men?
> Have you possess'd yourself of the Federal Constitution?
> have you sped through fleeting customs, popularities?
> Can you hold your hand against all seductions, follies, whirls,
> fierce contentions? are you very strong? are you really of the
>   whole People?
> Are you not of some coterie? some school or mere religion?
> Do you hold the like love for those hardening to maturity? for the
>   last-born? little and big? and for the errant?
>   —Walt Whitman, "Song of Myself"

BIBLIOGRAPHY

Acker, Kathy. *Blood and Guts in High School*. New York, 1978.

Adams, John Quincy. *Lectures on Rhetoric and Oratory*. Cambridge, MA, 1810.

Agamben, Giorgio. *Homo Sacer*. Trans. Daniel Heller-Roazen. Stanford, 1995.

Allen, Danielle S. *Talking to Strangers: Anxieties of Citizenship Since* Brown v. Board of Education. Chicago, 2004.

Althusser, Louis. "Ideology and Ideological State Apparatuses." In *Mapping Ideology*, ed. Slavoj Žižek, 100–40. London, 1994.

Ando, Clifford. *Imperial Ideology and Provincial Loyalty in the Roman Empire*. Berkeley and Los Angeles, 2000.

Appiah, Anthony. *The Ethics of Identity*. Princeton, 2004.

Arendt, Hannah. *The Human Condition*. New York, 1958.

———. *Between Past and Future: Six Exercises in Political Thought*. New York, 1961.

———. *The Life of the Mind*. New York, 1971.

———. *On Revolution*. New York, 1982.

Arthur, Marilyn B. "The Dream of a World Without Women: Poetics and the Circles of Order in the *Theogony* Prooemium." *Arethusa* 16 (1983): 97–116.

Asmis, Elizabeth. "The State as a Partnership: Cicero's Definition of *Res Publica* in His Work *On the State*." *History of Political Thought* 25 (2004): 569–99.

———. "A New Kind of Model: Cicero's Roman Constitution in *De Republica*." *AJP* 126 (2005): 377–416.

Atherton, Catherine. "Hand Over Fist: The Failure of Stoic Rhetoric." *CQ* 38 (1988): 392–427.

Axer, Jerzy. "Tribunal–Stage–Arena." *Rhetorica* 7 (1989): 299–311.

Badian, Ernst. "The Consuls: 179–49 BCE." *Chiron* 20 (1990): 371–413.

Bailyn, Bernard. *The Ideological Origins of the American Revolution*. New York, 1969.

Baldry, Harold. "Zeno's Ideal State." *JHS* 79 (1959): 207–28.

Balsdon, J.P.V.D. *Romans and Aliens*. Chapel Hill, 1979.

Barber, Benjamin. *Strong Democracy*. Berkeley and Los Angeles, 1985.

———. "Misreading Democracy: Peter Euben and the *Gorgias*." In *Demokratia*, ed. Josiah Ober and Charles Hedrick, 362–76. Princeton, 1996.

Barish, Jonas. "The Antitheatrical Prejudice." *Critical Quarterly* 8 (1966): 329–48.

———. "Exhibitionism and the Antitheatrical Prejudice." *English Literary History* 36 (1969): 1–29.

Baron, Hans. *The Crisis of the Early Italian Renaissance*. Princeton, 1966.

Barthes, Roland. *A Lover's Discourse*. New York, 1979.

———. "The Old Rhetoric: An Aide-Memoire." In *The Semiotic Challenge*, 11–94. New York, 1988.

Barton, Carlin A. *The Sorrows of the Ancient Romans: The Gladiator and the Monster.* Princeton, 1993.

———. *Roman Honor: The Fire in the Bones.* Berkeley and Los Angeles, 2001.

Bartsch, Shadi. *Actors in the Audience: Theatricality and Doublespeak from Nero to Hadrian.* Cambridge, MA, 1994.

Baumlin, James S. "Positioning Ethos in Historical and Contemporary Theory." In *Ethos: New Essays in Rhetorical and Critical Theory,* ed. James Baumlin, xi–xxxi. Dallas, 1994.

Beard, Charles. *The Economic Interpretation of the Constitution of the United States.* New York, 1913.

———. *Origins of Jeffersonian Democracy.* New York, 1916.

———. *The Economic Basis of Politics.* New York, 1922.

Beard, Mary. "Looking (Harder) for Roman Myth: Dumézil, Declamation, and the Problems of Definition." *Colloquium Rauricum 3: Mythos in mythenloser Gesellschaft,* ed. Fritz Graf, 44–64. Stuttgart, 1993.

———. "The Triumph of the Absurd: Roman Street Theatre." In *Rome the Cosmopolis,* ed. Catharine Edwards and Gregg Woolf, 21–43. Cambridge, 2003.

Behr, Charles. *Aelius Aristides and the Sacred Tales.* Amsterdam, 1968.

Bek, Lise. *Toward Paradise on Earth.* Rome, 1978.

Bell, Brenda. "Roman Literary Attitudes to Technical Terms." *Acta Classica* 34 (1991): 83–92.

Bender, John, and Wellbery, David. "Rhetoricality: On the Modernist Return of Rhetoric." In *The Ends of Rhetoric,* ed. John Bender and David Wellbery, 3–39. Stanford, 1990.

Benhabib, Seyla. *Situating the Self.* New York and London, 1992.

———. "Deliberative Rationality and Models of Democratic Legitimacy." *Constellations* 1 (1994): 25–53.

———. "Toward a Deliberative Model of Democratic Legitimacy." In *Democracy and Difference,* ed. Seyla Benhabib, 67–94. Princeton, 1996.

———. *The Claims of Culture: Equality and Diversity in the Global Era.* Princeton, 2002.

Berlin, Isaiah. *Four Essays on Liberty.* Oxford, 1979.

Blair, Carole. "Nietzsche's Lecture Notes on Rhetoric: A Translation." *Philosophy and Rhetoric* 16 (1983): 94–129.

Bloch, Maurice. Introduction, *Political Language and Oratory in Traditional Society,* ed. Maurice Bloch, 1–28. London, 1975.

Blondell, Ruby. *The Play of Character in Plato's Dialogues.* Cambridge, 2002.

Bloomer, W. Martin. "Schooling in Persona: Imagination and Subordination in Roman Education." *CA* 16 (1997): 57–78.

———. *Latinity and Literary Society at Rome.* Philadelphia, 1997.

———. "A Preface to the History of Declamation: Whose Speech? Whose History?" In *The Roman Cultural Revolution,* ed. Thomas Habinek and Alessandro Schiesaro, 199–215. Cambridge, 1998.

Bonner, S. F. *Roman Declamation in the Late Republic and Early Empire.* Berkeley, 1949.

Booth, Alan D. "The Appearance of the *Schola Grammatici.*" *Hermes* 106 (1978): 117–25.

Bourdieu, Pierre. *Outline of a Theory of Practice*. Cambridge, 1977.
———. *The Logic of Practice*. Stanford, 1990.
Braet, Antoine. "The Classical Doctrine of Status and the Rhetorical Theory of Argumentation." *Philosophy and Rhetoric* 20 (1984): 79–93.
Braund, Susanna Morton. "Vergil and the Cosmos: Religious and Philosophical Ideas." *The Cambridge Companion to Virgil*, ed. Charles Martindale, 204–21. Cambridge, 1997.
Braund, Susanna Morton, and Christopher Gill. *The Passions in Roman Thought and Literature*. Cambridge, 1997.
Brink, C. O. "Quintilian's *de Causis Corruptae Eloquentiae* and Tacitus' *Dialogus de Oratoribus*." *CQ* 39 (1989): 472–503.
Brody, Miriam. *Manly Writing: Gender, Rhetoric, and the Rise of Composition*. Carbondale, 1993.
Brown, Norman O. *Love's Body*. Los Angeles, 1966.
Brown, Peter. *Power and Persuasion in Late Antiquity: Towards a Christian Empire*. Madison, 1988.
Brown, Wendy. *Manhood and Politics*. Totowa, 1988.
———. *States of Injury*. Princeton, 1995.
Brunt, P. A. "Italian Aims at the Time of the Social War." *JRS* 55 (1965): 90–109.
———. "The Role of the Senate in the Augustan Regime." *CQ* 34 (1984): 423–44.
———. "*Libertas* in the Republic," In *The Fall of the Roman Republic and Related Essays*, 281–350. Oxford, 1988.
———. *The Fall of the Roman Republic and Related Essays*. Oxford, 1988.
Brunt, P. A., and J. M. Moore (eds.). *Res Gestae Divi Augusti*. Oxford, 1967.
Büchner, Karl. *Cicero*. Wiesbaden, 1962.
Butler, Judith. *Bodies That Matter*. London, 1993.
Butler, Shane. *The Hand of Cicero*. London, 2002.
Canovan, Margaret. "Patriotism Is Not Enough." In *The Demands of Citizenship*, ed. Catriona McKinnon and Iain Hampsher-Monk, 276–97. London, 2000.
Caplan, Harry. "The Decay of Eloquence at Rome in the First Century." In *Studies in Speech and Drama in Honor of Alexander M. Drummond*, 295–325. Ithaca, 1944.
Clarke, M. L. *Rhetoric at Rome: A Historical Survey*. London, 1968.
Classen, C. J. "*Virtutes Romanorum* nach dem Zeugnis der Münzen republikanischer Zeit." *Mitteilungen der Deutschen Archaeologischen Instituts* 93 (1986): 257–79.
Clausen, Wendell. "An Interpretation of the *Aeneid*." In *Virgil: A Collection of Critical Essays*, ed. Steele Commager, 75–88. Englewood Cliffs, 1966.
Cohen, Jean. "Discourse Ethics and Civil Society." *Philosophy and Social Criticism* 14 (1988): 315–37.
Cole, Thomas. "Who was Corax?" *ICS* 16 (1991): 65–84.
———. *The Origins of Rhetoric in Ancient Greece*. Baltimore, 1991.
Connolly, Joy. "Mastering Corruption: Constructions of Identity in Roman Oratory." In *Women and Slaves in Greco-Roman Culture*, ed. Sheila Murnaghan and Sandra Joshel, 130–51. London, 1998.

Connolly, Joy. "Problems of the Past in Imperial Greek Education." In *Education in Greco-Roman Antiquity*, ed. Yun Lee Too, 331–72. Leiden, 2001.

———. "Reclaiming the Theatrical in the Second Sophistic." *Helios* 28 (2001): 75–96.

———. "Like the Labors of Heracles: *andreia* and *paideia* in Imperial Greek Culture." In *Andreia: Ancient Constructions of Manly Courage*, ed. Ralph Rosen and Ineke Sluiter, 287–318. Leiden, 2003.

———. "The New World Order: Greek Rhetoric in Rome." In *Companion to Greek Rhetoric*, ed. Ian Worthington, 139–65. London, 2006.

———. "Crowd Politics." In *Crowds*, ed. Jeffrey Schnapp and Matthew Tiews, 77–96. Stanford, 2006.

———. "Virile Tongues: Rhetoric and Masculinity." In *Companion to Roman Rhetoric*, ed. William J. Dominik and Jon Hall, 83–97. London, 2006.

Constant, Benjamin. "The Liberty of the Ancients Compared With That of the Moderns." In *Political Writings*, ed. Biancamaria Fontana, 308–27. Cambridge, 1988.

Conte, Gian Biagio. *Genres and Readers*. Trans. Glenn W. Most. Baltimore, 1994.

Cooper, John. "Plato, Isocrates, and Cicero on the Independence of Oratory from Philosophy." In *Knowledge, Nature and the Good*, 43–64. Princeton, 2004.

Corbeill, Anthony. *Controlling Laughter*. Princeton, 1996.

———. "Rhetorical Education in Cicero's Youth." In *Brill's Companion to Cicero*, ed. James M. May, 23–48. Leiden, 2002.

———. *Nature Embodied*. Princeton, 2004.

Cox, Virginia. "Ciceronian Rhetoric in Italy, 1250–1360." *Rhetorica* 17 (1999): 239–88.

Crook, J. A. *Consilium Principis*. Cambridge, 1955.

Dagger, Richard. *Civic Virtues*. Oxford, 1997.

Danto, Arthur C. *The Philosophical Disenfranchisement of Art*. New York, 1986.

de Lauretis, Teresa. *Technologies of Gender*. Bloomington, IN, 1991.

de Ste. Croix, G.E.M. *The Class Struggle in the Ancient World*. Ithaca, 1981.

Dench, Emma. *Romulus' Asylum: Roman Identitics from the Age of Alexander to the Age of Hadrian*. Oxford, 2005.

Derrida, Jacques. "Plato's Pharmacy." In *Dissemination*, 61–84, Trans. Barbara Johnson. Chicago, 1981.

———. "Declarations of Independence." *New Political Science* 15 (1986): 7–15.

———. ". . . That Dangerous Supplement. . . ." In *Acts of Literature*, ed. Derek Attridge, 76–109. London, 1992.

Deslauriers, Marguerite. "Sex and Essence in Aristotle's Metaphysics and Biology." In *Feminist Interpretations of Aristotle: Re-Reading the Canon*, ed. Cynthia A. Freeland, 138–70. State Park, PA, 1998.

Dews, Peter. "Communicative Paradigms and the Question of Subjectivity." In *Habermas: A Critical Reader*, ed. Peter Dews, 87–117. London, 1999.

Di Stefano, Christine. "Autonomy in the Light of Difference." In *Revisioning the Political*, ed. Nancy J. Hirschmann and Christine Di Stefano, 95–116. Boulder, 1996.

Dieter, Otto A. L. "Stasis." *Speech Monographs* 17 (1950): 345–69.

Dietz, Mary G. "Context Is All: Feminism and Theories of Citizenship." In *Feminism and Politics*, ed. Anne Phillips, 378–400. Oxford, 1998.

Dolar, Mladen. "At First Sight." In *Gaze and Voice as Love Objects*, ed. Renata Salecl and Slavoj Žižek, 129–52. Chapel Hill, 1996.

Dollimore, Jonathan. *Sexual Dissidence*. Oxford, 1991.

Dominik, William (ed.). *Roman Eloquence: Rhetoric in Society and Literature*. New York and London, 1997.

———. "Tacitus and Pliny on Oratory." In *Companion to Roman Rhetoric*, ed. Jon Hall and William Dominik, 323–38. London, 2006.

Dowden, Kenneth. "Rhetoric and Religion: The Instance of Prayer." In *Companion to Greek Rhetoric*, ed. Ian Worthington, 320–35. London, 2006.

DuBois, Page. "Violence, Apathy, and the Rhetoric of Philosophy." In *Rethinking the History of Rhetoric*, ed. T. Poulakos, 119–34. Boulder, 1993.

———. "Asianism and the Theft of Enjoyment." In *Sappho Is Burning*, 163–94. Chicago, 1995.

Dugan, John. *Making a New Man: Ciceronian Self-Fashioning in the Rhetorical Works*. Oxford, 2005.

Dupont, Florence. *L'Acteur-roi, ou, Le Theatre dans la Rome antique*. Paris, 1985.

Dyck, Andrew. *A Commentary on Cicero's* De Officiis. Ann Arbor, 1996.

———. *A Commentary on Cicero's* De Legibus. Ann Arbor, 2004.

Eagleton, Terry. *Ideology of the Aesthetic*. London, 1990.

Eck, Werner. "Augustus' administrative Reformen: Pragmatismus oder systematisches Planen?" *Acta Classica* 9 (1986): 105–20.

———. "Senatorial Self-representation: Developments in the Augustan Period." In *Caesar Augustus: Seven Aspects*, ed. Fergus Millar and Erich Segal, 129–67. Oxford, 1984.

Eder, Walter. "Augustus and the Power of Tradition: The Augustan Principate as Binding Link between Republic and Empire." In *Between Republic and Empire: Interpretations of Augustus and his Principate*, ed. Kurt Raaflaub and Mark Toher, 71–122. Berkeley and Los Angeles, 1990.

Edwards, Catherine. *The Politics of Immorality in Ancient Rome*. Cambridge, 1993.

Elshtain, Jean Bethke. *Public Man, Private Woman*. Princeton, 1993.

Enders, Jody. "Delivering Delivery: Theatricality and the Emasculation of Eloquence." *Rhetorica* 15 (1997): 253–78.

Enos, Richard Leo, and Karen Rossi Schnakenberg. "Cicero Latinizes Hellenic Ethos." In *Ethos: New Essays in Rhetorical and Critical Theory*, ed. James Baumlin, 191–210. Dallas, 1994.

Euben, W. Peter. "Reading Democracy in Plato's *Gorgias*." In *Demokratia*, ed. Josiah Ober and Charles Hedrick, 327–60. Princeton, 1996.

Fairweather, Janet. *Seneca the Elder*. Cambridge, 1981.

———. "The Elder Seneca and Declamation." *ANRW* II.32.1 (1984): 514–56.

Fantham, Elaine. "Ciceronian *conciliare* and Aristotelian Ethos." *Phoenix* 27 (1973): 262–74.

Fantham, Elaine. "Imitation and Decline: Rhetorical Theory and Practice in the First Century after Christ." *CP* 73 (1978): 102–12.

———. "*Varietas* and *satietas*: *De orat.* 3.96.103 and the Limits of *ornatus*." *Rhetorica* 6 (1988): 275–90.

———. "The Concept of Nature and Human Nature in Quintilian's Psychology and Theory of Instruction." *Rhetorica* 13 (1995): 125–36.

———. "Orator and/et Actor." *Greek and Roman Actors*, ed. Pat Easterling and Edith Hall, 362–71. Cambridge, 2002.

———. *The Roman World of Cicero's* De Oratore. Oxford, 2004.

Farrell, Joseph. *Latin Language and Latin Culture*. Cambridge, 2001.

Farrell, Thomas B. *Norms of Rhetorical Culture*. New Haven, 1993.

Feig Vishnia, Rachel. *State, Society, and Popular Leaders in mid-Republican Rome, 241–167 B.C.* London, 1996.

Feldherr, Andrew. *Spectacle and Society in Livy's History*. Berkeley and Los Angeles, 1998.

Ferrante, Joan. *Woman as Image in Medieval Literature*. New York, 1975.

Ferrary, Jean-Louis. "The Statesman and the Law in the Political Philosophy of Cicero." In *Justice and Generosity: Studies in Hellenistic Social and Political Philosophy*, ed. André Laks and Malcolm Schofield, 48–73. Proceedings of the Sixth Symposium Hellenisticum. Cambridge, 1995.

Flaig, Egon. *Die Ritualisierte Politik: Zeichen, Gesten und Herrschaft im Alten Rom*. Göttingen, 2003.

Flax, Jane. *Disputed Subjects*. New York, 1993.

Fliegelman, Jay. *Declaring Independence: Jefferson, Natural Language, and the Culture of Performance*. Stanford, 1993.

Flory, Dan. "Stoic Psychology, Classical Rhetoric, and Theories of Imagination in Western Philosophy." *Philosophy and Rhetoric* 29 (1996): 147–67.

Flower, Harriet. *Ancestor Masks and Aristocratic Power in Roman Culture*. Oxford, 1996.

Fortenbaugh, William. "*Benevolentiam conciliare* and *animos permovere*: Some Remarks on Cicero's De Oratore 2.178–216." *Rhetorica* 6 (1988): 259–73.

———. "Cicero's Knowledge of the Rhetorical Treatises of Aristotle and Theophrastus." In *Cicero's Knowledge of the Peripatos*, ed. William Fortenbaugh and Peter Steinmetz, 39–60. New Brunswick, NJ, 1989.

———. "Cicero as a Reporter of Aristotelian and Theophrastean Rhetorical Doctrine." *Rhetorica* 23 (2005): 37–64.

Foucault, Michel. *Language, Counter-Memory, Practice*. Ithaca, 1977.

———. "The Order of Discourse." In *Language and Politics*, ed. Michael Shapiro, 108–38. New York, 1984.

———. *The History of Sexuality*. 3 vols. New York, 1984–1988.

———. "The Ethic of Care for the Self as a Practice of Freedom: An Interview with Michael Foucault on Jan. 20, 1984." In *The Final Foucault*, ed. J. Bernauer and D. Rasmussen, 1–20. Cambridge, MA, 1991.

Fowler, D. P. "Epicurean Anger." In *The Passions in Roman Thought and Literature*, ed. Susanna M. Braund and Christopher Gill, 16–35. Cambridge, 1997.

Fox, Matthew. "Dialogue and Irony in Cicero: Reading *De Republica.*" In *Intratextuality*, ed. Alison Sharrock and Helen Morales, 263–86. Oxford, 2000.

Frede, Dorothea. "Constitution and Citizenship: Peripatetic Influence on Cicero's Political Conception in the *De re publica.*" In *Cicero's Knowledge of the Peripatos*, ed. William W. Fortenbaugh and Peter Steinmetz, 77–100. New Brunswick, 1989.

Fustel de Coulanges, Numa Deis. *The Ancient City [La cité antique]*. Kitchener, ON, 2001.

Gaines, Robert. "Cicero's Response to the Philosophers in *De Oratore*, Book 1." In *Rhetoric and Pedagogy*, ed. Winifred Bryan Horner and Michael, Leff, 43–56. Mahwah, NJ, 1985.

Gaisser, Julia Haig. *Catullus and His Renaissance Readers*. Oxford, 1993.

Galinsky, Karl. *Augustan Culture*. Princeton, 1996.

Gardner, Jane F. *Being a Roman Citizen*. London and New York, 1993.

Gellner, Ernst. *Anthropology and Politics: Revolutions in the Sacred Grove.* London, 1996.

Giddens, Anthony. *Capitalism and Modern Social Theory*. Cambridge, 1973.

Gil, José. *Metamorphoses of the Body*, trans. Stephen Muecke. Minneapolis, 1998.

Gill, Christopher. "Passion as Madness in Roman Poetry." In *The Passions in Roman Thought and Literature*, ed. Susanna M. Braund and Christopher Gill, 213–41. Cambridge, 1997.

Gilmore, David. *Manhood in the Making: Cultural Concepts of Masculinity.* New Haven, 1990.

Gilson, Etienne. "Beredsamkeit und Weisheit bei Cicero." In *Das neue Cicerobild*, ed. Karl Büchner. Darmstadt, 1971. Also printed as "Éloquence et sagesse chez Cicéron," *Phoenix* 7 (1953): 1–19.

Gleason, Maud W. "The Semiotics of Gender: Physiognomy and Self-fashioning in the Second Century CE." In *Before Sexuality*, ed. David M. Halperin, John J. Winkler, and Froma I. Zeitlin, 389–416. Princeton, 1990.

———. *Making Men: Sophists and Self-Presentation in Ancient Rome.* Princeton, 1995.

Goerler, Woldemar. "From Athens to Tusculum: Gleaning the Background of Cicero's *De Oratore.*" *Rhetorica* 6 (1988): 215–35.

Goldberg, Sander. "Appreciating Aper: The Defence of Modernity in Tacitus' *Dialogus de oratoribus.*" *CQ* 49 (1999): 224–37.

Goldhill, Simon. "Programme Notes." In *Performance Culture and Athenian Democracy*, ed. Simon Goldhill and Robin Osborne, 1–29. Cambridge, 1999.

Gowing, Alain. *Empire and Memory*. Cambridge, 2005.

Graf, Fritz. "Gestures and Conventions: The Gestures of Roman Actors and Orators." In *A Cultural History of Gesture*, ed. Jan Bremmer and Herman Roodenburg, 36–58. Ithaca, NY, 1992.

Gramsci, Antonio. *Prison Notebooks*. Trans. Joseph A. Buttigieg and Antonio Callari. New York, 1991.

Greenblatt, Stephen. *Renaissance Self-Fashioning*. Chicago, 1980.

Grilli, Alberto. "Cicerone tra retorica e filosofia." In *Interpretare Cicerone: Percorsi della critica contemporanea: Atti del II Symposium Ciceronianum Arpinas*, ed. Emanuele Narducci, 53–65. Florence, 2002.

Grimshaw, Jean. "Practices of Freedom." In *Up Against Foucault*, ed. Caroline Ramazanoglu, 51–72. New York, 1993.

Grosz, Elizabeth. *Lacan: A Feminist Introduction*. London, 1990.

———. *Volatile Bodies: Toward a Corporeal Feminism*. Bloomington, IN, 1994.

Gruen, Erich. *Studies in Greek Culture and Roman Policy*. Berkeley and Los Angeles, 1990.

———. *Culture and National Identity in Republican Rome*. Ithaca, 1992.

Guite, Harold. "Cicero's Attitude to the Greeks." *G&R* 9 (1962): 142–59.

Gunderson, Erik. *Staging Masculinity*. Ann Arbor, 2000.

———. *Declamation, Paternity, and Roman Identity: Authority and the Rhetorical Self*. Cambridge, 2003.

Gustafson, Sandra. *Eloquence Is Power: Oratory and Performance in Early America*. Chapel Hill, 2000.

Gutmann, Amy, and Dennis Thompson. *Democracy and Disagreement*. Cambridge, MA, 1996.

Habermas, Jürgen. *Theory of Communicative Action*. Cambridge, 1985.

———. *Philosophical Discourse of Modernity*. Cambridge, MA, 1987.

———. *Moral Consciousness and Communicative Action*. Cambridge, MA, 1990.

Habinek, Thomas. "Greeks and Romans in Book 12 of Quintilian." *Ramus* 16 (1987): 192–202.

———. "Ideology for an Empire in the Prefaces of Cicero's Dialogues." In *Roman Literature and Ideology: Ramus Essays for J. P. Sullivan*, ed. A. J. Boyle, 55–67. Bendigo, 1995.

———. *The Politics of Latin Literature*. Princeton, 1998.

———. *Ancient Rhetoric and Oratory*. Oxford, 2005.

———. *The World of Roman Song*. Baltimore, 2005.

Hall, Jon. "Social Evasion and Aristocratic Manners in Cicero's *De Oratore*." *AJP* 117 (1996): 95–120.

Halliwell, Stephen. "Philosophy and Rhetoric." In *Persuasion: Greek Rhetoric in Action*, ed. Ian Worthington, 222–43. London, 1994.

Halperin, David M. "The Democratic Body." In *One Hundred Years of Homosexuality: And Other Essays on Greek Love*, 88–112. London, 1990.

Hamilton, Alexander. *Writings*, ed. Joanne Freeman. New York, 2001.

Hammer, Dean. "Hannah Arendt and Roman Political Thought: The Practice of Theory." *Political Theory* 30 (2002): 124–49.

Hankinson, R. J. "Stoic Epistemology." In *The Cambridge Companion to the Stoics*, ed. Brad Inwood, 59–84. Cambridge, 2003.

Hanson, Ann Ellis. "The Medical Writer's Woman." In *Before Sexuality*, ed. David M. Halperin, John J. Winkler, and Froma I. Zeitlin, 309–38. Princeton, 1990.

Hardin, Russell. "Deliberation: Method, Not Theory." In *Deliberative Politics: Essays on Democracy and Disagreement*, ed. Stephen Macedo, 103–19. Oxford, 1999.

Hardt, Michael, and Antonio Negri. *Multitude: War and Democracy in the Age of Empire*. New York, 2004.

Hariman, Robert. *Political Style: The Artistry of Power*. Chicago, 1995.

Harris, William. *Ancient Literacy*. Cambridge, MA, 1989.

———. *War and Imperialism in Republican Rome, 327–70 B.C.* Rev. ed. Oxford, 1992.

Hartz, Louis. *The Liberal Tradition in America*. New York, 1955.

Haynes, Holly. "Tacitus' Dangerous Word." *CA* 23 (2004): 23–61.

Heinze, R. "Auctoritas." *Hermes* 60 (1925): 348–66. Reprinted in *Vom Geist des Römertums*, 3rd ed. (1960).

Herzog, Don. "Some Questions for Republicans." *Political Theory* 14 (1986): 473–93.

Hesk, Jon. "The Rhetoric of Anti-Rhetoric in Athenian Oratory." In *Performance Culture and Athenian Democracy*, ed. Simon Goldhill and Robin Osborne, 201–30. Cambridge, 1999.

Hobbes, Thomas. *Man and Citizen (De Homine and De Cive)*, ed. Bernard Gert. Indianapolis, 1991.

———. *The Elements of Law*, ed. J.C.A. Gaskin. Oxford, 1994.

———. *Leviathan*, ed. Richard Tuck. Cambridge, 1996.

———. *De Cive*, ed. Bernard Gert. Indianapolis, 1998.

Hölkeskamp, Klaus-Joachim. *Senatus Populusque Romanus: Die politische Kulter der Republik*. Weisbaden, 2004.

Honig, Bonnie. "Declarations of Independence." In *The Rhetorical Republic: Governing Representations in American Politics*, ed. Frederick M. Dolan and Thomas L. Dumm, 201–25. Amherst, 1993.

Hopkins, Keith, and G. P. Burton. *Death and Renewal*. Cambridge, 1983.

Horsfall, Nicholas. *The Culture of the Roman Plebs*. London, 2003.

Hubbard, Thomas K. "Catullus 68: The Text as Self-Demystification." *Arethusa* 17 (1984): 29–49.

Hume, David. "Of the Standard of Taste." In *The Critical Tradition*, ed. David H. Richter. London, 1997.

Hyneman, Charles S., and Donald S. Lutz. *American Political Writing During the Founding Era*, vol. 1. Indianapolis, 1983.

Ignatieff, Michael. *Blood and Belonging: Journeys into the New Nationalism*. New York, 1995.

———. "Republicanism, ethnicity, and nationalism." In *The Demands of Citizenship*, ed. Catriona McKinnon and Iain Hampsher-Monk, 257–64. London, 2000.

Imholz, A. A. "Gladiatorial Metaphors in Cicero's *pro Sexto Roscio Amerino*." *CW* 65 (1972): 228–30.

Irigaray, Luce. *Speculum of the Other Woman*. New York, 1985.

Ivison, Duncan. "Modus Vivendi Citizenship." In *The Demands of Citizenship*, ed. Catriona McKinnon and Iain Hampsher-Monk, 123–43. London, 2000.

Jameson, Fredric. *The Political Unconscious*. Ithaca, 1982.

Jameson, Michael. "The Spectacular and the Obscure in Athenian Religion." In *Performance Culture and Athenian Democracy*, ed. Simon Goldhill and Robin Osborne, 321–40. Cambridge, 1999.

Jaeger, Werner. *Paideia: The Ideals of Greek Culture*. 3 vols. Berkeley, 1944.

Jarratt, Susan. *Rereading the Sophists: Classical Rhetoric Refigured*. Carbondale, IL, 1991.

Jed, Stephanie. *Chaste Thinking: The Rape of Lucretia and the Birth of Humanism*. Bloomington, IN, 1989.

Jehne, Martin. *Demokratie in Rom? Die Rolle des Volkes in der Politik der römischen Republik.* Historia Einzelschriften 96. Stuttgart, 1995.

Jones, Kathleen B. "Citizenship in a Woman-Friendly Polity." In *The Citizenship Debates,* ed. Gershon Shafir, 221–47. Minneapolis, 1998.

Kahn, Victoria. "'The Duty to Love': Passion and Obligation in Early Modern Political Theory." *Representations* 68 (1999): 26–49.

Kassell, R. *Aristotelis Ars Rhetorica.* Berlin, 1976.

Kastely, James L. "The Recalcitrance of Aggression: An Aporetic Moment in Cicero's *De inventione.*" *Rhetorica* 20 (2002): 235–62.

Kaster, Robert. *Emotion, Restraint, and Community in Ancient Rome.* Oxford, 2005.

Keith, Alison. "Slender Verse: Roman Elegy and Ancient Rhetorical Theory." *Mnemosyne* 52 (1999): 41–62.

Kelley, Robert. "Ideology and Political Culture from Jefferson to Nixon." *American Historical Review* 82 (1977): 531–62.

Kennedy, Duncan. " 'Augustan' and 'Anti-Augustan': Reflections on Terms of Reference." In *Roman Poetry and Propaganda in the Age of Augustus,* ed. Anton Powell, 26–58. Bristol, 1992.

Kennedy, George. *The Art of Persuasion in Greece.* Princeton, 1963.

———. *The Art of Rhetoric in the Roman World.* Princeton, 1978.

Koestenbaum, Wayne. "The Queen's Throat: (Homo) sexuality and the Art of Singing." In *Inside/Out: Lesbian Theories, Gay Theories,* ed. Diana Fuss, 205–34. London, 1991.

Krostenko, Brian. *Cicero, Catullus, and the Language of Social Performance.* Chicago, 2001.

Kymlicka, Will. *Contemporary Political Philosophy.* Oxford, 2002.

Laclau, Ernesto. "Identity and Hegemony: The Role of Universality in the Constitution of Political Logics." In *Contingency, Hegemony, Universality,* ed. Judith Butler, Ernesto Laclau, and Slavoj Žižek, 44–89. New York, 2000.

Laclau, Ernesto, and Chantal Mouffe. *Hegemony and Socialist Strategy.* London, 1985.

Lanham, Richard A. *The Motives of Eloquence: Literary Rhetoric in the Renaissance.* New Haven, 1976.

Leach, Eleanor W. "Ciceronian Bi-Marcus: Correspondence with M. Terentius Varro and L. Papirius Paetus in 46 B.C." *TAPA* 129 (1999): 139–79.

Leeman, A. D. *Orationis Ratio.* Amsterdam, 1963.

———. "L' hyperbole et l'ironie chez les romains en tant que mécanismes de défense et d' assimilation a l' égard de la culture grecque." In *Homages à Robert Schilling,* ed. H. Zenacker and G. Hentz, 347–55. Paris, 1983.

Leeman, A. D., and Harm Pinkster (eds.). *M. Tullius Cicero, De oratore libri III: Kommentar.* Heidelberg, 1981.

Lendon, J. E. *Empire of Honour: The Art of Government in the Roman World.* Oxford, 2002.

Lepore, Ettore. *Il princeps Ciceroniano e gli ideali politici della tarda Repubblica.* Naples, 1954.

Levene, D. S. "Sallust's 'Catiline' and Cato the Censor." *CQ* 50 (2000): 170–91.

Lintott, Andrew W. *The Constitution of the Roman Republic.* Oxford, 1999.

Liu, Alan. "The Power of Formalism: The New Historicism." *English Literary History* 56 (1989): 721–71.

Locke, John. *Two Treatises of Government*, ed. Peter Laslett. Cambridge, 1988.

Long, A. A. *Hellenistic Philosophy*. New York, 1974.

———. "Cicero's Politics in *De Officiis*." In *Justice and Generosity: Studies in Hellenistic Social and Political Philosophy*. Proceedings of the Sixth Symposium Hellenisticum, 213–40, ed. André Laks and Malcolm Schofield. Cambridge, 1995.

———. *Stoic Studies*. Cambridge, 1996.

Loraux, Nicole. *Children of Athena: Athenian Ideas about Citizenship and the Division between the Sexes*. Princeton, 1993.

Macedo, Stephen. *Liberal Virtues: Citizenship, Virtue, and Community in Liberal Constitutionalism*. Oxford, 1990.

Manville, Brook. "Toward a New Paradigm of Athenian Citizenship." In *Athenian Identity and Civic Ideology*, ed. Alan L. Boegehold and Adele Scafuro, 21–33. Baltimore, 1994.

Matthes, Melissa. *The Rape of Lucretia and the Founding of Republics*. University Park, MD, 2000.

May, James M. *Trials of Character: The Eloquence of Ciceronian Ethos*. Chapel Hill, 1988.

Mbembe, Achille. "Provisional Notes on the Postcolony." *Africa* 62 (1992): 1–37.

McClure, Kirstie. "The Odor of Judgment: Exemplarity, Propriety, and Politics in the Company of Hannah Arendt." In *Hannah Arendt and the Meaning of Politics*, ed. Craig Calhoun and John McGowan, 53–84. Minneapolis, 1997.

McCormick, John P. "Machiavelli Against Republicanism: On the Cambridge School's 'Guicciadinian Moments.' " *Political Theory* 31 (2003): 615–43.

McKinnon, Catriona, and Iain Hampsher-Monk (eds.). *The Demands of Citizenship*. London, 2000.

McKinnon, Catriona. "Civil Citizens." In *The Demands of Citizenship*, ed. Catriona McKinnon and Iain Hampsher-Monk, 144–64. London, 2000.

McNay, Lois. *Gender and Agency: Reconfiguring the Subject in Feminist and Social Theory*. Malden, MA, 2000.

Millar, Fergus. "State and Subject: The Impact of Monarchy." In *Caesar Augustus: Seven Aspects*, ed. Fergus Millar and Erich Segal, 37–60. Oxford, 1984.

———. "The Political Character of the Classical Roman Republic, 200–151 B.C." *JRS* 74 (1984): 1–19.

———. "Politics, Persuasion and the People before the Social War (150–90 B.C.)." *JRS* 76 (1986): 1–11.

Millar, Fergus. "Political Power in Mid-Republican Rome: Curia or Comitium?" *JRS* 79 (1989): 138–150.

———. *The Crowd in Rome in the Late Republic*. Ann Arbor, 1998.

Miles, Gary B. *Livy: Reconstructing Early Rome*. Ithaca, 1995.

Miller, D.A. "Pedagogy and Pederasty." *Raritan* 5 (1985): 14–21.

Miller, Fred D. "Naturalism." In *The Cambridge History of Greek and Roman Political Thought*, ed. Christopher Rowe and Malcolm Schofield, 321–43. Cambridge, 2000.

Miller, Paul Allen. *Lyric Texts and Lyric Consciousness: The Birth of a Genre from Archaic Greece to Augustan Rome*. London, 1994.

———. "Catullan Consciousness, the 'Care of the Self,' and the Force of the Negative in History." In *Rethinking Sexuality: Foucault and Classical Antiquity*, ed. David H. J. Larmour, Paul Allen Miller, and Charles Platter, 171–203. Princeton, 1998.

Minyard, J. D. *Lucretius and the Late Republic: An Essay in Roman Intellectual History*. Leiden, 1985.

Moatti, Claudia. *La Raison de Rome: Naissance de l'esprit critique à la fin de la république*. Paris, 1997.

Momigliano, Arnaldo. "Perizonius, Niebuhr, and the Character of Early Roman Tradition." *JRS* 47 (1957): 104–14.

Monoson, S. Sara. *Plato's Democratic Entanglements: Athenian Politics and the Practice of Philosophy*. Princeton, 2000.

Morgan, Llewellyn. "*Levi quidem de re*: Julius Caesar as Tyrant and Pedant." *JRS* 87 (1997): 23–40.

Morgan, Teresa. "A Good Man Skilled in Politics: Quintilian's Political Theory." In *Pedagogy and Power: Rhetorics of Classical Learning*, ed. Niall Livingstone and Yun Lee Too, 245–62. Cambridge, 1998.

Morstein-Marx, Robert. *Mass Oratory and Political Power in the Late Roman Republic*. Cambridge, 2004.

Mouffe, Chantal. "Hegemony and Ideology in Gramsci." In *Gramsci and Marxist Theory*, ed. Chantal Mouffe, 168–204. London, 1979.

Mouritsen, Henrik. *Italian Unification: A Study in Ancient and Modern Historiography*. London, 1998.

———. *Plebs and Politics in Late Republican Rome*. Cambridge, 2001.

Murphy, Trevor. "Privileged Knowledge: Valerius Soranus and the Secret Name of Rome." In *Rituals in Ink,* ed. Abssandro Barchiesi Jörg Rüpke, and Susan Stephens, 127–37. Munich, 2004.

Naipaul, V. S. *A Bend in the River*. New York, 1979.

Narducci, Emanuele. *Cicerone e l'eloquenza Romana: Retorica e progetto culturale*. Roma, 1997.

———. "*Orator* and the Definition of the Ideal Orator," trans. James M. May. In *Brill's Companion to Cicero: Oratory and Rhetoric*, ed. James M. May, 427–43. Leiden, 2002.

Nederman, Cary. "Nature, Sin, and the Origins of Society: The Ciceronian Tradition in Medieval Political Thought." *Journal of the History of Ideas* 49 (1988): 3–26.

Nicolet, Claude. *The World of the Citizen in Republican Rome*. Berkeley and Los Angeles, 1980.

Nippel, Wilfried. "Policing Rome." *JRS* 72 (1984): 20–29.

———. "Ancient and Modern Republicanism." In *The Invention of the Modern Republic*, ed. Biancamaria Fontana, 6–26. Cambridge, 1994.

———. *Public Order in Ancient Rome*. Cambridge, 1995.

Nock, Arthur Darby. "A Feature of Roman Religion." In *Roman Religion*, ed. Clifford Ando, 84–97. Edinburgh, 2003.

Norden, Eduard. *Die Antike Kunstprosa*. Stuttgart, 1958.

North, Helen. "Combing and Curling: *Orator summus Plato.*" *ICS* 16 (1991): 201–19.

North, J. A. "The Roman Counter-Revolution." *JRS* 79 (1989): 151–56.

———. "Politics and Aristocracy in the Roman Republic." *CP* 85 (1990): 277–87.

Nussbaum, Martha. *The Therapy of Desire.* Princeton, 1994.

———. *For Love of Country: Debating the Limits of Patriotism.* Boston, 1996.

———. "Duties of Justice, Duties of Material Aid: Cicero's Problematic Legacy." *Journal of Political Philosophy* 8 (2000): 176–206.

Ober, Josiah. *Mass and Elite in Democratic Athens.* Princeton, 1989.

———. "Power and Oratory in Democratic Athens." In *Persuasion: Greek Rhetoric in Action,* ed. Ian Worthington, 85–108. London, 1994.

———. *The Athenian Revolution.* Princeton, 1996.

———. *Political Dissent in Democratic Athens: Intellectual Critics of Popular Rule.* Princeton, 1998.

O'Gorman, Ellen. *Irony and Misreading in the* Annals *of Tacitus.* Cambridge, 2000.

Okin, Susan Moller. *Women in Western Political Thought.* Princeton, 1975.

Oliensis, Ellen. "Canidia, Canicula, and the Decorum of Horace's Epodes." *Arethusa* 24 (1991): 107–38.

Oravec, Christine, and Michael Salvador. "The Duality of Rhetoric: Theory as Discursive Practice." In *Rethinking the History of Rhetoric,* ed. T. Poulakos, 173–92. Boulder, 1993.

Ortner, Sherry B. "Is Female to Male as Nature Is to Culture?" In *Women, Culture, and Society,* ed. Louise Lamphere and Michelle Zimbalist Rosaldo, 67–88. Stanford, 1974.

O'Sullivan, Neil. "Caecilius, the 'Canons' of Writers, and the Origins of Atticism." In *Roman Eloquence,* ed. William J. Dominik, 32–49. London, 1997.

Parker, Patricia. *Literary Fat Ladies.* London, 1987.

———. "Virile Style." In *Premodern Sexualities,* ed. Carla Freccero and Louise Fradenburg, 201–22. London, 1986.

———. "On the Tongue: Crossgendering, Effeminacy, and the Art of Words." *Style* 23 (1989): 445–65.

Parry, Adam. "The Two Voices of Vergil's *Aeneid.*" *Arion* 2 (1963): 66–80.

Pateman, Carole. *The Disorder of Women: Democracy, Feminism, and Political Theory.* Stanford, 1990.

Paxson, James. "Personification's Gender." *Rhetorica* 16 (1988): 149–79.

Perkins, Judith. *The Suffering Self: Pain and Narrative Representation in the Early Christian Era.* London, 1995.

Petrochilos, Nicholas. *Roman Attitudes to the Greeks.* Athens, 1974.

Pettit, Philip. *Republicanism: A Theory of Freedom and Government.* Oxford, 1997.

Phillips, Anne. "Feminism and Republicanism: Is This a Plausible Alliance?" *Journal of Political Philosophy* 8 (2000): 279–93.

Philp, Mark. "Motivating Liberal Citizenship." In *The Demands of Citizenship,* ed. Catriona McKinnon and Iain Hampsher-Monk, 165–89. London, 2000.

Pina Polo, Francisco. "Procedures and Functions of Civil and Military *Contiones.*" *Klio* 77 (1995): 203–16.

———. *Contra Arma Verbis: Der Redner vor dem Volk in der später römischen Republik.* Trans. E. Liess. Stuttgart, 1996.

Pocock, J. G. A. "Time, Institutions, and Action: An Essay on Traditions and Their Understanding." In *Politics, Language, and Time,* 233–72. New York, 1971.

———. *The Machiavellian Moment: Florentine Political Thought and the Atlantic Republican Tradition.* Princeton, 1975.

———. "Verbalizing as a Political Act: Toward a Politics of Speech." In *Language and Politics,* ed. Michael J. Shapiro, 25–43. New York, 1984.

———. "Virtues, Rights, and Manners." In *Virtue, Commerce, and History: Essays on Political Thought and History, Chiefly in the Eighteenth Century,* 37–50. Cambridge, 1985.

———. "Civic Humanism and Its Role in Anglo-American Political Thought." In *Politics, Language, and Time: Essays on Political Thought and History,* 80–103. Chicago, 1989.

———. "The Ideal of Citizenship Since Classical Times." In *Theorizing Citizenship,* ed. Ronald Beiner, 29–52. New York, 1995.

Powell, J. G. F. (ed.). *Cicero the Philosopher.* Oxford, 1995.

Prescott, H. W. "The Unity of Catullus LXVIII." *TAPA* 71 (1940): 473–500.

Probyn, Elspeth. *Sexing the Self.* Routledge, 1993.

Putnam, Michael. "Possessiveness, Sexuality, and Heroism in the *Aeneid.*" *Vergilius* 31 (1985): 1–21.

———. "Anger, Blindness and Insight." *Apeiron* 23 (1990): 10–15.

Quint, David. *Epic and Empire.* Princeton, 1993.

Raaflaub, Kurt A., and L. J. Samons. "Opposition to Augustus." In *Between Republic and Empire: Interpretations of Augustus and his Principate,* ed. K. Raaflaub and M. Toher, 417–54. Berkeley and Los Angeles, 1990.

Ramage, Edwin. *Urbanitas: Ancient Sophistication and Refinement.* Cincinnati, 1973.

Rawson, Elizabeth. *Intellectual Life in the Late Roman Republic.* London, 1985.

———. "The First Latin Annalists." In *Roman Culture and Society: The Collected Papers of Elizabeth Rawson,* 254–71. Oxford, 1991.

———."The Introduction of Logical Organization in Roman Prose Literature." In *Roman Culture and Society: The Collected Papers of Elizabeth Rawson,* 324–51. Oxford, 1991.

———. "L. Crassus and Cicero: the Formation of a Statesman." In *Roman Culture and Society: The Collected Papers of Elizabeth Rawson,* 16–33. Oxford, 1991.

———. "Scipio, Laelius, Furius, and the Ancestral Religion." In *Roman Culture and Society: The Collected Papers of Elizabeth Rawson,* 80–101. Oxford, 1991.

Rebhorn, Wayne. "Baldesar Castiglione, Thomas Wilson, and the Courtly Body of Renaissance Rhetoric." *Rhetorica* 11 (1993): 241–73.

Remer, Gary. "Political Oratory and Conversation: Cicero versus Deliberative Democracy." *Political Theory* 27 (1999): 39–64.

Rich, John. "Fear, Greed, and Glory: The Causes of Roman War Making in the Middle Republic." In *Roman Imperialism: Readings and Sources*, ed. Craige B. Champion, 46–66. Oxford, 2004.

Richardson, Emeline Hill, and L. *"Ad cohibendum bracchium toga:* An Archaeological Examination of Cicero, *pro Caelio* 5.11." *YCS* 19 (1966): 255–68.

Richlin, Amy. *The Garden of Priapus: Sexuality and Aggression in Roman Humor*. Oxford, 1992.

———. "Gender and Rhetoric: Producing Manhood in the Schools." In *Roman Eloquence*, ed. William Dominik, 90–110. London, 1997.

Riggsby, Andrew. "Pliny on Cicero and Oratory: Self-fashioning in the Public Eye." *AJP* 116 (1995): 123–35.

———. "Self and Community in the Younger Pliny." *Arethusa* 31 (1988): 75–97.

———. *Crime and Community in Ciceronian Rome*. Austin, 1999.

Rodgers, Daniel T. "Republicanism: The Career of a Concept." *Journal of American History* 79 (1992): 11–38.

Roller, Matthew. *Constructing Autocracy: Aristocrats and Emperors in Julio-Claudian Rome*. Princeton, 2001.

Rorty, Richard. "The Historiography of Philosophy: Four Genres." In *Philosophy in History: Essays on the Historiography of Philosophy*, ed. Richard Rorty, J. B. Schneewind, and Quentin Skinner, 49–75. Cambridge, 1984.

Rousseau, Jean-Jacques. *The Social Contract and Other Later Political Writings*, ed. Victor Gourevitch. Cambridge, 1997.

Rousselle, Aline. *Porneia: On Desire and the Body in Antiquity*. London, 1988.

Russell, D.A. *Criticism in Antiquity*. Berkeley and Los Angeles, 1981.

———. "Ethos in Oratory and Rhetoric." In *Characterization and Individuality in Greek Literature*, ed. C. Pelling, 197–212. Oxford, 1990.

Rutledge, Steven H. "Oratory and Politics in the Empire." In *Companion to Roman Rhetoric*, ed. Jon Hall and William Dominik, 109–21. London, 2006.

Said, Edward. *Culture and Imperialism*. New York, 1993.

Saxonhouse, Arlene. *Fear of Diversity: The Birth of Political Science in Ancient Greek Thought*. Chicago, 1992.

Schofield, Malcolm. *The Stoic Idea of the City*. Chicago, 1999.

———. "Cicero's Definition of the *res publica*." In *Cicero the Philosopher*, ed. J. G. F. Powell, 63–83. Oxford, 1995.

Schütrümpf, Eckart. "Platonic Elements in the Structure of Cicero's *De Orat.* Book 1." *Rhetorica* 6 (1988): 237–58.

———. "Cicero's *De Orat.* 1 and the Greek Philosophical Tradition." *Rheinisches Museum* 133 (1990): 310–21.

Sedley, David. "Philosophical Allegiance in the Greco-Roman World." In *Philosophia Togata*, ed. Miriam Griffin and Jonathan Barnes, 97–119. Oxford, 1989.

Selden, Daniel L. *"Ceveat lector:* Catullus and the Rhetoric of Performance." In *Innovations of Antiquity*, ed. Ralph J. Hexter and Daniel L. Selden, 461–512. London, 1992.

Seigel, Jerrold. *Rhetoric and Philosophy in Renaissance Humanism: The Union of Eloquence and Wisdom, Petrarch to Valla*. Princeton, 1968.

Seigel, Jerrold. "Civic Humanism or Ciceronian Rhetoric?" *Past and Present* 34 (1966): 3–48.

Serres, Michel. *Rome: The Book of Foundations.* Trans. Felicia McCarren. Stanford, 1991.

Sherwin-White, A. N. *The Roman Citizenship.* Oxford, 1973.

Shaftesbury, Anthony Ashley-Cooper. *Characteristicks of Men, Manners, Opinions, Times.* 3 vols. Indianapolis, 2001.

Shklar, Judith. *Ordinary Vices.* Cambridge, MA, 1984.

Sidorsky, David. "The Third Concept of Liberty and the Politics of Identity." *Partisan Review* 68 (2001): 536–61.

Sinclair, Patrick. "The *Sententia* in the *Rhetorica ad Herennium*: A Study in the Sociology of Rhetoric." *AJP* 114 (1993): 561–80.

———. "Political Declensions in Latin Grammar and Oratory 55 BCE–CE 39." In *Roman Literature and Ideology: Ramus Essays for J. P. Sullivan,* ed. A. J. Boyle, 92–109. Bendigo, Australia, 1995.

Skinner, Marilyn. *Catullus in Verona.* Cincinnati, 2003.

Skinner, Quentin. *The Foundations of Modern Political Thought.* Vol. 1, *The Renaissance.* Cambridge, 1978.

———. "The State." In *Political Innovation and Conceptual Change,* ed. Terence Ball, James Farr, and Russell L. Hanson, 90–1313. Cambridge, 1989.

———. *Reason and Rhetoric in the Philosophy of Hobbes.* Cambridge, 1996.

———. *Liberty Before Liberalism.* Cambridge, 1998.

Smith, Adam. *The Theory of Moral Sentiments.* Indianapolis, 1976.

Solmsen, Friedrich. "Aristotle and Cicero on the Orator's Playing Upon the Feelings." *CP* 33 (1938): 390–404.

———. "The Aristotelian Tradition in Ancient Rhetoric." *AJP* 62 (1941): 35–50, 169–90.

Springborg, Patricia. "Republicanism, Freedom from Domination, and the Cambridge Contextual Historians." *Political Studies* 49 (2001): 851–76.

Staffhorst, Ulrich. "Helen in jedem Weibe? Zum Proeemium des 2. Buches von Ciceros Schrift *de Inventione.*" *Gymnasium* 99 (1992): 193–200.

Steinmetz, Peter. "Beobachtungen zu Ciceros philosophischem Standpunkt." In *Cicero's Knowledge of the Peripatos,* ed. William Fortenbaugh and Peter Steinmetz, 1–22. New Brunswick, NJ, 1989.

Sunstein, Cass. *Republic.com.* Princeton, 2001.

Sussman, L. A. "The Elder Seneca and Declamation." *ANRW* II.32.1 (1984): 557–77.

Swearingen, C. Jan. *Rhetoric and Irony: Western Literacy and Western Lies.* Oxford, 1991.

Syme, Ronald. *The Roman Revolution.* Oxford, 1939.

Tambornino, John. *The Corporeal Turn: Passion, Necessity, Politics.* London, 2002.

Taussig, Michael. *The Magic of the State.* London, 1997.

Taylor, Charles. *Sources of the Self.* Cambridge, MA, 1999.

Taylor, Lily Ross. *Roman Voting Assemblies.* Ann Arbor, 1991.

Too, Yun Lee. *The Rhetoric of Identity in Isocrates: Text, Power, Pedagogy.* Cambridge, 1995.

Toohey, Peter. "Eros and Eloquence: Modes of Amatory Persuasion in Ovid's *Ars Amatoria*." In *Roman Eloquence: Rhetoric in Society and Literature*, ed. William J. Dominik, 198–211. New York, 1997.

Treggiari, Susan. "Home and Forum: Cicero Between Public and Private." *TAPA* 128 (1998): 1–23.

Trenchard, John, and Thomas Gordon. *Cato's Letters*, ed. Ronald Hamowy. Indianapolis, 1995.

Tully, James. "The Challenge of Reimagining Citizenship and Belonging in Multicultural and Multinational Societies." In *The Demands of Citizenship*, ed. Catriona McKinnon and Iain Hampsher-Monk, 212–34. London, 2000.

Turner, Bryan S. "Citizenship Studies: A General Theory." *Citizenship Studies* 1 (1997): 5–18.

Vanderbroeck, P. J. J. *Popular Leadership and Collective Behavior in the Late Roman Republic (ca. 80–50 B.C.)*. Amsterdam, 1987.

Vasaly, Ann. "The Masks of Rhetoric." *Rhetorica* 3 (1985): 1–20.

———. *Representations: Images of the World in Ciceronian Oratory*. Berkeley and Los Angeles, 1993.

Vickers, B. F. *In Defence of Rhetoric*. Oxford, 1988.

Viroli, Maurizio. *For Love of Country: An Essay on Patriotism and Nationalism*. Oxford, 1995.

———. *Republicanism*. New York, 1999.

Wallace-Hadrill, Andrew. "*Mutatio morum*: the idea of a cultural revolution." In *The Roman Cultural Revolution*, ed. T. Habinek and A. Schiesaro, 3–22. Cambridge, 1997.

Walters, Jonathan. "Invading the Roman Body: Manliness and Impenetrability in Roman Thought." In *Roman Sexualities*, ed. Judith P. Hallett and Marilyn B. Skinner, 29–43. Princeton, 1997.

Walzer, Michael. "Citizenship." In *Political Innovation and Conceptual Change*, ed. Terence Ball, James Farr, and Russell L. Hanson, 211–19. Cambridge, 1989.

Ward, John O. "Rhetorical Theory and the Rise and Decline of *Dictamen* in the Middle Ages and Early Renaissance." *Rhetorica* 19 (2001): 175–223.

Weber, Max. *Economy and Society*, vol. 1, ed. Guenther Roth and Claus Wittich. Berkeley and Los Angeles, 1978.

Wieruszowski, Helene. *Politics and Culture in Medieval Spain and Italy*. Rome, 1971.

Wilamowitz-Moellendorf, Ulrich. "Asianismus und Atticismus." *Hermes* 35 (1900): 1–52.

Wilkins, A. S. (ed.). *M. Tulli Ciceronis: Rhetorica*. Oxford, 1935.

Williams, Gordon. *Change and Decline: Roman Literature in the Early Empire*. Berkeley and Los Angeles, 1978.

Williams, Raymond. *Marxism and Literature*. Oxford, 1977.

———. *The Sociology of Culture*. Chicago, 1981.

Wills, Garry. "John Wayne's Body." *The New Yorker*, August 19, 1996, 38–49.

Wingrove, Elizabeth Rose. *Rousseau's Republican Romance*. Princeton, 2000.

Winterbottom, Michael. "Quintilian and the *vir bonus*." *Journal of Roman Studies* 54 (1964): 90–97.

——— (ed.). *The Elder Seneca: Controversiae and Suasoriae*. Cambridge, 1974.

Wirszubski, Chaim. "Cicero's *cum Dignitate Otium*: A Reconsideration." *JRS* 44 (1954): 1–13.

———. *Libertas as a Political Idea at Rome*. Cambridge, 1960.

Wisse, Jakob. *Ethos and Pathos: From Aristotle to Cicero*. Amsterdam, 1989.

———. "The Intellectual Background of Cicero's Rhetorical Works." In *Brill's Companion to Cicero: Oratory and Rhetoric*, ed. James M. May, 331–74. Leiden, 2002.

———. "*De Oratore*: Rhetoric, Philosophy, and the Making of the Ideal Orator." In *Brill's Companion to Cicero: Oratory and Rhetoric*, ed. James M. May, 375–400. Leiden, 2002.

Wohl, Victoria. *Love Among the Ruins: The Erotics of Democracy in Classical Athens*. Princeton, 1992.

Wood, Gordon S. *The Creation of the American Republic, 1776–1787*. Chapel Hill, 1998.

Wood, Neal. *Cicero's Social and Political Thought*. Berkeley and Los Angeles, 1988.

Wright, M. R. "Cicero on Self-love and Love of Humanity." In *Cicero the Philosopher*, ed. J. G. F. Powell, 171–96. Oxford, 1995.

Yakobson, Alexander. "*Petitio et Largitio*: Popular Participation in the Centuriate Assembly of the Late Republic." *JRS* 82 (1992): 32–52.

Yavetz, Zvi. "*Existimatio, Fama*, and the Ides of March." *HSCP* 78 (1974): 35–65.

Yeatman, Anna. "Feminism and Citizenship." In *Culture and Citizenship*, ed. Nick Stevenson, 138–53. London, 2001.

Young, Iris Marion. *Justice and the Politics of Difference*. Princeton, 1990.

———. *Inclusion and Democracy*. Oxford, 2000.

Zeitlin, Froma I. "The Power of Aphrodite: Eros and the Boundaries of the Self in the *Hippolytus*." *Directions in Euripidean Criticism*, ed. Peter Burian, 52–111, 187–206. Durham, 1985.

———. "Playing the Other: Theatre, Theatricality and the Feminine in Greek Drama." In *Nothing to Do with Dionysos? Athenian Drama in Its Social Context*, ed. John J. Winkler and Froma Zeitlin, 63–96. Princeton, 1990.

Zetzel, James. "Plato With Pillows." In *Myth, History, and Culture in Republican Rome*, ed. David Braund and Christopher Gill, 119–38. Exeter, 2003.

———. "Citizen and Commonwealth in *De Re Publica*, Book 4." In *Cicero's Republic*, ed. J. G. F. Powell and J. A. North, 83–97. London, 2001.

Žižek, Slavoj. *The Sublime Object of Ideology*. London, 1989.

———. *The Plague of Fantasies*. London, 1997.

———. *The Ticklish Subject*. London, 1999.

ANCIENT SOURCES

Bennett, Charles Edwin (ed.). *Tacitus: Dialogus de Oratoribus*. New Rochelle, NY, 1983.

Buchheit, V. (ed.). *Quintilianus: Institutio Oratoria*. Stuttgart, 1959.

Courtney, Edward. *Fragmentary Latin Poets*. Oxford, 2003.

Hendrickson, G. L., and Hubbell, H. M. *Cicero: Brutus and Orator*. Cambridge, MA, 1939.

Kassel, R. *Aristotelis Ars Rhetorica*. Berlin, 1976.

Kaster, Robert (trans.-ed.). *Suetonius: De Grammaticis et Rhetoribus*. Oxford, 1995.

Malcovati, Henri. *Oratorum Romanorum Fragmenta: Liberae Rei Publicae*. Turin, 1953.

Mynors, R.A.B. (ed.). *C.Valerii Catulli Carmina*. Oxford, 1958.

Ogilvie, Robert Maxwell (ed.). *Titi Livi: Ab Urbe Condita*. Vol. 1. Oxford, 1974.

Reynolds, L. D. (ed.). *M. Tulli Ciceronis: De Finibus Bonorum et Malorum Libri Quinque*. Oxford, 1998.

Sutton, E. W., and H. Rackham. *Cicero: On the Orator*. 2 vols. Cambridge, MA, 1942.

Von Arnim, Hans (ed.). *Stoicorum Veterum Fragmenta*. 3 vols. Leipzig, 1903–5.

Wilkins, A. S. (ed.). *M. Tulli Ciceronis: Rhetorica*. Oxford, 1935.

Winterbottom, Michael (ed.-trans.). *The Elder Seneca: Controversiae and Suasoriae*. Cambridge, MA, 1974.

INDEX

CPSIA information can be obtained at www.ICGtesting.com
Printed in the USA
BVOW10*0510190813

328696BV00004B/70/P